Legal Philosophies

For my son Hugh

Legal Philosophies

Second Edition

J W Harris BCL, MA, PhD
Professor of Law at the University of Oxford
Fellow of Keble College, Oxford

OXFORD
UNIVERSITY PRESS

OXFORD
UNIVERSITY PRESS

Great Clarendon Street, Oxford OX2 6DP

Oxford University Press is a department of the University of Oxford.
It furthers the University's objective of excellence in research, scholarship,
and education by publishing worldwide in

Oxford New York

Auckland Cape Town Dar es Salaam Hong Kong Karachi
Kuala Lumpur Madrid Melbourne Mexico City Nairobi
New Delhi Shanghai Taipei Toronto

With offices in

Argentina Austria Brazil Chile Czech Republic France Greece
Guatemala Hungary Italy Japan Poland Portugal Singapore
South Korea Switzerland Thailand Turkey Ukraine Vietnam

Oxford is a registered trade mark of Oxford University Press
in the UK and in certain other countries

Published in the United States
by Oxford University Press Inc., New York

© Oxford University Press 2004

British Library Cataloguing in Publication Data

Data available

Library of Congress Cataloging in Publication Data

Data available

ISBN: 978-0-406-50716-7

5 7 9 10 8 6 4

Printed in Great Britain by
Antony Rowe Ltd
Chippenham, Wilts

Preface to the second edition

Since the first edition of this book was written, seventeen years ago, there have been many developments in the theoretical and practical problems addressed by legal philosophers. At that time, the labels 'Critical Legal Studies' and 'Feminist Jurisprudence' were scarcely known. New sections have accordingly been added to chapters 8 and 20. Philosophers have discovered new terms in which to debate the ancient search for the foundations of the objectivity of morals, hence the new section on 'Moral Truth' in chapter 2; and a new section on 'Communitarianism' in chapter 20 takes account of a revived theoretical and political invocation of the demands of 'community' in opposition to individualist liberalism.

Michael Hartney's translation of Hans Kelsen's last posthumously published work, *General Theory of Norms*, the posthumously published postscript to the second edition of Herbert Hart's *The Concept of Law* and the publication of Ronald Dworkin's *Law's Empire* have led to the complete rewriting of chapters 6, 9 and 14. Thanks largely to the initiatives of Joseph Raz, the relation of law to other departments of practical reasoning has taken on fresh vitality, and a new section on 'Law's Normativity' is included in chapter 9.

Law's proper place as the enforcer of moral standards has been set new challenges by developments in embryonic research and the practice of surrogacy, taken account of in chapter 10. The House of Lords' path-breaking repudiation of its previous attitude to Parliamentary materials in interpreting statutes has been explored in chapter 12. Alterations, minor or substantial, appear throughout the rest of the book.

The purpose of the book remains the same: to provide a bill of fare for the beginner in jurisprudence, moral or political philosophy. I gave my reasons for believing such an introductory work to be needed in the preface to the first edition. Students, with whom the book has proved popular, have agreed with me. Some of my colleagues have not. I have encountered objections of two kinds, the first of which arouses my sympathy more than the second. First, it has been pointed out to me that there are idle students who will suppose – some of whom, it seems, have claimed even after the event – that it is possible to score adequate marks in an examination by using this book alone. I should be sorry for that. The book is intended to whet the appetite for further reading. The second objection runs like this: students should be provided with initial summaries of the pertinent arguments on either side of important questions and of the views of leading theorists, true; but they should obtain them by attending the lectures of their mentors, not by reading books. A colleague at a distinguished Ivy League faculty in the United States told me, 'quite frankly', that he used the book himself as a basis for preparing lectures, but that he did all he could to keep it out of the university's student bookshop. If your professor is of that way of thinking, better keep this book between plain covers!

J. W. HARRIS
Keble College
Oxford

January 1997

Preface to the first edition

This book is intended for the beginner in legal philosophy, legal theory or jurisprudence. It has been written with the needs of the law student primarily in mind. It may also be useful to students of politics, or of moral and political philosophy; for no detailed knowledge of any branch of the law is required in order to follow the lines of argument discussed.

Before they embark on a new legal course, such as contract or land law, law students are commonly recommended to read some introductory work which covers the ground of the course in outline. An overview of the terrain, before undertaking detailed study, is thought desirable. In the case of legal philosophy, legal theory or jurisprudence, there is even more need for such an introductory book; for, not only is the subject matter strange to the student, but he finds that he is now expected to employ critical criteria of a wholly new kind. In other law courses, he has learned that 'information' must be supported by citation of statutes or cases, and that 'critical comment' consists either in the analytical exposition of the implications of these same sources or else in matching them with 'policy'. Now, in 'jurisprudence', so much that was taken for granted or left unsaid about the law is put before him. 'Information' appears to consist in acquaintance with the views of a very heterogeneous collection of theorists and philosophers; and 'critical comment' appears to range from the minutiae of textual exegesis, to the deepest questions about the nature of man or society as to which – perish the thought! – he is expected to take up an overt moral or political stance. Besides these difficulties of method, jurisprudence is daunting because there is so much of it. There is no end to the literature of philosophy, politics and social theory which might have a bearing on the issues comprised in it. Oh for the security of a case and statute reading list which, if long, might at least be regarded as definitive.

This book may help to absorb the first shock. It can be read through as a survey of the ground. It covers a wider range of topics than most single courses in legal philosophy, legal theory or jurisprudence are likely to encompass. Selection will be essential for issues to be dealt with at all adequately, but a glance at the full menu may help.

Portions of the book may also be read, week by week, as an introduction to different topics in a course. Each chapter has been designed, so far as possible, to stand on its own – although cross-references have been made where crucial intersections of theme seemed to require them. There is a select bibliography for each chapter so that the subject can be more fully explored.

No introductory work can make legal philosophies simple, and this book does not try to do so. It attempts two things, apart from providing a general survey; first, to set out the major contentions on either side of a debate, leaving the student to pass his own judgment; secondly, to indicate by what sorts of criteria someone who knows something of the law. but little of philosophy, is supposed to judge jurisprudential issues.

J. W. HARRIS
Keble College
Oxford

September 1980

Contents

Table of abbreviations

The following is a list of the abbreviations used for periodicals referred to in this book:

Ad L Rev	Adelaide Law Review
AJ	*Acta Juridica* (South Africa)
Am Anth	American Anthropologist
Am Econ Rev	American Economic Review
Am J Comp L	American Journal of Comparative Law
Am J Jur	American Journal of Jurisprudence
Am L Rev	American Law Review
Am Phil Q	American Philosophical Quarterly
Am PS Rev	American Political Science Review
ARSP	Archives für Rechts-und Socialphilosophie
Br J L Soc	British Journal of Law and Society
Calif L Rev	California Law Review
Can Bar Rev	Canadian Bar Review
Card L Rev	Cardozo Law Review
China Q	China Quarterly
CLJ	Cambridge Law Journal
CLP	Current Legal Problems
Colum LRev	Columbia Law Review
Duc U L Rev	Ducane University Law Review
Duke LJ	Duke Law Journal
Ga L Rev	Georgia Law Review
GST	Grotius Society Transactions
GTLJ	Georgetown Law Journal
Harv L Rev	Harvard Law Review
HKLJ	Hong Kong Law Journal

Hof LR	Hofstra Law Review
ICLQ	International Comparative Law Quarterly
IESS	International Encyclopaedia of the Social Sciences
IJE	International Journal of Ethics
Is L Rev	Israel Law Review
J Law Soc	Journal of Law and Society
JCL	Journal of Comparative Law
JL Econ	Journal of Law and Economics
JLE	Journal of Legal Education
JLS	Journal of Legal Studies
JPE	Journal of Political Economy
J Phil	Journal of Philosophy
JSPTL	Journal of the Society of Public Teachers of Law
Jur Rev	Juridical Review
LQR	Law Quarterly Review
LS	Legal Studies
LS Rev	Law and Society Review
McGill LJ	McGill Law Journal
Mich L Rev	Michigan Law Review
Minn L Rev	Minnesota Law Review
Miss L Rev	Missouri Law Review
MLR	Modern Law Review
NILQ	Northern Ireland Law Quarterly
NLF	Natural Law Forum
NY U L Rev	New York University Law Review
OJLS	Oxford Journal of Legal Studies
PPA	Philosophy and Public Affairs
RJ	Ratio Juris
Rut L Rev	Rutgers Law Review
S Cali LR	Southern California Law Review
Scand S L	Scandinavian Studies in Law
Stan L Rev	Stanford Law Review
Tas U L Rev	Tasmania University Law Review
Tex LR	Texas Law Review
Tul L Rev	Tulane Law Review
U Br Col L Rev	University of British Columbia Law Review
U Chi L Rev	University of Chicago Law Review
U G LJ	University of Ghana Law Journal
U Pa L Rev	University of Pennsylvania Law Review
U Tor LJ	University of Toronto Law Journal
Vand L Rev	Vanderbilt Law Review
Vill L Rev	Villanova Law Review
Virg L Rev	Virginia Law Review
Wis LR	Wisconsin Law Review
Yale LJ	Yale Law Journal

1 What is jurisprudence about?

Jurisprudence is a ragbag. Into it are cast all kinds of general speculations about the law. What is it for? What does it achieve? Should we value it? How is it to be improved? Is it dispensable? Who makes it? Where do we find it? What is its relation to morality, to justice, to politics, to social practices, or to naked force? Should we obey it? Whom does it serve? These are the questions of which general jurisprudence is comprised. They can be ignored, but they will not go away.

In his daily round, the legal practitioner can usually push aside such questions together with the office cat. But now and then they will jump on his desk. Here is client Jones, storming in with some story about his neighbour's appalling behaviour.

—Yes, well, we might try to take out an injunction – though it's not certain that what he did amounts to what the law regards as a nuisance.

—Not certain! Can't you look it up?

—The law isn't something you just look up.

—What have you got all those books for then?

—They help ... anyway, we'll have to convince the county court judge that your neighbour was acting unreasonably.

—I know the judge. A sound man! He'll agree with me.

—But he's got to apply the law. It's not just a question of the particular judge – or, at least ... you may be sure that you're in the right, but we're not here concerned with questions of abstract justice.

—What sort of justice, then?

—Look, I don't think you'll be entitled to legal aid, so you must decide ...

—I know, the law's up for sale, unless some political do-gooder has decided you're poor enough to have it on a plate. You'll be asking me next: 'How much are your principles worth?' The law's supposed to protect people like me against people like him.

—No it isn't. It is supposed to do equal justice to all.

—But you just said ...

—This sort of discussion is all very well, Mr Jones, and outside office hours I'd be glad to pursue it. Right now, we have to decide on your best course of action.

—I know what I'm going to do. I'll let down the tyres on that great monstrosity he parks outside.

—You can't do that, it's illegal!

—Why should I be the only one to obey the law? Anyway, I can't see the police bothering with a thing like that and he's not likely to waste his time coming to see someone like you.

—That's not the point. Just because you think your neighbour has been antisocial, that's no reason for you to be it too.

—So now you're preaching!

It is sometimes said that the justification for teaching jurisprudence to law students is that it will make them better lawyers. Worldly practitioners tend to be cynical about that. People acquire those technical skills of legal reasoning and legal argumentation which make up the concept of 'good lawyer' by immersing themselves in substantive legal subjects. They might concede that, when issues about human rights are forced on the attention of courts, or when judges are directed by legislation to apply the 'just' or 'fair' solution, some instruction about what these notions might mean would be useful for judges, advocates and advisers. But high-flown philosophical speculation is (they might say) not the stuff of the lawyer's trade. The trouble is, however, that there is no dividing line between everyday moral problems immanent in the interpretation and application of the law and the general agenda of philosophy. In any case, every lawyer is also a citizen and, as such, does he not have a responsibility to form some conception of the worthwhileness of what he does?

Jurisprudence has to do, not primarily with the lawyer's role as a technician, but with any need he may feel to give a good account of his life's work – either to fellow citizens, or to himself, or to any gods there be. What is it that is so special about legal reasoning as against any other kind of reasoning? (see chapter 15, below). Does the lawyer contribute to the maintenance of the rule of law? If so, is the rule of law such a worthwhile ideal anyway? (see chapter 11, below). Does the lawyer's role vary from one kind of society to another? (see chapter 19, below). Of course, any lawyer may rest his case at the bar of conscience on his technique alone, and assert that it requires no justification. I once heard a

New York lawyer interviewed about his practice in advising suspected Mafia families, and that is what he did: 'I just do a job, like a surgeon.' Is that enough? Surgeons might not be flattered.

Whether for his craft or for his well-being as an informed citizen, a lawyer should be familiar with the social dimensions of law. But what are they? What does it mean to say that a thing like 'law' has a 'social context'? (see chapter 18, below). It is commonly urged that the lawyer should not be too parochial. He should not assume that the law of the modern state is the only kind of law. Why not? (see chapter 17, below).

The won't-go-away questions are not and should not be the lawyer's preserve. Everyone has a right to ask whether the ideal of the rule of law has value; whether there is any moral duty to obey the law (see chapter 16, below); whether the law ought to diminish our liberty for our own physical or moral good (see chapter 10, below); what it is, if anything, that justifies the institution of punishment (see chapter 5, below). 'Out of office hours', we all stand on the same (usually shaky) ground when we debate the merits of proposed legislation in terms of the public good (see chapter 4, below), or of justice – whether liberal, communitarian or feminist – (see chapter 20, below). By 'we' I mean lawyers and non-lawyers. It may be that moral and political philosophers are better informed. Jurisprudence has to entrench upon these disciplines at many points, as well as upon those of social and political theory. It is a scavenger, as well as a ragbag; having no perimeter to its field of inquiry, save that what is studied must have a bearing on some general speculation about law.

If jurisprudence has a heartland all its own, it is legal theory. Much discussion about the moral claims of the law (and moral claims on the law) takes the concept of law itself for granted. Yet, answers to such questions may turn on what picture of law we have. Legal theory asks: What is the nature of law (everywhere, or just in the modern state)? Some would claim that this question deserves an answer in and for itself. For others, the question is important but subsidiary – when we have defined law, we can describe its functions and its values; or, we should choose between competing definitions of law by reference to the functions we believe it has or the values we wish it to serve.

Writers make different assumptions about the proper relationship of legal theory to issues of legal philosophy – that is, between an investigation of the nature of law and a discussion of the value implications of law. For Bentham and Austin, law should be defined in terms of political facts, so that it may be laid bare for criticism in terms of utility (see chapter 3, below). For Hart, the diverse social functions of the law must be incorporated into our conception of law, so that any judgments we make about it are not deflected by a distorting mirror (see chapter 9, below). For Kelsen, pure information about legal prescriptions must be separated from intrusive value judgments of all kinds (see chapter 6, below). Despite the obscurities of his esoteric language, Kelsen is the true friend of the practitioner who wants to be called on to describe the law and nothing but the law *in office hours*. For the natural lawyers and for Fuller and for Dworkin – each in their very different ways – such a practitioner cannot be satisfied. What 'the law is' is so intimately connected with what, morally speaking, 'the law ought to be' that our picture of it must include some conception of moral truth (see chapters 2, 11 and 14, below). For the 'realist', all the pictures of law we have are illusions; and for the advocate of 'critical legal studies' they serve only to mask illegitimate domination (see chapter 8, below).

General jurisprudence contributes to the training of a lawyer *qua* citizen and of the citizen *qua* legal critic. 'Particular jurisprudence' may, however, bear more directly on the professional lawyer's concerns. General jurisprudence deals with speculations about the law; particular jurisprudence, with speculations about particular legal concepts. Every lawyer has from time to time to analyse terms of art appearing in legal materials. When is a concept employed in the law fit for jurisprudential analysis as distinct from ordinary legal elucidation? I suggest that no line is to be drawn. There is a continuum from very concrete questions – like, what does this word mean in the context of this statute? – to very general questions – like, what is the essence of a legal right? Roughly, particular jurisprudence concerns itself with terms which are common both to different systems of law and to different branches of law. 'Base fee' is not such a concept, not because it is not difficult, but because it is peculiar to the common law. 'Rape' is not such a concept, because though it appears in all systems, it is peculiar to criminal law. Particular jurisprudence fastens on terms which are inter-branch and inter-systemic – like right, duty, possession, person and so on. Opinions vary as to the value of such analyses for the practising lawyer, but they were certainly intended to assist him (see chapter 7, below).

The two concepts investigated by particular jurisprudence which have the best claim to the attention of the practising lawyer – as indeed to that of the political scientist – are those of 'precedent' and 'legislative intention'. All modern legal systems have to deal with statutory interpretation and have some notion of precedent. The investigation of the version of these concepts employed by any particular system turns out to involve a special mixture of constitutional and conceptual issues (see chapters 12 and 13, below).

All these questions, then, are what jurisprudence is about. Whether the word 'jurisprudence' is a good baggage label for them matters not at all. Sometimes this word is used as a heavy word for the study or knowledge of the law. There was a time when it was used in England to stand merely for the analysis of legal concepts. In French, 'la Jurisprudence' signifies what we call case law; and 'theorie generale du droit' covers much of the same ground as what is here called jurisprudence. I believe that use of 'jurisprudence' to stand for general speculations of all kinds about the law is now fairly common in modern English usage; that 'legal theory' is used to cover inquiries into the nature of law; and that 'legal philosophy' means that branch of practical philosophy which investigates the value implications of describing something as 'legal'. Whether labels matter when it comes to the word 'law' itself – a question which is highly controversial in the areas of 'primitive law' and 'living law' (see chapters 17 and 18, below) – it is surely the case that labels do not matter in assigning the proper fields for 'jurisprudence', 'legal theory' and 'legal philosophy'. It is the won't-go-away questions which count.

This book does not break up the subject according to a systematic plan. That would be impossible without prejudging crucial questions – such as whether 'the relations of law to morality' constitute a topic separate from 'the nature of 'law'. Some chapters deal with particular questions (like the duty to obey the law), some with topics involving clusters of questions (like statutory interpretation), some with schools of thought (like the historical school), and some with individual theorists. My object is to introduce the reader to a bill of fare. On controversial matters, I have tried to state both sides of a question leaving it to the reader to provide an answer; but one cannot always disguise one's own view. I hope at least to have exemplified how jurists argue so that, if she wants to, the reader can join in. Welcome to the feast.

2 Natural law and moral truth

1 Natural law

One facet of common discourse assumes a correlation between 'good' and 'what comes naturally'. Parental affection, heterosexual love, support for aged kin and comradely interdependence are natural and therefore good. That which ignores or distorts human nature is bad. Lawyers, on occasion, have been prepared to listen to such 'naturalistic' arguments, especially where an issue is not covered by the arguments from authority with which lawyers are more familiar. In a case of first impression in 1970, an English judge held that a 'marriage' between a man and a person who had undergone a 'sex change' was a nullity since it could not involve the natural, biologically-determined consequences of marriage.:

> 'Since marriage is essentially a relationship between man and woman, the validity of the marriage in this case depends, in my judgment, upon whether the respondent is or is not a woman ... Having regard to the essentially heterosexual character of the relationship which is called marriage, the criteria must, in my judgment, be biological, for even the most extreme degree of transsexualism in a male or the most severe hormonal imbalance which can exist in a person with male chromosomes, male gonads and male genitalia cannot reproduce a person who is naturally capable of performing the essential role of a woman in marriage.'[1]

The jurists who developed the law of the Roman empire made frequent references to the nature of the case as a basis for settling matters not covered by authority. The compilers of the *Corpus Juris* of the emperor Justinian

1   *Corbett v Corbett* [1971] P 83 at 106 per Ormerod J.

in 533 AD employed the adjective *naturalis* as a classificatory peg, distinguishing 'natural' obligations and transactions from their counterparts in the *Jus Civile*. Parallel with, and sometimes infusing, these lawyer-like references to the natural, the philosophy of the ancient world had evolved a conception of natural law.

The classical doctrine of natural law, though it would support the naturalistic arguments and classifications of the lawyers, has much more far-reaching implications. It speaks of a law of nature which has characteristics quite different from those of the ordinary laws familiar to practitioners. First, it is universal and immutable. In consequence, it is available at all times and in all places for those whose office it is to enact or develop law. In other words, it is one conception of 'justice', in the sense in which justice stands for the righting of wrongs and the proper distribution of benefits and burdens within a political community. Secondly, it is a 'higher' law. It has a relationship of superiority towards laws promulgated by political authorities. This means that it determines whether ordinary laws are morally binding on subjects. These first two characteristics emphasise the 'legal' quality of natural law. If it were merely a system of private ethics, it would not *eo ipse* be mete for enactment by legislatures and judges and would not set criteria for obedience. Thirdly, it is discoverable by reason. Herein lies the 'natural' quality of natural law. The stoics, the school which elaborated the doctrine, viewed all things, including man, as having natural essences or ends. The reflective intellect possessed direct knowledge of these qualities from which conclusions might be drawn, by rational steps, about what justice requires. Aristotle had claimed that it was natural to man to be a member of a *polis* – often crudely paraphrased as the view that man is a 'political animal' or 'social animal'. That being so, his nature requires rules setting up political organisations and imposing mutual forbearances for the common good.

The most famous summary of the classical natural law doctrine is the following statement of the stoic position given by Cicero in the first century BC:

> 'True law is right reason in agreement with Nature; it is of universal application, unchanging and everlasting; it summons to duty by its commands, and averts from wrong-doing by its prohibitions. And it does not lay its commands or prohibitions upon good men in vain, though neither have any effect on the wicked. It is a sin to try to alter this law, nor is it allowable to attempt to repeal any part of it, and it is impossible to abolish it entirely. We cannot be freed from its obligations by Senate or People, and we need not look outside ourselves for an expounder or interpreter of it. And there will not be different laws at Rome and at Athens, or different laws now and in the future, but one eternal and unchangeable law will be valid for

all nations and for all times, and there will be one master and one ruler, that is, God, over us all, for He is the author of this law, its promulgator, and its enforcing judge.'[2]

Natural law was eventually prayed in aid by the Christian church. The New Testament spoke of divine grace and individual redemption, but was rather thin on political blue-prints. Some of the fathers of the church were pessimistic about human institutions. Given the sinful condition of man since the fall, his political arrangements were likely to be defective. St Augustine (354-430) asked rhetorically:

'Set justice aside, then, and what are kingdoms but fair thievish purchases?'[3]

Medieval scholars were more optimistic. The fall had not taken away man's ability to appreciate his own good, and to reason therefrom to the good society. The Roman Catholic church eventually adopted the views of the Dominican jurist St Thomas Aquinas (1225-1274). Aquinas synthesised Christian revelation with the pre-Christian doctrine of natural law. His legal theory encompasses four types of law. 'Eternal law' comprises God-given rules governing all creation. 'Natural law' is that segment of eternal law which is discoverable through the special process of reasoning mapped out by the pagan authors – intuitions of the natural and deductions drawn therefrom. 'Divine law' has been revealed in Scripture. 'Human law' consists of rules, supportable by reason, but articulated by human authorities for the common good. As to the interrelation between these different types of law, two crucial propositions stand out in Thomist philosophy. First, human laws derive their legal quality, their power to bind in conscience, from natural law. Man's natural end being social, a community prescription which is, in reason, directed to the common good has, by nature, the quality of law. In some instances, the content of law is deducible from first principles of natural law; for the rest, the legislator has the freedom of an architect. Secondly, any purported law which is in conflict with natural or divine law is a mere corruption of law and so not binding by virtue of its own legal quality. Nevertheless, even if an enactment is contrary to natural law and so 'unjust', obedience may still be proper to avoid bad example or civil disturbance:

'But in human affairs a thing is said to be just when it accords aright with the rule of reason: and ... the first rule of reason is the natural law. Thus all humanly enacted laws are in accord with reason to the

2   *De Republica* iii, xxii, 33.
3   *City of God* 4, 4.

extent that they derive from the natural law. And if a human law is at variance in any particular with the natural law, it is no longer legal, but rather a corruption of law.

But it should be noted that there are two ways in which anything may derive from natural law. First, as a conclusion from more general principles. Secondly, as a determination of certain general features. The former is similar to the method of the sciences in which demonstrative conclusions are drawn from first principles. The second way is like to that of the arts in which some common form is determined to a particular instance: as, for example, when an architect, starting from the general idea of a house, then goes on to design the particular plan of this or that house ...

Man is bound to obey secular Rulers to the extent that the order of justice requires. For this reason if such rulers have no just title to power, but have usurped it, or if they command things to be done which are unjust, their subjects are not obliged to obey them; except, perhaps, in certain special cases when it is a matter of avoiding scandal or some particular danger.'[4]

Aquinas's theory gives political rulers quite a lot of room for manoeuvre. So long as what they lay down is guided by a reasoned assessment of the common good, it has the power to bind in conscience. Only the first principles of natural law – such as 'Do harm to no man' – are immutable. Specific deductions from first principles might vary. Furthermore, natural law could be added to. Thus, although by nature all men were equally free and all things were held in common, positive law could introduce the legal concepts of slavery and private property. The effect of the theory is to clothe all legislation with presumptive moral status; and even where positive law conflicted with natural law, compliance might still be morally required.

As a topic in the history of ideas (in the fields of ethics and of political and legal philosophy), there can be no doubt of the importance of the doctrine of natural law. It is through the medium of this doctrine that the Roman Catholic church claims to be able to speak authoritatively on ethical questions to all men. In 1968, Pope Paul VI appealed to it as support for the view that artificial means of birth control are not allowable:

'The Church, calling men back to the observance of the norms of natural law, as interpreted by her constant doctrine, teaches that each and every marriage act must remain open to the transmission of life ...

4   *Selected Political Writings* (D'Entreves ed) pp 121, 179.

We believe that the men of our day are particularly capable of seizing the deeply reasonable and human character of this fundamental principle.'[5]

So far as political philosophy is concerned, the Thomist version of natural law is seen as conservative compared with the revolutionary implications to which the doctrine later gave rise. Aquinas showed how the bindingness of positive law actually derived from natural law, so long as flexible notions like the rationally-conceived common good were not overstepped; and he thus threw over positive law a halo of moral sanctity. Later writers, using the same process of reasoning from nature, evolved the conception of natural rights, infringement of which entitled citizens to revolt. The American colonists in 1776 justified their overthrow of British rule on the ground that the colonial government had impaired rights to 'life, liberty and the pursuit of happiness', it being 'self-evident' that man was endowed with such rights. The French National Assembly in 1789 made a similar appeal to 'simple and indisputable' principles, which showed that men had natural rights to 'liberty, property, security and resistance to oppression'. Such rights were evident to reason, taking the nature of man as its starting-point. Intermingled with such naturalistic reasoning was 'contractarian' reasoning, that is, the view that political rights and obligations could be conceived of in terms of a social contract. But the two modes of philosophising must be distinguished, since writers who shared the concept of social contract took very different views of the significance of 'nature'. Thomas Hobbes (1588-1679) rejected the view that sovereigns could be made politically accountable by reference to any supra-state concept of justice. Men enjoy natural liberty (including the right to make pre-emptive strikes against any of their neighbours) only in a state of nature in which the life of man is 'solitary, poor, nasty, brutish, and short'.[6]

By the social contract, according to Hobbes, citizens surrendered natural liberty, and subjected themselves to an unlimited state sovereign. John Locke (1632-1704), on the other hand, argued that there were natural rights which survived the entry into civil society constituted by the social contract, and failure to protect them was a ground on which governments could be changed. The most complex amalgam of contract and nature is that of Jean-Jacques Rousseau (1712-1778). For him there were natural rights which nothing could take away; but, provided the social contract invested the 'general will' with all legislative power, there could be no question of positive law entrenching on rights. The general will subsumed

---

5   *Humanae Vitae* paras 11 and 12.
6   *Leviathan* p 186.

all wills, so that every man willed what the law stipulated – even if, on occasion, someone had to be 'forced to be free'.

A natural rights argument as such, like a natural law argument, bases its claims about what ought to be done by governments on the nature of man. A contractarian argument, as such, bases such claims on what citizens did (or notionally would) agree to. These are rival conceptions of justice. The most celebrated modern contractarian theory of justice, that of John Rawls, is considered in chapter 20, below. In that chapter we shall also investigate Robert Nozick's version of Locke's argument that private property arises by just steps from a state-of-nature in which all resources are held in common.

So far as legal philosophy is concerned, academic jurists up to the end of the eighteenth century commonly incorporated the doctrine of natural law. Generally, however, this was no more than a gloss without detailed implications, as it is in the *Corpus Juris* of Justinian. Sir William Blackstone (1723-1780) begins his *Commentaries on the Laws of England* with an assertion of all the leading tenets of the classical doctrine – natural law willed by God and discoverable by reason; positive law deriving its binding force from natural law; positive law in conflict with natural law being a nullity; and adds in the concept of social contract for good measure. Yet this acceptance of natural law had little effect on his detailed exposition of English law.

On the European continent, however, whole expository statements of law purported to be based on natural law. This was of particular importance in the area of what we now call 'public international law'. Civilian academic lawyers were expounders of Roman law. In the sphere of private law, there were authoritative texts enough in the *Corpus Juris* and the commentaries written upon it to make appeals direct to naturalistic reason unnecessary – although the texts themselves contained such references. But the emergence of comity between sovereign and equal states gave renaissance lawyers a new problem. How could law, not made by princes, bind princes among themselves? The answer was to redeploy the classical Roman concept of *Ius Gentium*. This originally referred to the law which Roman authorities enforced in dealings between citizens and foreigners, or between foreigners, as opposed to the *Ius Civile* which was applicable between citizens. It now came to cover relations of war and peace, treaty-making and allegiance, and so on. But it is one thing to find a label; from where was to come the content? Only from natural law, that is, from propositions which, it seemed to these authors, no one in reason could dispute. In this way writers like Grotius (1583-1645) and Puffendorf (1632-1694) discovered or – if naturalistic arguments are unsound – 'created' new law for a new era. Natural law was increasingly secularised, in that its rational (as distinct from revealed) basis was stressed. Even if God did not exist, Grotius said, natural law would have the same content; and just as

God cannot cause that two times two shall not be four, so he cannot cause the intrinsically evil to be not evil.

Granted its historical importance, what is twentieth-century man to make of the classical doctrine of natural law? One's answer to that depends, in the first instance, on what one makes of two assertions about the relation of law to morality which together led to the eclipse of natural law thinking during the nineteenth century, and dissatisfaction with which has led, in some quarters, to its recent revival. These assertions generally go under the names of 'noncognitivism' and 'legal positivism'.

Noncognitivism is the view that there is no rational procedure by which we can objectively know what is morally right and wrong. We cannot derive an 'ought' from an 'is'. No amount of information about the facts of the world or of human nature provides proof that anything ought to be done or not done. In the English-speaking world, the paternity of this doctrine is generally attributed to the Scottish philosopher, David Hume (1711-1776). In his *Treatise of Human Nature*, first published in 1739, he wrote:

> 'In every system of morality, which I have hitherto met with, I have always remark'd, that the author proceeds for some time in the ordinary way of reasoning, and establishes the being of a God, or makes observations concerning human affairs; when of a sudden I am surpriz'd to find, that instead of the usual copulations of propositions, *is*, and *is not*, I meet with no proposition that is not connected with an *ought*, or an *ought not*. This change is imperceptible; but is, however, of the last consequence. For as this *ought*, or *ought not*, expresses some new relation or affirmation, 'tis necessary that it sho'ld be observ'd and explain'd; and at the same time that a reason should be given, for what seems altogether inconceivable, how this new relation can be a deduction from others, which are entirely different from it. But as authors do not commonly use this precaution, I shall presume to recommend it to the readers; and am persuaded, that this small attention wo'ld subvert all the vulgar systems of morality, and let us see, that the distinction of vice and virtue is not founded merely on the relations of objects nor is perceiv'd by reason'.[7]

For many jurists, Hume's point is a knock-down argument against all forms of natural law thinking; for does it not show that reason can tell us nothing about justice or political obligation? It must, however, be borne in mind that, according to the standard interpretation of the passage just quoted, Hume was making only a logical point – an assertion about the

7   *A Treatise of Human Nature* p 521.

logically necessary relationship between propositions. It merely deprives natural lawyers of that most revered of philosophic weapons, the deductive syllogism.

A syllogism comprises three elements: a major premise, say, 'All men are mortal'; a minor premise, 'Socrates is a man'; and a conclusion, 'Socrates is mortal'. Given the premises, one cannot deny the conclusion without self-contradiction. Therefore, the conclusion follows, with logical necessity, from the premises. Since Hume, few would be prepared to defend the following syllogism: 'All animals rear their young'; 'Men are animals'; therefore, 'Men *ought* to rear their young'. Granted the first two steps, the conclusion does not follow for the simple reason that it contains a copula not contained in the premises, namely, the 'ought'. Thus, even if we accept all that Aristotle said about man's social nature as factually correct, it does not follow, logically, that he is under any kind of obligation to other members of his community. If we grant that, biologically, the primary function of sexual relations is begetting of offspring, it does not follow, logically, that artificial means of contraception are morally wrong.

Two matters must be taken into account in order to set Hume's point in a proper relationship to the whole field of human reasoning. First, if syllogistic, deductive demonstration is the only kind of acceptable 'proof', then one has to be sceptical, as Hume was, about all the assertions of natural science. Not only do *ought*-assertions not follow from *is*-assertions, but no proposition about the future follows from any number of propositions about the past. From the fact that the sun has always risen in the east, it does not follow, as a matter of logical necessity, that it will do so tomorrow. Only mathematical deductions from definitional axioms meet the test of logical necessity. Philosophers have had to find other, non-syllogistic criteria of proof to support the rationality of natural science. Secondly, and more importantly for our assessment of the claims of natural law, if those engaged in a discussion can begin by agreeing on some *ought*-proposition as major premise, then, given factual propositions as minor premises, they can go on to deduce *ought*-conclusions. If I say that killing the innocent is wrong and you disagree, we can get no further. But if we both accept the major premise, we may make progress. Perhaps there are normative premises about which all those who ever debate do agree – about the dignity of man requiring that all be provided with a minimum of security, clothing, food, freedom of self-expression and so on. Only if there are not does Hume's *is/ought* cleavage scupper natural law in port. Hume himself does not appear to have been a subscriber to the extreme relativism of later writers who contend that all our moral opinions are dependent on our personal experience and circumstances. His remark about reason being the 'slave of the passions' is sometimes cited in support of 'emotivism', the view that normative discourse is nothing more than an expression of feelings, equivalent to cries of 'ouch!'.

But it may have meant no more than that our emotions – which could be universally shared emotions – must give us the normative premises from which reasoning may then proceed:

> 'Tho' the rules of justice be *artificial*, they are not *arbitrary*. Nor is the expression improper to call them *Laws of Nature*; if by natural we understand what is common to any species, or even if we confine it to mean what is inseparable from the species.'[8]

In his recent comprehensive restatement of natural law theory, John Finnis denies that the true classical doctrine ever purported to derive 'ought' from 'is'. He concedes that the stoic doctrine, renaissance theorists and indeed Catholic writers on natural law down almost to the present day, did claim to draw normative inferences from nature and in that sense confused fact and value. But he argues that this was not true of Aristotle – who, on the contrary, clearly differentiated between 'speculative reason' (reasoning about what is the case) and 'practical reason' (reasoning about what ought to be done); and it was not true of Aquinas – whose ethical theory was misunderstood by later writers. Basing himself primarily upon his interpretation of Aquinas, Finnis claims that the 'classical doctrine' takes as its first step towards normative conclusions, not some observation of human or other nature, but a reflective grasp of what is self-evidently good for men:

> 'When discerning what is good ... intelligence is operating in a different way, yielding a different logic, from when it is discerning what is the case (historically, scientifically, or metaphysically); but there is no good reason for asserting that the latter operations of intelligence are more rational than the former ...
>   The basic forms of good grasped by practical understanding are what is good for human beings with the nature they have. Aquinas considers that practical reasoning begins not by understanding this nature from the outside, as it were, by way of psychological, anthropological, or metaphysical observations and judgments defining human nature, but by experiencing one's nature, so to speak, from the inside, in the form of one's inclinations. But again, there is no process of inference. One does not judge that "I have (or everybody has) an inclination to find out about things" and then infer that therefore "knowledge is a good to be pursued". Rather, by a simple act of non-inferential understanding one grasps that the object of the inclination which one experiences is an instance of a general form of good, for oneself (and others like one).'[9]

8   *A Treatise of Human Nature* p 536.
9   *Natural Law and Natural Rights* p 34.'

Expanding and clarifying Aquinas's approach, Finnis proceeds to set out his own theory of natural law. He argues that there are certain 'basic forms of human flourishing' which are in one way or another used by everyone who considers what to do, however unsound his conclusions. These include 'life', 'knowledge', 'play', 'aesthetic experience', 'friendship', 'practical reasonableness', and 'religion'. There are, secondly, a set of 'basic methodological requirements' of practical reasonableness which, taken together, provide the criteria for distinguishing ways of acting that are morally right or wrong. These include 'pursuit of goods', 'a coherent plan of life', 'no arbitrary preferences amongst values', 'no arbitrary preferences amongst persons', 'detachment and commitment', 'the (limited) relevance of consequences', 'respect for every basic value in every act', 'the requirements of the common good', and 'following one's conscience'. These basic goods and methodological requirements together constitute the universal and unchanging principles of natural law. Because of them, objective knowledge of morality is possible. 'Justice' consists of the concrete implications of the requirement to foster the 'common good' (in the sense of the set of conditions which enable the members of a community to realise the basic values for themselves and to attain any other reasonable objectives they may have). People may reasonably differ as to details, and the justice of arrangements varies with circumstances. Nevertheless, Finnis argues, the basic goods and methodological requirements are sufficiently precise to rule out many kinds of injustice. In their light one can arrive at certain absolute duties, with correlative absolute natural (human) rights – rights not to be tortured, not to have one's life taken directly as a means to any further end, not to be positively lied to (in situations in which factual communication is reasonably expected), not to be condemned on knowingly false charges, not to be deprived of one's procreative capacity; and the right to be taken into respectful consideration in any assessment of what the common good requires.

Finnis contends that most jurists have misunderstood classical natural law doctrine. It appealed, not to inferences drawn from facts about human nature, but to judgments people can make because they are endowed with a special faculty of practical reasoning as part of their nature. One may wonder what difference this makes. When we reflect on our own and other people's inclinations in order to gain self-evident knowledge about universal goods, are not assumptions of fact about human nature inevitably going to form part of the content of the reflection? Perhaps the Thomist writers of the seventeenth century and afterwards, although they changed Aquinas's conceptual structure, were nevertheless drawing out the implications of his theory. Finnis himself appeals to facts of human experience and psychology when working out the requirements of 'practical reasonableness'. He gives two reasons for maintaining that a regime of private ownership (including of means of production) is in most times and places a requirement of justice. The first is the good of 'personal autonomy in community'. The second is the rule of human experience that resources are more productively exploited by private than by public enterprise. He argues that 'public morality' limitations on the exercise of rights are justified in the light of psychological facts about the egotistic nature of sexual drives. On the general question of specifying and demarcating rights, he says:

> 'There is, I think, no alternative but to hold in one's mind's eye some pattern, or range of patterns, of human character, conduct, and interaction in community, and then to choose such specification of rights as tends to favour that pattern, or range of patterns.'[10]

Finnis stresses that our knowledge of self-evident human goods is not innate. It comes to us, to all of us, only if we have had sufficient experience and are willing to engage in reasoning reflection. It may be that such reflection must embrace an indissoluble mixture of what human beings are like and what is good for them – at least if it is to yield principles sufficiently concrete to be useful guides to moral deliberation. Even if this process does affront the *is/ought* cleavage, that only shows that we are not dealing with logical necessities. We can still call the process 'reasoning'. If it will yield basic principles to which all who engage in it must reasonably assent, then there is a natural system of morality.

The second fundamental assault on natural law doctrine is 'legal positivism'. This expression is used in many ways, but most of its adherents would at least subscribe to the following two propositions. First, no element of moral value enters into the definition of law. Secondly, legal provisions are identified by empirically-observable criteria, such as legislation, decided cases and custom. Their contention is that there is no law but positive law, and therefore no such thing as 'natural law'. Whether or not there are criteria of morality or justice by which we can assess the merits of positive law, what law is is one thing, its goodness or badness another.

Legal positivists have appealed to two features of legal practice in support of their anti-natural law stance, one empirical, and one programmatic. When practising lawyers describe the law to clients, they do not give, and would not be thanked for giving, their views about what the law ought to be. They look up the books, and from them state what the law is. As to programmes of reform, we need to know what the law is before we can formulate ways of changing it. If, in stating the law, we base our reasoning on inferences from morality rather than on known source materials, we may smuggle in controversial moral claims. Better

10   *Natural Law and Natural Rights* p 219.

to set out the law as it is, and then go on to give our reasons why the law is right or in what ways it should be changed. The issues of justice and of the morally-binding nature of positive law raise questions as to which there is no specifically juristic answer. Lawyers, *qua* lawyers, have nothing special to say about them; so these issues should not be presented in the guise of a supposed higher law.

Bentham, the founder of English legal positivism, appealed in just this way to legal practice when refuting the natural law theory espoused by Blackstone. By insisting that human law derives its validity from natural law, Blackstone merely warded off criticism of the law. If the law could not be shown to conflict with natural law, it was valid. Although Blackstone repeated the classical view that laws contrary to natural law are a nullity, he gave no example of any such purported enactment in England, but only the hypothetical example of a law which allowed or enjoined us to commit murder. On this frail example, Bentham turned the heavy guns of his characteristic irony:

> 'Murder is *killing* under certain *circumstances*. Is the human law then to be allowed to define, *in denier resort*, what shall be those *circumstances*, or is it not? If yes, the case of a "human law allowing or enjoining us to commit it", is a case that is not so much as supposable: if no, adieu to all human laws: to the fire with our Statutes at large, our Reports, our Institutes, and all that we have hitherto been used to call our law books; our law books, the only law books we can be safe in trusting to, are Puffendorf and the Bible.'[11]

Critics of legal positivism answer as follows. Issues of justice and of the duty to obey cannot be separated from legal science in the way positivists suggest. When we describe the law on many questions, we have to refer to moral considerations. And this is not just a matter of filling in gaps. It is systematically part of the function of lawyers, and especially of judges, to answer two questions in one: 'What is the law?' and 'What does justice require?' As we shall see in chapter 14, Ronald Dworkin argues in this way, but without invoking any higher (natural) law.

What Bentham says about burning law books is a travesty. The classical doctrine distinguished *mala in se*, like murder and theft, where the principles of positive law are deduced from or founded on objective moral principles; and *mala prohibita*, regulatory offences which are more or less at the discretion of the legislature. In the case of the latter, we clearly find the law in the positive sources; and even with the former, matters of definition and penalty are left to positive law. For Finnis, although the

11 *Fragment on Government* ch 4, para 18, n 1.

'focal meaning' of law refers to rules aimed at coordinating the common good, that is in no way inconsistent with the fact that any practitioner turns first to legislation and case law. He argues that the central claim about positive law deriving its legal quality from natural law is a support, not an undermining, of positive law. He maintains that his theory of natural law enables one to found both the reasonable claims, and the limits, of authority on objective moral principles; for it can be rationally demonstrated that the problems of 'coordination in community' require legislative determination. Similarly (he argues) the principles of the rule of law, discussed in chapter 11, below, can be shown to be based on 'practical reasonableness':

> 'The tradition of natural law theorizing is not concerned to minimize the range and determinacy of positive law or the general sufficiency of positive sources as solvents of legal problems. Rather, the concern of the tradition ... has been to show that the act of "positing" law ... is an act which can and should be guided by "moral" principles and rules; that those moral norms are a matter of objective reasonableness, not of whim, convention, or mere "decision"; and that those same moral norms justify (a) the very institution of positive law, (b) the main institutions, techniques, and modalities within that tradition (e.g. separation of powers), and (c) the main institutions regulated and sustained by law (e.g. government, contract, property, marriage, and criminal liability). What truly characterises the tradition is that it is not content merely to observe the historical or sociological fact that "morality" thus affects "law", but instead seeks to determine what the requirements of practical reasonableness really are, so as to afford a rational basis for the activities of legislators, judges, and citizens.'[12]

Finnis also claims that the slogan '*lex iniusta non est lex*' has been misrepresented by critics of natural law doctrine. An unjust law is not a 'nullity', in the sense of being something one can totally disregard. It merely lacks, prima facie, the power to bind in conscience which laws usually possess; and there can be a moral duty to obey even unjust laws if not doing so might lead to the weakening of a legal system which is on the whole just.

Arguments for and against a prima facie duty to obey the law are considered in chapter 16, below. It should be mentioned, however, that some advocates of natural law would give a much more robust interpretation to the nullity doctrine. According to this view, *lex iniusta non est lex* is not merely a guide to conscientious disobedience, but also

12   *Natural Law and Natural Rights* p 290.

a moral blue pencil for use by legal science. Where laws are (or were) sufficiently heinous, lawyers, *qua* lawyers, can disregard them. This view gained adherents as the direct consequence of the Nazi nightmare. In some of the decisions of German courts since the establishing of the Federal Republic, Nazi legislation has been declared invalid, inter alia, because it was incompatible with fundamental justice. A majority of the House of Lords has indicated that it would refuse to recognise a Nazi law depriving Jewish citizens of German nationality (even though it passed the normal criteria of recognition specified in the English rules relating to conflict of laws) simply because it was flagrantly unjust.[13]

The doctrine proclaimed at the Nuremberg war trials – that superior orders constitute no defence to 'crimes against humanity' – can also be understood as moral blue pencil; although there was no explicit appeal to natural law.

H.L.A. Hart argued against the natural-law implications of the post-Nazi experience, contending that the best way to deal with 'offenders' who claim the shield of Nazi 'law' is frankly to enact retrospective legislation. He believed that the statement of law and its criticism should not be confused. However, he found a 'core of good sense' in natural law doctrine:

'For it is a truth of some importance that for the adequate description not only of law but of many other social institutions, a place must be reserved, besides definitions and ordinary statements of fact, for a third category of statements: those the truth of which is contingent on human beings and the world they live in retaining the salient characteristics which they have.'[14]

The most important characteristic is that men wish to survive. They are not members of suicide clubs. That supplies the 'ought' of a major premise. The minor premises come from certain indisputable observations ('truisms') about man and the world. First, men are mutually vulnerable. Second, unlike nation states, they are approximately equal in their abilities to help and harm each other. Third, they have limited altruism, being neither angels nor devils. Fourth, they live in a world with limited resources. Fifth, they suffer from weakness of intellect and will which means that achievement of their aims requires a special coordination of their activities. On the basis of these universal truths, Hart concludes that all human societies have, and must necessarily have, rules restricting violence, some property system which entails rules restricting theft, and

13 *Oppenheimer v Cattermole* [1976] AC 249.
14 *The Concept of Law* (2nd edn) pp 199-200.

some system of promising which entails rules restricting deceit. These are the 'minimum content of natural law'.

Is the 'natural law' label appropriately employed in this context? If all societies have these rules, then no society can ever be called unjust and no government legitimately resisted for not having them. The only normative mileage one could make out of this minimum content would be an argument against dispensing with social organisation altogether, a refutation of some forms of anarchism. The minimum content does not appear to require that the exercise of force be politically centralised. It is consistent with a system of rules that protects only one group (by institutionalising slavery or racial oppression); and with any kind of property regime, public or private – although not with the final stage envisaged by Marxist theory, in which there would be production to abundance and so no restrictions on any use of material things (see chapter 19, below). It has to be consistent with much variation in social organisation in order for its claim to descriptive universality to be true. One might call it a 'sociological' conception of natural law. Sociology provides generalisations based on proven information. The minimum content gives us generalisations based on 'truisms', facts so obvious that they need no proof. If a Martian came to earth, we might take him to one side and begin his sociological education as follows: 'Now I know that you Martian chaps are all armour-plated crabs and so couldn't hurt each other if you tried, and also that you are so rational and benevolent that you can plan your lives without cooperative institutions, and that you only eat red mud of which you have an inexhaustible supply. Things are otherwise with us.'

2   Moral truth

There may be a lot to be said for sociology-for-Martians, precisely because it tells us humans basic truths our dreamers sometimes forget. But the classical doctrine of natural law goes much further. It requires us to look at man and his world in as much detail as we can, and to apply to the information we have a special kind of moral reasoning which we all share. If we do that, so the doctrine contends, we will arrive at concepts of man and of communities (national and international), which will provide a consistent critical touchstone for all political arrangements including laws. That system of justice arrived at in that way the doctrine calls 'natural law'. It is 'natural' by virtue of the sort of reasoning which reveals it. It is a higher 'law', both because it provides criteria of justice for legislatures and judges, and also because it tells us when we are morally required to obey the prescriptions of political superiors and when we are not.

The reader may not be convinced. She may be sceptical about the whole idea of objective moral truth. There are two familiar grounds for such scepticism. One appeals to anthropological information, and the other invokes the value of 'tolerance'. Do we not observe that different peoples, both in the past and at the present day, have incompatible opinions about what is morally required or permitted? Anyone is entitled to his or her own moral beliefs, but is it not an impertinence to suggest that other people's opinions are 'wrong'? Added to these popular grounds for scepticism, there are weighty philosophical objections to supposed moral objectivism. There is the Humean is/ought cleavage to which reference has already been made. In addition, there is what might be called 'scienticism'. The natural sciences, with their procedures of observation and repeatable experiments, can alone tell us what objective facts there are 'out there'. There is something 'queer', as J.L. Mackie put it, in supposing that there could as well be 'moral facts'. Morality is not part of the furniture of the universe. Such noncognitivism about morals may be combined with either 'relativism', the view that a moral judgment expresses only the speaker's (or his group's) opinion; or 'emotivism', the claim that such judgments evince the speaker's emotions.

If moral scepticism is right, what should we make of political controversy, calls for legal reform, or condemnations of governments? Should someone announce: 'The following is my opinion ... If you disagree, there is nothing more to be said'? Shall we say that, for our part, we are revolted by genocide and ethnic cleansing; but there is simply no way of demonstrating that those who practise such things are in the wrong? In particular, is all the talk of 'human rights' mere rhetoric or, worse, cultural imperialism?

The history of Western political thought contains various suggestions for providing moral foundations from which individual or governmental action may be appraised, which are not dependent on any special faculty to grasp the self-evident. Usually, they make no appeal to a higher law.

In the eighteenth century Immanuel Kant (1724-1804) turned away from the state-of-nature theorising of the previous century in favour of working out the implications of rational human agency. As he argued, if one acted morally at all, one was committed to a 'categorical imperative': one must act in accordance with a rule which one willed to be a universal law of conduct. A modern variant of Kantianism is espoused by Alan Gewirth, and Deryck Beyleveld and Roger Brownsword have offered a sophisticated version of 'natural law' based on Gewirth's moral theory. They maintain that concepts such as law must have an essence – it is not just a question of words; and that true law, as opposed to rules enforced by naked power, must conform to those principles to which any rational agent is committed. They are happy to embrace, as Finnis is not, the maxim that an unjust 'law' is not law.

Kantian notions of 'agent rationality' and 'universalisability' are problematic. If someone dumps litter but complains when other people do so, it seems appropriate to say that he is inconsistent. Is he, however, acting 'irrationally' in the way that a person who does not want to be burnt, but nevertheless puts his hand in a fire, is acting irrationally? If I have a selfish end in view and take appropriate steps to achieve it, can it be demonstrated by any process of abstract reasoning that my conduct is objectively wrong? Even if we accept that universalisability is intrinsic to rational reflection about what ought to be done, there remains the problem of the level at which universalisation is to come in.

> Jones says: 'Only I ought to park a car on that spot!'
> 'Universalise, please, Mr Jones.'
> 'Because I am a resident, and only residents should park.' Or
> 'Because mine is a small car, and only small cars should be parked there.' Or
> 'Because I am a member of the Church of England and parking should be restricted to Anglicans.'

The trouble with Kantianism, in the view of its critics, is that abstract agency is an inadequate basis for substantive moral principles. If we approve or condemn any of the Jones alternatives we do so because we introduce concrete moral content from some non-Kantian basis.

One need not be committted to abstract rational demonstration in order to put forward moral foundations. One can offer reasons addressed to the members of a particular culture (or to all humanity) which, one supposes, make some foundational position *plausible*. Believers in divine revelation do that when they appeal to faith. Bentham proceeded in just this way when commending utilitarianism: it could not be 'proved', he said, but bear in mind that if you rejected it you must be favouring the misery, rather than the happiness, of the greatest number. We shall see in chapter 4 that utilitarianism is supported or denied by invoking its allegedly obvious attractive or unattractive implications.

In a similar way, one can take particular values, either one by one or in clusters, to be features of just human association and draw arguments from them, on the assumption that, as starting-points, they will seem plausible to one's addressee. In that way, in chapter 16, the question whether there is a moral duty to obey the law is debated. Such a procedure is sometimes called 'intuitionistic'. But that does not mean that the proponent is simply announcing 'I happen to believe ... and that's enough.' He supposes that the values in question are facets of true morality and that (if need be) he can show this to be plausible by reasons which appeal to the human condition, short of logical or scientific demonstration. As we shall see in chapter 20, liberals, communitarians and feminists proceed in this way when invoking competing conceptions of justice.

Appeal to the plausible as a source of values does not violate the Humean cleavage, since it purports to supply ought-premises; and it leaves aside as irrelevant the objection from 'scienticism'. What about 'tolerance'? The moral sceptic may suggest that if we attribute objectivity to values, on any ground, we are intolerant of those who disagree. On closer examination, however, this is not an argument for scepticism at all; but rather the espousal of a competitor, supposedly objective, value. The advocate of toleration, as a political value, insists on institutions which prevent the intolerant from enforcing their opinions on others, because such enforcement is 'wrong'. For example, according to Mill's 'harm' principle, people should be free to do what they like so long as they don't harm others, it being assumed, of course, that harming others is morally objectionable. This is discussed in chapter 10, below, where its plausibility is tested by working out its implications and the implications of competing, paternalistic values. Similarly, the implications of the widely-shared belief that punishment must be retributively just are compared, in chapter 5, with other approaches to the proper moral basis for state coercion.

What of the anthropological ground for scepticism – it just is the case that people differ in time and place about moral matters? That might be countered by 'conventionalism'. At least we all agree that such-and-such is a good rule or a valuable feature of human association, so let's proceed from there. That might suffice for politics within a particular culture, or even globally. Hume, as we have seen, was prepared to employ the label 'natural law' for those rules of justice to which there was universal assent. One problem is that, while conventions may be widely shared, there may be dissenters; and majority opinion does not appear to found moral truth, any more than widespread disagreement establishes that there can be no such thing as moral truth. Another difficulty is that, so far as concrete rules are concerned, conventions may always be culture-bound.

Hart's minimum content of natural law only suggested that all communities must have rules about violence, theft and deception, not the particular prohibitions which such rules should contain.

When we invoke 'human rights' in political controversies, we may appeal to nothing but conventionalism. We leave aside whether there are natural rights to which all human beings at all times have been entitled. We notice that there are a number of international and supra-national treaties, and particular constitutional provisions or doctrines of case law, in which human rights have been asserted. Then we call on governments to live up to their commitments. The trouble is that this will not help if we are voicing attacks, on the basis of invasion of human rights, against governments which have not signed up to the particular right in question; nor, more importantly, if we are arguing for one, rather than another, interpretation of some abstract statement about human rights. How can one affirm that failure to provide some level of welfare, or mucking up the environment, or the practice of female circumcision, violates human rights, in the teeth of someone who has not already agreed to the precise terms of one's formulation of the right, without invoking moral truth?

It might be possible to do so by reference to what we may call 'deep conventionalism'. Modern political culture, it might be said, gives universal lip-service to abstract notions of autonomy and equality. Governments do not go on record as announcing, either: 'Our subjects are mere pawns for us to manipulate as we please'; or: 'Some people are inherently inferior kinds of human being'. Then the deep-conventionalist may seek to show why particular commitments, about which there is controversy, follow from a true understanding of 'autonomy' or 'equality'. Much of contemporary moral and political philosophy proceeds in this way. At an abstract level, it is described as a 'coherentist', as opposed to a 'foundationalist' approach to moral truth.

Would that have been enough for Nuremberg? If failure to carry through some abstract principle which you already affirm is the only basis for moral condemnation, can we say either that the Nazis, or the European slave-traders of the past, were acting wrongly? They did go on record as affirming that jews, or negroes, were sub-human.

Perhaps we might combine deep conventionalism with a commitment to enforce its prescriptions only retrospectively in favour of living (or recently murdered) victims. That would enable us to punish war criminals, while rejecting as ahistorical any suggestion that xenophobes or racists of the long-distant past behaved wickedly. Where, though, do we draw the historical line at which retrospective condemnation is to stop? I once heard a fundamentalist preacher expounding the Book of Joshua to the following effect: God's people had disobeyed him by failing to exterminate completely those they found already dwelling in the promised land. Of course, said the preacher, we were not to take this as a warrant for genocide in our day. A lawyer colleague whispered to me: 'He is distinguishing a bad precedent!'

The last two decades have witnessed a revival of a debate, usually joined at a high level of meta-ethical abstractness, between supporters and opponents of 'moral realism'. ('Real' is used in the sense in which it figures in Plato's philosophy, and has nothing to do with the sceptical 'realism' discussed in chapter 8, below.) Moral realists maintain that all engaged in moral controversy are, by the nature of their disputatious claims, committed to the view that there is a supra-temporal and convention-independent normative reality. Just as in the natural sciences we do not say that exploded theories were correct (as distinct from being believed to be correct) in their day, but rather that we now know that they mistook the truth; so too, over disputed questions of morals or politics, we engage in a discourse which supposes that there is a truth to be found.

We are all of us – constitution-makers, legislators, judges and commentators – engaged on the same quest for that which is, really, right or just. Roughly the contention is that, since we all argue as if there is a moral truth, then there is a moral truth. Michael Moore has made moral realism the basis of what he calls a 'natural law theory of interpretation'.

Modern moral realists deny that they are committed to spooky metaphysics. To the sceptic's point that morals are not part of the furniture of the universe, they answer 'So what!' Indeed, they purport to up-end the moral sceptic in his own metaphysical wheelbarrow: 'If you maintain that there can be no moral truth because there is nothing out there, it is you who have invented the out-thereness in which nothing is. You have trundled on this wheelbarrow of other-worldly goings-on, and you can jolly well sit in it! We realists take discourse as we find it, and the reality presupposed in discourse is the only ontology we need.' Anti-realists answer that the moral realists have misrepresented ethical discourse or, even if they have not, they are not entitled to found upon it their special ontological claims, about there being moral facts which 'exist' in some way parallel to the way in which tables and chairs exist.

I shall explore these abstruse matters no further here. Suffice it to say that, whether you adopt a sceptical, relativist, conventionalist or realist position, the chances are that life will force you into political and moral debates with other people – certainly, if you have anything to do with the law. You will invoke reasons which seem in point, whether they refer to some conventional commitments you share with those you address, or whether, given the intuitions we have and other facts of our human circumstances, they just seem plausible. That will do for most purposes, either if there is or there is not such a thing as moral truth and (if there is) whatever its real foundation may be.

Bibliography

Natural law

Aquinas St T. *Selected Political Writings* (D'Entreves (ed), Dawson trans, 1959) pp. 103-180

Augustine St *City of God* (Tasker (ed), Healey trans, 1944) bk 4, chs 3-4; bk 19, chs 5-6, 15-17, 21, 24-25.

Bentham J. *A Fragment on Government* (Burns and Hart (eds), 1977)

Blackstone W. *Commentaries on the Laws of England* (16th edn, 1825) vol I, intro., s. 2

Brown B. F. 'Natural Law: Dynamic Basis of Law and Morals in the Twentieth Century' (1957) 31 Tul L Rev 491

Buckle S. *Natural Law and the Theory of Property: Grotius to Hume* (1991)

Davitt T. E. 'Law as a Means to an End – Thomas Aquinas' (1960-1) 14 Vand L Rev 65

D'Entreves A. P. *Natural Law* (2nd edn, 1970)

Finnis J. M. *Natural Law and Natural Rights* (1980)

Friedmann W. *Legal Theory* (5th edn, 1967) chs 7-17, 28, 30

George R. P. (ed) *Natural Law Theory* (1992)

Hart H. L. A. *The Concept of Law* (2nd edn, 1994) ch 9

Hittinger R. *A Critique of the New Natural Law Theory* (1987)

Hobbes T. *Leviathan* (MacPherson (ed), 1968) chs 13-18

Hook S. (ed) *Law and Philosophy* (1964) Pt 2

Hudson W. D. *The Is/Ought Question* (1969)

Hume D. *A Treatise of Human Nature* (Mossner (ed)) Book III

Jolowicz H. F. *Lectures on Jurisprudence* (Jolowicz J. A. (ed), 1963) chs 2-5

Jones J W *Historical Introduction to the Theory of Law* (1956) ch 4

Locke J *Second Treatise of Government* (Gough (ed), 1976) chs 2, 7-9, 19

Maine H. J. S. *Ancient Law* (Pollock (ed), 1930) chs 3-4

Maritain J. *The Rights of Man and Natural Law* (1954)

McCoubrey H. *The Development of Naturalist Legal Theory* (1987)

O'Connor D. J. *Aquinas and Natural Law* (1967)

O'Meara J. 'Natural Law and Everyday Law' (1960) 5 NLF 83

Oppenheim F. E. 'The Natural Law Thesis' (1957) 51 Am PS Rev 41

Perry M. *Morality, Politics, and Law* (1988) ch 1

Pollock F. *Essays in the Law* (1922) ch 2

Ross A. *On Law and Justice* (1958) chs 10-11

Sklar J. N. *Legalism* (1964) Pt I

Tuck R. *Natural Rights Theories* (1979)

Weinrib L. L. *Natural Law and Justice* (1987)

Wild J. D. *Plato's Modern Enemies and the Theory of Natural Law* (1953) chs 3-8

Wright R. A. 'Natural Law and International Law' in Sayre (ed) *Interpretations of Modern Legal Philosophies* (1947)

Moral truth

Bayefsky A. F. 'Cultural Sovereignty, Relativism, and International Human Rights: New Excuses for Old Strategies' (1996) 9 RJ 42

Beyleveld D. and Brownsword R. *Law as a Moral Judgment* (2nd edn, 1994)

Brink D. O. *Moral Realism and the Foundation of Ethics* (1989)

Claude R. P. and Weston B. H. (eds) *Human Rights in the World Community* (2nd edn, 1992)

Copp D. and Zimmerman J. (eds) *Morality, Reason and Truth* (1985)

Finnis J. M. *Fundamentals of Ethics* (1983) ch 3

Foot P. 'Moral Realism and Moral Dilemma' (1983) 80 J. Phil 379

Gewirth A. *Reason and Morality* (1978)

Hare R. M. *Moral Thinking* (1981)

Hill T. E. 'The Kantian Conception of Autonomy' in Christman (ed) *The Inner Citadel* (1989)

Honderich T. (ed) *Morality and Objectivity* (1985)

Hurley S. L. *Natural Reasons, Personality and Polity* (1989)

Kant I. *Critique of Practical Reason* (Abbott trans, 1879)

Lycan E. G. *Judgement and Justification* (1988)

Mackie J. L. *Ethics: Inventing Right and Wrong* (1977)

Moore M. S. 'Moral Reality' (1982) Wis LR 1061
   – A Natural Law Theory of Interpretation' (1985) 58 S. Cali LR 227

Munzer S. R. 'Realistic Limits on Realist Interpretation' (1985) 58 S. Cali LR 459

Nagel T. *The View From Nowhere* (1985)

Nino C. S. *The Ethics of Human Rights* (1991)

Patterson D. *Law and Truth* (1996)

Perry T. *Moral Reasoning and Truth* (1976)

Sayre-McCord G. (ed) *Essays in Moral Realism* (1988)

Stavropoulos N. *Objectivity in Law* (1996)

Waldron J. 'The Irrelevance of Moral Objectivity' in George (ed) *Natural Law Theory* (1992)

Watson F. 'Free Agency' in Christman (ed) *The Inner Citadel* (1989)

3 The command theory of law

We all know that from time to time the law makes demands of us. We may often think these demands reasonable; but sometimes we regard them as quirkish or arbitrary or even outrageous. Is there not then a difference between our perceptions of what the law requires, and our views as to what it would be reasonable to require? The assumption that there is such a difference, and the working out of the implications of the difference, have been the hallmarks of the theoretical tradition known as legal positivism. According to legal positivism, law is not some set of propositions derivable by reasoning from the nature of things, as the natural lawyers seemed to suppose. One version of this approach saw law as the commands of political superiors, of the state sovereign. This is the command theory of law.

The English founder of this theory of law was Jeremy Bentham (1748-1832). Bentham was a philosopher and reformer dedicated to the principle of utility: that every act or law should be judged, as to its goodness or badness, solely by reference to its consequences in terms of human happiness. He was anti-traditionalist from an early age, and was shocked to the core when in his 'teens he attended lectures by Sir William Blackstone and heard all the complexities and anomalous accretions of the contemporary common law defended in the name of reason. The root cause of all such unmerited praise seemed to him to be the confusion of law as it is with law as it ought to be, and for that the theory of natural law was largely to blame. It was necessary to define law in terms of facts, the political facts of power, human prescriptions, punishments and rewards. That done, one could devise a scientific theory of legislation based on the principle of utility.

Analysis for its own sake was never Bentham's aim. He believed that all law could be analytically reduced to a 'logic of the will', in which every human act could be seen either as commanded or prohibited, or not commanded or not prohibited, by the law. Where an act was commanded or prohibited, it was the subject of a legal duty. 'Duty' was the lowest common denominator of all laws. All other legal concepts, such as right, power and property, were to be translatable into their relationships to duties. Having decided, on the basis of utility, what acts ought to be made the subject of duties, and what incentive to compliance (whether punishment or reward) was desirable, scientific codes could be worked out.

In fact, most of what Bentham wrote by way of explaining the nature of law was not published in his lifetime. Elements of a command theory appeared in *A Fragment on Government* (1776) and *An Introduction to the Principles of Morals and Legislation* (1789). But his major work on legal theory remained in manuscript form until it was discovered by Charles Everett more than a century after Bentham's death. This work was first published in 1945 as *The Limits of Jurisprudence Defined*, and later in a definitive edition as *Of Laws in General* (1970). Bentham's lifetime publications were principally concerned with issues of moral and political philosophy and with programmes for institutional and economic reform.

The popularising of the command theory of law was left to Bentham's disciple, John Austin (1790-1859).

Austin was appointed in 1827 to the first chair of jurisprudence at the newly created University College in London. Six of his lectures were published in 1832 as *The Province of Jurisprudence Determined*. This book is generally cited as the standard exposition of the command theory of law. Austin's later lectures were published posthumously. They applied the theory of law set out in *The Province* to a wide range of legal concepts. For the next half century and more, a series of writers sought to refine the conceptual analysis appearing in these lectures, and they became known as the school of 'analytical jurisprudence'. Today, analysis of concepts flourishes, but the Austinian basis for it has largely been rejected (see chapter 7, below).

Even if the law as it is can be apprehended separately from some vision of what it ought to be – and that is a large question – in what value-free 'facts' is our apprehension to be anchored? There are books, judges, court officials, policemen, prisons. A factual definition of law which purports to be universal, to apply in all countries at all times – or at any rate, as Austin said, in all the 'maturer systems' – will have to give us universal facts, broad sociological and political generalisations about institutions. Where do we start?

Bentham and Austin started with concepts they found in political philosophy. Since the Renaissance, political philosophers like Bodin and Hobbes had explained those traditional puzzles of their discipline – the sources of political authority and political obligation – in terms of a sovereign who gave commands. Bentham and Austin took over these concepts and turned them to new purposes. In their hands, the sovereign was not he who by divine or natural right could tell us what we ought to do. The sovereign was identified by the fact that he was obeyed, and his commands were those facts which people call 'laws'.

1   Laws as commands

Austin's book determines the province of jurisprudence. That is to say, it sets a fence round those sorts of entities whose terminology is worthy of analysis by anyone seeking enlightenment about standard legal processes.

The first step, in drawing the definitional boundary, was to exclude everything which was not deliberately laid down, everything which was not a 'command' as Austin defined that term:

> 'The ideas or notions comprehended by the term command are the following. (1) A wish or desire conceived by a rational being, that another rational being shall do or forbear. (2) An evil to proceed from the former, and to be incurred by the latter, in case the latter comply not with the wish. (3) An expression or intimation of the wish by words or other signs.' [1]

On this basis, so-called 'customary law' was to be excluded from the province of jurisprudence, unless it had been adopted as the content of a wish by some state organ. The same was true of public international law and of conventional constitutional law.

The next step was to exclude those commands which were not laws. Only 'rules' (that is, general commands as opposed to particular commands) were 'laws properly so called':

> 'Every *law* or *rule* (taken with the largest signification which can be given to the term *properly*) is a *command*. Or, rather, laws or rules, properly so called, are a *species* of commands.[2] ... Now where it obliges *generally* to acts or forbearances of a *class*, a command is a law or rule. But where it obliges to a *specific* act or forbearance, or to acts or forbearances which it determines *specifically* or *individually*, a command is occasional or particular.'[3]

Finally, there must be excluded from the province of jurisprudence all those laws properly so called which are not 'positive laws', that is, which

1   *Province* p 17.
2   *Province* p 13.
3   *Province* p 19.

were laid down by someone other than the sovereign or his subordinates. This excluded divine laws (the general commands of God), and also laws laid down by private individuals (such as the general commands of an employer). Austin uses the expression 'positive morality' to stand both for general commands of non-sovereign human beings, and also for those so-called 'rules' which are supported by public opinion but are not commands of anyone. In delimiting positive law, he draws the line between those general commands of individuals which are to be attributed to the sovereign and those which are not, in terms of commands being issued 'in pursuance of legal rights'. This appears to mean that general commands issued for a man's own benefit are not positive laws, while those issued in a fiduciary capacity are; for Austin indicates that the term 'positive law' encompasses the commands of a guardian, but not those of a master:

> 'Positive laws, or laws strictly so called, are established directly or immediately by authors of three kinds: – by monarchs, or sovereign bodies, as supreme political superiors: by men in a state of subjection, as subordinate political superiors: by subjects, as private persons, in pursuance of legal rights. But every positive law, or every law strictly so called, is a direct or circuitous command of a monarch or sovereign number ... to a person or persons in a state of subjection to its author.'[4]

Austin's underlying assumption seems to be that only general commands of the sovereign and his subordinates are enforced in courts and written about in law books. We must therefore demarcate them, analyse the terms they use, see how these terms relate to each other – this is jurisprudence. The demarcation may be represented in the following diagrams.

Diagram 1   Commands

Particular commands	General commands (otherwise called 'laws properly so called' or 'rules' simpliciter)		
	Commands of God ('divine laws')	Commands of the sovereign ('positive laws')	Commands of others ('positive morality')

4   *Province* p 134.

Diagram 2   Laws by analogy

Laws by a close analogy ('positive morality' – for example, laws of honour, public international law, constitutional law, customary law)	Laws by a remote analogy (for example, laws of physics)

These diagrams show that Austin excluded from the definition of positive law many things which others have thought a proper subject of jurisprudential inquiry, especially customary law, constitutional law and international law. His reason for excluding them was that they were not commands. Yet there were three other things which Austin wanted to reserve for the province of jurisprudence, even though he recognised that they did not meet his definition of 'command'. These were repealing laws, declarative laws and 'imperfect laws', that is, laws prescribing acts but without sanction. (The last mentioned, Austin believed, were to be found in Roman, but not contemporary, law.) It would be inappropriate to charge him with inconsistency, since the three non-command types are expressly stated to be exceptions. But he can be charged with lack of largeness of aim, with providing too narrow a backcloth against which to depict law. Will we get a good picture if we only analyse the concepts used in statutes, judicial decisions and Roman law texts? Austin evidently thought we would, so repealing and declaratory statutes and imperfect laws came in, while the concepts of conventional constitutional law, international treaties and mere custom were out. Nowadays, many analytic jurists take the view that the concepts employed in familiar legal texts should be compared with, and explained in the light of, concepts found, not merely in conventional 'laws' of all kinds, but in morality, games and other rule-governed practices.

Less important criticisms concern terminology. It was rather odd of Austin to use the expression 'law properly so called' in a sense wider than 'positive law' or 'law simply so called', and even odder to use 'positive morality' in two senses, as standing for general commands of private people not given in pursuance of legal rights and also for all varieties of rules set by opinion. Call them what you like. What matters is: should they be within an illuminating model of law or without it? And if without, how related to it?

As for general commands of God ('divine laws'), Austin as a unitarian believed that God's law was the mark of what law ought to be; and as a utilitarian, he believed that God's law was discoverable by asking which rules would have best consequences in terms of human happiness. They were not part of the picture of law as it is. Whether he was right about that is part of the large positivist-versus-natural-lawyer controversy.

None of the criticisms of Austin, in terms of largeness of aim, have been as persistent and damning as attacks mounted against the cornerstone of the first diagram, the concept of command itself. Austin said that every command comprises three elements: a wish, a sanction, and an expression of the wish; and every command which is a law comprises a fourth element, generality. Some critics make the point that his definition of command does not square with the way the word 'command' is used in ordinary language. Do we not speak of 'commands' in contexts where the commander owes his authority to respect rather than to the power to punish?

That criticism based on the true meaning of the word 'command' is misplaced can be easily demonstrated. Supposing one accepted – nobody does, but let's suppose – that the laws of the modern state do have just those elements in terms of which Austin defines general commands, and no others. Then Austin's legal theory would be accurate and definitive and it would be a very small point that his own use of the middle term 'command' diverged from any dictionary definition. Conversely, if his use of 'command' matched ordinary usage, but the laws of the state have none of the elements, his theory is false. His is a command theory of law, using 'command' in his sense; it is not a theory about what it is to 'command' in any other sense.

If his theory were right, then every positive law would contain the four elements of wish, sanction, expression of wish, and generality – as well as a fifth element of 'emanation from a sovereign person or body' (to be considered in the next section). To test it, we must look to see whether each of these elements is present in every law, or whether laws contain further elements not specified by his definition.

When we say that something is required by law, are we committing ourselves to the proposition that some political superior entertains a wish that the conduct in question be performed? Certainly not, if 'conceiving a wish' is understood in a psychological sense. As many critics have pointed out, no one has the psychological capacity to make compliance with every legal duty the content of a separate wish. Is there some other, non-psychological sense of conceiving a wish such that the sovereign may be said to do it in regard to every law? Austin says that the sovereign's wish that instructions emanating from subordinates – like judges and deputy legislators – be carried out is manifested by the fact that the sovereign punishes breaches. Similarly, the sovereign shows his desire that the laws of previous sovereigns should be obeyed by not repealing them and enforcing compliance with them. This is his much criticised idea of 'circuitous' commanding. So the sovereign's wish is not a brute psychological fact. It is a construct made up out of other facts, like punishing or not repealing. It may be urged in Austin's defence that the brute facts of legal life are too complicated for the empirical basis of law to be stateable directly in terms of them. We need simplified pictures made up of constructive, second-order 'facts', that is, 'models'. But is 'circuitous commanding' a good model? That depends on how illuminating we find it in depicting the relationships between the administration of law and political power. If we think that, in essence all law enforcement gives effect to the desires of political superiors, maybe it is not so bad. But if the relationship between what the law achieves and the diffusion of political power among officeholders is much more complicated, the model distorts.

It is the second element of command/laws (the sanction) which has attracted most attention. Is it true that all laws have sanctions? Austin analyses all legal concepts in terms of wish, sanction and sovereign. Particular attention has been paid to his analysis of legal duty. He says that a person is under a duty if the sovereign has expressed a wish and has the power and purpose to inflict an evil. One has a legal obligation when one is, by virtue of threatened punishment, 'obliged' to act.

Discussions of 'legal duty' typically give rise to three quite separate issues. First, when does a legal duty (as opposed to any other kind of duty) arise? Second, what motivates people to comply with legal duties? Third, ought one to act in accordance with one's legal duties? Austin is certainly not concerned with the third of these questions when he defines duty in terms of sanction – he does not say that might is right. Critics have accused him of confusing the first and second. Sometimes, it is true, he indicates that sanction is a motive. But he tells us that the smallest chance of the smallest evil is sufficient for a duty to exist, and it is reasonable to conclude that his primary concern is the first issue. One is under a legal duty when, and only when, the sovereign has stipulated a sanction; why one obeys, and whether one ought to obey, are different questions. In so far as positive law recognises duties where there are no sanctions, the command model is incomplete – as Austin himself recognised by stating that the province of jurisprudence should encompass 'imperfect laws'.

Much more important is the objection that there are many laws which do not impose duties at all, such as laws empowering people to make wills or contracts. Austin dealt with this difficulty by asserting that, in such cases, people are the addressees of conditional commands, subject to the sanction of nullity – if you want to make a will, sign it in the presence of two witnesses or it will have no legal effect. Such a rendering, argued H.L.A. Hart, distorts the 'social function' of such provisions; for they empower people to do things, they don't make demands – they are 'power-conferring rules'. If a concept of law should capture, not merely the political and social facts underlying all legal institutions, but also their typical functions, the command theory is undoubtedly deficient. The law does many other things apart from making demands on us. But whether one can type different sorts of laws by reference to different functions is more problematical. As we shall see in connection with Hart's concept of law (chapter 9, below), it is not historically accurate to regard the introduction of the Wills Act formalities as a measure designed to empower people to do what they could not do before. Whether the common perception of such formality provisions is one of 'the law's demands' or 'the law's assistance' is a complex issue about social attitudes. The general question of ascribing social functions to the law is discussed in chapter 18, below.

As to the third element of Austin's command conception of law – an expression of wish by words or other signs – it can be objected that much of the language of statutes and judgments does not look like wish-expressive language. If a section contains a definition, the language is very far from anything like: 'My desire is that people act in the following way'. Austin tells us that commands are distinguished from other significations of desire, not by their imperative form, but by the power and purpose to inflict a penalty if the desire be disregarded. But that does not seem to meet the objection that much legislative language is not expressive of any desire, imperative or otherwise. Perhaps we can extend Austin's point, and interpret the third element as entirely dependent on the second: if the legislator has penalties in mind, then (for that reason) any language he uses must be reconstructed as expressive of a legislative intention that people shall do or forbear. The third element thus means merely that, before there can be a command and hence a law, the legislator must have taken some overt step beyond conceiving in his own bosom a wish and a purpose to punish.

The fourth element (generality) can be attacked for excluding from the province of jurisprudence particular judicial orders and statutes dealing with a finite number of actions. Actual examples of the latter may be rare; but it is common enough for a judge to issue a one-off order requiring X to do Y. As we shall see in chapter 6, below, Kelsen argues that such 'particular norms' ought to be comprised within a theory of law.

2   The sovereign

Because positive laws are (according to Austin) a species of commands, they comprise the four elements of wish, sanction, expression of wish and generality. Because they all emanate from a sovereign person or body, there is a fifth element, that of identifiable political superiors who entertain and express the wish and purpose to inflict the punishment.

It is important to distinguish the use which the command theory of law makes of the concept of sovereignty from the employment of that concept within legal rules. Sovereignty is an important concept in constitutional law. Some constitutions vest supreme legislative power in a particular body, like the Queen in Parliament, and 'sovereignty' is the term used to stand for this vesting. Rules of public international law vest rights and duties in 'states', but only if they are 'sovereign and independent'. Austin was not seeking to explicate either of these particular legal conceptions of sovereignty – so that it is not enough to refute his theory to point out, for example, that some constitutions do not employ the conception. For him, the sovereign is a pre-legal political fact, in terms of which law and all legal concepts are definable. (Although occasionally, conceptions of 'sovereignty' similar to Austin's may be used to supplement English rules for the recognition of foreign law – as when the House of Lords recognised East German law, even though they were bound to accept that East Germany was not a sovereign state, by treating the East German government as a delegate of the recognised sovereign, the USSR.)[5]

Austin defines the sovereign as a person or body of persons who receives habitual obedience within a political society – a society whose numbers are not extremely small – and who renders habitual obedience to no one else. Laws are defined as the sovereign's general commands. It ought to follow from these definitions that, if one wants to discover the positive law of Ruritania, all one has to do is find out who is habitually obeyed there and then collate his or their general commands. Finding out the sovereign person or body will be a sociological exercise. One will note that there are people giving directions to others, that there are people obeying others; but in any political society there will be discoverable one person or body whose orders are generally obeyed and who obeys orders from no other.

Since legal concepts are defined in terms of the sovereign's commands it follows, Austin argued, that there could be no legal limitation on the sovereign, and no division of sovereign power. Being under a duty is defined as being commanded by the sovereign; so no precept purporting to limit the sovereign could itself have the status of law. In particular, the sovereign could not be bound by laws promulgated by previous sovereigns. Austin's definitions exclude the idea of continuity of law from one sovereign to another. Anything which a former sovereign commanded is law today only if our present sovereign has re-commanded it:

'Even though it sprung directly from another fountain or source, it is a positive law, or a law strictly so called, by the institution of that present sovereign in the character of political superior. Or (borrowing the language of Hobbes) "The legislator is he, not by whose authority the law was first made, but by whose authority it continues to be a law".'[6]

5   *Carl Zeiss Stiftung v Rayner and Keeler Ltd* [1967] 1 AC 853.
6   *Province* p 193.

Although Austin correctly drew out the implications for illimitability and indivisibility which flowed from his assumed pre-legal sovereign, he did not himself apply the sociological test of habitual obedience in discovering who the sovereign was. His definition required him to look at the facts of command and obedience. His practice was to look at constitutional rules. This was his greatest inconsistency and points up the most important flaw in the command theory. Imagine one were oneself asked to discover, by inquiry into the facts of political life, who is that person or body of persons who is habitually obeyed (gets their way) in Britain in our day or in Austin's. There would be no easy answer, and answers given by political scientists are likely to be equivocal or coloured by assumptions about the propriety of certain kinds of political power. Probably, there is not and was not any single group to fit the bill; or if there is or was some readily identifiable ruling class, it is not their general commands which are collated in law books and cited in courts.

Austin, ignoring his definition, sought the sovereign in the United Kingdom and the United States by reference to the constitution. In his early lectures, he assumed that the sovereign in the United Kingdom was that body composed of the king, all the peers and all the members of the House of Commons – that is, 'parliament' viewed as a collection of people, not a constitutional abstraction. Then he saw a difficulty, in that there would be no sovereign during prorogations. His final conclusion was that the United Kingdom sovereign was a body constituted of king, peers and all electors. In the United States, since not Congress but the States have the power to change the written constitution, he found the sovereign body to be the combined members of the electors of all the states' governments. Some body!

If there were nothing else amiss with the command theory of law, the fallacy of the concept of a personal sovereign would alone necessitate its rejection. There are difficulties in spelling out how a legislative body (as such) can entertain and express wishes; but they may not be insurmountable, as we shall see when considering the conception of 'legislative intention' universally employed in statutory interpretation (chapter 12, below). A rule-free identification of a commanding body is, however, impossible, as Austin's own practice makes clear. He says that the members of the sovereign body, while acting in their sovereign capacity, might issue commands to themselves in their private capacity. But how is one to distinguish a man's 'acting like a legislator' or 'acting like an elector' from any other things he does except by reference to rules which tell you what counts as legislating or voting? Certainly, the distinction cannot be referred to others' habitual obedience. A child may habitually obey its father. The brightest child would find it difficult to say when his obedience was rendered to his father, *qua* father, and when it was not.

Even if laws are commands, their source is determined by constitutional rules and practices not capable of reduction to habitual obedience of a person. If these rules and practices (or some of them) are distinguishable as 'laws', then there is no need to predicate illimitability or indivisibility of legislative power. Rejection of Austin's simple sovereignty model is not now controversial. But, as we shall see in other chapters, there is no agreement as to whether laws are or are not in some sense 'commands', nor as to what the true test of legal pedigree is, or whether any such test is, can or should be applied.

W.L. Morison insists that all Austin's claims about political societies – everywhere there is a single person or body to whom habitual obedience is rendered; that person or body conceives wishes in a psychological sense; such wishes are directed to every facet of legally regulated conduct; – are to be understood as straightforward empirical claims. If so, they are manifestly false and the wonder is that Austin, and his mentor Bentham, could have believed them. On the other hand, Bentham's notion of the 'logic of the will' points to another interpretation. Lawyers commonly approach their work with the assumption that legal materials should, if possible, be understood as constituting a consistent and coherent whole. Is that because they personify 'the law' as if a single rational will underlay all its pronouncements? One might then suggest (as I have done), a partial rescue measure for the failings of the command theory: its advocates had, at the back of their minds, a conception of 'sovereign will', not as a fact of political experience, but as a constructive metaphor. As such it would need to be compared with other foundations for, or condemnations of, holistic legal interpretation, considered in later chapters of this book.

Bibliography

Austin J. *The Province of Jurisprudence Determined* (1954) lectures 1, 5-6

Bentham J. *An Introduction to the Principles of Morals and Legislation* (Burns and Hart (eds), 1970) ch 17 *Of Laws in General* (Hart (ed), 1970) chs 1-2, 19, appendix (a)

Bryce J. *Studies in History and Jurisprudence* (1901) vol 11, ch 10

Buckland W. W. *Some Reflections on Jurisprudence* (1945) chs 1, 5, 9-10

Davies H. and Holdcroft D. *Jurisprudence: Text and Commentary* (1991) ch 2

Eastwood R. A. and Keeton G. W. *The Austinian Theories of Law and Sovereignty* (1929)

Harris J. W. 'The Concept of Sovereign Will' (1977) AJ 1

Hart H. L. A. *The Concept of Law* (2nd edn, 1994) chs 2-4

－　*Essays on Bentham* (1982) chs 5 and 9

Heuston R. V. F. 'Sovereignty' in Guest (ed) *Oxford Essays in Jurisprudence* (1961)

Jones J. W. *Historical Introduction to the Theory of Law* (1956) ch 3

Manning C. A. W. 'Austin to-day; or 'The Province of Jurisprudence' Re-examined' in Jennings (ed) *Modern Theories of Law* (1933)

Moles R. N. *Definition and Rule in Legal Theory* (1987) chs 1 and 2

Morison W. L. *John Austin* (1982)

Paulson S. L. 'Classical Legal Positivism at Nuremberg' (1975) PPA 132

Postema G. *Bentham and the Common Law Tradition* (1986) pt 2

Raz J. *The Concept of a Legal System* (2nd edn, 1980) pp. 5-43

Rees W. J. 'The Theory of Sovereignty Restated' in Laslett (ed) *Philosophy, Politics and Society* (1956)

Ruben E. 'Austin's Political Pamphlets' in Attwooll (ed) *Perspectives in Jurisprudence* (1977)

Rumble W. *The Thought of John Austin* (1985)

Samek R. A. *The Legal Point of View* (1974) ch 6

Stone J. *Legal System and Lawyers' Reasonings* (1964) ch 2

Stumpff S. E. 'Austin's Theory of the Separation of Law and Morals' (1960-61) 14 Vand L Rev 117

Tapper C. F. H. 'Austin on Sanctions' (1965) 23 CLJ 271

4 Utilitarianism and the economic analysis of law

The student of jurisprudence will, in many contexts, be referred to arguments deriving from utilitarian moral philosophy. John Rawls, in advancing a theory of substantive justice, seeks to refute the view that the rightness of social institutions is to be measured only by utility (see chapter 20, below). In the context of the philosophy of punishment, the two views generally contrasted are those of retribution and utility (see chapter 5, below). Utilitarian arguments are among those considered in assessing whether or not there is a moral duty to obey the law (see chapter 16, below), and whether the conventional morality of a community should be legally enforced (see chapter 10, below). In the context of legal reasoning, one of the criteria suggested for determining what rules judges should lay down is utility (see chapter 15, below). We saw in the last chapter that, in devising a command theory of law, Bentham was seeking a definition in terms of fact (in contrast to natural law) so that a proper basis might be laid for scientific legislation based on utility.

Moral philosophers have subjected utilitarianism to minute critical analysis. All that is attempted in this chapter is, first, a sketch of the classic theory put forward by Bentham, with a discussion of criticisms of utilitarianism based on that sketch; and secondly, an outline of the modern economic analysis of law which parallels the utilitarian approach, but in a form which is supposed to insulate it against some of these criticisms.

1 Utilitarianism

'The greatest happiness of the greatest number' is a maxim adopted by Bentham to popularise his philosophy. It is, however, as he recognised, somewhat inaccurate. A measure may be justified by utility which increases the happiness of a few greatly even though it marginally diminishes that of the many:

'By the principle of utility is meant that principle which approves or disapproves of every action whatsoever, according to the tendency which it appears to have to augment or diminish the happiness of the party whose interest is in question: or, what is the same thing in other words, to promote or to oppose that happiness.'[1]

The happiness of an individual will be augmented if there is an addition to the sum total of his pleasures greater than any addition to the sum total of his pains. The interest of the community is comprised of all interests of the individuals of which it is composed. Therefore, the happiness of the community will be increased if the total of all the pleasures of all its members is augmented to a greater extent than their pains. Bentham lists 14 pleasures and 12 pains as a comprehensive account of happiness-relevant consequences. When assessing the rightness of any proposed action, one notes which items on this list will result from it, and measures the value of each particular lot of pleasure or pain by reference to seven criteria: intensity, duration, certainty, propinquity, fecundity, purity and extent.

'*Intense, long, certain, speedy, fruitful, pure* – such marks in *pleasures* and in *pains* endure. Such pleasures seek, if *private* be thy end: If it be *public*, wide let them *extend. Such pains* avoid, whichever be thy view: If pains *must* come, let them *extend* to few.'[2]

Bentham advances the principle of utility as the sole proper basis for morality and legislation. Both the rightness of every act we do in private life, and the rightness of public measures of all kinds, should be tested by his 'felicific calculus'. His philosophy is anticonventionalist and universalist. The mere fact that overwhelming opinion in a community has held something to be right or wrong is no warrant for moral approval or condemnation; only the test of utility can decide. And, although what the law is differs from one society to another, what it ought to be is in principle everywhere the same, namely, legislation which passes the utilitarian test.

He begins his advocacy of the principle of utility with some psychological assumptions which today look rather crude. He believes that all that men desire are pleasures and the avoidance of pains, and that men are motivated to do whatever they do by their desires:

'Nature has placed mankind under the governance of two sovereign masters, pain and pleasure. It is for them alone to point out what we

1 *An Introduction to the Principles of Morals and Legislation* ch 1 (2).
2 *Introduction* ch 4(2)n.

ought to do, as well as to determine what we shall do. On the one hand the standard of right and wrong, on the other the chain of causes and effects, are fastened to their throne ... *The principle of utility* recognises this subjection, and assumes it for the foundation of that system, the object of which is to rear the fabric of felicity by the hands of reason and of law. Systems which attempt to question it, deal in sounds instead of sense, in caprice instead of reason, in darkness instead of light.'[3]

It might be thought from this that Bentham is substituting his own natural law for other systems, that he is deriving an 'ought' from an 'is'. This he denies, saying of the principle of utility:

'Is it susceptible of any direct proof? It should seem not: for that which is used to prove every thing else, cannot itself be proved: a chain of proofs must have their commencement somewhere. To give such proof is as impossible as it is needless.'[4]

The object of Bentham's psychology is, therefore, not proof but advocacy. He commends the principle of utility as a moral principle which, he thinks, any reader will find preferable to any other, given the truth of his assertions about human nature. Three aspects of this advocacy can be distinguished. First, since men desire only happiness, they must approve a principle which affirms that they ought to have what they want. Secondly, if one will accept the principle of utility, then all disputes about right and wrong will be reduced to disagreements about future matters of fact, and hence morals and legislation become scientific. Utilitarians are concerned only with consequences; they will know how to value consequences; so all that any two of them can be at issue about are what consequences a certain act or measure will in fact bring about. Thirdly, since men are only motivated by pain and pleasure, properly drafted legislation can produce a coincidence between the interests of the individual and the interests of the community. Given appropriate rewards and punishments laid down by law, we can achieve a fortunate state of affairs in which a man will draw the same conclusions about the rightness of any proposed action of his, whether he calculates the effect only upon his own happiness or upon that of the community.

Benthamite utilitarianism was an important part of the political culture of the first half of nineteenth-century Britain, and reforms (creditable or otherwise) have been attributed to its influence. The sweeping away of archaic legal procedures and the pruning of pointlessly severe punishments

3   *Introduction* ch 1 (1).
4   *Introduction* ch 1 (11).

may owe something to it. But so too may the New Poor Law introduced in 1834, with its notorious 'less eligibility' principle – workhouse conditions should always be worse than those resulting from the least remunerative employment, otherwise there would be no incentive to work.

Utilitarians, after Bentham, have modified many of his assertions. John Stuart Mill was an avowed utilitarian, but rejected Bentham's view that all pleasures were to count the same. Since, Mill argued, people educated to appreciate intellectual and aesthetic pleasures always value them more than sensual pleasures, they should be counted as intrinsically of more worth. Probably no one today would wish to be tied to Bentham's list of pleasures and pains and no one would accept the grandiose simplicity of his psychological assumptions. Nonetheless, those who take utilitarian positions tend to reflect the spirit of his advocacy of the principle. Why should we accept that actions are morally required unless their consequences are good for people – meet their demonstrable needs and desires, or cater for their satisfactions? Why should we accept any principle as morally appropriate merely because someone or some body of people say it is right? And if two disputants have different moral philosophies or political programmes to recommend, is not the best ground for discussion achieved if each is required to set out what consequences she maintains will follow from acceptance of her view? And even if rationalistic motivation is not to be hoped for, should not public measures seek to balance conflicting aspirations by giving as much satisfaction to each as possible?

Bentham advocated the same test, the principle of utility, for both private acts and public measures. Yet his own definition speaks only of 'actions'. He was evidently not aware of the distinction which later philosophers have drawn between 'act-utilitarianism' and 'rule-utilitarianism'. For the former, an act is right if it has best consequences. For the latter, an act is right if required or permitted by a rule where the general following of that rule would have best consequences. Austin accepted the principle of utility, but believed it should be applied to rules. 'Our rules would be fashioned on utility; our conduct, on our rules.'[5] He regarded 'the laws of God' as the test of what positive laws ought to be. Where they are not revealed in scripture, they are those rules which will promote human happiness (it being assumed that God wills the welfare of his creatures). Creative judicial decisions generally are, and should be, dictated by the consequences any decision would have were it universalised into a rule.

In the context of legal philosophy, the version of utilitarianism most often appealed to is 'ideal rule-utilitarianism'. This stipulates that an action is right if required or permitted by a rule, where that rule, if obeyed by all

5 *Province* p 47.

to whom it applies, would have better consequences (or at least as good consequences) compared with any other rule governing the same act. It appears to have advantages over act-utilitarianism. Where a judge is deciding whether liability-in-damages should be imposed for some activity, if he views his decision as a single act the relevant consequences might include the effect on the particular defendant who is poor; and hence by act-utilitarian reasoning the award should not be made. But it might be that a rule requiring all judges to award damages in such circumstances would have good consequences, so that the award would be right by rule-utilitarian reasoning.

Many objections have been raised to utilitarianism of all kinds. Here are a few.

First, the felicific calculus is impracticable. No one can know all the consequences of his acts and it would often be foolish to try to assess them. Received moral precepts provide more practical guides to action. This objection tells less in the context of deliberate rulemaking by legislators or judges than in the sphere of private morality. Even so, are not the results of research into expected consequences of public measures commonly contradictory and often proved wrong? Does that mean we should not try to calculate consequences?

Secondly, the pleasures and pains of different people are not intra-commensural. Supposing all agree that the effect of proposed legislation would be marginally to increase the average take-home pay, at the cost of marginally increasing the number of those out of work. How do we balance the satisfactions of the majority against the different kind of distress caused to the minority? When a judge is deciding whether or not to issue an injunction against an alleged nuisance, how is the enjoyment of one who likes late-night noisy parties to be weighed against the discomfort of his neighbours? We shall see that those who advocate an economic analysis of law believe that such problems are in principle soluble.

Thirdly, the principle of utility is unworthy. Satisfaction of all human desires should not be the aim of our morality. Some pleasures are gross and some forms of suffering are ennobling. Bentham was aware that ruling out any particular kinds of pleasure or pain from the calculus would entail making pre-utilitarian value judgments, and so he tried to include them all. For example, his list includes 'the pleasures of malevolence'. This led him into difficulties with his theory of punishment; for he wanted to maintain the position that punishment is in itself evil and can only be justified by the prevention of greater evil. Why is not pure retribution a good by virtue of satisfying feelings of vengeance? Bentham's answer was that 'No such pleasure is ever produced by punishment as can be equivalent to the pain.'[6] But is that not a distinct value judgment rather than a plausible generalisation from the facts of human experience? Some take the view that our satisfactions cannot be the only test of what is right, but must themselves be judged by some higher value, such as human dignity. Supposing it could be shown that women living in purdah would lead less happy lives were they to be allowed into the outside world – it might still be argued that it is right to free them.

Fourthly, are not human desires and satisfactions capable of manipulation? If so, how can the issue of how to mould them be decided by utility? If by education or advertising a person can be brought to desire things which he would not have desired otherwise, and to cease to want other things, can judgment be passed on the manipulation programmes in terms of a principle which merely refers us to maximising satisfactions? Is it an answer to say that the felicific calculus includes, not merely all the things we want, but all the things we might come to want given alternative measures of education and indoctrination?

Fifthly, whose interests are in question? There may be various utilitarian answers to a problem, depending on whether we include as relevant beneficiaries the members of a national community, all mankind, present and future generations, or all sentient creatures. Utility cannot itself dictate where to draw the line. On the issue of abortion on demand, for instance, if the interest of the foetus does not count, abortion ought clearly to be allowed; if it does count, very heavy considerations must weigh on the other side before the loss of future satisfactions involved in the destruction of the foetus can be justified. More bizarre problems have been raised by asking whether the persons whose interests are in question include all those who could possibly be begotten. If so, then so long as any addition to the population would give the new individual satisfactions which would outweigh the dissatisfactions to others resulting from his demands on resources, then there is a duty to beget him. Not merely is birth control ruled out, but we all have a duty to procreate to the maximum. Because of this argument, modern utilitarians often appeal to a principle of *average* utility – you maximise the average satisfactions of the people who now exist. It is not clear whether this justifies killing off the extremely miserable, provided this can be done without causing fear or other pains to the rest.

In the light of such objections and many others, there are not many today who base all their moral and political judgments on strictly utilitarian reasoning. Yet it is also true that utilitarian considerations are seldom ignored. Consequences are usually accepted to be among the morally-relevant considerations of private acts and public measures.

2 The economic analysis of law

Some of the objections to utilitarianism can be met if, instead of concerning ourselves with the messy business of actual human psychology, we simplify our task with a few definitional assumptions. This is what has been attempted in the economic analysis of law which has grown up (principally in the United States) during the past 30 years. The felicific calculus is difficult because one cannot be sure how people will react to alternative measures. The answer of economic analysis is to make an assumption. Man is a rational maximiser of his satisfactions. The entire theory is premised on this definition. If he will achieve more of what he wants to achieve by taking step X rather than step Y, *homo economicus* will, by definition, take step X; to do otherwise would, by definition, be acting irrationally. The felicific calculus is also problematic because of empirical difficulties in finding out what people do in fact want. No problem! For the economic analysis of law, what I want is, by definition, what I am willing to pay for – either in money, or by the deployment of some other resource that I have such as time and effort. The utility calculus is objectionable in principle because the advantages to some cannot be measured against the disadvantages to others. But this is not so, according to economic analysis; for all that happens to us can be reduced to things we will pay to have or pay to be without, the solvent of a hypothetical market. Where Bentham spoke of the greatest happiness of the greatest number, the economic analyst speaks of the 'efficient' solution.

It is important to distinguish the merits claimed for real markets in relation to particular areas of law from the global subjection of all law to economic models based on notional markets. From the days of Adam Smith (1723-1790) to the present, advocates of free-market economics have maintained that a society's wealth will be augmented most effectively if resources are privately owned and owners are free to trade them as they choose. Adherents of modern economic analysis of law take this to be axiomatic. Indeed, the connection between markets and property has induced stipulatively wide definitions of the term 'property' among some members of the school: any right which a person may agree not to insist on (whether personal, familial or political) should be styled a 'property' right, because the right-holder has control over the effects of the exercise of the right on others (its 'externalities'). Even more characteristic of the school is the importance it attaches to notional markets. Its adherents seek to draw implications for legal 'wrongs' of all kinds from notional re-allocations within a total wealth-pie taken to be fixed at a particular moment of time. Granted zero transaction costs, every right would end up vested in the person who values it most – value being determined by each party's willingness to pay. Where transaction costs frustrate such re-allocations, the law should impose the 'efficient' solution.

In a path-breaking article on 'The Problem of Social Cost', published in 1960, R.H. Coase applied this approach to nuisance law. If we have to decide whether a factory-owner should or should not be enjoined from emitting smoke which interferes with the amenities of neighbouring householders, there is, Coase suggested, no reason for beginning with a prior assumption that the detrimental effects are a 'cost' to the neighbours as against regarding a restraint on emissions as a 'cost' to the factory-owner. In the real world, any bargaining about the matter between the factory-owner and the neighbours will be impracticable. He would have to find all the neighbours who might be affected and negotiate with them or their representatives. Some cussed individual, knowing that others were prepared to settle for a certain sum, might 'hold out' for a much larger one, realising that he had the factory-owner over a barrel. Or suppose that most of the neighbours were willing to buy off the factory-owner, but a few 'free-riders' sought to benefit from the deal without making their contributions.

Multi-party negotiations and problems of hold-outs and free-riders contribute to 'transaction costs'. Imagine, however, that there were no such costs. Then ask whether the factory-owner would buy out the neighbours (supposing that the law banned the emissions), or the neighbours would pay him not to make the smoke (supposing that the general law imposed no restraint). Coase's revolutionary insight is that the answer will be the same either way. If the factory-owner is willing to pay more for the freedom to pour out the smoke than the neighbours will pay to be spared it, he will (in the imagined world of zero transaction costs) end up with the right to do it whether the legal starting-point was nuisance-liability or no nuisance-liability. If that would be so on the notional market, it is the efficient solution and the law should impose it: the factory-owner should be free to emit the smoke and the neighbours should be required to put up with it, even though (real transactions being impossible) the neighbours will receive no compensation for their 'detriment'.

Coase's theorem has been applied, with modifications, across the whole sweep of substantive and procedural law. It has captured the imagination of the school precisely because it yields conclusions, based on a theoretical economic model, which, on the face of it, seem counter-intuitive. The benighted layman may suppose that, even if a factory-owner's activities are, all things considered, in the public interest, he ought to bear the cost of compensating those who suffer from them. Coase's analysis purports to demonstrate that such a supposition may, where real transactions are impracticable, stand in the way of rights being accorded to those who would (if they could) pay most for them.

Adherents of the school do not claim for economic analysis what Bentham claimed for utility, namely, that it is the sole test of law's goodness or badness. Nevertheless, it is taken to have a prima facie normative status. Justice may require that some non-efficient solution to a legal problem be adopted; but the onus lies on anyone arguing for this to demonstrate why it should. Critics of economic analysis contest the merits even of real markets in relation to particular areas of social life.

More importantly, they deny that 'efficiency', in the specialised sense in which it depends on notional markets, has any normative force at all. Suppose we concede that real markets, at least sometimes, have moral merits in that people are kept to their promises, and instrumental merits, because the production of goods and services can be maximised in no other way. Why should anyone be treated as if he had made a bargain when he has not made one, especially if the practical consequence is that he is denied the price he would (notionally) have contracted to receive?

In his celebrated textbook, Richard Posner argues that, quite apart from the normative implications of both real and notional markets, economic analysis of law has great explanatory and predictive power. He cites the formula propounded by Justice Learned Hand as the test for negligence:

> 'The defendant is guilty of negligence if the loss caused by the accident, multiplied by the probability of the accident's occurring, exceeds the burden of the precautions that the defendant might have taken to avert it.'[7]

Posner maintains that, even when the surface language of judicial opinions is not overtly economic, the underlying rationale of common law adjudication is economic in nature:

> '[Common law] doctrines form a system for inducing people to behave efficiently, not only in explicit markets, but across the whole range of social interactions. In settings in which the cost of voluntary transactions is low, common law doctrines create incentives for people to channel their transactions through the market ... In settings in which the cost of allocating resources by voluntary transactions is prohibitively high making the market an infeasible method of allocating resources, the common law prices behaviour in such a way as to mimick the market.'[8]

The layman might think that the law penalises conduct such as murder, assault, rape and theft because such things have always been thought to be morally wrong. In the language of natural law, such actions are termed *mala in se*, as distinct from *mala prohibita* (regulatory offences created in the service of some particular policy goal). The true basis of legal prohibition is, Posner argues, quite different. Economic efficiency, not some other normative conception, is what determines legal prohibition. So-called *mala in se* are examples of *coerced transactions*. Some value is transferred from the victim to the delinquent without proper bargaining.

7   *United States v Carroll Towing Company* 159 F 2d 169 at 173(1947).
8   Posner *Economic Analysis of Law* (4th edn) pp 251-2.

The law penalises the thief, not because theft is in some non-economic sense 'wrong', but in order to persuade the thief to use the market. Posner concedes that there are problems with the assessment of damages in the case of some serious assaults, since there is no available market in maiming and mutilation. Nonetheless, he maintains that 'intentional torts' and serious crimes all fall foul of the overriding principle that, when transaction costs are low, people must use the market. Whether the law penalises through tortious liability or criminal sanction is merely a question of technique. The reason for punishment is that the cost to the delinquent needs to be greater than mere compensation in order to provide him with the necessary incentive to refrain. Posner expressly follows Bentham's cost-benefit analysis of punishment.

Posner goes through the common law, branch by branch, demonstrating its economic logic. When it comes to statutes, he finds, on the whole, that – although those manning legislative and administrative agencies are themselves motivated by utility – the rules they produce are inefficient. They are the result of pressures brought to bear by competing interest-groups, and the resulting compromises do not maximise total satisfactions. In particular, the substitution of administrative or adjudicatory processes for low-cost market transactions is inefficient. Posner casts a jaundiced eye on modern consumer law, whether originating from statute or cases. If manufacturers and sellers of products cannot contract out of liability, they will either take cost-unjustified steps to improve their products, raising the price more than the cost of the defects to the consumer; or they will add in the cost of anticipated damages and raise the price that way. The result will be that the total value of the transactions to all concerned is reduced – especially if the consumer is a 'risk preferrer', that is, someone who would like to pay less and take the chance of defects. Fraud, incapacity and duress are valid grounds for interfering with freedom of contract, for here the consumer is prevented from acting as a rational maximiser; but the other more comprehensive grounds of intervention recognised by modern law are unfortunate.

> 'If "unconscionability" means that a court may nullify a contract if it considers the consideration inadequate or the terms otherwise one-sided, the basic principle of encouraging market rather than surrogate legal transactions where (market) transaction costs are low is badly compromised. Economic analysis reveals no grounds other than fraud, incapacity, and duress (the last narrowly defined) for allowing a party to repudiate the bargain that he made in entering into the contract.'[9]

9   *Economic Analysis of Law* p 116.

Many lawyers will agree that economic analysis does throw interesting light on particular areas. Critics have suggested, however, that its explanatory power is not as inclusive, even in relation to the common law, as its advocates suggest. Does the above explanation of the law's penalising serious offences (in terms of 'coerced transactions') carry conviction? Is the following Posnerian explanation of the no-duty-to-rescue rule illuminating or fanciful? With no liability, strong swimmers often do rescue people. This increases total values, because the person drowning would pay a large sum to be rescued if there were a market; and the rescuer achieves satisfactions through being recognised as an altruist. If strong swimmers were liable for failure to rescue, there would be an incentive to keep off the beach. They would no longer receive recognition as altruists, and they would avoid situations in which they would be forced either to incur the resource-costs of rescue, or pay damages or fines. There would consequently be less rescues, and so a diminution in total values. The no-liability rule is therefore efficient.

The normative implications of economic analysis of law are, perhaps, most challenging when it is claimed that a real (not just a notional) market should be introduced in respect of some sensitive area of social interaction which has hitherto been subjected to non-market considerations. For example, Posner argues that there ought to be a market in the production of babies for adoption. The demand and supply would eventually equalise. Poor adopters would be better off, because the prices charged by producing mothers in circumstances of open competition would be less exacting than criteria of wealth currently applied to prospective adopters by adoption agencies. Such an analysis at least requires us to ask why it is that this proposal is, at present, generally looked on with horror.

The strength of economic analysis, as of its utilitarian parent, is its appeal to the intuition: other things being equal, why not give people what they want? Its methodological weaknesses, some would argue, are its artificial equation of 'what people want' with 'willingness to pay', its assumptions about rational maximisers and its invocation of notional markets across the entire field of problems of human interaction. More substantively, is the law's only function that of ministering even to real markets? Does it not have to balance competing claims to power and influence by people who are bound to lose out in any competition based on market competence? And, above all, can any philosophy of law be adequate which side-steps the crucial questions of substantive justice involved in the distribution of wealth? (See chapter 20, below)

Bibliography

Utilitarianism

Austin J. *The Province of Jurisprudence Determined* (1954) lectures 2-4
Bentham J. *An Introduction to the Principles of Morals and Legislation*
(Burns and Hart (eds), 1970) chs 1-5
Brandt R. B. *Morality, Utilitarianism and Rights* (1992)
Christman J. (ed) *The Inner Citadel* (1989) pt 3
Frey R. G. (ed) *Utility and Rights* (1985)
Griffin J. *Well-being: Its Meaning, Measurement and Moral Importance*
(1986)
Hodgson D. H. *Consequences of Utilitarianism* (1967)
Lyons D. B. *Forms and Limits of Utilitarianism* (1965)
    –   *In the Interests of the Governed* (revised edn, 1991) chs 1-5
Mill J. S. *Utilitarianism* (Lindsay (ed), 1960)
Quinton A. M. *Utilitarian Ethics* (1973)
Regan D. *Utilitarianism and Cooperation* (1980)
Sartorius R. E. *Individual Conduct and Social Norms* (1975) ch 2
Scheffler S. (ed) *Consequentialism and its Critics* (1988)
Sen A. and Williams B. (eds) *Utilitarianism and Beyond* (1982)
Smart J. C. and Williams B. *Utilitarianism: For and Against* (1973)
Stephen L. *The English Utilitarians* (1900)
Wasserstrom R. A. *The Judicial Decision* (1961) chs 6-8

The economic analysis of law

Baker C. E. 'The Ideology of the Economic Analysis of Law' (1975) 5
PPA 3
Becker G. S. *The Economic Approach to Human Behaviour* (1976) Pt 3
Barzel Y. *Economic Analysis of Property Rights* (1989)
Bowles R. 'Creeping Economism: a Counter-view' (1978) 5 Br J L Soc
96
Buchanan J. M. 'Good Economics – Bad Law' (1974) 60 Virg L Rev 483
Calabresi G. 'Some Thoughts on Risk Distribution and the Law of Torts'
(1961) 70 Yale LJ 499
Calabresi G. and Melamed A. D. 'Property Rules, Liability Rules, and
Inalienability: One View of the Cathedral' (1972) 85 Harv L Rev 1089
Coase R. H. 'The Problem of Social Cost' (1960) 3 J L Econ 1
Coleman J. *Markets, Morals and the Law* (1988) pt 2
Cranston R. 'Creeping Economism: Some Thoughts on Law and
Economics' (1977) 4 Br J L Soc 103
Demsetz H. 'Toward a Theory of Property Rights' (1967) 57 Am Econ
Rev 347
Dworkin R. M. *A Matter of Principle* (1985) chs 12 and 13

Epstein R. A. 'A Theory of Strict Liability' (1973) 2 JLS 151

Harris J. W. *Property and Justice* (1996) pp. 145-49, 293-301

Jerdingham D. H. 'The Coase Theorem and the Psychology of Common Law Thought' (1983) 56 S. Cali LR 711

Kennedy D. and Michelman F. I. 'Are Property and Contract Efficient?' (1980) 8 Hof LR 711

Leff A. A. 'Economic Analysis of Law: Some Realism about Nominalism' (1974) 60 Virg L Rev 451

Mishan E. J. 'Evaluation of Life and Limb: a Theoretical Approach' (1971) JPE 687

Moles R. (ed) *Law and Economics* (1988)

Ogus A. I. and Veljanovski C. G. (eds) *Readings in the Economics of Law and Regulation* (1984)

Pennock J. R. and Chapman J. W. (eds) *Nomos xxiv: Ethics, Economics and the Law* (1982)

Posner R. *Economic Analysis of Law* (4th edn, 1992)
- *The Economics of Justice* (1983)
- 'Dworkin's Critique of Wealth Maximization' in Cohen (ed) *Ronald Dworkin and Contemporary Jurisprudence* (1984)

5 Punishment

In *Crime and Punishment,* Dostoevsky puts the following views in the mouths of his characters:

Marmeladoff: Mr Lebeziatnikoff, who is up to all the ideas of our day, explained lately that pity is now actually prohibited by science, an opinion current in England, the headquarters of political economy.

Sonia (to Raskolnikoff): You must make atonement, so that you may be redeemed thereby ... You shall have it (her cross) at the moment of your expiation.

Porphyrius (to Raskolnikoff): *You cannot do without us* ... I am even of opinion that, after careful consideration, you will make up your mind to make atonement ... In truth, Rodion Romanovitch, suffering is a grand thing ... There lies a theory in suffering.

The 'theory' to which Porphyrius refers is that of retributive punishment. According to this theory, justice requires that a man should suffer because of, and in proportion to, his moral wrongdoing. The political economists in England, to whom Dostoevsky was passionately opposed, were the utilitarian disciples of Bentham, who had written (as we saw in the last chapter) that all punishment was in itself an evil, and could only be justified as far as it prevented some greater evil. From a utilitarian point of view, the pain of punishment may be outweighed by its good consequences if it deters the offender from offending again, or if it deters others from committing the like offence, or if it can be made the occasion for reforming the offender, or if it results in a dangerous person being removed from society. For retributivists, whatever other purposes are served by a penal system, it only exacts justice so far as it gives an offender his moral deserts. Welfare consequences are irrelevant from the point of view of retributive justice. Kant expressed the matter graphically:

> 'Even if a Civil Society resolved to dissolve itself with the consent of all its members – as might be supposed in the case of a People inhabiting an island resolving to separate and scatter themselves throughout the whole world – the last Murderer lying in the prison ought to be executed before the resolution was carried out. This ought to be done in order that every one may realise the desert of his deeds, and that bloodguiltiness may not remain upon the people; for otherwise they might all be regarded as participators in the murder as a public violation of Justice.'[1]

Thus, the philosophers and moralists have divided themselves on the issue of punishment: retributivists versus utilitarians. The numbers on each side vary. Forty years ago there were very few confessed retributivists in the English-speaking world; now they are perhaps in the majority. Not that every writer takes his stand firmly at one end or other of the tug-of-war, and there are many combinations and variants. The discussion is not exclusively jurisprudential since plenty of punishment goes on outside the law. It bears on legal institutions in four contexts: legislation; judicial 'legislation'; sentencing; and institution-evaluation.

First, in debating the merits of proposed legislation which seeks to penalise or de-penalise some activity, one may ask whether the measure is supposed to be justified by its good consequences, or whether it is aimed at more perfectly realising the state's duty to punish wrongdoing. Such discussion overlaps with issues raised in chapter 10, below, about freedom and the enforcement of morals.

Secondly, in the judicial elucidation of the criminal law, conceptions of what punishment is for play a role. In this context, no consistent commitment to utilitarian or retributive views emerges. On one view, as we shall see, the insistence on proof of intent or recklessness (*mens rea*) in serious crimes, and the admissibility of exculpatory defences (like capacity or duress), are justified on retributive but not on utilitarian grounds. Certainly the judges commonly speak of both as 'requirements of justice'. In two recent decisions, senior English judges have been divided about the relative weight to be given to such 'retributive' considerations as compared with general consequentialist arguments. In 1975, a majority of the House of Lords laid down, for the first time, that duress could be a complete defence to a charge of murder in the second degree.[2] In 1987,

1   *The Philosophy of Law* p 198.
2   *Director of Public Prosecutions for Northern Ireland v Lynch* [1975] AC 653.

the House unanimously overruled this decision and held that duress could never be a defence to any charge of murder.[3] The minority judges in the first case and the majority in the second stressed the bad consequences of allowing people to go free on the ground that, when they killed or assisted in killing, they were acting under the threat of death from a terrorist or gang-leader. To do this would be a 'terrorist's charter'. It would mean that any such leader could comfort his followers: 'If you are caught, you need only tell the truth, that I would have shot you if you had not obeyed; and they will have to let you go'. Lord Wilberforce (speaking for the majority in the first case) and Lord Hailsham LC in the second case, however, invoked retributive considerations, but took diametrically opposed views on whether the actor deserved punishment. Lord Wilberforce said:

> 'The judges have always assumed responsibility for deciding questions of principle relating to criminal liability and guilt, and particularly for setting the standards by which the law expects normal men to act. In all such matters as capacity, sanity, drunkenness, coercion, necessity, provocation, self-defence, the common law, through the judges, accepts and sets the standards of right-thinking men of normal firmness and humanity at a level which people can accept and respect ... A law, which requires innocent victims of terrorist threats to be tried for murder and convicted as murderers, is an unjust law.'[4]

Lord Hailsham LC said:

> 'I have known in my own lifetime of too many acts of heroism by ordinary human beings of no more than ordinary fortitude to regard a law as either "just" or "humane" which withdraws the protection of the criminal law from the innocent victim and casts the cloak of its protection upon the coward and the poltroon in the name of a "concession to human frailty".'[5]

So far as drunkenness is concerned, the House of Lords preferred general arguments of utility to specific arguments based on retributive justice. Before the decision in *DPP v Majewski*,[6] the predominant view among academic writers was that one who was too drunk to know what he was doing should not be convicted of a crime whose definition included *mens rea*. 'Logic' – that is, the consistent application of the *mens rea*

---

3   *R v Howe* [1987] AC 417.
4   [1975] AC 653 at 684-685.
5   [1987] AC 417 at 432.
6   [1977] AC 443

principle – required that he could not be justly held accountable. The House unanimously rejected this view. Men who got into such dangerous conditions could not be left at large. Since we have no crime of 'getting dangerously drunk', the only way to protect the community was to convict a man of a crime of 'basic intent' (such as an assault) even though he had no control at the time of the offence. Lord Edmund-Davies said:

> 'It is at this point pertinent to pause to consider why legal systems exist. The universal object of a system of law is obvious – the establishment and maintenance of order.'[7]

The third jurisprudential context for conceptions of what justifies punishment is the area of sentencing. In the great majority of crimes, the courts have a wide discretion up to a statutory maximum. English judges adopt both retributive and utilitarian considerations. The Court of Appeal has laid down four principles to be applied in sentencing: retribution, deterrence (as regards both the offender and others), prevention, and rehabilitation – retribution being required so that society through its courts can show its abhorrence of particular types of crime.[8] The reasons for pronouncing sentence given by first instance judges contain variants of all these criteria: 'You have shown no remorse', that is, you are especially wicked and deserve heavy punishment (retribution); 'You broke a special relationship of trust' (ditto); 'I am not unsympathetic, having regard to the circumstances which led you to act as you did, but it must be made clear that this sort of thing is not to be tolerated' (deterrent); 'It is to be hoped that you take advantage of this further period of probation to undertake a proper training course' (rehabilitation); 'Such people as you are a danger to the community if left at large' (prevention). Superior courts vary sentences on appeal, sometimes because they take a different view of the deterrent, reformatory or preventative consequences, sometimes because the sentence is out of line with other sentences and so retributively unjust.

The three contexts so far considered presuppose a typical background of a criminal law and a criminal enforcement process. Could we not have something radically different, a system of 'treatment' rather than punishment, or no organised state force at all? As we shall see in chapter 19, below, Lenin envisaged a future classless society where such delinquents as remain will be dealt with by the spontaneous reaction of their fellows. Our fourth type of question considers whether 'punishment' is justifiable at all.

7   Ibid at 495.
8   *R v Sargeant* [1974] 60 Cr App Rep 74.

At this point, we are liable to run up against a 'definitional stop' argument: 'That system might be better, but it wouldn't be punishment, so it is not relevant to the philosophy of punishment.' Definitions ought not to block off fundamental questions in that way. Nevertheless, we have to pay some attention to the definition of punishment expressed or implied in some arguments about justification of punishment, just to see whether all alternatives have been considered.

John Rawls offered the following definition:

> 'A person is said to suffer punishment whenever he is legally deprived of some of the normal rights of a citizen on the ground that he has violated a rule of law, the violation having been established by a trial according to the due process of law, provided that the deprivation is carried out by the recognised legal authorities of the State, that the rule of law clearly specifies both the offence and the attached penalty, that the courts construe statutes strictly, and that the statute was on the book prior to the time of the offence.'[9]

Rawls, using this definition, purports to avoid the retributive/utilitarian dilemma. He argues that, whatever justifies punishment in general, a punishment in a particular case is justified simply by reference to the practice of punishment. He conjures up an alternative practice – for which he coins the word 'telishment' – in which officials would have discretion to subject any individual they thought fit to deprivation if that would (in their view) advance the general good. He argues that, not merely would telishment be incompatible with retributivism, but that utilitarian considerations are likely to favour 'punishment' as against 'telishment', because the consequences of the latter practice would be so bad.

Might it not be possible, however, to devise a system of 'punishment' which lacks some of the features contained in Rawls's definition, but is still quite different from 'telishment'? Whether it would be preferable to Rawlsian punishment might depend on the importance we attach to the rule-of-law elements incorporated into his definition (see chapter 11, below). In 1974, the House of Lords declared that the crime of 'conspiracy to effect a public mischief' was unknown to the law. Lord Simon of Glaisdale said:

> 'In effect the concept enjoins an English criminal court to act like a "people's court" in a totalitarian regime, and to declare punishable and to punish conduct held at large to be 'extremely injurious to the public".'[10]

---

9   'Two Concepts of Rules' in Acton *The Philosophy of Punishment* pp. 111-112.
10   *DPP   v Withers* [1975] AC 842 at 870.

'Punishment' by a 'people's court' need not be telishment. There may be no precise rules defining offences, but there may be fairly well-established criteria of 'guilt'. A Marxist revolutionary court may have a clear programme for delineating 'class enemies' who are to be eliminated or subjected to special disadvantages. An Islamic revolutionary court is more likely to justify its penalties directly by reference to considerations of retributive justice – punishment mete for evil-doers.

In considering whether we need criminal law in order to perform what Lord Edmund-Davies calls 'the universal object of a system of law', viz 'the establishment and maintenance of order', one popular *non sequitur* must be got out of the way. It is sometimes argued that, since most offenders continue to commit crimes after serving their sentences, it follows that deterrents do not work. But, of course, the conclusion does not follow. Other people may have been deterred from committing their first crime. Such evidence as there is, for instance from police strikes, suggests that crime would be much greater were there no criminal law enforcement at all. This still leaves open for debate the Marxist contention that, if only people were properly re-educated, there would be no need for institutionalised law enforcement. Acceptance of that view must at present rest on faith.

Consider a much more modest departure from our present punishing practices, that of Lady Wootton. The system she advocated would be one of universal strict liability. Pre-announced rules would define the external manifestations of anti-social conduct, and a court would have to find whether these had been met in any particular case. But whether or not the person before the court had acted 'intentionally' would not be considered at the 'conviction' stage. The court, having found that a person had performed the prohibited conduct, would hand him over to sentence commissioners, trained social scientists who would be qualified to decide on the appropriate treatment taking into account, if they thought fit, the fact that he had acted deliberately or accidentally. This system would be far removed from 'telishment'. It is not clear whether it would come within Rawls's definition of punishment, but Lady Wootton was clear that she would not wish it to be called 'punishment' precisely because of the retributive associations of that word. She would like what she regarded as the essentially religious concept of responsibility to 'wither away'. She believed that her system would be preferable, on utilitarian grounds, to our present punishment practices. It would be forward-looking towards treatment, and not backward-looking towards moral guilt at the time of the offence. It would enable suitable treatment measures to be taken in the case of people who, under our present system, are not prosecuted because *mens rea* cannot be proved.

'If the object of the criminal law is to prevent the occurrence of socially damaging actions, it would be absurd to turn a blind eye to those which were due to carelessness, negligence or even accident.'[11]

Whether the requirement of *mens rea* is based on retributive grounds is a question which has provoked much controversy. Bentham argued that *mens rea* and the general defences were required by utility. His point was that, since the object of laying down penalties was to threaten just enough harm to deter from harm, it would be pointless to threaten those who could not help acting as they did. H.L.A. Hart rejected this 'economy of threats' argument, on the ground that, although one who did not deliberately break the law could not himself have been deterred, punishing him might deter others. To that some would rejoin that the especially acute suffering involved in being punished for what you could not help would outweigh any deterrent advantages.

Hart himself believed that *mens rea* is supportable on a modified retributive basis. He argued that the 'justifying aim' of punishment is utilitarian, the protection of society and so on; but this aim should be limited by reference to what he called 'retribution in distribution'. Even if punishing one who was not at fault would produce a net utility gain, we should not allow it. We should defer to the popular conception of justice which requires that only the blameworthy should be subjected to state penalising. He further conceded that a rough retributive scale of maximum punishments should be used to limit sentences even where longer sentences would be justified on utilitarian grounds. Does this concede too much to the retributivists? If we are sure that burglars are deterrable, but that baby batterers are not, is there not a (utilitarian) case for giving the former much longer sentences than the latter even if we think that their crimes are morally less culpable?

Issues raised in the debate between retributivists and utilitarians bear on all the four contexts we have been discussing. They cannot be eliminated, as some philosophers appear to suggest, by focusing attention on 'decisions under a practice', where the judge has merely to perform his role-duty of applying the law. In sentencing, and in hard cases where the issue is what the law should be held to be, retributive justice and social consequences offer their competing allures. Nevertheless, if Hart and English judges are correct, it is not necessary to come down bang on one side or the other.

What are the general arguments for each view? Perusal of the writers may give the impression that the chief arguments are brick-bats thrown at the other party. Utilitarians argue that retributivists are cruel. They favour infliction of suffering when it cannot be proved that any good will be done by it. They believe, says Bentham, in a 'vengeful and splenetic deity'. Or

11   *Crime and the Criminal Law* (2nd edn) p 47.

else, they talk in mysterious metaphysical terms, as Hegel does when he speaks of punishment as the 'annulment' of a crime. They rely on loose language about 'paying one's debts to society', in order to draw an inappropriate analogy between reparation and retribution – whereas, although it is true that someone who damages another has a duty to make good (a duty supportable on utilitarian grounds), moral wrongdoing, as such, does not give rise to a 'debt'. Above all, not only do retributivists regard infliction of punishment as justified simply by being morally deserved, but they hold the curious belief that it is possible to measure such desert by reference to the harm done and the degree of responsibility – witness the *lex talionis,* 'an eye for an eye, a tooth for a tooth'.

To such charges retributivists reply in various ways. Retribution is not cruel, because it treats a man with dignity, regarding him as a responsible agent. It gives him a chance to expiate his crime by suffering, so the analogy with debts is not inappropriate. Alternatively, far from being cruel, retribution is the offender's right. How else is the breach between him and society to be healed? Or, at least retribution is not needlessly cruel, since society must denounce crimes in an emphatic way, and the only available method is retributive sentencing. As to *lex talionis,* of course the exact equivalent of harm cannot be meted out to most offenders – you cannot defraud the fraudster, or rape the rapist. But you can insist on proportionality: that is, given that punishments of a certain magnitude are customarily imposed for certain offences, you can insist on less for lesser offences and more for graver ones. Above all, the retributivist appeals to 'justice' as understood by the overwhelming majority of mankind through all ages.

Someone who is intellectually convinced of the barrenness of the idea of 'just retributive punishment' may nevertheless find it difficult to shake off its psychological hold. I have met the following dilemma experienced by students taking parallel courses in penology and legal philosophy. Criminological research has established that men fall into two groups: those who would never commit rape whether there was a law against it or not; and those who will commit this offence, and are never deterred by fear of punishment. Punishment is never warranted on retributive grounds. Therefore, rape should be removed from the catalogue of offences: 'oh, but that can't be right!'

Appeal to popular notions of justice seems particularly effective when the retributivist swings into the attack. 'Justice' is held up as a shield against those who would coerce us for what they consider to be community good. Any coercion going beyond our deserts is unjust. Furthermore, the retributivist may have a multi-principled ethic which allows him to temper justice with mercy, while the strict utilitarian must decide what is best, all things considered, by reference to consequences, and thereafter regard any 'mitigation' as morally unacceptable.

Utilitarians, argues the retributivist, would support 'punishing' the innocent if that could be seen to produce the greatest good. Here is Lady Wootton, a utilitarian, suggesting that we ditch responsibility. This would mean that, if a semi-illiterate widow inserts incorrect information in her supplementary benefits claim form, she could be brought before a court even though all concerned have no doubt that she did not mean to defraud. She would, of course, be told that this was not 'punishment', that she was not liable to 'conviction' but merely to be found a suitable case for treatment. She could tell the sentence commissioners about her mistake and, if they believed her, they would probably require no more by way of treatment than that she attend literacy classes: 'It's for your own good, dear!' The retributivist believes that no such assurance would meet her complaint that 'It's not just; it wasn't my fault!'

Why should we stop with strict liability? If medical science advances to the point where it can accurately predict that a certain kind of individual is biologically predisposed to commit serious crime, why wait for him to do so? Would not utilitarianism recommend his humane incarceration? The retributivists might raise a similar point in the context of what one might call 'social defence arguments'. It is sometimes contended – for example, with criminal damage or petty theft by members of disadvantaged groups – that society is to blame, not the offender. What follows? From a retributivist point of view, if it is really true that what was done was not morally wrong, there should be no punishment; or if it was less wrong than would have been the case but for the social conditions, less sentence. But from a utilitarian point of view, perhaps, since such acts are harmful, those who are inevitably (because of their background) going to offend should be removed from society forthwith – into humane labour colonies or retraining camps. We would explain to the members of the disadvantaged group: 'It's not your fault that you will inevitably inflict damage; this is best for everyone'. Will they not reply: 'Who says I will? It's unjust.' Kant's major argument against a utilitarian theory of punishment is that it treats men as mere means, not both as means and ends. Only a conception of retributively just punishment accords with respect for men as autonomous individuals. Apart from this point of principle, are utilitarians in any better case, in the matter of being able to calculate consequences, than are retributivists in being able to provide objective scales of desert?

To all of this utilitarians might answer that a careful calculation of social consequences will take proper account of the distress which would be caused to people by what the retributivists call 'unjust' measures. As the economic analysis of law demonstrates (see chapter 4, above), things like 'distress' are in principle measurable, by asking what people would pay to have them removed; whereas no measure is even in principle available for the retributivists' notion of subjective moral guilt. In any case, scientific progress is impossible if we insist on haltering it by untutored conceptions of 'justice'. It was necessary to fly in the face of popular retributivist sentiment in order to abolish the death penalty. We must do so again to get rid of the idea of personal responsibility.

Utilitarians are generally against the death penalty because there is no satisfactory evidence of its deterrent effect. Retributivists are divided about it. The traditional view, supported by Kant and Hegel, was that executing murderers was a clear case of just deserts. On the other hand, Dostoevsky, with his more individualistic view of the redemptive quality of punishment, ruled it out.

The retributivist-utilitarian debate will not go away. Even a radical critic who takes the view that nothing justifies our present punishing practices is still likely to employ the language of retributive or utilitarian justification when the spotlight is turned on particular topics of social concern. For any future that one can foresee, both will be embedded in our political and moral culture.

Bibliography

Acton H. B. (ed) *The Philosophy of Punishment* (1969)

Ashworth A. *Criminal Justice and Deserved Sentences* (1989)

Bedau H. A., Hirsch A. V., Wasserstrom R. A. 'The New Retributivism (A Symposium)' (1978) 85 J Phil 601

Bentham J. *An Introduction to the Principles of Morals and Legislation* (Burns and Hart (eds), 1970) ch 13

Braithwaite J. and Pettit P. *Not Just Deserts: a Republican Theory of Criminal Justice* (1990)

Clarke M. J. 'The Impact of Social Science on Conceptions of Responsibility' (1975) 2 Br J L Soc 32

Duff A. and Garland D. *A Reader on Punishment* (1994)

Gavison R. (ed) *Issues in Contemporary Jurisprudence* (1987) pt 3

Haag E. van Den *Punishing Criminals* (1975)

Hart H. L. A. *Punishment and Responsibility* (1968)

Hegel G. W. F. *Elements of the Philosophy of Right* (Nisbet trans, 1991) pp 119-31

Hirsch A. V. *Censure and Sanctions* (1993)

Honderich T. *Punishment: The Supposed Justifications* (1969)

Kant I. *The Philosophy of Law* (Hastie trans, 1887) pp. 194-205
   – *The Metaphysical Elements of Justice* (Ladd trans, 1965) pp. 99-107

Klenig J. *Punishment and Desert* (1973)

Lacey N. *State Punishment* (1987)

Lyons D. *Ethics and the Rule of Law* (1984) ch 5

Lucas J. R. *On Justice* (1980) ch 6

Morison J. 'Har's Excuses: Problems with a Compromise Theory of Punishment' in Leith and Ingram (eds) *The Jurisprudence of Orthodoxy* (1988)

Morris H. 'Persons and Punishment' (1968) 52 Monist 475

Murphy J. G. *Retribution, Justice and Therapy* (1979)

Ross A. *On Guilt, Responsibility and Punishment* (1975)

Sher G. *Desert* (1987) ch 5

Solomon R. C. and Murphy M. C. (eds) *What is Justice?* (1990) pt 4

Walker N. *Why Punish?* (1991)

Wootton B. *Crime and the Criminal Law* (2nd edn, 1981)

6 Kelsen's pure theory of law

(The following exchange takes place at the office of a travel agent soon after the democratic government of a holiday island country has been ousted by a military coup whose leaders have promulgated a constitution and effectively taken over all aspects of government.)

Traveller: 'Are you saying that I ought to pay the new airport tax on arrival?'
Agent: 'That's the new regulation.'
Traveller: 'Yes, I know that. But do you mean that I ought to pay?'
Agent: 'Well, they won't let you through unless … '
Traveller: 'I am not asking you for predictions. Ought I to pay?'
Agent: 'Morally, of course, given the undemocratic and unjust nature of the regime … '
Traveller: 'I am not interested in your subjective political opinions. Answer my question.'
Agent: 'On the assumption that they were entitled to launch the coup and promulgate their constitution, you ought to pay.'

REVOLUTIONARY'S DILEMMA

Joe: 'So I drive the car with the bomb down the High Street. Where do I go next?'
Bill: 'Straight on to the traffic lights. Whatever you do, don't turn right before the cinema, or you'll make yourself conspicuous.'
Joe: 'Why?'

Bill: 'Because turning right there is now illegal. Ouch! Why are you hitting me?'
Joe: 'You said "illegal". That means their regulations and their constitution ought to be obeyed.'
Bill: 'That isn't what I meant to say!'
Joe: 'It is the meaning of what you said. Haven't you read your Kelsen? Just watch your language in future!'

Soon after the first world war, news in the philosophic world was coming out of Austria. In Vienna, thinkers were suggesting new ways of looking at old problems – demarcating factual (verifiable, scientific) statements from other kinds of assertion. One of these was Hans Kelsen (1881-1973), whose 'pure theory of law' became, in terms of international reputation, the most famous contribution to legal philosophy of our century. The first edition of Kelsen's *Reine Rechtslehre*, published in 1934, was not translated into English until 1992, under the title *Introduction to the Problems of Legal Theory*, although extracts from this work appeared in the 1930s in the Law Quarterly Review. Much of the English-speaking literature on Kelsen relates to his *General Theory of Law and State*, published in 1945. The second edition of *Reine Rechtslehre*, originally published in 1960, was translated as *The Pure Theory of Law* in 1967. His posthumously published *General Theory of Norms*, translated in 1991, contains the final version of his theory.

There were many important changes in the theory, some of which will be touched on later in this chapter. One feature, however, remains constant: the pre-occupation with statements which convey information about positive law – the 'thousands of statements' in which the law is 'daily' invoked.[1] (Kelsen frequently refers to this phenomenon as 'juristic cognition', 'juristic thinking', or 'legal science'. But it is clear that it encompasses all legal-information-giving statements, whether made by lawyers or not.) Such statements should not be understood as referring to moral values. As a relativist, Kelsen denied that there could be objective assertions about morals. On the other hand, describing conduct as 'legal' or 'illegal', or making statements about legal rights and duties, was not the same thing as conveying information about past, present or future matters of fact. These were amoral 'ought' assertions. They took place against a background of effective administration of coercion within a territory, but they referred directly to a system of 'ought' meaning-contents which the information-giver assumed to be objectively binding – that is, they described a hierarchy of 'valid' norms rooted, not in justice, but in some historical starting-point (the promulgation of the 'historically first constitution').

1   *Introduction to the Problems of Legal Theory* p 35. *Pure Theory of Law* p 104.

The following, then, is Kelsen's picture of a society in which there is to be found that social phenomenon we call 'law'. We see individuals or groups purporting to issue prescriptions about how other people ought to decree measures of coercion – the forcible deprivation of life, liberty, health or economic values. We find that, generally speaking, when members of the community fulfil the conditions contained in these prescriptions, coercive measures are indeed decreed and implemented. These facts could be interpreted merely 'sociologically' not 'juristically'. They could be portrayed as a series of events, of power relations operating on the level of cause and effect. But that would be to leave out of account the daily phenomenon of law-talk, so that the social scientist could hardly be said to have explained what was going on. Apart from the prescribers and the enforcers, there are countless people out there conveying information about what, according to law, ought to be done. Working inductively from this universal phenomenon we find, Kelsen says, that whenever people measure conduct by 'legality' they are talking as though those who promulgated the historically first constitution had been empowered to set the ultimate terms for the exercise of coercion within the territory – the admission extracted from the travel agent in the first scenario I invented at the beginning of this chapter. This characteristic assumption of law-talk Kelsen has called 'presupposing a basic norm'. Does it entail that anyone who allows words like 'legal' or 'illegal' to pass his lips is thereby committing himself to an assumption that the law is objectively binding, as revolutionary Joe supposed in the second scenario? Questions of that kind have bedevilled Kelsen's explanation of the law's normativity. I shall turn to them later.

1   Why 'pure'?

Kelsen believed that statements of positive law were not statements of moral or political value, nor yet statements of fact; and it was the business of theory to work out a conception of law which would reflect this feature of discourse. Hence ethical or sociological definitions of law were to be rejected. In a sense the word 'pure' in 'the pure theory of law' has got into the wrong place. Kelsen's is a theory about pure legal-information-giving. The theory itself cannot be pure. It is sound, or it is not.

Kelsen maintained that much legal text-writing tended to smuggle in the writer's own value judgments, and part of the explanation for that was that legal language used concepts which morals and politics and social sciences also employ – like duty, state and person. The thing to do was to isolate the norms of positive law, which alone could be the subject matter of objective (scientific) description, and then define 'legal' uses of such concepts in terms of those norms. A legal norm characteristically provided that if certain conduct was performed, an official should apply some measure of coercion. To say that someone has a legal duty is therefore to say no more than that some norm of positive law makes the opposite conduct the condition for coercion to be applied to him. The 'state', as a legal concept, means just the personification ('hypo-statisation') of all the legal norms valid within a territory. A 'person', as a legal concept, means some entity (human or otherwise) to whose actions or existence legal norms attach consequences.

It is, said Kelsen, not the business of the science of law 'to approve or disapprove its subject'.[2] Let lawyers stick to their last. If asked for information about the law, they can, scientifically, only describe norms – the circumstances under which, by law, coercion is stipulated. Whether conduct is, by any other criterion, right or wrong is a private and wholly subjective value judgment; the lawyer's attitude as to that is no different from everyone else's. If it is not clear whether, by existing norms, conduct is the condition of sanctions, but the law empowers judges to decide the question at their discretion, then legal science must report just that – the law authorises the court to create a particular norm ordering a sanction in this case. Whether the judge ought so to 'legislate' is a question of legal politics. He has the authority, but how he exercises it is beyond science to lay down.

Legal commentators commonly support their descriptions of the law by reference to the purposes or functions of the law. They suggest that a particular interpretation is correct, having regard to the motives of the legislature or the social function the law is supposed to serve. Such psychological and political matters cannot be objectively known and should therefore, Kelsen argues, not be part of objective legal science. The only 'function' which can, objectively, be attributed to all legal systems is that which appears on the face of legal norms. Reading the legal texts will show that coercive acts by one man against another are always either the condition for the application of sanctions ('delicts'), or else they are prescribed by legal norms ('sanctions'). So the only universal function is the monopolisation of force within the legal order – not justice, but peace. The purposes of legislators are multifarious. The technique for achieving them is always the same – the discouraging of conduct by attaching a sanction to it. This overall technique breaks down into three particular techniques, typical of different branches of the law or of particular economic regimes. The penal technique makes conduct (offences) the condition of sanctions to the delinquent. The administrative technique stipulates that coercive measures should be taken – such as the internment of the insane or those considered politically undesirable – without any particular conduct by the person against whom the measures are applied being laid down as a condition. The civil technique stipulates

2 *Pure Theory of Law* p 68.

as the conditions for coercive measures (like awards of damages) both the conduct of the delinquent (breach of contract or tort) and the decision of some party to sue. This latter technique is typical of capitalist economic regimes. The term 'legal right', in its strict sense, refers to the fact that some norm makes the application of coercion conditional on someone's choice to sue.

Thus, the 'pure' theory recommends that all positive law should be viewed as a system of norms stipulating that, under certain conditions, a coercive measure ought to be applied. Is such a view practicable, and, if practicable, is it desirable?

Can all the products of legislation – provisions setting up institutions, rules about formalities for transactions, conceptual definitions, and so on – be reduced to the Kelsenian canonical form of: 'if ... then a sanction ought to be applied'? Kelsen supposed that they could. Procedural requirements relating to legislation can be rewritten for example: 'If a bill has been duly voted on and promulgated ... then the court should order (the sanction stipulated in the bill)'. Rules relating to the formation of contracts or wills may be rendered: 'If there has been an offer and an acceptance, and if there was consideration, etc, and if breach and suit followed, then ... sanctions'; or: 'If a will has been validly made and the executors will not deliver the property to the legatee, and he has claimed it, then the court should order them to deliver'.

Kelsen recognises that there may be products of legislation which cannot be reconstructed in this way. If an act contains congratulatory remarks about a statesman, or purely 'ideological' provisions about the existence of God or the sovereign will of the people, it is unlikely that civil or criminal wrongs will only be punishable if such provisions are complied with. If a statute provided: 'Winston Churchill was a great man', but did not go on to make the denial of this the condition for punishment, the provision would, for that reason, be what Kelsen calls 'legally irrelevant material'. Legislation, and particularly constitutions, do contain ideological pronouncements, as well as indications of the conditions under which state force is to be applied, but only the latter are part of positive law. The Kelsenian canonical norm-structure is supposed to provide a litmus paper test for distinguishing the legally relevant from the legally irrelevant.

Is this reconstruction desirable? Principles which cannot be represented as parts of sanction-stipulating norms may, some would argue, still be 'legal' in the sense that they can be used by judges to justify decisions in 'hard cases' (see chapter 14, below). To this Kelsen replied that such suggestions come from those who 'engage in highly subjective evaluation of law under the banner of objective legal cognition'.[3] Or it may be argued that there are 'legal' sentiments ('living law') which would be left out by Kelsen's source-bound definition (see chapter 18, below). To this Kelsen answers that, in order to distinguish sociology of law from a general sociology of society, one must begin with his juridical definition. 'The function of the legal norm for the sociology of law is to designate its own particular object, and lift it out of the whole of social events.'[4]

2 Sanctions

For Kelsen, the coercive measures stipulated by legal norms are the deprivation of life, liberty, health or property – that is, capital punishment, imprisonment, corporal punishment, or fines, damages, and other orders about handing over specific property. Unlike Austin (see chapter 3, above), he is quite clear on one point. It is no part of his theory that sanctions in fact provide a motive for compliance. Law is not distinguished from customary morality by the fact that it is enforced by coercion. It is distinguished in that it stipulates that coercion ought to be applied. Both legal and moral norms contain 'oughts', but a moral norm stipulates, for example, 'People ought not to steal'; whereas a legal norm stipulates 'If people steal, they ought to be punished'. Moral norms are addressed directly to citizens. Legal norms are addressed only to officials. It may be that people would comply with the conduct which is the content of a legal duty even if there were no sanctions. It may be that people comply with moral norms out of fear of social reactions. Sanctions (coercive measures) are the hallmark of law because they appear on the face of legal norms, not because of their supposed psychological effectiveness.

At the same time, legal science is not totally unconcerned with whether sanctions in fact occur. Although, by stating that such and such is a legal norm, the lawyer does not commit himself to a prediction that anyone will be punished, his statements about the validity of legal norms presuppose effectiveness in two ways. First, although a legal norm is valid from the moment of its enactment, it will (Kelsen argues) lose its validity if it has been ineffective for a long time – this is a generalisation of the civil law doctrine of 'desuetude' which, as it happens, does not apply in common law countries. Secondly, no norm can be valid unless it is a member of a system of norms which is, by and large, effective. In these two ways, effectiveness conditions validity. But how do we measure effectiveness? By two criteria: first, is the norm 'obeyed' (in the sense that conduct conditioning the sanction is not performed); secondly, when disobedience occurs, is the sanction applied? A legal scientist, performing his proper objective role, cannot describe laws emanating from the

4   *What is Justice?* p 270.

government of Taiwan as the law of mainland China, because disobedience of Taiwanese laws is never matched by the application of sanctions on the mainland.

Unlike Austin, Kelsen did not limit his theory to the laws of modern states. He asserted that everywhere at all times the word 'law' is used to stand for a system of coercive rules. In the context of primitive societies, the laws stipulated blood revenge. In public international law, the sanctions are war and military reprisals. Everything which is distinctly 'legal' about primitive societies or the international community must be slotted in as conditions for norms requiring kinship groups, or states, to take these drastic measures. Few would follow Kelsen here. The organisers of tribal initiations, or the instructors of diplomats, would be sorely perplexed if they were asked to sieve through the information they give and pick out only that which had a bearing on the propriety of killing. In these contexts, then, because Kelsen's theory cannot separate out any significant system of rules, the theory distorts.

Many critics would assert that the theory also distorts the positive law of modern states, by virtue of the overemphasis on sanctions. It may be denied that there is a conceptual connection between 'law' and 'coercion'. Raz maintains that law is distinguished from other institutions by its claim to ultimate authority not by its monopolisation of force, so that the rules of a church might constitute a legal system. (See chapter 9, below.) Fuller goes further: any enterprise of subjecting human conduct to the governance of rules is a legal system, so that universities and clubs have 'laws'. (See chapter 11, below.) It should be noted, however, that Dworkin does accept the conceptual connection, although for him the concept of law refers to justified coercion, whereas for Kelsen it points to organised coercion. (See chapter 14, below.)

Even conceding that positive law is distinguished from other systems of rules by its coercive nature, do we really have to conceive of every rule as directing officials to take away life, liberty, health or property? One objection is based on cumbersomeness. Given Kelsen's reconstruction, you could not make a small point, eg that a contract relating to land needs to be made in writing, without placing it alongside the rest of the law on contract-formation and breach, all as the conditions for a direction to a judge to award damages or specific performance. Assessing this criticism is one of those things which turns on what one thinks Kelsen was really trying to say. If he meant that law books, solicitors and counsel should rewrite what they say in this cumbersome form, he was recommending what in practice cannot be done. If instead, as seems more plausible, he meant only that the deep structure of sanction-stipulating norms must be kept in mind, so that, on demand, any information about formalities or whatever could be related to circumstances in which damages or an order for specific performance would or would not lie, the objection from cumbersomeness is misplaced.

A second objection runs like this. The legal system is overall coercive, true. But the law has many functions wherein coercive enforcement is very much in the background, such as the enunciation of new standards – for example, in the areas of racial or sexual discrimination. A citizen will ask, and a lawyer will tell him, when it is or is not lawful to discriminate. The matter of sanctions will often never arise. We should split up laws into different types, depending on different legal functions. To this criticism we shall return in discussing Hart's concept of law (see chapter 9, below).

A third criticism fastens on the subsidiary role which Kelsen's coercive form gives to the concept of legal duty. If legislative material in terms makes conduct 'obligatory', but stipulates no sanction for failure to perform the conduct in question, then, by Kelsen's theory, there is no legal duty. If a statute stated that a public authority is to provide certain facilities, but there was in the law no sanction should they not, the duty is merely political-ideological – has the same status as if contained in a manifesto. But can that be right? Surely, the criticisms to which an authority will be subjected if it breaches what a statute ordered it to do will be of a different kind from those which will be made if, for any other reason, the critic thinks it has acted inadequately. It will be said to be 'flouting the law'.

Furthermore, so critics argue, specific conduct may be made the condition for a sanction where it is not thought of as the subject of a 'duty'. If the law states that, should anyone import canned octopus, an official shall levy on him a payment of £1 per ton, the non-importing will be termed a 'duty' and the £1 per ton a 'fine', only if the object of the legislation was to prohibit the importation. If the legislature had revenue-raising in mind, neither importing nor not importing will be said to be the subject of an obligation, and the payment will be termed a 'tax'. The purity of the theory, as represented in its canonical sanction-stipulating form, prevents us from inquiring into the motives of the legislature; so law conceived in terms of the theory cannot account for these differences in duty-terminology.

Kelsen might have replied to this charge – though I think he never did – 'So much the worse for your slipshod, ideologically-loaded terminology!' If a man is told that, by law, if he imports so much, he must pay so much, that is all the legal information he requires. Compare the situation with library or parking 'fines'. If I return my book late, am told how much is owing and pay up, and then the attendant tells me: 'You were at fault, acting wrongly, not doing your duty, when you kept the book over time', may I not answer: 'Mind your own business. You've told me the rules, and applied them.'

Kelsen's final views on the individuation of legal norms are obscure. Prior to the second edition of *Reine Rechtslehre*, he had said that all legal norms were 'depsychologised commands' addressed to officials. From 1960 onwards, he divided norms of all kinds, those of positive law and of positive morality, into four kinds: commanding, permitting, authorising (empowering)[5], and derogating. Derogating norms repeal norms. What is not clear is whether the other three types constitute independent norms in the case of law. Authorising (empowering) norms confer power to create law. Some commentators read the 1960-onwards revision as entailing that all norms addressed to officials must be of this type, since implementing sanctions always involves the creation of law; and, unless there is some further norm directing a sanction to be applied to an official if he failed to implement the first norm, the first norm could not be said to impose a duty and hence would not be a command. But then Kelsen also said in the second edition of *Reine Rechslehre* that if we treat a prescription as a norm we interpret its 'subjective meaning' as its 'objective meaning', which would suggest that mandatory stipulations addressed to officials are commanding norms. As to permitting norms, he gave the example of self-defence, which some have taken to imply that legal norms need not (after all) be addressed to officials.

In his last work, *General Theory of Norms*, Kelsen makes it clear that all stipulations addressed to citizens must, if they are to carry legal 'oughts', be dependent on primary norms addressed to officials. 'If the legislator were to command that loans be repaid or to forbid committing theft, without attaching a sanction to the non-repayment of loans or the commission of theft, he would merely be expressing a legally irrelevant wish; the repayment of loans and the avoidance of theft would not be legally commanded.'[6]

Furthermore, in this last book Kelsen deploys, alongside the usual concept of duty (conduct which is the opposite of that which is the stipulated condition of a sanction), what looks like a special role concept of duty specifically for judges. 'Judges are empowered by statutes to apply general legal norms to concrete cases. As a rule they are also commanded to do so. A judge violates the duties of his office if he refrains from making use of his power in a concrete case: he acts illegally.'[7]

So far as one can read a consistent position into Kelsen's final legal-norm typology, it would appear to be this. All primary legal norms are addressed to officials. If the implementing of the coercive measures they stipulate involves the creation of individual norms, they are empowering

---

5　The German verb *ermachtigen* is translated 'to authorise' in *Pure theory of law* and 'to empower' in *General Theory of Norms*.

6　*General Theory of Norms* p 97.

7　Op cit p 103.

norms. If they are mandatory in content, they are also commanding norms. Kelsen gives no examples of primary permissive legal norms; but presumably they would be ones which permitted officials to apply coercion in circumstances which would not create further norms – perhaps, where a police officer is permitted to search suspects. Citizens, as distinct from officials, are the subject of secondary, dependent legal norms, which may be commanding, empowering or (as with self-defence) permissive in character.

Thus to say that X, a citizen, is under a legal duty to ... is the same thing as saying that if X does not ... the law stipulates a sanction against X. Even if such an analysis can be imposed on a body of given legal material, it will be inapplicable to concepts used in judicial reasoning where the law is unsettled. Such reasoning commonly starts from the assumption that X had a legal duty to do something, and then goes on to discuss whether any particular failure to perform it should be made the subject of a sanction. The reasoning would be circular if duty were defined as liability to sanction. Similar objections may be raised against Kelsen's reductionist analysis of other legal concepts in terms of sanctions. It will not work if the concept is presupposed as a step in reasoning leading to a conclusion about sanctions.

Moreover, a major internal weakness in Kelsen's theory comes to light when we relate his sanction-dependent concept of duty to his concept of effectiveness (the latter being, as we have seen, a condition of validity). In the case of the importer of canned octopus, or that of the library or parking fine, how are we to measure the effectiveness of the norms unless we can say, as a matter distinct from the sanction, that the intention was to prevent the conditioning conduct, or merely to tax it? If importation, parking or late returning increase, but the payments are always collected, the rules are effective if intended to tax, but not so if intended to prohibit. The attaching of coercion to certain types of conduct is not a mere 'technique' designed to achieve *any* purpose. Often it has an immediate purpose of making the conduct illegal, something one is duty-bound not to do. The concept of 'duty' must therefore stand on its own feet, as something distinct from the concept of sanction. A theory of law must define duty and sanction separately.

3   The basic norm

Kelsen said that there were two things universally true of law: that it was coercive, and that it was a system of norms. For a legal norm to be described as 'valid' it must be a member of a system. The reason for the validity of a norm was always another norm. If it were said that a byelaw was valid, the reason for that would be a statute. The reason for the statute's validity might be a written constitution conferring legislative power on the legislature. The constitution might be valid because it had been promulgated in accordance with some historically prior constitution. Eventually, one must get back to a historical starting-point for norm-creation, beyond which the chain of validation cannot go. At that point it was possible to make sense of legal-information-giving only by inserting the theoretical construct of a presupposed basic norm, which empowered those who promulgated the historically first constitution:

> 'If the historically first constitution was posited by the resolution of an assembly, then it is the individuals forming this assembly who are empowered by the basic norm; if the historically first constitution arose by way of custom, then it is this custom, or to be more exact, it is the individuals whose behaviour forms the custom creating the historically first constitution, who were empowered by the basic norm.'[8]

If public international law is regarded as law, then, argued Kelsen, legal science must interpret it as forming one system with national law. Either it is subsumed under national law, or national law is subsumed under it. In the latter case, the effective constitution of a state is authorised by the principle of effectiveness, a principle of customary international law; and the only true basic norm is that which authorises the creation by states of customary and treaty-made international law – that coercive measures should be applied in ways states have customarily recognised as 'legal'.

Just as validity is traced up, so authority may be traced down. The basic norm authorises the promulgators of the constitution, the constitution authorises the legislature; and so on. The law is a 'dynamic' system, in that the contents of lower norms are, within limits, chosen by the norm-creator. But the norm is only valid because the choice is authorised by a higher norm. The process of dynamic derivation produces gradually increased 'concretisation' as one moves down the ladder. For Kelsen, contracts, wills and settlements produce legal norms. So long as their makers act within legal powers, they create particular concretisations of higher norms. So too with judges. When a judge passes a sentence he creates an individual norm. Indeed, every act of norm-application is an act of norm-creation, except the final carrying out of a coercive measure.I suggest the following simplified model of norm-concretisation as an example of how Kelsenian reconstruction would apply to a particular case.

Concretisation of Kelsenian norms

(1) Basic norm of UK legal order: Coercive acts ought to be carried out only in the ways provided for in the historically first constitution which custom has established.

8   *General Theory of Norms* p 255.

(2) Constitutional norm contained within the historically first constitution: Coercive acts ought to be carried out in accordance with statutes enacted by the Queen in Parliament.

(3) General norm created by statute: Where, pursuant to a contract of sale of goods, the seller neglects or refuses to deliver the goods to the buyer, and the buyer elects to sue, the seller ought to be condemned to pay damages.[9]

(4) Particular norm created by contract between Smith and Brown: If Smith neglects or refuses to deliver his prize rabbit (Wundabun) to Brown, and Brown elects to sue, Smith ought to be condemned to pay damages.

(5) Particular concretised norm created by county court judge on Brown's suing Smith: If Smith fails to pay damages of £50 within 28 days of this order, and Brown issues a warrant of execution, the bailiff ought to levy execution upon the goods of Smith.

(6) Particular fully concretised norm created by Brown's issuing warrant of execution: Bailiff, levy execution upon the goods of Smith.

For Kelsen, legal science gives information in terms of norms at many levels of generalisation. Smith and Brown and the bailiff will be informed of, and act against the background of, 'law' at the level of concreteness indicated by norms (4), (5) and (6). The textwriter on sale of goods will describe the law at the level of norm (3), and the constitutional lawyer that of norm (2). It is the theorist alone who is concerned with norm (1), the basic norm itself.

The concept of the basic norm has given rise to four kinds of question: What is its nature? What is its content? What is its function? How do we choose between competing basic norms?

Kelsen asserted that the basic norm differs from all other legal norms in that it is not posited by an act of norm-creation. It is not the product of legislation, but is assumed by anyone who purports to describe valid law. If he is speaking of American law, he assumes that the rules must derive only from the constitution promulgated by the fathers of the constitution in the 18th century, and so presupposes a norm which confers ultimate legislative power upon that body of men. If he is speaking of English law, he is assuming that the laws can only originate in the sources hallowed by the UK customary constitution, and so is presupposing a norm which confers ultimate legislative power on custom.

The basic norm is a 'fiction' in the sense of Vaihinger's philosophy of 'as if', that is 'a cognitive device used when one is unable to attain one's cognitive goal with the material at hand'.[10] The travel agent at Kelsen Tours Ltd was forced to invoke it because only in that way could he explain the sense in which the traveller 'ought' to pay the airport tax. The

9 Sale of Goods Act 1979, ss 2, 51.
10 *General Theory of Norms* p 256.

basic norm is not a psychological or sociological phenomenon. Unlike Hart's rule of recognition (see chapter 9, below), it does not stand for a complex social practice and is not consciously accepted by legal officials from an 'internal point of view'. It is invented by theory as an inductive inference from the universal practice of law-information-giving. Of course, it cannot explain how the law could be said to be X, not by reference to sources, but in virtue of arguments based on justice or policy. For Kelsen, all such matters are 'legal politics', not susceptible to scientific cognition.

As to content, the notion of a 'historically first' constitution has the disadvantage that it appears to suggest that all ultimate sources presupposed by legal cognition must have crystallised at a particular historical date. I have suggested that it would be more consistent with Kelsen's own methodology to conceive of the basic norm as listing and ranking various independent sources, such as legislation and precedent, so that changes in the basic norm may be more accurately depicted. American lawyers presuppose that rulings of the Supreme Court on questions of constitutional interpretation prevail over enactments of Congress. That was not laid down when the constitution was first ratified, but came about as the result of the Court's ruling in *Marbury v Madison*.[11] Kelsen's brief discussion of customary constitutions in *Pure Theory of Law* and earlier writings can be taken to imply that, in their case, the presupposed basic norm never changes unless the customary constitution is replaced by a written constitution, as I supposed was his view in my 1971 Cambridge Law Journal article. A better reading, as I now think in the light of what he says in *General Theory of Norms*, is that a customary constitution may be replaced by another customary constitution in ways not provided for in the first constitution, when there would be a change in the presuppositions made when legal information is given and hence a change in the basic norm. Before the enactment of the European Communities Act 1972 it was a settled feature of the UK customary constitution that Parliament could not bind successor parliaments, at least as to matters of legal content. That statute provided that legislation emanating from the institutions of what is now the European Union should prevail over UK legislation. If it is now accepted, in any description of UK law, that our parliament could not, constitutionally, repeal the 1972 Act in such a way as to reverse the ranking of European and UK sources, then, at some time between 1972 and the present day, there occurred a change in presupposed constitutional foundations – a change in the basic norm, a technical (Kelsenian) 'revolution'. (See also the discussion of changes in precedent practices in chapter 12, below.)

As to the function of the basic norm, Kelsen says that it founds the validity of the legal order. Some critics have charged him with circularity:

11   Cranch 137 (1803).

we identify legal norms, ultimately, by reference to the basic norm; but we can only say what basic norm is presupposed by working backwards from the legal norms which we have first identified. To this charge Kelsen responded in his 1965 Stanford Law Review article. Effectively enforced acts of purported legislation come first and, indeed, could be recorded, sociologically, without the help of any basic norm. But if we interpret them juristically, by speaking of their contents as 'legally binding', then we presuppose a basic norm. That presupposition adds a top-dressing of 'oughtness' to the power-facts on the ground.

'Validity', for Kelsen, denotes both system-membership and bindingness. If we separate these elements, we have two functions of the basic norm. It both explains how, when giving information about the law, we fit legal bits and pieces into a whole; and it also explains the sense in which law 'ought' to be obeyed (the law's normativity).

When the lawyer comes to her work, she assumes (before she starts) that she can produce a conclusion about the legality or illegality of conduct. This entails, Kelsen argues, that she systematises the products of particular acts of will within a hierarchical dynamic structure founded on a historically first constitution, and hence presupposes some basic norm. Up to and including the second edition of *Reine Rechtslehre*, Kelsen also asserted that legal cognition presupposes the elimination of contradiction (drawing an analogy with Kant's theory of knowledge). In the normative logic which he expounded in essays published after 1960 and in his *General Theory of Norms*, he resiled from this latter claim. Scientific cognition required that contradictory norms be simultaneously described as valid. I suggest that this change was mistaken. If it is true that lawyers presuppose hierarchy among legislative sources, surely it is also true that they assume the following: one cannot say that the law on a point is quite clear, in that it predicates of a judge issuing a particular coercive order both that the judge is applying, and that he is flouting, the law. What is true is that one may not be able to say for sure what the law requires, precisely because there appear to be contradictory provisions. In so far as one knows for certain what the law is, one 'knows' it as a non-contradictory field of meaning.

As to the second function of the basic norm, the attribution of bindingness, we face the revolutionary's dilemma set out in the second scenario at the beginning of this chapter. Bill was giving useful information to Joe but, according to Joe's reading of Kelsen, if Bill used legal terminology to convey that information he would inevitably imply that the hated regime's pronouncements ought to be obeyed. Joe, and many commentators, have taken Kelsen to mean that when we ascribe validity to the law we imply that, in some sense or from some point of view, it is morally binding. (See the discussion of Raz on 'point of view' in chapter 9, below.) Warrant for that interpretation is provided by Kelsen's oft-repeated claim that only by presupposing the basic norm can we distinguish the command of a taxman from that of a gangster if the commands have the same content; and also by his occasional references to anarchists not presupposing the basic norm, or to communists not presupposing the basic norm of a capitalist legal order. If persons who disapprove of the law do not presuppose the basic norm, does that not imply that those who do presuppose it thereby endow the law with moral legitimacy? So when Joe told Bill to 'watch his language in future', he meant that Bill must convey information about the facts of prescription and enforcement, but should not use words like 'illegal'.

On the other hand, in a celebrated passage in the second edition of *Reine Rechtslehre*, Kelsen says of his suggestion that anarchists do not presuppose the basic norm that it was 'misleading'. 'Even an anarchist, if he were a professor of law, could describe positive law as a system of valid norms.'[12] I have argued that the 'oughtness' which Kelsen attributes to law is 'pallid normativity'. To say that conduct is 'illegal' carries no value implications. A Kelsenian 'ought' is exclusively will-relative. It treats a subjective prescription as an objective measure of conduct, that is all. It could not entail value, in the sense of critical morals or politics, for Kelsen was a relativist about such things. We might suppose that there are many reasons, having to do with critical values, for distinguishing the demands of a taxman from those of a gangster. Kelsen's contention that the only ground of distinction is the presupposition of a basic norm merely confirms his moral relativism, and his peculiar (pallid) conception of 'ought'. We shall see (in chapter 16, below) that it is controvertial whether one can find moral grounds for a duty to obey the law. For Kelsen, since there are no such things as 'true' moral considerations, such an enquiry is 'unscientific'. The only cognitive 'oughts' there can be are those which clothe effective prescriptions with an assumed, amoral, pallid normativity.

The issue of choosing between competing basic norms arises from the efficacy pre-condition of its presupposition by legal science. Supposing the effectively enforced law would fit different basic norms equally well, what then? For example, it may be that current UK law would have precisely the same content whether one derived the validity of legislation emanating from the European Union either from the 1972 European Communities Act as an ultimate source, or from the various treaties constituting the Union as ultimate sources. Again (critics have argued) when the UK parliament conferred independence on former British dominions, you could just as well relate the law in force in the new state back to the UK constitution as treat the newly independent state as being possessed of a distinct legal system. Kelsen never addressed such problems. However, in the context of the relationship between municipal

12   *Pure Theory of Law* p 218 (n).

and international law, he asserted (as we have seen) that the same legal material could be interpreted either as ultimately founded on one source or another. Perhaps a similar approach could be taken in these other contexts. Immediately after dominion independence, it may have been unclear whether, should the UK parliament purport to legislate for the territory in ways incompatible with the dominion's constitution, that legislation would have been enforced by local courts. We can be sure that that would not be so today, so that at some stage – and it hardly now matters when – a change in the basic norm came about. Similarly, perhaps, it is now the case, or some day will be true, that English courts would refuse to implement parliamentary legislation which expressly purported to repeal the 1972 Act and to override European Union law. That is the point at which, according to the efficacy test, there comes about a breach in constitutional continuity and hence a change in the basic norm. (Of course, basic-norm-theorising says nothing about whether any particular new constitutional start would be a good thing. It merely provides the logical frame for such questions.)

To illustrate changes in the basic norm, Kelsen himself cites only instances in which the efficacy test is clearly satisfied, cases of successful revolution. He says that when a revolution occurs, when the old laws cease to be effectively enforced and laws promulgated by the rebels are enforced instead, then lawyers presuppose a new basic norm authorising the revolutionary constitution. Kelsen does not say that it is right or desirable that lawyers should do this, but merely that they do do it. His is a descriptive theory. It has been criticised for making efficacy the only test for legal recognition of revolutions. Surely, it has been argued, lawyers take other things into account – such as the justice of the revolutionary cause, or the approval or disapproval of the populace – not just the fact of enforcement? Whether Kelsen, or his critics, correctly describe what lawyers do in such contexts is a question for historians.

Much more controversial has been the implication drawn from Kelsen's theory by judges in revolutionary situations. The theory was expressly cited, following a coup in Pakistan in 1958, one in Uganda in 1965 and the Rhodesian Unilateral Declaration of Independence in 1965, as justifying judicial recognition of new regimes.[13]

These decisions, and the theory they purport to apply, have had a bad press. In general, it has been said that, so interpreted, Kelsen's theory amounts to 'might is right' – actually, it should be 'Might is law'. In particular, the unpopularity of the Smith regime in Rhodesia has been reflected by distaste for the whole idea of measuring legality by effectiveness. Apart from the attacks of juristic critics, some courts have

---

13 *State v Dosso* [1958] 2 Pakistan SCR 180; *Uganda v Commissioner of Prisons, ex p Matovu* [1966] EA 514; *Madzimambuto v Lardner-Burke NO* [1968] 2 SA 284.

repudiated the theory. In 1970, the Supreme Court of Nigeria refused to apply Kelsen's theory of revolutions. It held that a military coup of 1966 was not a true revolution, so that the legislative capacity of new institutions was limited by reference to the pre-existing constitution.[14] In 1972, the Supreme Court of Pakistan rejected Kelsen's theory, repudiating its earlier decision. It held that it was through judicial recognition alone that a new legislative organ acquired competence; and that this should be accorded only if a revolutionary constitution embodied the will of the people.[15] In the Nigerian case, the court's decision was immediately overturned by new legislation declaring that the 1966 coup had been revolutionary. In the Pakistan case, the court was in the happy position of adjudicating on the legality of one coup after it had been superseded by another.

There is no doubt that Kelsen did not expressly authorise judicial use of his theory. However, drawing out the implications of his view that efficacy is a pre-condition of legal validity, should we not say that the judge who stays in office will inevitably render support to the effective regime, since, be it good or bad, the only law is effectively enforced law? If that is right, then when an effective revolution occurs, the only true choice for judges or other officials is either to resign or to stay on and – like the French traffic police who remained on duty after the German invasion – inevitably to consolidate the new regime. This would mean that the British Government in 1965 gave (through its Governor) inconsistent directives to Rhodesian officials when they were told to carry on with their normal tasks, but not to recognise the new regime. If effectiveness is a pre-condition for law, then the British Government was disingenuous when it said to the black majority, in effect: 'We will not use force to oust the rebel authorities; but, don't worry, they are not legal.'

Bibliography

Beyleveld D. and Brownsword R. *Law as a Moral Judgment* (1986) ch 6
Brookfield F. M. 'The Courts, Kelsen, and the Rhodesian Revolution' (1969) 19 U Tor LJ 326

---

14   *E. O. Lakami and Kimelomo Ola v A-G (Western State)*; see A. Ojo 'The Search for the Grundnorm in Nigeria: the Lakanmi Case' (1971) 20 ICLQ 117.

15   *Asma Jilani v Government of Punjab* (Pak Leg decisions 1972, Supreme Court of Pakistan); see T.K.K. Iyer 'Constitutional Law in Pakistan: Kelsen and the Courts' (1973) 21 Am J of Comp L 759. The Court of Appeal in Ghana has refused to apply Kelsen's theory that, when a basic norm changes, all norms are made new: *E. K. Sallah v A-G* [1970] CC 54 at 55; see T. and F. S. Tsikata 'Kelsen and others in the Court of Appeal' (1970) 7 U G LJ 142, and S. K. Date-bah 'Jurisprudence's Day in Court in Ghana' (1971) 20 ICLQ 315.

Dias R. W. M. *Jurisprudence* (4th edn 1976) ch 16

Dworkin R. M. 'Comments on the Unity of Law Doctrine (a Response)' in Kiefer and Munitz (eds) *Ethics and Social Justice* (1970)

Ebenstein W. *The Pure Theory of Law* (1945)

Eckhoff T. and Sunby N. K. 'The Notion of Basic Norm(s) in Jurisprudence' (1975) Scand S L 123

Eekelaar J. M. 'Principles of Revolutionary Legality' in Simpson (ed) *Oxford Essays in Jurisprudence* (2nd series, 1973)

Finnis J. M. 'Revolutions and Continuity of Law' in Simpson (ed) *Oxford Essays in Jurisprudence* (2nd series, 1973)

Gianformaggio L. (ed) *Hans Kelsen's Legal Theory* (1990)

Golding M. P. 'Kelsen and the Concept of "Legal System" 'in Summers (ed) *More Essays in Legal Philosophy* (1971)

Guest S. 'Three Judicial Doctrines of Total Recognition of Revolutionary Governments' (1980) AJ 1

Harris J. W. 'When and Why Does the Grundnorm Change?' (1971) 29 CLJ 103
 – 'Kelsen's Concept of Authority' (1977) 36 CLJ 353
 – *Law and Legal Science* (1979) ss. 5, 9-17
 – 'Kelsen, Revolutions and Normativity' in Attwooll (ed) *Shaping Revolution* (1991)
 – 'The Basic Norm and the Basic Law' (1994) HKLJ 207
 – 'Kelsen's Pallid Normativity' (1996) 9 RJ 94

Hart H. L. A. *Essays in Jurisprudence and Philosophy* (1983) chs 14 and 15

Hughes G. B. J. 'Validity and the Basic Norm' (1971) 59 Calif L Rev 695

Ingram P. 'Effectiveness' (1989) 69 ARSP 484

Kelsen H. 'Law as a Specific Social Technique' (1941) 9 U Chi L Rev 75
 – *General Theory of Law and State* (Wedberg trans, 1945)
 – *What is Justice?* (1957)
 – 'Sovereignty and International Law' (1960) 48 GTLJ 627
 – 'Professor Stone and the Pure Theory of Law: a Reply' (1965) 17 Stan L Rev 1128
 – 'On the Pure Theory of Law' (1966) 1 Is L Rev 1
 – *Pure Theory of Law* (Knight trans, 1967)
 – *Essays in Legal and .Moral Philosophy* (Head trans, 1973)
 – *General Theory of Norms* (Hartney trans, 1991)
 – *Introduction to the Problems of Legal Theory* (Paulson trans, 1992)

MacCormick D. N. 'Legal Obligation and the Imperative Fallacy' in Simpson (ed) *Oxford Essays in Jurisprudence* (2nd series, 1973)

Maher G. 'Custom and Constitutions' (1981) 1 OJLS 167

Moore R. *Legal Norms and Legal Science* (1978)

Munzer S. R. *Legal Validity* (1972) pp. 15-25, 45-50

Nino C. 'Some Confusions Around Kelsen's Concept of Validity' (1978) ARSP 357

Paulson S. L. 'Material and Formal Authorisation in Kelsen's Pure Theory' (1980) 39 CLJ 172
- 'The Neo-Kantian Dimension of Kelsen's Pure Theory of Law' (1992) 12 OJLS 311

Raz J. *The Concept of a Legal System* (2nd edn, 1980) pp. 93-120
- *The Authority of Law* (1979) chs 7 and 8

Stewart I. 'Closure and the Legal Norm' (1987) 50 MLR 908

Stone J. *Legal System and Lawyers'Reasonings* (1964) ch 3

Tur R. and Twining W. (eds) *Essays on Kelsen* (1986)

Wilson A. 'The Imperative Fallacy in Kelsen's Theory' (1981) 44 MLR 270

Woozley A. D. 'Legal Duties, Offences and Sanctions' (1968) 77 Mind 461

7 Legal concepts

1 Hohfeld's analysis

A little jurisprudence can be a dangerous thing. Some years ago, I was taking a short cut across a field. A young lady riding a horse politely asked me never to do so again, as this was private property so I was a trespasser. I knew that she had no possessory rights herself in the field, being neither owner nor lessee but merely one of several people licensed to keep a horse there. So, bethinking me of my Hohfeldian analysis, I replied: 'I may be a trespasser as against the lessees, but as against you I owe no duty not to cross this field.' Her rejoinder was that a trespasser was a trespasser – which is to say: 'It's all very well reducing legal rules to bilateral legal relations for some purposes, but when we are discussing the demands which honour makes of a law-abiding citizen, such reductionism is inappropriate.' On another occasion, I was attending a seminar given by radical social scientists on welfare rights. I asked whether the rights one should press for should be seen primarily in terms of the will-theory or the interest theory of rights – that is, were we concerned to give the disadvantaged more dignity by making their choices the determinants of how official action should affect their lives, or was the idea simply to see that certain basic needs were met. The reaction was that such pettyfogging analysis was not called for. 'Welfare rights' was an ideological commitment, a slogan. It was an on-going movement, to whose wheels every good man and true should simply put his shoulder.

Chastened by these and similar experiences, I turn in this chapter to the immense jurisprudential literature which has been devoted to the analysis of leading legal concepts. As mentioned in chapter 3, above, the modern approach to this enterprise in English-speaking countries began with Bentham and Austin. Bentham believed that 'expository jurisprudence' should turn its hand to explaining the significance of the basic building bricks used in legal prescriptions such as 'right', 'duty', 'power', 'property' and so on; what Austin was to call 'the principles, notions and distinctions' common to 'mature systems'. For Bentham, the objective was purely practical. We should not only explain the part played by these concepts in the law, but we should reconstruct – where necessary, stipulating how words should be used – in the interests of greater clarity of thought and with a view to reform and codification. Later exponents of the method have sometimes appeared to overlook this pragmatic side of analytic endeavour, and have taken the view that scientific analysis was an end in itself. The most celebrated of English-speaking 20th century analysts, however, was fully conversant with the pragmatic objective. In the early years of the century, the American jurist, Wesley Newcombe Hohfeld, sought to reduce all legal quantities to their lowest common denominators. In doing this, he (unlike Bentham) did not have codification in mind; but he did believe that his analysis would facilitate the resolution of practical problems in judicial reasoning.

In *Fundamental Legal Conceptions as Applied in Judicial Reasoning*, Hohfeld expounds the lowest common denominators of the law in terms of legal relations. These consist of two squares of correlation and opposition.

Right	Duty
Privilege	No-Right

Power	Liability
Immunity	Disability

Within these squares, every horizontal represents a correlation, and every diagonal an opposition. To say that X has a duty to entails that he has this duty as against someone, Y, who has the correlative right; and also that he has no privilege not to as against Y. To say that A has a power entails that he can by his voluntary act change the legal relations of some other person, B, who has the correlative liability; and that it is not true that A has a disability as against B's legal relations, correlating with an immunity of B.

It is implicit in Hohfeld's analysis that the universe of discourse, which is the subject matter of judicial reasoning, consists of two things only: either some other-regarding act or omission of a person, or some relation-regarding voluntary act of a person. Here is a man putting an envelope into a pillarbox. For the purpose of judicial reasoning, ask not: 'Is this act unlawful?', for it might be a tort against one person – for instance, if it represents the publication of a libel – but be perfectly lawful as against everyone else. Ask: 'Was this act the subject of a duty as against some other individual – say, the man's employer – or was it privileged as against that other individual?' It must be one or the other; for, as between A and B, every act of B must either be the subject of a duty – when A has a right that it be done – or it must be the subject of a privilege – when A has a 'no-right' that it be done. The only other question one can ask about the posting of the letter is: 'Was it the exercise of a power as against the legal relations of some other person?' If the person posting the letter is A, and B had previously posted a letter making A an offer, then the posting of the letter is an exercise of a power by A. It creates a contract. That means that, whereas before the posting of the letter of acceptance B did not have certain contractual rights and duties, afterwards he did. A's power to create these contractual relations is correlative to B's liability to have them created. Either A has this power or he does not, power being the opposite of a disability. If, for instance, the offer had been effectively revoked before the letter was posted, then, as to posting the letter and its effect on the relations of B, A would have a disability correlating with B's immunity.

Hohfeld gives many examples of the application of this analysis, both hypothetical, and related to the facts of reported cases. From his treatment of these examples, it becomes apparent that three kinds of advantage are being claimed for the analysis. First, it enables real normative choices to be disentangled from verbal confusions. Hohfeld cites cases having to do with trade competition and labour disputes. In such areas, he says, there is a temptation to move from the proposition that 'I have a right to trade' to 'so you have a duty not to impede my trading'. Such false logic would be avoided if we realise that the word 'right' is used loosely to stand for the four dissimilar relations of right-duty, privilege-no-right, power-liability, and immunity-disability. What people mean by 'I have a right to trade' is that, in carrying on my business, I do no man any legal wrong. As against every other person, each of my trading activities is privileged; as regards each such activity, every person has a no-right that I shall not do it. From that nothing follows about my rights regarding other people's actions. My privilege (my absence of duty) concerns my actions only. Any alleged 'rights' I may have, in the strict sense of that term, concern other people's activities. From my privilege to trade, it does not follow that I have a right that X shall not commit a certain act even if that act makes it more difficult for me to trade. It may be desirable that there should be such a right, but we should beware of thinking that there must be merely because my trading activities are privileged. Hohfeld would have approved of the distinctions drawn – though not necessarily of the normative choices made – in English cases on the 'right to picket'. It was pointed out that legislation which provided that picketers commit no tort or other unlawful act did not entail that picketers had any enforceable claim that those going to work should stop and listen. [1]

The second claimed advantage relates to change in judicial language. Hohfeld believed that his terminology was not too far removed from that

1   *Broome v DPP* [1974] AC 587; *Kavanagh v Hiscock* [1974] QB 600.

employed in the cases. Within the eight basic terms, the only invention was the hyphen in 'no-right'. If judges (and lawyers in general) would only employ his terminology, clarity would reign. As to this hope, he has had no more success than other stipulators about use of legal terms. In the picket cases just referred to, a Hohfeldian point was made, but not in Hohfeldian language. The picketers were said to have been clothed with an 'immunity' not a 'privilege'. For Hohfeld, 'immunity' should only be used where we have in mind a situation in which X's legal relations cannot be changed by Y – for example, constitutional 'immunities' covering those relations which the legislature is disabled from altering. Of course, the fact that judges, legislators and lawyers in general have not used his words does not establish that things might not have been clearer if they had. Some American writers have deliberately employed his terminology, both in the analysis of private law and in analysing the laws of primitive communities. *The American Law Institute's Restatement* also makes use of it.

The third advantage concerns the activity of other jurists. In the light of his analysis, so Hohfeld believed, juristic problems concerning the nature of such compound concepts as rights *in rem* and legal personality, and the problem of the relation between law and equity, could be dissolved.

'Rights *in rem*' should not be distinguished from 'rights *in personam*' by being thought of as rights over things, nor even as rights against the world. Every notion in the law must be reduced to combinations of bilateral relations. Every such relation has three elements: X, X's act or omission so far as it affects Y or Y's legal relations, and Y. Thus, a so called 'right *in rem*' was one of a bundle of similar relations between a property owner and each and every other member of the community. If I own Blackacre, this means that I have a right that X not enter on Blackacre without my leave, and a similar right against Y, Z and everyone else. It also means that I have a privilege myself to walk on Blackacre (or do any of an indefinite class of other acts in relation to Blackacre), correlating with X's no-right that I shall not walk, and a similar privilege correlating with Y's, Z's and everyone else's no-right. I also have a power to change X's legal relations by conveying Blackacre to him, correlating with his liability to have his relations changed. I have a similar power in relation to Y, Z and the rest. I have an immunity against having my relations changed by someone else conveying away Blackacre, which correlates with X's disability, and a similar immunity correlating with Y's, Z's and everyone else's disability. 'Ownership' then turns out to be constituted by a bundle of rights, privileges, powers and immunities. Hohfeld recommended the term 'multital' relation for any relation forming part of such a bundle, indicating that it was accompanied by an indefinite class of similar relations. Where I have rights of a certain tenor against only a finite class, we should speak of a 'paucital' relation; and if only against one individual, a 'unital' relation.

Such a treatment of 'rights in *rem*' would (Hohfeld contended) dispose of two sorts of juristic puzzles. It will enable us to understand how ownership can be limited or fragmented, and it will dissolve the problem about having property in non-tangible things. If I have licensed X to walk on my land, or granted him a right of way, then, as against him, I have no right that he shall not enter; but my multital rights about entry subsist against everyone else. If the law prohibits me from developing the land without planning permission, then, as to those actions comprised in 'development', I no longer have multital privileges so far as planning enforcement officers are concerned. As to non-tangible things, we need not worry ourselves about questions like: Is a reputation, or a marital status, 'property'? If I can sue anyone, or most people, who defame me, then I have a multital right that each person is not to defame me. In the days when it was possible to sue anyone who alienated my wife's affections, I had multital rights regarding such conduct. Knowing the bundles of legal relations involved, it matters not a whit how we classify 'property'.

In a similar way, Hohfeld argued that there was no problem about the concept of legal personality, once we recognised that rules relating to so-called 'juristic persons' actually create bundles of relations between stockholders and company officers. And the problem about the simultaneous existence in one piece of property of legal and equitable ownership could be side-stepped by asking of any particular action: Is it the breach of a duty owed to X at common law and/or in equity? If both systems give the same answer, there was no conflict. If the common law said 'no' and equity 'yes', then the common law was *pro tanto* repealed. A tenant for life who is not impeachable for waste commits no breach of duty to the remainderman at common law if he cuts down ornamental trees; but he does in equity. Since equity prevails over common law, the common law rule on this point has been abrogated.

Is Hohfeld's analysis an accurate description of, or an acceptable prescription for, the use of concepts in judicial reasoning? Should judicial reasoning be the sole focus of an analysis of legal concepts? These two questions interweave, in an often confusing way, the particular charges levelled at Hohfeld's analysis.

Two minor matters need not detain us long. First, perhaps Hohfeld could have picked better words, departing less from ordinary usage. 'Liberty' might be preferable to 'privilege'. 'Liability' sounds odd when applied to a situation of material advantage – like my 'liability' to have my legal relations changed by someone's leaving me a fortune. Second, as Glanville Williams points out, the accurate opposition (logical contradictory) to 'duty' should be 'liberty not'. Either I am under a duty to as against someone, or I am privileged or at liberty 'not' to . More important criticisms concern three matters: first, Hohfeld's insistence on correlativity; second, his failure to make clear the relationship between 'primary' ('antecedent'), 'secondary' ('remedial') and 'tertiary' ('adjectival') legal relations; third, his failure to investigate the essence of concepts, particularly that of a 'right'.

Older analytical jurists, like Bentham and Austin, took the view that there were some legal duties as to which there were no correlative rights. Critics of Hohfeld have asked whether the duties imposed by the criminal law or other areas of public law necessarily correlate with rights of individuals to claim performances of those duties. As to 'privileges', what is the point of insisting that every act which the law does not prohibit me from performing correlates with someone's 'no-right'? The law permits me to blow my nose. Why describe this legal situation in terms of multital privileges correlating with every other citizen's no-right that I should not do so? As to 'liabilities', my legal relations may change because of some occurrence which is not another's voluntary act – for instance, if a tree set on fire by lightning brings about a new duty to take care. Before the lightning struck, was I not subject to a 'liability' which did not correlate with a 'power'?

Nothing in Hohfeld's writings meets these sorts of criticism directly, but the implicit answer is clear enough. Correlativity is essential, as part of the law's lowest common denominators, on the assumption that every judicial question concerns two people. For then we ask, not 'Was such-and-such conduct required, prohibited or permitted by law?' but rather 'Was some complainant (civil plaintiff, tax collector, public prosecutor or whoever) entitled to demand that another person do or forebear, or was he not so entitled?' Whether I am at liberty to blow my nose will never come to court; but if it did – say, I was an actor claiming compensation for unfair dismissal and my inappropriate nose-blowing was alleged as a proper ground for my dismissal – then the issue would be whether as to some other person I was or was not privileged to do it. Lightning cannot be joined as a defendant. It is only where my legal relations have been allegedly changed by someone's voluntary act that the question whether they were validly changed or not will arise; and the issue will always be between two persons, deciding whether there was power/liability, or disability/ immunity.

Is that defence of the insistence on correlativity sustainable? Do judges ever say 'duty', 'right' and so on, where the concept is not being employed dispositively as to an issue between X and Y? One possible example concerns summonses for directions by trustees. Trustees may ask the court: 'Given this rather obscure settlement and the facts which have arisen, what should/may we do now?' Can that question (must that question) and its answer be translated into: 'What can one or more individual beneficiaries insist that we do, or as to which of the things we do can some (but perhaps not others) raise no complaint?' Similar questions can be raised about declaratory judgments, or any other proceedings not based on a straightforward *lis*.

Even where litigation is wholly adversary, judges employ terms like 'right' and 'duty', not merely in announcing their conclusions, but in the reasoning leading to such conclusions. In the latter context, it seems impossible to interpret such terms as correlations. It has been frequently ruled that citizens cannot bring civil actions for breach of statutory duties unless they protect 'private rights'. Supposing a judge concludes: 'This breach infringed the plaintiff's private right; accordingly, he has a right to demand that the defendant desist from further breaches and I grant him an injunction.' If we interpret the first reference to 'right' in Hohfeldian terms, we would achieve the tautology: 'The plaintiff has a right to demand compliance because he has a right to demand compliance.' Where 'private right' is referred to as a reason for allowing a right to sue, what must be meant is something like 'private interest', a non-Hohfeldian, non-relational conception of right.

Similar non-Hohfeldian analysis of terms is required where reference to a general, uncorrelated 'duty' is given as a reason for recognising a certain relationship. In one case[2] the duty of the police to promote free flow of traffic was a reason for holding that a constable could (in an emergency) order a man to drive the wrong way down a one-way street. In another case[3] a local authority's statutory duty to protect areas of natural beauty was a reason why it should be granted an interim injunction to restrain breach of a tree preservation order. It might be argued that, in the interests of clarity, different terms should be used as substitutes for 'right' and 'duty' where the context is not that of correlation. Is that practical? Or is judicial reasoning necessarily infused with moral and political ideas about private right and public duty, for which some non-Hohfeldian analysis is essential?

One might try to meet objections of this kind by restating Hohfeld's position in the light of American legal realism (see chapter 8, below). M. Radin takes this course. He insists that judicial reasoning is always to be read backwards. The court concludes (for inscrutable motives) that one party can or cannot make a claim against another. Anything it says about the pre-litigation legal position in purported justification of its decision can only be relevant so far as it concerns the two parties. Consistently with realist premises, there is no law but the law for the parties to a litigated dispute.

Whether Hohfeld would have accepted this characterisation of his analysis is unclear. He indicated that 'primary' relations are replaced by 'secondary' relations once a breach of duty occurs, and the latter by 'tertiary' relations once litigation begins. However,

2   *Johnson v Phillips* [1975] 3 All ER 682.
3   *Kent County Council v Batchelor* [1978] 3 All ER 980.

'All primary, or antecedent, relations and all secondary, or remedial, relations can, in general, be ascertained only by inference from the purely adjective judicial processes, that is, by inference from either affirmative or negative action regularly to be had from the particular court from which a judgment or decree may be sought.'[4]

The first major criticism of Hohfeld concerns correlativity, the second concerns these levels of legal relations. Is the content of primary relations dependent on that of secondary and tertiary relations? Hohfeld says that if X is under a duty to deliver goods to Y and fails to do so, then secondary relations arise under which X is under a duty to pay damages to Y. But since contracts of this kind are not specifically enforceable, why did he not reach the 'realist' conclusion advocated by Holmes, that X's duty from the start was merely either to deliver or to pay damages? Further, Hohfeld does not make clear whether the replacement of primary by secondary relations is itself a 'change' in relations capable of being the subject of a power/liability, or disability/immunity, relation. If it is, then every duty-breaking act is itself the exercise of a power, since it converts someone's primary right into a remedial right. So is every filing of a defence, or other step in pleadings, which turns remedial into adjectival relations – the latter involving, apparently, legal relations between litigants and judges and other officials. Conversely, on this reading, every 'privilege' involves an 'immunity'; since if I am free, as against you, to act in a certain way, then I am immune from having this primary relationship changed into a remedial relationship by your suing me. In that case, the courts do employ Hohfeldian terminology when they speak of picketers' 'immunities'.

We do not know how realist Hohfeld meant to be. Most of his examples, however, suggest that he intended substantive legal relations to be analysed as a distinct field of discourse from remedial and adjectival relations. In that case, his analysis is unacceptable to the extent that judicial reasoning does employ concepts like right or duty in a non-relational sense. Hohfeld claimed that failing to see concepts his way may obscure normative choices. I have myself made the converse claim in the context of the English law of trusts, namely, that insisting on seeing concepts Hohfeld's way has obscured normative choices – that insisting that the sort of 'duty' in terms of which a trust is defined is a relational duty has miscued judicial reasoning.[5]

So far we have discussed criticisms within the bounds of Hohfeld's own particular context, that is, concepts 'as applied in judicial reasoning'. He can be attacked, not for technical error, but for lack of largeness of aim, in that the fundamental conceptions examined are employed in many other

4   (1913) 11 Mich L Rev 537, 569, n 34.
5   (1971) 87 LQR 31.

contexts. Legal rights and duties are spoken of outside courts. If a man asks his solicitor: 'Do I break the law by doing such and such?' he might be surprised to receive the answer: 'Break it, as against whom?' Furthermore, the significance of legal concepts is not limited to their use by lawyers. When we criticise the law, or use it as a model for right conduct, we do not have to (and commonly do not) reduce it to paired relations. If we debate whether the law should make the wearing of seat-belts compulsory, we conceive of 'duty' as something required, not as something due to some particular individual or individuals. Those who think that one ought to obey the law make similar assumptions about the non-relatedness of duty – that was the point of the young lady equestrian's comment mentioned at the beginning of this chapter: 'A trespasser is a trespasser!' One of the matters which concerns a legal sociologist is whether points of legal duty actually correspond to how people behave, or how they think they should behave. There is no question here of reducing duty rules to relational pairings.

The third type of criticism mentioned above concerns Hohfeld's failure to investigate the essence of concepts. The charge is one of arbitrary reductionism. Hohfeld insists that concepts like 'property' and 'corporate person' must be understood in terms of multital paired relations. But that means that we do not even ask whether there is something essential in the idea of property or legal personality which might explain why legal reasoning has taken the form it has and point to the kinds of political philosophy which underpin it. Hohfeld assumes that all legal concepts belong to one kind of legal system:

'Since, in any sovereign state, there must, in the last analysis, be but a single system of *genuine law,* since the various principles and rules of that system must be consistent with one another, and since, accordingly, all *genuine* jural relations must be consistent with one another, two conflicting rules, the one "legal" and the other "equitable", cannot be valid at the same moment of time; one must be valid and determinative to the exclusion of the other.'[6]

I have argued (in *Law and Legal Science)* that the total significance of legal concepts cannot be expressed in terms of legal material frozen at a point of time in 'momentary legal systems'. Legal reasoning deploys legal concepts as part of the 'doctrine model of rationality'; and in that context the concepts exist as part of non-momentary (historic) legal systems, in which the pull of liberal conceptions of property rights and the tension between legal and equitable ownership may be permanent features.

6   (1913) 11 Mich L Rev 537, 557.

In particular, it can be urged that Hohfeld's analytic squares fail to bring out the essence of the concept of a legal right. He says that we should distinguish four senses in which the word 'right' is sometimes used – right, privilege, power, immunity – but does not pose the question whether there is some underlying idea which explains all these uses. He does not take sides in the time-honoured debate between those who favour a 'will' or an 'interest' conception of 'right'. H.L.A. Hart and Neil MacCormick exemplify these positions. Hart argues that the essence of a legal right is a legally protected 'choice'. He bases this contention largely on its utility to legal science. When lawyers are giving information about the law, they may be able to say all that needs saying in terms of duties. But sometimes the existence or operation of a duty is made dependent on the choice of an individual. This special feature needs to be conveyed by some characteristic terminology, and the word 'right' is apt for the job. In the context of criminal and public law, what is required of someone is not usually dependent on another's choice; so there is no special point in talking about 'rights' not to be murdered or 'rights' that others should pay taxes. On the other hand, in the typical civil law context, I may release someone from their duty under a contract, or agree not to sue for a tort, so that I am made mini-sovereign over his legal duty. 'Legal right' should normally be reserved for this situation.

MacCormick replies: first, there are sometimes rights without duties; second, evaluative and critical discourse about the law presupposes an interest conception of rights (for example, 'children's rights'). As to the first point, he cites Scottish legislation concerning intestate succession which refers to the 'rights' of successors in situations where the corresponding duty-holding executors have not been appointed. To this it might be rejoined that, even before the executor is appointed, the 'right' correlates with a duty-shaped gap; and that it is called a right precisely because, once the executor is appointed, it is for the successor to choose whether to enforce or waive it.

MacCormick's second point raises more fundamental issues about the nature of analytic enterprise. Should we analyse legal concepts by reference to the use of words in the law, or also by reference to use of the words in discourse about the law? Can one separate the tasks, for example, by speaking of 'legal rights' as one sort of thing, and 'moral/political rights' as another? Philosophers have recently distinguished 'concepts' from 'conceptions' in the following way. A 'concept' is that essential thing for which a word stands, though different people may have conflicting 'conceptions' or 'ideas' about it. Thus, the debate between will theorists and interest theorists assumes that there is some notion to be sought to which the word 'right' corresponds, though they have competing conceptions of what that notion is. The other view, that you can have quite different concepts which, for reasons of the history of language, just happen to be represented by the same word, is at present unfashionable. As Hohfeld never saw the issue in these terms, we cannot be sure what he would have said to it. But a modern apologist for him might take the view that there is no need to assume any underlying essence for the four terms he distinguished as right, privilege, power and immunity, merely because usage commonly terms them all 'rights'.

2 Analysis in general

General jurisprudence raises questions of all kinds about law, which may involve analysis of the concept of law and of other legal concepts. Particular jurisprudence is concerned with the analysis of legal concepts other than the concept of law itself. Substantive legal commentaries and legal arguments also engage in the analysis of legal concepts. It was suggested in chapter 1 that there is a *continuum* between particular jurisprudence and ordinary critical legal science; but that, as a rough guide, an analysis is 'jurisprudential' if a term is investigated, not with a view to ascertaining its meaning within a particular context, but on the basis that it stands for a concept which is common both to different legal systems and to several branches of the law. It therefore encompasses terms like 'right', 'duty', 'possession', 'ownership', 'contract', 'person', 'intention', 'fault', 'cause' and so on.

Hohfeld's is the most celebrated of modern essays in particular jurisprudence. It is not possible here to survey the issues which have been raised by other analyses of particular concepts. What needs to be stressed is that some other kinds of analysis presuppose quite different procedures. Hohfeld followed in the tradition started by Bentham, of analysing a legal concept by asking how it is employed in the law and how it ought to be employed in the interests of greater clarity. This is the tradition of logical atomism. The law is dissected into logically distinct packets of information, and our problem in analysing different concepts is to decide what labels to give the different packets.

Another older tradition seeks the essence of legal concepts by asking for true definitions. This is the tradition of 'real' essences. It used to be fashionable, for example, to debate whether or not there was some reality to which the concept of corporate personality corresponds. If there was not, the concept must be 'fictional'. Hart attacked this approach in his 'Definition and Theory in Jurisprudence'. We must beware, he said, of theory raised 'on the back of definition'. The metaphysical connotations of the 'real essences' approach is uncongenial to the modern mind. But it can be defended by anyone prepared to take up an avowed ideological stance. Supposing one holds that there are good political philosophical grounds for according to certain groups – those which exhibit a certain kind of internal cohesion and which play an important role in political life

– rights and duties similar to those which one's philosophy accords to human beings. Then one may give voice to this view by a conceptual dogma: that sort of cohesion and that sort of importance is the real essence of legal personality.

A third tradition is that of 'nominal essences'. Legal concepts have essences, but these depend solely on the function of words in language. Hart suggested that the right sort of question to ask about concepts should not be of the form: 'What is a …?' but rather: 'What functions are performed by sentences containing the word … ?' During the 1950s, he brought to bear on the analysis of legal concepts the methods of 'ordinary language philosophy' which were then dominant among Oxford philosophers. Followers of this approach seek insights into the nature of legal concepts by careful attention to all the subtle variations of language, comparing uses of the same word inside and outside the law. Hart himself appeared to move away from this approach in the direction of logical atomism. In discussing Bentham's conception of legal rights, he assumed that the most important criterion for testing the analysis of a legal concept is usefulness in giving legal information – although he still accepted that employment of the one word 'right' must indicate some underlying unity between the senses he so carefully differentiated.

Perhaps all three traditions – logical atomism, real essences, or nominal essences – have something to offer. What matters is to know what we are about in any particular analytic enterprise. If we are analysing 'intention', are we recommending a clearer terminology, reflecting some prior breakdown of legal categories? Or are we relating the law to psychological reality? Or are we exploring the functions of the word 'intention' and its cognates? With 'contract', are we slotting a term into an overall breakdown of the law of obligations? Or are we anchoring it to that central device which, as the economic analysis of law reveals (see chapter 4, above), really maximises efficiency? Or are we drawing on the wealth of philosophic literature which deals with the function of expressions like 'I promise'? As for 'property', should that be a term given technical stipulative use within a code? Or is analysis of it dependent on its proper place within a philosophy of justice? (See chapter 20, below.) Or shall we look for its essence by collating uses of the word? In the case of 'rights', Hohfeld, as we have seen, wanted different senses clearly distinguished in the interests of clarity; and one criticism was that 'right' must have an essence. But is it a nominal or a real (ideological) one? As we shall see in chapter 14, below, Dworkin believes it is the latter. He makes no claim that his analysis of 'rights' corresponds with the way that word is used by lawyers or non-lawyers. He advocates a liberal, individualistic philosophy, and believes that this same philosophy already infuses legal reasoning; on that basis he produces an answer to the question: 'What are legal rights?'

Perhaps one should give up particular jurisprudence altogether. Two sorts of argument might tend to this conclusion. It might be contended that the meaning of a legal term varies from context to context, so that any general analysis of it is unwarranted – as D. Harris argues is the case with 'possession'. Or it might be contended that words simply do not stand for ideas at all. This is the view put forward by Glanville Williams, on the basis of a semantic theory popularised by Ogden and Richards. He agrees with Olivecrona (see chapter 8, below) that the function of words is to influence action: we find out what words 'mean' by asking what pictures they bring to the mind and what impulses they stimulate.

Alf Ross advances a more specific argument for the view that words like 'ownership' stand for nothing. We could, he says, rewrite all the rules of law which employ this term without using it. The law says: 'If X has completed a valid purchase, he is owner'; and: 'If X is owner, he can sue for recovery'. One could eliminate the middle man and rewrite the law: 'If X has completed a valid purchase, he can sue for recovery'. This would be inconvenient, but the fact that it would be possible proves that it is 'nonsense' to attribute meaning to the term 'ownership', that it is 'without semantic reference'. Ross cites, as illustration, an island community where people believe in a magical form of contamination known as 'tu-tu'. If you eat the chief's food you become tu-tu. If you become tu-tu, you have to undergo a purification ceremony. Now, says Ross, one could rewrite the rule: 'If you eat the chief's food, you must undergo a purification ceremony'. So, just as tu-tu is meaningless, so is ownership.

In response to these objections to particular jurisprudence, consider the following argument in favour of analysing general legal concepts. Legal terms may be used, not merely to express legal rules, but as steps in reasoning towards legal decisions. We cannot grasp the significance of a legal concept without placing it in a dynamic as well as static context. If the rules of Ross's islanders are all clear, no doubt his suggested rewriting would be possible. But supposing some new issue arose? Supposing someone ate food belonging to the chief's son and some said that that made him tu-tu, while others denied it. The elders – or whoever settled disputed issues of law – would argue out the question in terms of what tu-tu really is. We outsiders consider tu-tu meaningless, but for them it is not – and, understanding the magical metaphysic from the inside, their 'lawyers' would know what sorts of argument were relevant to it. Similarly, open questions in our law are sometimes settled by reference to what the judges think 'possession', or 'ownership' or 'person' mean. Arguments of many kinds push the law into developments which stretch the meaning of terms. But if the terms themselves impose limits on such developments, they cannot be meaningless. The common law of larceny was nailed to the concept of 'possession'. To be a thief, a person had to acquire possession of goods feloniously, and so theft could not be committed by one who was in possession before he formed a felonious intent. The judges were able to bring dishonest servants within the net, by asserting that someone who was entrusted with goods by his master did not acquire possession but merely detention. But where goods were entrusted to a servant by a third party for the master, it was felt that one could not deny that the servant (rather than the master) was in possession; so that if the servant dishonestly appropriated he did not steal. The crime of embezzlement had to be invented to plug a hole created by nothing except the outer limits of a concept.

Certainly, dogmatic particular jurisprudence has been overdone in the past. Sometimes it has been argued that a … just is … and so any legal rule employing the term must be given a particular interpretation. Furthermore, jurisprudence textbooks have tended to collate uses of terms without any very clear indication of the purpose of the exercise. But so long as legal reasoning by reference to conceptual doctrine continues, broad-scale conceptual analysis is likely to have its place.

Bibliography

Hohfeld's analysis

Attwooll E. 'Liberties, Rights and Powers' in Attwooll (ed) *Perspectives in Jurisprudence* (1977)

Feinberg J. 'Duties, Rights, and Claims' (1966) Am Phil Q 142

Finnis J. M. 'Some Professorial Fallacies About Right' (1972) 4 Ad L Rev 377

Haksar V. 'The Nature of Rights' (1978) 64 ARSP 183

Halpin A. K. W. 'Hohfeld's Conceptions: From Eight to Two' (1985) 44 CLJ 435.

Harris J. W. *Law and Legal Science* (1979) s 3

Hart H. L. A. *Essays on Bentham* (1982) ch 7

Hohfeld W. *N. Fundamental Legal Conceptions as Applied in Judicial Reasoning* (1946)
- 'Relations between Equity and Law' (1913) 11 Mich L Rev 537
- 'Supplemental Note on the Conflict of Law and Equity' (1917) 26 Yale LJ 767

Kamba W. J. 'Legal Theory and Hohfeld's Analysis of a Legal Right' (1974) Jur Rev 249

Kocourek A. *Jural Relations* (2nd edn, 1928) chs 1-2

Lyons D. B. 'Rights, Claimants and Beneficiaries' (1969) Am Phil Q 173

MacCormick D. N. *Legal Right and Social Democracy* (1982) ch 8
- 'Rights in Legislation' in Hacker and Raz (eds) *Law, Morality, and Society* (1977)

Radin M. 'A Re-statement of Hohfeld' (1938) 51 Harv L Rev 1141

Raz J. *The Morality of Freedom* (1986) ch 7
- *Ethics in the Public Domain* (1994) ch 11
Singer J. W. 'The Legal Rights Debate in Analytical Jurisprudence' (1982) Wis LR 975
Stone R. L. 'An Analysis of Hohfeld' (1963) 48 Minn L Rev 313
Sumner L. R. *The Moral Foundation of Rights* (1987) ch 2
White A. R. *Rights* (1984)
Williams G. L. 'The Concept of Legal Liberty' in Summers (ed) *Essays in Legal Philosophy* (1968)

Analysis in general

Atiyah P. *Promises, Morals and Law* (1981)
Bodenheimer E. 'Modern Analytical Jurisprudence and the Limits of its Usefulness' (1955-56) 104 U Pa L Rev 1080
Cohen J. 'The Value of Value Symbols in Law' (1952) 52 Col L Rev 893
Fitzgerald P. J. *Salmond on Jurisprudence* (12th edn, 1966) Book 3
Fried C. *Contract As Promise* (1981)
Harris D. 'The Concept of Possession in English Law' in Guest (ed) *Oxford Essays in Jurisprudence* (1961)
Harris J. W. *Property and Justice* (1996) pt 1
Hart H. L. A. 'The Ascription of Responsibility and Rights' in Flew (ed) *Logic and Language* (1951)
- 'Definition and Theory in Jurisprudence' (1954) 70 LQR 37 (reprinted in *Essays in Jurisprudence and Philosophy* ch 1)
- 'Analytical Jurisprudence in Mid-Twentieth Century: a Reply to Professor Bodenheimer' (1957) 105 U Pa L Rev 953
Hart H. L. A. and Honoré A. M. *Causation in the Law* (2nd edn, 1973)
Honoré A. M. 'Ownership' in Guest (ed) *Oxford Essays in Jurisprudence* (1961) (reprinted in *Making Law Bind* (1987) ch 8)
Kelly D. St L. 'Legal Concepts, Logical Functions and Statements of Fact' (1968) 3 Tas U L Rev 43
Munzer S. R. *A Theory of Property* (1990) ch 2
Paton G. W. *A Textbook of Jurisprudence* (4th edn, 1972) Books 4-6
Ross A. 'Tu-tu' (1957) 70 Harv L Rev 812
Simpson A. W. B. 'The Analysis of Legal Concepts' (1964) 80 LQR 535
Waldron J. *The Right to Private Property* (1988) ch 2
Williams G. L. 'Language and the Law' (1945) 61 LQR 71, 189, 293, 384; (1946) 62 LQR 387
Wolff M. 'On the Nature of Legal Persons' (1938) 54 LQR 494

8 Legal realism and critical legal studies

One suspects that cynicism about the law and lawyers has always been common among non-lawyers. Novelists and playwrights have attested to it. Dickens, in *Bleak House,* stated that the one great principle of English law was to provide work for lawyers. Molière's plays pillory lawyers and doctors alike; but whereas medical science now has a measure of awesome respect, the layman is generally still cynical about the law. In this century, two traditions of legal writers have come to the fore, many of whose conclusions are grist to the mill of those who suspect that, beneath a panoply of rhetoric, judges do what they like; or that a lot of legal words are jargon designed to bamboozle and impoverish the average citizen.

These traditions, one in the United States and one in Scandinavia, have been called 'realist'. As it happens, this is an inept label in the context of the history of philosophy. The term 'realist' was applied to followers of Plato, who taught that the things of everyday life are but imperfect copies of 'real' (ideal) forms which transcend our senses. (The 'moral realists', discussed in chapter 1, above, invoke this terminology.) The legal 'realists' are in the opposite camp. They attack what they claim to be only too prevalent in traditional legal science, the conception of law as a 'brooding omnipresence in the sky'. They say that lawyers commonly talk of 'rules' as though they were genuine entities, occupying some world other than the world of time and space (the universe of 'law'); and that legal concepts, like 'right', 'duty' or 'possession', are treated as if these words had some metaphysical essence as their counterpart in that same other legal world. Such mythology must be dispelled, and the scientific truth brought to light. Like other truth-seekers, however, they find it easier to agree on the falsity to be dismissed than on the 'reality' which is to be substituted.

Both American and Scandinavian realists are commonly adopted as targets by English jurists; but in the United States the Scandinavian variety is largely ignored. In that country there has arisen over the past 20 years a category of legal scholarship which claims heirship to American legal realism and combines it with a leftist onslaught on the perceived evils of modern western societies. It calls itself 'the critical legal studies movement'.

1 American legal realism

The intellectual inspiration of the realist movement in America is generally credited to Oliver Wendell Holmes (1841-1935), who was a Justice of the Supreme Court from 1902. Holmes was no cynic. He did not believe that judges can do what they like, for he delivered judgments in which he pronounced himself bound to hold that the law was not as he would like it to be. He was a great expert in the common law and in American constitutional law, and a moderate, liberal reformer. But aphorisms of his have been cited again and again by those who wish to debunk over-conceptualism in legal thinking: 'The life of the law has not been logic, it has been experience.' Law should be viewed 'from the stance of the bad man'. 'The prophecies of what the courts will do in fact, and nothing more pretentious, are what I mean by the law.'

What Holmes was attacking was the idea that all inherited legal provisions could be rationally defended, and any tendency to expound 'law' which did not have a direct bearing on courts' decisions. Much of the law, he believed, had been invented in a historical context which had now been superseded, and the real purposes it served under changed conditions should be constantly reviewed. In no circumstances should it be claimed that the law, according to some conceptually deductive process, was one thing, if the practice of the courts suggested that it was something else.

A similar court-centred bias for American jurisprudence was insisted upon by Holmes's academic contemporary, John Chipman Gray (1839-1915). Gray, too, was no legal revolutionary. He wrote books about property law of a fairly traditional kind. But, as a theorist, he insisted that the law was comprised of the rules laid down by the courts, and that statutes and other legal materials were merely 'sources' of this law.

In the heyday of self-conscious 'realist' attacks on conventional modes of conceptualisation, in the 1920s and 30s, something more fundamentally iconoclastic appeared to be offered. Members of the movement, like Karl Llewellyn (1893-1962), warned readers against 'paper rules', against merely reading the law off from the books. Law, said Llewellyn, was 'what officials do about disputes'. We should have regard to different styles of judicial interpretation of source materials prevalent at different places and in different epochs, and to all information that social research might provide about actual decisions. Mere 'rules' would often not tell us much about decisions, because they are capable of being construed in different ways, and because different rules could be selected from the mass available to support decisions arrived at for reasons which had nothing to do with rules.

In his later writings, Llewellyn softened his critique. We could find, he said, in the history of the common law, as well as a 'formal style' (which pretended to deduce conclusions from rules), also an admirable 'grand style', wherein far-sighted judges looked beyond the rules to over-arching considerations of justice and wise dictates of policy. There were 'law jobs' to be done in which rules, if kept within bounds, had a proper role to play. Any lawyer who soaked himself in the 'folkways' of a particular appellate court would acquire a sense of how the jobs got themselves done and could be expected to make correct predictions of outcomes eight times out of ten.

The writer commonly considered to be the most extreme of all the American realists was Judge Jerome Frank (1889-1957). Frank criticised authors like Llewellyn for what he called their 'upper courtitis'. They were merely 'rule-sceptics', whereas he, Frank, was a 'fact-sceptic'. What he meant by this was that, even if rules are clear as to interpretation, in lower courts they may have precious little determining effect on decisions because a tribunal of fact, particularly a jury, can always find the facts as it pleases so that a rule will give the decision it wants. What actually causes the tribunal to decide the way it does are conscious and subconscious attitudes, beliefs and prejudices, which are peculiar to the parties, the witnesses and the facts of each case. Rules are little more than pretty playthings. Frank's conclusion was:

> 'For any particular lay person, the law, with respect to any particular set of facts, is a decision of a court with respect to those facts so far as that decision affects that particular person. Until a court has passed on those facts no law on that subject is yet in existence.'[1]

Critical discussion of American realism, as a movement, has often been bedevilled by questions about how seriously we are supposed to take statements like that just quoted from Frank. Frank himself tells us that he is not intending to give a definition of 'law' suitable for all purposes; and also that his case is deliberately overstated. Minimally, realists say only that 'rules' are not all that matter in the administration of justice, and there has probably never been a theorist who denied that. More positively, the movement has had some influence in directing research towards non-rule-governed operations – towards studies of the personal background of judges, the actual workings of the jury system, the practical importance

---

1   *Law and the Modern Mind* p 50.

of availability of legal representation, and the consequences of formality in procedure. But these matters were not altogether neglected before the movement began.

In so far as the pronouncements of leading members of the movement have a general significance for our picture of law, this must be demonstrated by taking such definitions as Frank's at their face value. Two crucial theses emerge: first, rules by *their nature* cannot control decisions by courts and other officials; second, the overriding function of law is the settlement of disputes.

These theses are connected. Viewed from the standpoint of a court, there is a dispute and legal rules are supposed, in most cases, to provide the answer. Frank asserts that judges and others delude themselves about this. They have a psychological need for security, a childish hang-over, which is satisfied by a belief that 'the law' (a father figure) dictates what is to happen. This must be a delusion, because decisions are actually caused by a multiplicity of motives operating on the finder of facts, which leads him to find suitable facts to fit the rules that will support the decision. These motives would produce the same decision whatever the rules. Accordingly, in the interest of truth, the idea that there is 'law' before the decision should be dropped.

The anti-rule causal thesis is almost impossible to test by experiment. You would need, say, 10 motorists, all charged with speeding at more than 30 miles per hour in a built-up area, but charged before tribunals whose prejudices were thought to vary. Let five actually have been driving at 60 miles per hour, and five at 20. One would note variables, like the appearance of the witnesses, their class accents and so forth. Given that rules have no effect, there is no likelihood that those who were in fact speeding will be convicted, while those who were not will be acquitted. Is this plausible?

It might be thought that this would not be a fair test of Frank's position, because he is concerned with cases where issues of fact or law are likely to be raised, and in my example the excess over the speed limit or the falling short of it would be so patent that the speeders would plead guilty and the non-speeders would never be prosecuted. Such a suggestion raises another difficult issue, this time of evaluation. Are all those occasions on which rules have an effect without producing a dispute less important, and so not indicative of the true function of the law, than those occasions on which a dispute arises? The court-centred view of American realists is to be compared with the view that the function of law is to guide or coerce behaviour through rules, and that settling disputes is only a subsidiary function.

Further, precisely how is it that a decision settles a dispute? Presumably, through some order being made by the judge requiring a party to pay damages, to give up property, to desist from some activity, to go to gaol and so on. But if rules of the legislature have no determinative effect over disputes, ought we not also to assume that orders of judges have none over later disputes involving the same issue – for example, if a judgment creditor alleges that he has not been paid? If a statute is not a pre-existing rule for judge X, why is judge X's order a pre-existing rule for judge Y or sheriff Z? Perhaps Frank's realist definition could be taken further. 'For any particular lay person, the law, with respect to any particular set of facts, is some coercive measure by a state official actually being applied to that person.'

If one is merely a rule-sceptic and not a fact-sceptic, one could be a 'realist' only about difficult cases. The thesis would be that, although clear cases are governed by rules, whenever the law is uncertain we should abandon 'legal reasoning' in favour of behaviour-prediction. As we shall see in chapters 14 and 15, below, the nature of judicial reasoning in unclear cases is highly controversial. Legal standards other than rules evidently play some part. A 'realist' approach to this problem would require us to concentrate, not on the reasons judges give for their decisions, but on the motives which actually influence them; not on what they say, but on what they do. In an extreme form, it would regard all legal reasoning as mere surface talk. I have come across practitioners who, in their cups, talk about judges in just this way: 'You wouldn't get very far with that argument before judge X, given the way he feels about deserting husbands (or trade unions, or whatever)!' If it is systematically true that, whenever there is an arguable point, arguments based on the purpose of a rule, or Parliament's intention, or some legal principle, might as well not have been advanced because the judge's prejudices alone determine his decision, then perhaps law is (as F. Rodell argues) a 'high-class racket'. When teased with this inference, your cynical practitioner may well pull up, and say that it is of course only in relation to some kinds of dispute that judges reach the conclusions they wish whatever the arguments, and that for the most part decisions are influenced by well-reasoned advocacy. If that were not so there would, for example, be no agitation for the extension of legally-aided representation to tribunals. Do we believe him?

There remains the difficulty, which many critics of realism have pointed out, that if legal science is to be transformed into a science of prediction, just what are judges supposed to do? Practitioners may predict judicial decisions, but judges themselves cannot. They must purport to justify. The best advice which Frank could offer was that they should be as conscientious as possible in introspecting about their motives. At least they should be clear that justice in the case at bar (whatever 'justice' means, see chapter 20, below) is their goal, not some solution dictated by 'justice according to law'.

If the belief that rules matter, inside and outside courts, were to be totally discredited, it would not merely confirm the cynicism that many share about the law; it would also lead to total pessimism about the utility of law reform. Why bother to change the rules? The only possible 'law reform' would be to substitute officials with desirable prejudices for those officials we have. Judges, old or new, would automatically have complete discretion, but we might as well make this plain by giving it to the new ones expressly – for rules to guide them would not guide them.

Another criticism commonly advanced against realists is that, without rules, how do we know who are officials, for are they not appointed according to rules? To this it might be answered that we have psychological triggers of various kinds which make us view individuals acting in certain formal ways as dispute-settling officials. The topic of 'jurisdiction' should be concerned with deference reactions to wigs and gowns, not with rules. Would this mean that, if we were ever unsure whether a court had jurisdiction, these kinds of reactions, not the paper rules, would settle the question?

But then the realist case was never intended to be as extreme as it sounds. This makes an assessment of its contribution to theory difficult. Llewellyn denied that it had theoretical implications of any kind:

'Realism is *not* a philosophy, but a technology ... What realism was, and is, is a method nothing more.'[2]

The 'method' employed by members of the movement was a mixture of recording data about judicial practices, and intuitions based on what Llewellyn called 'horse sense'. As we shall see in chapter 18, below, it is questionable whether sociological research related to law presupposes any conception of law different from that the realists so vehemently denounced.

2 Scandinavian legal realism

If we are unhappy with the idea that rules are abstract entities, alleged to 'exist' as part of some legal system, one way of anchoring 'the law' in 'reality' is to equate it with the behaviour of officials – that is the approach of extreme American realism. Another way is to identify the law with psychological occurrences – the sensations produced in people's minds as the result of legal words. The latter is the course taken by a school commonly called 'Scandinavian realists'. This school derives its inspiration from the Swedish professor, Axel Hagerstrom (1868-1939).

Hagerstrom's own contributions to jurisprudence and moral philosophy were largely destructive. He was at pains to point out the 'metaphysical' elements in others' theories. He found suspect all accounts of law and morals which included assertions that a moral or legal rule actually exists;

2   *The Common Law Tradition* p 510.

for such talk must assume that there is some non-natural sense in which things could exist, and therefore presupposes a world alongside or superior to the physical world. In fact, he said, value judgments about right and wrong are purely emotive. They merely express our feelings of like or dislike. Similarly in law, an assertion that there exists a binding rule mystifies the truth, for 'bindingness' as a quality has no counterpart in sense-experience. His historical researches convinced him that, in primitive law, men really believed in magical powers and bonds to which the words 'right' and 'duty' (or 'obligation') corresponded. As law developed, belief in these magical entities faded away but still people went on using these nouns with the same psychological effect as they had had over their more credulous ancestors. The assertion that one has 'a right' produces a sensation of power; and the assertion that someone has 'an obligation' typically produces in him feelings of constraint.

This sceptical approach to legal rules and legal concepts has been developed by writers of the school, the two most well-known of whom in the English-speaking world are the Swede, Karl Olivecrona (1897-1980), and the Dane, Alf Ross (1899-1979). Each of these authors seeks to build up a picture of law, starting with the insights which Hagerstrom provided. They share with him the assumption that the only 'reality' to which 'law' may correspond is a psychological reality.

Olivecrona equates law with 'independent imperatives'. It is false, he argues, to think of the law as the commands of an actual person, for no human being could go about commanding all that is contained in the law; and to identify the commander of the law with the 'state' or the 'people' is to deal in abstractions and therefore in unrealities. What actually occurs when legislation is enacted is that a proposal, such as a bill, is subjected to certain formal acts of voting, signing and promulgation. Because of the hold these formalities have over people's minds, the contents of the bill acquire a special psychological effectiveness. A legal provision contains two elements: an idea of an action ('stealing'), and some imperative symbol ('ought', 'duty', 'offence'). The provision itself is just words on paper. The 'reality' to which 'scientific' discourse about law must correspond consists of the psychological reactions of individuals – the ideas of imaginary actions and the sensations of compulsion and restraint produced when a provision is brought to our auditory or visual attention:

'In reality, the law of a country consists of an immense mass of ideas concerning human behaviour, accumulated during centuries through the contributions of innumerable collaborators. These ideas have been expressed in imperative form by their originators, especially through formal legislation, and are being preserved in the same form in books of law. The ideas are again and again revived in human minds, accompanied by the imperative expression: "This line of conduct *shall* be taken" or something else to the same effect.'[3]

Olivecrona takes the same view of the overall function of the law as does Kelsen, namely the monopoly of force in the hands of state officials (see chapter 6, above). But in order to understand how this really works, he says, we must reject Kelsen's conception of law as 'norms' set over against reality. Legal rules must be placed within the world of cause and effect, and this is only possible if they are understood as psychological phenomena. He envisages a society in which it is felt desirable by those in power to make some new form of activity the subject of prohibition. Rules will be promulgated forbidding the conduct in question, coupled with the threat of sanctions. Initially, those to whom the prohibitions are addressed will calculate, on each occasion of temptation, whether the gains of disobedience are worth the risk of sanction. But the human personality cannot withstand constant warring between temptation and fear; so eventually both will be pushed into the subconscious, and will be replaced in the conscious mind by some arational imperative symbol, such as 'ought not'. Once the rule has been internalised in this way, there is usually no need for the actual threat of force. The idea of the prohibited act will come to the mind, if at all, already imprinted with a disapprobative symbol. Olivecrona suggests that this is the way in which most of our so-called 'moral' standards were created – that is, he reverses the common assumption about the historical relationship between morality and law. In the education of children, internalised rules will be directly transmitted in the typical form of idea plus ought-symbol; and the community may well attach the psychologically-loaded term 'moral' as well as the term 'legal' to them. But the special advantage of the psychological hold which 'legal' has over our minds is that it enables the powerholders in society to introduce new standards – employing the psychologically-loaded legislative formalities – which will gain some ascendancy over our personalities even without actual threat of force. Force is necessary if the internalisation process is to be maintained; but most of the time it can be kept in the background. Law and force are thus associated in two ways. First, law gains its initial psychological hold, and from time to time strengthens the hold it has, by the application of sanctions. Secondly, the content of legal provisions determine exclusively the circumstances in which the exercise of force is thought proper.

To many other legal philosophers language is important because of the light it throws on the true nature of concepts: we discover what 'right' or 'duty' stand for by examining how such terms are employed. For

---

3   *Law as Fact* (1st edn) p 48.

Olivecrona, language is important because of its use as a technique of social control. Such terms are 'hollow' since they refer to nothing, but they have psychological effects. When lawyers purport to provide information about the law, what they are really doing is to re-echo the way in which the crucial terms ring in the 'common mind' of the community.

> 'Legal language is not a descriptive language. It is a directive, influential language serving as an instrument of social control. The "hollow" words are like signposts with which people have been taught to associate ideas concerning their own behaviour and that of others.'[4]

Some support for these claims might be derived from widely shared opinions that law has an educative role. If legislation attaches the label 'illegal' to conduct such as sexual or racial discrimination, may that not change people's attitudes quite apart from specific calculations about the likelihood of sanctions? Then wielding legal language is a fear substitute, as Olivecrona supposed it was. On the other hand, opinions of this sort may be no more than unproven guesswork. The recent burgeoning of literature on legal semiotics points to a multiplicity of ways in which legal texts may be deployed in different kinds of discourse. It is a gross over-simplification to speak of a single 'common mind', or to represent control over texts as a uni-directional power relationship.

One of the chief criticisms of Olivecrona is that he reaches empirical generalisations through armchair theorising rather than through empirical research. He concludes that what underlies the law must be such and such psychological cause-and-effect relations because only if we assume this can legal language be given any meaning. Study of words thus tells us something about the psychological life of man. Many have questioned whether law creates morals in the way he says it does. Why is it, for example, that murder has always been regarded as more heinous than theft even though for centuries capital punishment was meted out for both? Is it not mere guesswork to insist that the existence of an 'ought' idea in a person's mind is evidence that he, or his forebears, must have repressed the temptation to perform an act so as to be free of the fear of sanctions? Empirical studies, based on questionnaires directed to popular knowledge and opinion about law, have become more common in recent years – see the discussion of 'living law' in chapter 18, below. It can be argued that we should base our psychological generalisations on them rather than on speculation about concepts. On the other hand, conclusions based on such researches are unlikely to give a total picture (an interpretative model) of the functions of law in society. Research demonstrating ignorance of

4   *Law As Fact* (2nd edn) p 251.

positive law is of great value for those concerned with education about law, but can hardly tell us what effect law has on those who are not ignorant of it. Olivecrona's principal thesis would be falsified if it could be shown that, notwithstanding regular and well-publicised enforcement of a legal provision, automatic reactions of rightness or wrongness do not emerge. In so far as any thesis can be said to have been confirmed by modern research it is that normative views do not coincide with the law, and that they vary between age bands and social groups.

Another criticism of Scandinavian realism relates to the operation of law on the intellectual level. Even if it is true that legal rules achieve effects through internalisation, surely textwriters, practitioners and judges who describe 'the law' are not purporting to discuss the psychological lives of citizens? Surely, too, when lawyers perform logical operations on the law – such as deducing a particular prescription from a more general one – they are not making contentions about ways in which people 'feel bound'? If I work out the complexities of the schedules to various Finance Acts, using a calculator to do the sums where necessary, and conclude that my client is liable now to pay so much tax, I would not expect to be told that I thereby committed myself to the view that he or some official had already (or would ever have) any particular sensations of compulsion in regard to the matter.

Alf Ross modified the principal tenets of Scandinavian realism to meet just these kinds of objection. 'Law in action', he says, is just what Olivecrona described; but when legal science speaks of 'law' it does not refer, directly, to the psychological lives of the citizenry. The 'directives' which it describes constitute a 'scheme of interpretation' which enables one to predict the behaviour of officials. The ought ideas in the law, as they pass from the mind of law teacher to student, are 'ought' moulds with no stimulating effect; but armed with them, the student can tell what judges will do for he knows that, in the judicial mind, they will set off sensations of compulsion. To assert that such and such provision is valid law means no more than this: if the provision in question were to be cited to a judge, it would influence his decision. Ross coupled with the 'realism' of the Hagerstrom tradition a view of epistemology inherited from that movement of the 1920s and 30s known as 'logical positivism'. According to the high priests of logical positivism, sentences which were not mere tautologies could only be meaningful if the propositions they expressed were capable of verification. Ross believed that his view of legal science met this criterion. If when one says that there is a valid rule one intends to say that some entity independent of the world of time and space 'exists' and has some non-natural quality of 'bindingness', one is talking meaningless metaphysics as the realists had shown. But if (argues Ross) one means that a particular psychological phenomenon will, predictably, occur in the spiritual lives of judges, then one's assertion is one about this world and, consistently with logical positivism, it can be tested by experiment in the courts.

It will be seen that, at least in his discussion of legal science, Ross, like the American realists but unlike other Scandinavian realists, is specifically court-centred. Consequently, the same complaints of circularity have been raised against him: how can a judge's view of the law be interpreted as a prediction of what the judge will himself decide? But Ross differs from the American realists precisely by insisting that decisions which concur with pre-existing rules do show that the rules effectively control decisions: if they did not, then the verification he insists on would not be supplied. Ross and Frank agree that it is my lawyer's business to predict what courts will do; but Frank says that they are to beware of rules as grounds for prediction, while Ross says rules 'exist' just because they are good grounds for prediction. Neither appears to explain what happens when a judge announces: 'The law on this point is clearly as follows ... and therefore, alas, I must find for the defendant.' Such a judge, when he states what the law is, is not, on the face of it, making any kind of prediction.

3   The critical legal studies movement

The insights of American legal realism were absorbed fairly painlessly in university law schools. In so far as they debunked the idea that solutions to difficult legal questions could be sought from an inner logic of the law, they were merely attacking that which, from any other perspective, we should decry with the universal boo! word of American jurisprudence – 'formalism'. During the past 20 years, however, a ferment of controversy within the academy has been provoked by a coterie of left-wing scholars who style themselves 'the critical legal studies movement'. Its members are disenchanted with the institutions of modern western democracies. They deplore the hierarchical structures of social power and the differentiation of social roles fostered in the work-place, the class room, the family and in the process of political decision-making. If they had reserved their critiques for their extra-curricular activities, eyebrows would scarcely have been raised. But they have brought them into the law school. They have criticised colleagues, whether conservative or reformist, for their perpetuation of the myth that there exists a special kind of intellectual endeavour known as 'legal reasoning', which is separate from open-ended political controversy. Their colleagues teach students to interpret the rulings in cases widely or narrowly, depending on how (if at all) they can be made to fit coherently with the rest of a discrete body of law. These colleagues recommend that statutes should be viewed in the light of their purposes, that we should attend to those principles which can be seen to underlie legal materials and that we must be ever attentive to 'policy' (viewed as circumscribed choices between alternative legal developments, all to be measured by common sense evaluations of consequences). The benighted colleagues further suppose that acquiring skill in these matters is the point of legal education and that expertise in them should be the basis upon which appointments and promotions within the legal academy are made.

All of this is anathema to crits. What has it to do with the burgeoning discontent of the powerless, or with movements of radical protest such as those which emerged during the period of the war in Vietnam? The remedy, however, is not to put aside the law books as irrelevant to real life. On the contrary, crits pore over reported cases as assiduously as any of those they attack. But they do so with a different motivation. They seek to 'deconstruct' or 'trash' the law by showing how the materials to hand could be manipulated either way, that coherent exposition is an illusion, that there are no purposes, principles or policy constraints with any dispositive bite, and that consequently every outcome is arbitrary. That is what law students should be taught and it is acceptance of this message which should be taken into account in appointments and promotions.

Where other scholars find dissonant elements within legal materials susceptible to reformulation in the light of principle or policy, crits find irreconcilable 'contradictions' within 'legal liberalism'. Beginning with Duncan Kennedy's seminal article on 'Form and Substance in Private Law Adjudication' of 1976, members of the movement have laid stress on the ambivalence between clear-cut rules and vaguer standards, it being shown that either kind of provision could equally well be invoked to settle any issue so that the choice between solutions is without rational basis. 'Contradictions' have been everywhere unearthed: between intentionalism and determinism in the criminal law; between public and private in domestic relations law; between ownership and collective-resource-use in property law; between consensual contracting and job security in employment law: and so on.

The arbitrariness of conventional legal doctrinal reasoning is not its worst failing. More importantly, it serves to legitimate existing power structures, even when it is deployed by someone who thinks he is forwarding progressive causes. Suppose one were to argue that the rights which the law presently confers upon employees should be broadly construed, that would only serve to buttress the assumption that the appropriate starting-point is control over the working environment by employers. If one argues that the underlying principles of the law confer property rights on dependant members of a family, one simply legitimises the whole notion of dependence.

For some members of the movement all legal discourse is inherently suspect because it substitutes its constructed categories for the reality of diverse human interactions. A multiplicity of relations are forced into the categories of contract, crime, property or family. All the talk of 'rights' serves only to depict real people as abstract entities, subsisting apart from their communities. The more abstract the 'right' invoked, the less determinate will it be in practice. Hence, for example, Mark Tushnet argues that the left in Britain is properly opposed to the adoption of a bill of rights: it would serve only to 'enhance the political power of the privileged without bolstering the position of the Left'.[5] On the other hand, the view that all 'rights' talk is to be avoided has been denounced as short-sighted by Kimberle Crenshaw, who argues that it can and should be used against the liberal establishment, as was done on behalf of black Americans in the civil rights movement.

Appeal is sometimes made, eclectically, to social theorists, such as Michel Foucault, Jurgen Habermas and Richard Rorty who, in various ways, have stressed that systems of communication 'create' rather than 'reflect' social reality. Other members of the movement have discounted any need for high-level theory about legal discourse. (See Kennedy's celebrated renunciation of it in 'Roll Over Beethoven'). The main thing is to dissipate reliance on conventional doctrinal distinctions and to introduce as much broad-scale political critique into one's scholarship and teaching as possible. Consequently, deconstruction of law should be prized for its own sake. This facet of crits thinking is sometimes absorbed within a wider movement in art, literature and philosophy known as 'post-modernism', as advocated by writers such as Jean Francois Lyotard. The programme for post-modernists comprises the rejection of all attempts since the enlightenment to relate the human condition to broad expository narratives. There is no such thing as 'sound theory' and no such entity as 'the human subject'. Once we appreciate that, we will be liberated to think about concrete relationships and to swap with one another any number of constructions, or reconstructions, of them.

Some members of the critical legal studies movement ally themselves with feminist critiques of liberal legalism, discussed in chapter 20, below. Others invoke Marxist concepts of class and of capitalist domination (see chapter 19, below). Generally, however, they distance themselves from Marxist economic-instrumentalism and from Marxist historicism. A traditional Marxist would regard law as primarily super-structure, something determined by relations of production, and therefore not worthy of study divorced from examination of the underlying economy. For crits the law is very important precisely because of its power to project a discourse which gives an appearance of inevitability and naturalness to dehumanising structures. They are in one way less optimistic than traditional Marxists in that they do not prophesy the triumph of the oppressed. In another sense they are more optimistic. Once we appreciate the roles of legal doctrine and legal discourse in buttressing the status quo,

5   (1984) 62 Tex LR 1363 at 1381.

we can think out and implement a new, freer social world. The human mind has the capacity to transcend the fetters of existing legal and economic structures.

Few crits have been willing to speculate about the new law and new legal institutions which might come about in a better tomorrow. I was once told by a leading member of the movement that this is so because, since there would inevitably be disagreement about the matter, it would divide the movement and so blunt its critical edge. A sketch of such a vision does, however, appear in the essay on the movement written by its most renowned banner-holder, Roberto Unger.

Unger suggests that existing political and legal institutions should be replaced by new ones within an 'empowered democracy', a society committtted to 'super liberalism'. Wealth would be much more evenly spread than in contemporary societies, but there would be no centralised command economy. A rotating capital fund would be made available on an experimental basis to enterprises, and educational measures would be adopted to promote individuals' 'negative capabilities' – that is, the power to resist stereotyping and domination by others. The new society would build on the best insights of liberalism and socialism by furnishing its members with immunity rights against governmental interference, solidarity rights to associate with others, and provisional market rights. There would also be added 'destabilisation rights', which would empower individuals to smash, and to prevent the re-emergence of, existing systems of social hierarchy and differentiation. These rights would not be enforced by courts of the traditional kind (which now are staffed by judges whose role self-image includes the assumption that juridical reasoning stands apart from all-things-considered political controversy). They would be enforced by more informal agencies, with the help of a new breed of lawyers:

'If legal doctrine is acknowledged to be continuous with other modes of normative argument, if the institutional plan that decrees the existence of a distinct judiciary alongside only one or two other branches of government is reconstructed, and if long before this reconstruction the belief in a logic of inherent institutional roles is abandoned, legal expertise can survive only as a loose collection of different types of insight and responsibility.'[6]

Unger is not explicit as to how destabilisation rights would interact with the other three kinds of right, nor as to the nature of the populist institutions which would enforce them. On a worst case scenario, everyone would be at the mercy of vociferous popular assemblies empowered to decide what

6 *The Critical Legal Studies Movement* p 111.

ought to be done to her or to her resources or to her family relationships, to ensure the destruction of what her fellow citizens deemed to be undesirable hierarchy or differentiation. But perhaps that is to lack faith in Unger's vision of a reconstituted humanity.

Pending the achievement of the empowered democracy there is, according to Unger, work for the legal scholar to do and pitfalls for her to avoid. She must espouse 'deviationist' or 'critical' doctrine. She needs to refute the spurious claims of 'objectivism', that is, any suggestion that existing legal materials sustain a defensible scheme of human association. She will do that by showing, in relation to any branch of law, that there are equally matched principles and counter-principles, and that beneath these there are irreconcilable ideological assumptions. She can deploy an immanent critique of the existing law by demonstrating how some of the counter-principles could be expanded so as to disrupt what is taken to be settled in other areas:

> '[T]he crucial feature of deviationist doctrine is the willingness to recognise and develop the conflicts between principles and counterprinciples that can be found in any body of law. Critical doctrine does this by finding in these disharmonies the elements of broader contests among prescriptive conceptions of society.'[7]

What she must resist, however, is any temptation to go along with the notion of objective legal outcomes, even if, on occasion, that might serve the interests of some disadvantaged individual or group. Joining them only encourages them:

> 'The appeal to a spurious conceptual necessity may prove tactically expedient. In the end, however, it always represents a defeat for our cause, no matter who may be the temporary victors in the broadened doctrinal debate.'[8]

Critical legal studies is aimed at legal scholars and their pupils. It is not to be supposed that, given our existing institutions, an advocate or a judge could embody its message wholesale into his submissions or his judgments.

> 'I submit that the court should exacerbate the disharmonies of the law and disrupt the crippling effect of all available legal discourse!'

> 'Certainly. Among the purely arbitrary choices open to me, I will select that which, so far as I can see, has the best chance of dissolving

7   Op cit, p 17.
8   Op cit, p 57.

social hierarchy and differentiation – while making it clear that I do not invoke any "correct" legal solution!'

There could be no such thing as a crit judge, sitting in the kind of courts we now have. So much the worse, a crit might say, for our existing institutions. As Unger puts it:

'So when asked whether deviationst doctrine can suitably be used by judges, we answer as follows. We are neither servants of the state ... nor their technical assistants. We have no stake in finding a pre-established harmony between moral compulsions and institutional constraints. We know, moreover, that the received views of institutional propriety count for little except as arguments to use against those who depart too far from professional consensus.'[9]

(This jibe, it seems, is specifically directed against the interpretive theory espoused by Ronald Dworkin, according to which it is possible to arrive at a 'fit' between extant legal materials and defensible principles of political morality – see chapter 14, below.)

There is no evidence that students who have sat at the feet of the critical scholars and then accepted posts in firms handling corporation or tax law have taken with them any special attitude towards their clients' affairs. What of that! The radical scholar is revolted by the notion of playing poodle to the demands of legal practice. It is for him to spill the beans about the spurious nature of legal reasoning and the horrible legitimising effects of legal discourse. Let the 'liberal' respond, if he can, by demonstrating that legalism, revised or reformed, has more to offer by way of incremental justice than either deconstruction for its own sake or even the envisioned domain of Unger's 'empowered democracy'.

Bibliography

American Legal Realism

Ackerman B. A. *Reconstructing American Law* (1984) ch 2
Fisher W. W., Horwitz M. J. and Reed T. A. (eds) *American Legal Realism* (1993)
Frank J. *Law and The Modern Mind* (2nd edn, 1963)
    – *Courts on Trial* (1949)
Fuller L. L. 'American Legal Realism' (1934) 82 U Pa L Rev 429
Garlan E. N. *Legal Realism and Justice* (1944)
Grant G. 'Legal Realism: its Cause and Cure' (1961) 70 Yale LJ 1037

9   Op cit, p 19.

Gray J. C. *The Nature and Sources of the Law* (2nd edn, 1963)
Hart H. L. A. *The Concept of Law (2nd edn,* 1994) ch 7
Holmes O. W. 'The Path of the Law' (1897) 10 Harv L Rev 457
Hunt A. *The Sociological Movement in Law* (1978) ch 2
Llewellyn K. N. 'A Realistic Jurisprudence: the Next Step' (1930) 30
    Colum L Rev 431
    –   'Some Realism about Realism' (1931) 44 Harv L Rev 1222
    –   'The Normative, the Legal and the Law Jobs: the Problem of
        Juristic Method' (1940) 49 Yale LJ 1355
    –   *The Bramble Bush* (revised edn, 1951)
    –   *The Common Law Tradition* (1960)
    –   *Jurisprudence: Realism in Theory and Practice* (1962)
Llewellyn K. N., Adler M. J., Cook W. W. 'Law and the Modern Mind (a
    Symposium)' (1931) 31 Colum L Rev 82
McDougall M. S. 'Fuller versus the American Legal Realists: an
    Intervention' (1941) 50 Yale LJ 827
Pound R. 'The Call for a Realist Jurisprudence' (1931) 44 Harv L Rev
    697
Rumble W. E. *American Legal Realism* (1968)
Rodell F. *Woe Unto You Lawyers* (1957)
Schubert G. 'Behavioral Jurisprudence' (1968) 2 LS Rev 407
Singer J. 'Legal Realism Now' (1988) 76 Calif L Rev 465
Taylor E. H. 'H. L. A. Hart's Concept of Law in the Perspective of
    American Legal Realism' (1972) 35 MLR 606
Twining W. *Karl Llewellyn and the Realist Movement* (1973)
Yntema H. 'American Legal Realism in Retrospect' (1960) 9 Vand L Rev
    317

Scandinavian Legal Realism

Castberg F. *Problems of Legal Philosophy* (2nd edn, 1957) pp 27-37
Hagerstrom A. *Inquiries into the Nature of Law and Morals* (Olivecrona
    (ed), Broad trans, 1953)
Harris J. W. *Law and Legal Science* (1979) ss. 6, 17
    –   'Olivecrona on Law and Language – the Search for Legal
        Culture' (1982) Tiddsskrift for Rettsvitenskap 625
Hart H. L. A. *Essays in Jurisprudence and Philosophy* (1983) ch 6
Jackson B. S. 'On scholarly developments in Legal Semiotics' (1990) 3
    RJ 415
Lewis J. U. 'Karl Olivecrona: "Factual Realism" and Reasons for Obeying
    a Law' (1970) 5 U Br Col L Rev 281
Lundstedt A. V. *Legal Thinking Revised* (1956)
MacCormack G. 'Scandinavian Realism' (1970) Jur Rev 33

- 'Hagerstrom on Rights and Duties' (1971) Jur Rev 59
Merrills J. G. 'Law, Morals and the Psychological Nexus' (1969) 19 U Tor LJ 46
Olivecrona K. *Law As Fact* (1939)
- *Law As Fact* (2nd edn, 1971)
- 'Legal Language and Reality' in Newman (ed) *Essays in Honor of Roscoe Pound* (1962)
- 'The Imperative Element in Law' (1964) 18 Rut L Rev 794
- 'Bentham's Veil of Mystery' (1978) 31 CLP 227
Pasmore L. 'Axel Hagerstrom and his Disciples' in Sawer (ed) *Studies in the Sociology of Law* (1961)
Ross A. *Towards a Realistic Jurisprudence* (1946)
- *On Law and Justice* (1958) chs 1-4
- *Directive and Norms* (1968) ch 4
Simmonds N. E. 'The Legal Philosophy of Axel Hagerstrom' (1976) Jur Rev 210

Critical Legal Studies

Altman A. *Critical Legal Studies: a Liberal Critique* (1990)
Boyle J. *Critical Legal Studies* (1992)
Carrington P. 'Of Law and the River' (1984) 34 JLE 222
Crenshaw K. 'Race, Reform and Retrenchment' (1988) 101 Harv L Rev 1331
Douzinas C. and Warrington R. (eds) *Postmodern Jurisprudence* (1991)
Finnis J. M. 'On "The Critical Legal Studies Movement"' in Eekelaar and Bell (eds) *Oxford Essays in Jurisprudence* (3rd series, 1987)
FitzPatrick P. and Hunt A. (eds) *Critical Legal Studies* (1987)
Gabel P. and Kennedy D. 'Roll Over Beethoven' (1984) 36 Stan L Rev 1
Harris J. W. 'Unger's Critique of Formalism in Legal Reasoning' (1989) 52 MLR 42
Hunt A. 'The Theory of Critical Legal Studies' (1986) 6 OJLS 1
Hutchinson A. C. *Dwelling on the Threshold* (1988)
Kairys D. (ed) *The Politics of Law* (1982)
Kelman M. *A Guide to Critical Legal Studies* (1987)
Kennedy D. 'Form and Substance in Private Law Adjudication' (1976) 89 Harv L Rev 1685
Krygier M. 'Critical Legal Studies and Social Theory – a Response to Alan Hunt' (1987) 7 OJLS 26
MacCormick D. N. 'Reconstruction after Deconstruction' (1990) 10 OJLS 539
Peller G. 'The Metaphysics of American Law' (1985) 73 Calif L Rev 1151
Symposia
- 1984 36 Stan L Rev

–   1984 62 Tex LR
–   1987 14 J Law and Soc
Tushnet M. 'Following the Rules Laid Down' (1983) 96 Harv L Rev 781
Unger R. M. *The Critical Legal Studies Movement* (1983)
–   'Legal Analysis as Institutional Imagination' (1996) 59 MLR 1

9 Hart's concept of law

'Notwithstanding its concern with analysis the book may also be regarded as an essay in descriptive sociology; for the suggestion that inquiries into the meanings of words merely throw light on words is false.'[1]

The late professor H.L.A. Hart (1907-92) broke new ground in analytical jurisprudence with his book, *The Concept of Law*, first published in 1961. We saw (in chapter 7, above) that Hart rejected theory raised 'on the back of definition'. The way to analyse legal concepts was to explore the ways in which terms standing for those concepts were used inside and outside the law. Not only would this method avoid the unnecessary puzzles to which other methods of analysis had led; it would also draw attention to important features of social life. Linguistic practices were good sociological evidence. From what has been called 'the method of ordinary language analysis' we are to expect both conceptual and sociological information. This chapter considers how far Hart's book succeeded in these respects, as regards legal rules and legal systems and the general problem of the normativity of law. We take account of responses to criticisms which Hart offered in subsequent writings, especially in the postscript to the posthumously published second edition of *The Concept of Law*.

1 Legal rules as social rules

Hart says that when a social group is said to have a 'rule', two things are true. First, the members generally perform certain actions. That is the 'external aspect' of the rule. If that were all, what would be present would

1 H. L. A. Hart *The Concept of Law* (2nd edn) p v.

be merely a 'habit'. There must, secondly, be an 'internal aspect', that is, a 'critical reflective attitude' shared by most members of the group towards the conduct in question. This internal aspect is manifested by criticisms made by members of the group against those who deviate or threaten to deviate from standard behaviour, by demands for conformity, and by acknowledgements that the line of conduct in question is indeed proper. Language exhibits the manifestation of this internal attitude by the use of a special kind of 'normative' vocabulary – you ought to do this, you must do that, such and such is right (or wrong). What emerges from this analysis is an explanation of the concept of a rule in terms of a particular kind of social situation: rules as social rules.

There were many kinds of such rules, relating to etiquette, games, morals and so on. An important category were those rules which are 'conceived and spoken of' as imposing obligations. We find that people use a special type of normative term – 'duty' or 'obligation' – when 'the general demand for conformity is insistent and the social pressure brought to bear upon those who deviate or threaten to deviate is great'.[2] Obligation rules differ from other rules in two further respects: they are associated with some prized feature of social life, and it is generally recognised that what they require may conflict with a person's interests.

Obligation rules were divisible into sub-categories. If the social pressure brought to bear upon those who deviate includes physical sanctions, they represent a (possibly primitive) kind of law. But if the strong social pressure does not go that far, then they are rules forming part of the morality of the group. In a 'pre-legal' society, there may be no more by way of legal rules than obligation rules of the coercive type. Inevitably, there must be some such obligation rules in any society. For society to survive, there must be legal obligation rules restricting violence, theft and deception. Men always find such rules necessary because of man's nature as a partly selfish but partly co-operative creature, his typical wish to survive, and the limited resources of the world. As we saw in chapter 2, above, Hart describes these necessary rules as 'the minimum content of natural law'.

If a society has no more than obligation rules it will not be able, Hart says, to cope satisfactorily with the need to change rules from time to time, with the need to decide on disputed questions, and with the need for criteria to determine which rules are rightly regarded as obligation rules and which not. These needs can only be satisfied by the introduction of rules of change, adjudication and recognition. Their introduction represents a step from the pre-legal to a legal world. A 'legal system' comprises both legal obligation rules ('primary legal rules'), and 'secondary legal rules' – like the rules of change, adjudication and recognition. Secondary rules do not

2   Op cit, p 86.

impose duties. They are 'power-conferring' rules. They are 'parasitic on' primary rules.

A wealth of critical literature has been devoted to this picture of law. Some critics have objected to the whole analysis of rules in terms of social rules. How can all rules be understood as combinations of patterns of behaviour and attitudes? Surely personal moral rules at least must be some other kind of rule. If a strict vegetarian tells you that he subscribes to a rule according to which eating animal products is wrong, he is not committing himself to any statement about the practices of any particular group. In the postcript to the second edition of *The Concept of Law*, Hart acknowledged that his 'practice theory' of rules is not 'a sound explanation of morality, either individual or social'.[3] Even if all members of a social group were vegetarians, their rules would not be social rules because they would each condemn meat-eating out of personal conviction. A social rule arises where the fact that conduct is conventionally accepted is part of the reason for the participants in a practice to regard it as a standard of assessment. Such is the case with ordinary social customs and (Hart continues to insist) with certain important legal rules – including the rule of recognition, which is a form of judicial customary rule. Enacted legal rules, by contrast, though they are identifiable as valid legal rules by the criteria contained in the rule of recognition, 'may exist as legal rules from the moment of their enactment before any occasion for their practice has arisen and the practice theory is not applicable to them'.[4]

To those social rules to which the analysis does apply, how illuminating is the notion of an 'internal' attitude? It is proffered as a better explanation of legal discourse than either Austin's command model or the predictive analysis of the American legal realists. Furthermore, Hart indicates that it is not a psychological concept, not a mere 'feeling of being bound'. He rejects the internalisation-of-rules analysis made by the Scandinavian realists (see chapter 8, above). Nor does the internal point of view consist in moral approval of the rule, for, he says, people may accept rules out of fear, self-interest or habit. Even the 'acceptance' by judges of secondary rules does not consist of moral approval (or even pretended moral approval), but merely of a 'settled disposition' to act in accordance with an established practice which they join upon taking office.[5] It may be that the so-called 'internal' aspect of rules consists exclusively of the criticisms, demands and acknowledgments which people make, that is, of speech acts. The point of the concept would then be, not to suggest that rule-governed practices require psychological internalisation of rules or convergence of

3   Op cit, p 256.
4   Ibid.
5   *Essays on Bentham* pp 155-59.

group approval, but to make a functional generalisation about linguistic usage. When you have social rules, there will be expressions whose function is to draw attention to the rules or to apply them – 'off-side', 'out', 'wrong', 'unlawful', 'guilty'.

Against this understanding of his concept stands the fact that Hart speaks of the internal attitude as 'critical' and 'reflective'. Neil MacCormick suggests that these adjectives represent two features of Hart's internal point of view. One is 'cognitive', awareness of a standard of conduct – hence, 'reflective'. The other is 'volitional' – hence 'critical'. MacCormick aligns Hart with a category of social theory known as 'hermeneutic', one which insists that social actions and institutions can be understood only by interpreting the meaning they have for those engaged in them. Is it true that use of normative terminology is good evidence for the existence of such a double-edged attitude, at least when it is applied to those social rules to which (in the end) Hart supposed his 'practice theory' of rules to be confined?

Austin explained rules like those relating to the formation of contracts and wills in terms of conditional commands backed by the sanction of nullity (see chapter 3, above). Hart maintains that this distorts their social functions. Power-conferring rules have a function different from that of duty-imposing rules. They enable, not require, us to do things. It has been argued that Hart's own category of secondary rules distorts social functions by bracketing together rules with very different functions – for example, rules conferring capacities or defining rights with rules of legislation, adjudication and administration. Can it be said that all secondary rules confer powers? What about the rule of recognition? Are not judges bound to accept that 'Whatever the Queen in Parliament enacts is law'? And is it an oversimplification to describe all secondary rules as 'about' or 'parasitic' on primary rules? Surely, rules governing legislation enable secondary, power-conferring rules relating to contracts and wills to be changed?

The functions of law are manifold. Clearly Hart did not suppose that there were only two, for he indicated that three types of rule (those of change, adjudication and recognition) met different needs. The term 'power-conferring' may be no more than a misleading catalogue label. In any case, should one try to categorise different types of rules by reference to distinguishable social functions? As we shall see in chapter 18, below, it is far from easy to give an objective account of the functions of law. It is even more difficult to pair each function with a particular kind of legal rule. It may be that some legal rules perform more than one function, or that a single function requires a cluster of different kinds of rules. When we speak of a rule's 'function', we may mean that which it was historically introduced to achieve, or the use made of it in contemporary society. Clearly, when the Statute of Frauds (1677) was enacted and certain formalities stipulated for will-making, the object was not to enable people to do something (make wills) which they could not do before. As to the uses made today of these formality provisions, our characterisation depends on evidence and evaluation. Maybe they do enable people to make secure provision for their families, or maybe they inhibit people from making informal 'wills'.

2   The union of primary and secondary rules

Hart offers no definition of a legal system, but he tells us that the 'union of primary and secondary rules' is at its heart. It may not answer peripheral questions – like whether primitive systems or public international law should, without qualification, be described as 'law'. But it will explain much that has puzzled both the jurist and the political theorist. On the analytic plane, it explains the use of concepts such as 'validity'. Common to positivist writers in general is the thesis that there are in legal systems criteria by reference to which 'laws' can be distinguished from other things. Hart's version states that rules are members of a legal system if, but only if, they meet the criteria laid down by the rule of recognition.

Some confusion has been caused by Hart's use of the expression 'rule of recognition' sometimes in the singular and sometimes in the plural. So far as the positivist thesis is concerned, it seems that it is one rule for each legal system. Like Kelsen's basic norm it enables the products of law-creating acts to be described as a system. However, as Hart claims, the rule of recognition exists 'as a social practice', and is not a mere 'presupposition'. A further difference is that, while Kelsen formulates his basic norm in terms of the historically first constitution, Hart formulates his rule of recognition in terms of listed criteria. He does not spell out the rule for any system. He indicates that the rule of recognition in the United Kingdom is 'Whatever the Queen in Parliament enacts is law'. But elsewhere he states that precedents would be further criteria listed by the rule, albeit the rule would indicate that statutes prevail over them. Thus it is implicit that the rule of recognition will contain a full list of all criteria – statute, precedent, custom and so on – with an indication of their mutual ranking.

The analytic function of the concept of the union of primary and secondary rules is rejected by some anti-positivists. If it is not possible to articulate all the criteria by reference to which rules are identified as legal, then 'validity' cannot be merely a concept which relates a particular rule to a master rule. In the postscript, Hart considers it sufficient to defend only 'soft positivism': rules of recognition generally provide factual criteria enabling legal rules to be identified but they may, contingently, announce tests of validity which refer to the conformity of laws with substantive moral values or principles. As we shall see in chapter 14, below, Dworkin argues that moral criteria enter, not merely occasionally, but systematically, into the identification of law. Hart states that, in the penumbral area of uncertainty left by valid rules, a judge may have to reach beyond the law for reasons to justify his decision. Dworkin denies this, arguing that there are principles based on community morality which, collectively, provide the right answer in 'hard cases'. Such principles are applied because, as well as being moral, they are also legal. Therefore, no test of 'pedigree', such as the rule of recognition, can serve to distinguish law from morality or to draw lines around the legal system.

Others have objected, not to the possibility of a positivist test of validity, but to Hart's version of it. How is one to discover a rule of recognition existing 'as a social practice'? As we have seen, Hart tells us that we can find out whether there is a social rule about some behaviour by seeing whether members of a group criticise their own and others' conduct by reference to some standard. Do we find that those who administer the legal system make criticisms by reference to a single, all-embracing standard, a rule which sets out all the criteria for legal validity in a ranked order?

Even more attention has been paid to the non-analytic uses of Hart's concept of the 'union of primary and secondary rules' – that is, to its contribution to 'descriptive sociology' as compared with the light it throws on the use of terms. Like Austin's concept of 'habitual obedience' and Kelsen's concept of 'by and large effectiveness', the union of primary and secondary rules incorporates what may be called an 'existence thesis' about legal systems:

> 'There are therefore two minimum conditions necessary and sufficient for the existence of a legal system. On the one hand, those rules of behaviour which are valid according to the system's ultimate criteria of validity must be generally obeyed, and, on the other hand, its rules of recognition specifying the criteria of legal validity and its rules of change and adjudication must be effectively accepted as common public standards of official behaviour by its officials.'[6]

The significance of this existence thesis is not altogether clear. Some have treated it as a developmental thesis. As we have seen, Hart envisages a pre-legal society (one without secondary rules) in which defects of three kinds emerge: uncertainty about which rules are members of the system, rigidity through lack of any recognised means of changing the rules, and diffuseness of social pressure when disputes arise about the application of rules. These three defects are matched by the introduction of rules of

6   *The Concept of Law* (2nd edn) p 116.

recognition, change and adjudication respectively. Hart cites anthropological works in the notes to this discussion, which might suggest that he is presenting a picture of historical developments. If so, it can be criticised by showing that 'primitive systems' do not lack secondary rules of the three kinds he mentions, or on the grounds that their introduction was not the result of observed 'defects'. But perhaps Hart's existence thesis is not developmental, and he postulates only an imaginary situation in which secondary rules do not exist in order to point up their functions.

Hart's existence thesis can be treated as heuristic or diagnostic – that is, it enables one to recognise legal systems when one finds them, and it enables one to express a diagnosis about a marginal case of 'legal system'. If we want to know whether a society has yet attained a legal system, Hart has provided a test. If a country is in a state of turmoil and the political scientist is trying to assess whether it has that social grace commonly known as 'law', wheel in the patient and apply this two-pronged stethoscope – 'Are your primary rules generally obeyed?' 'Do your officials accept your secondary rules?' It is questionable whether Hart himself had this sort of application of his existence thesis in mind. He indicates that social arrangements may more or less approximate the standard arrangements, and that there may be little point in drawing a sharp line between 'legal system' and 'non-legal system'.

So perhaps the existence thesis is merely informative. It provides us with information, in large-scale terms, about what happens in political societies. We might apply the same 'sociology for Martians' critique that we used in chapter 2, above, in connection with Hart's minimum content of natural law. Picture a Martian coming to earth and, astounded by the prevalence of normative utterances and coercive institutions, asking: 'What's all this law about?' We will get across the heart of the matter if we explain the nature of rules as social rules, secondly, distinguish primary from secondary rules, and finally, tell him that a legal system exists when the primary rules are generally obeyed and the secondary rules accepted by officials. Of course, there are no Martians; but there are students of institutions interested in distinguishing the central features of legal systems from peripheral ones, without going exhaustively into the detail of particular provisions.

Are general obedience to primary rules and official acceptance of secondary rules the most important features of legal systems? To some extent, this must be a matter of evaluation. No attempt to extrude the universally significant from among a welter of social detail can be otherwise. Lawyers concentrate on rules. Other social scientists may see careers, role-structures and institutional frameworks. Hart's picture should be compared with that of other social theorists, such as those discussed in chapter 19, below.

3   Law's normativity

Hart's invocation of the 'internal' point of view has, for English-speaking jurists, focused attention on the alleged inherent normativity of positive law. That issue must be distinguished from the question (discussed in chapter 14, below) of whether there are values exterior to the law from which a moral obligation to obey the law can be derived. Law's inherent normativity refers to an alleged conceptual connection between 'legal duty' and 'ought'. If you say that there is a legal duty to do something, it is part of the meaning of what you say that, in some sense of 'ought', the thing 'ought' to be done.

This is not a question as to which all natural law theorists are necessarily ranged on one side while all legal positivists are on the other. Finnis, for example, claims that, given law's role as forwarder of the common good, we should understand the 'focal meaning' of law from the morally concerned man's point of view; but he nevertheless accepts that the concept of 'legal duty' is applicable across the board to all positive enactments, just or unjust – so that, merely by saying that there is a legal duty, one has not settled the question whether the prescribed conduct ought to be carried out. (See chapter 2, above.) Kelsen, on the other hand, the arch proponent of legal positivism, always maintained the conceptual connection between 'legality' and 'ought' – although (as we saw in chapter 6, above), 'ought' for him entailed no more than that the subjective meaning of a prescription was interpreted as its objective meaning: it implicated nothing in the way of objective moral values, because, for Kelsen, no such values were admissible to 'scientific' cognition.

The early English positivists, Bentham and Austin, did not present positive law as inherently normative. They equated 'legal duty' with 'commanded by the sovereign' or 'liability to a sanction' (see chapter 3, above). Hart criticised this command model on the ground that it failed to distinguish 'being obliged' from 'having an obligation'. The latter expression evidenced the internal point of view from which a prescription was viewed as an appropriate standard for measuring conduct. Some critics of Hart have insisted that his admission of law's normativity is incompatible with his legal positivism. J. C. Smith, for example, maintains that people only speak of the law as imposing 'duties' when they conceive the rules in question to be morally binding. M. J. Detmold goes much further. He claims that all 'practical' discourse – all assertions about what ought to be done – *must* be unified. There is no sense in which it can be maintained that, morally, one should do something, but that 'legally' (or from any other point of view) one should do the opposite. Those who occupy official roles can never, logically, shelter behind the law when their moral convictions run counter to it. Thus, Detmold argues, a Roman Catholic judge who issues a decree of divorce (pursuant to law) misunderstands his role as a judge.[7] He insists that a judge who thinks capital punishment is morally wrong cannot pass a sentence of death whatever the statute may say.[8] By Detmold's logic of the unity of practical discourse, the converse would presumably follow: if a judge supposed that, morally, a prisoner ought to hang, he must pass sentence of death even if legislation has abolished capital punishment.

What exit might a legal positivist (who subscribes to the normativity of law) seek from these seemingly bizarre implications (otherwise than via Kelsen's 'pallid' normativity)? The most celebrated exponent, in the English-speaking world, of the view that a strictly positivistic conception of law can be combined with the recognition that law and morals share the same concepts, is to be found in Joseph Raz's 'authority' legal theory. Raz espouses a 'strong' version of what he calls the 'sources thesis': the existence and content of every law is to be found by answering questions of fact (perhaps, difficult questions) about social institutions, conventions and the intentions of actors in the legal process. What the law is as to any matter never involves value judgments, although legal institutions (including courts) are often vested with power to fill gaps in the law and gap-filling does involve value judgments. Raz rejects 'soft' positivism.

Why should we look at the law in that way? Because, says Raz, it is of the essence of law that it claims supremacy over all other guidance-systems about what we ought to do – that is, the concept of 'law' is tied to that of 'authority'. Raz does not suppose that law has the authority it claims. On the contrary, he argues that there are no good grounds for a general moral obligation to obey the law. The conceptual truth is that law is a system of prescriptions, identified by their recognition by law-applying institutions, which *purport* to constitute ultimate authority. This claim to authority, not the monopolisation of coercion, is the hallmark of law so that, for example, the rules of a religious order, if recognised by its institutions as the ultimate test of what ought to be done, would constitute a legal system.[9]

Raz's authority theory of law is grounded in a much wider conception of practical reasoning, the core of which is the notion of 'reasons for action'. To say that something ought to be done, is to say that there is a reason to act in that way. A conclusionary judgment that something ought to be done refers to the balance of all applicable reasons. Mandatory rules enter the picture in the following way. The existence of such a rule constitutes a second-order reason against acting on the balance of first-order reasons. It constitutes an 'exclusionary reason'. If I am considering what to do in matters small or great – whether to park my car on a double-

7   Detmold *The Unity of Law and Morality* p 37.
8   Op cit, pp. 22-28.
9   Raz *Practical Reason and Norms* p 151.

yellow line, whether to pay the poll tax, whether to participate in sado-masochistic sex – I might, if left to myself, reach a conclusion on a balance of reasons (prudential, moral or religious) about what I ought to do. If there is a mandatory legal rule on the subject, however, then, from the point of view of those who staff legal institutions, the existence of that rule is a reason for me not to act on my own assessment of the balance of reasons, but to defer to that rule. Strict positivism follows from this theory because, if the existence or content of any law were dependent on a value assessment, the law would not be fulfilling its definitional role of providing authoritative guidance. It would instead be allowing the issue to be settled on the balance of first-order reasons. (Non-mandatory legal rules, like Hart's power-conferring rules, add reasons for action but are not exclusionary reasons. Raz argues that it is possible to 'individuate' laws (break down the contents of a legal system into distinct bits) if we have regard to law's normative functions, the provision of reasons for action, rather than Hart's description of its various social functions.)

What, then, about the conceptual connection with morality? Raz notes that we say of laws, not merely that they require things to be done or omitted, but that they impose 'duties'. Since there can be only one meaning for the concept of 'duty', we must be making the same kind of claim whether we are speaking of legal or moral or religious duties. We must be saying that there exists a mandatory rule which excludes all first-order reasoning about the matter. To explain how it is that a person might say that there is a legal duty while denying that (or remaining agnostic as to whether) the conduct in question is morally required, Raz introduces the idea of 'detached' statements. A person invoking duty may be making a committed statement – that is, he may fully accept the authority of the relevant mandatory rule. Instead, however, he may be making a detached statement, from the point of view of someone who does accept that authority (while he himself does not). For example, someone who is not an orthodox Jew, but who is well informed about the religious obligations of orthodox Jewry, might tell a less well-informed practising Jew what, from the addressee's point of view, the addressee ought to do. Or a non-vegetarian might warn his vegetarian colleague not to eat a certain dish because it contains meat. Similarly, argues Raz, it is often the case that when we describe the law, we adopt the point of view of the 'legal man' – one who believes that the full range of his moral duties coincides with the provisions of positive law. (A problem with this analogy, as it seems to me, is this. The adviser of the orthodox Jew or of the vegetarian knows, though he does not share, the value system of the person to whom he is speaking. The hypothetical 'legal man', in contrast, has no value system. He is not one who supposes that there are good extra-legal moral grounds for obeying a particular system of law and, on those grounds, accepts its moral authority. He is, by definition, one who clothes law with morality even though he has no law-independent conception of what morality is.)

Raz's idea of 'detached statement' is his explanation of Kelsen's 'rechtsatz'; and his idea of the hypothetical 'legal man' is the equivalent of Kelsen's presupposed basic norm. However, where Kelsen's legal 'oughts' are amoral and will-relative, for Raz the concept of legal duty is a fully moral concept, albeit that it is frequently deployed only in a detached way. Hart, in writings subsequent to the publication of the first edition of *The Concept of Law*, gave a qualified endorsement to Raz's suggestion. He recognised that his book appeared to suggest that there could be only two kinds of statement about the law: external ones, which merely record the facts on the ground; and internal ones, wherein the law is invoked as a standard of conduct. Hart now accepted a third kind, 'detached statements'. However, disagreeing with Raz, he insisted that neither internal nor detached statements need deploy moral concepts. The internal point of view might be adopted by someone for reasons of self-interest or habit. The detached statement did not involve appeals to the law as a moral standard, but rather invoked the point of view of someone who, for whatever reason, measured conduct by the 'law's demands'.[10]

There is, according to Hart, no compelling ground for assuming that the concept of 'duty' has the same meaning in law as it does in morals. Legal 'duty' refers only to what is demanded by positive law. How then is his final view different from that of the command model which he so trenchantly criticised? I have suggested that, for Hart, normativity hovers over the law, rather than being intrinsic to it. To say that there is a legal duty, in and of itself, means only that the law demands something. Nevertheless, people often invoke the law as a standard, or give information from the point of view of people who do. That sociological explanation of the law's normativity was something left out of account by the command model. Consistently with this view, one can make sense of such claims as that, as to conduct X, there is, technically, a legal duty to perform it, but, nevertheless, there is no reason why (from any point of view) one 'ought' to do it. One may consider that such assertions are morally mistaken; but can one claim that, by virtue of the law's inherent normativity, they are a misuse of language? Even judges may, exceptionally, speak in this way. The Court of Appeal once ruled that, even though fire engine drivers who jump traffic lights in order to rescue someone from a burning building were acting contrary to law, far from being prosecuted, they should be congratulated.[11] Is one who asserts the presence of 'legal duties' in the case of either trivial or manifestly unjust positive enactments, and who combines this terminology with a denial that there is any sense in which what is prescribed 'ought' to be done, thereby misusing the concept of 'legal duty'? Or should we give up the conceptual connection between law and 'ought'?

10 Hart *Essays on Bentham* pp 153-61; *Essays in Jurisprudence and Philosophy* pp 9-10.
11 *Buckoke v Greater London Council* [1971] 1 Ch 655.

Bibliography

Alexy R. 'On Necessary Relations Between Law and Morality' (1989) 2 RJ 168

Cohen L. J. 'H. L. A. Hart: *The Concept of Law*' (1962) 71 Mind 395

Coleman J. L. 'Negative and Positive Positivism' (1982) 11 JLS 140

Detmold M. J. *The Unity of Law and Morality* (1986) ch 2

Duff R. A. 'Legal Obligation and the Moral Nature of Law' (1980) Jur Rev 61

Dworkin R. M. *Taking Rights Seriously* (revised edn, 1978) chs 2-3

Edgeworth B. 'Legal Positivism and the Philosophy of Language' (1986) 6 LS 115

Gavison R. (ed) *Issues in Contemporary Legal Philosophy* (1987) chs 1-3

George R. P. (ed) *The Autonomy of Law* (1996)

Greenawalt K. 'Hart's Rule of Recognition and the United States' (1988) 1 RJ 40

Hacker P. M. S. 'Hart's Philosophy of Law' in Hacker and Raz (eds) *Law, Morality, and Society* (1977)

Harris J. W. *Law and Legal Science* (1979) s 7

Hart H. L. A. *The Concept of Law* (2nd edn, Bulloch and Raz (eds), 1994)
 – *Essays on Bentham* (1982) pp 141-61
 – *Essays in Jurisprudence and Philosophy* (1983) pp 1-16

Hill R. E. 'Legal Validity and Legal Obligation' (1970) 80 Yale LJ 47

Kanowicz L. 'The Place of Sanctions in Professor Hart's Concept of Law' (1966-67) Duc U L Rev 1

Krygier M. 'The Concept of Law and Legal Theory' (1982) 2 OJLS 155

MacCormick D. N. *Legal Reasoning and Legal Theory* (1978) appendix
 – *HLA Hart* (1981)

Martin M. *The Legal Philosophy of HLA Hart* (1986)

Raz J. *The Authority of law* (1979) chs 2-3
 – *The Concept of a Legal System* (2nd edn, 1980) postcript
 – *The Morality of Freedom* (1986) chs 2-4
 – *Practical Reason and Norms* (2nd edn, 1990) chs 2 and 5
 – *Ethics in the Public Domain* (1994) chs 8 and 9

Samek R. A. *The Legal Point of View* (1974) chs 8-9

Sartorius R. E. 'Hart's Concept of Law' in Summers (ed) *More Essays in Legal Philosophy* (1971)

Smith J. C. *Legal Obligation* (1976) ch 2

Soper P. *A Theory of Law* (1982) ch 2

Summers R. S. 'Professor H. L. A. Hart's Concept of Law' (1963) Duke LJ 629

Tapper C. F. H. 'Powers and Secondary Rules of Change' in Simpson (ed) *Oxford Essays in Jurisprudence* (2nd series, 1973)

Waluchow W. J. *Inclusive Legal Positivism* (1994) chs 4 and 8

Warnock G. J. *The Object of Morality* (1971) ch 4

10 Freedom and the enforcement of morals

We all think that freedom is a value, and public debate about law often mentions it. Sometimes, people say that freedom is something the law can promote. Often this is done in the context of recommended constitutional restraints on state power. More generally, it is claimed that the law is needed to secure one man's freedom from his neighbour's invasion; or that community institutions, including law, are necessary to secure freedom from want. On the other hand, law may be seen as the enemy of freedom, as a set of prescriptions which necessarily detract from natural liberty. From this stance, any restraint on liberty to do what one likes is seen as something requiring justification. If the legislature wishes to make the wearing of seat-belts or crash-helmets compulsory, or to restrict the free sale of drugs or pornographic literature, it had better have a good reason.

Political rhetoric appeals to 'freedom' in many contexts, and the rhetoric may become embodied in legal principle. The movement towards decolonisation and national self-determination – the demand that men should only be ruled, for good or ill, by their co-culturals – appealed to freedom; and international charters have made the principle of self-determination a principle of international law. The liberal heritage of western democracies lays great stress on freedoms of expression – of speech, assembly and criticism – regarding them as both goods in themselves and as necessary means to arriving at policies best suited to the public good. Such freedoms are often embodied in written constitutions, or, as with the European Convention on Human Rights and Fundamental Freedoms, in the basic documents of supra-national institutions.

Discussions of freedom, on the level of moral or political philosophy, revolve around such questions as: Why do we value freedom? What is its relation to other values – pre-eminent or subordinate? Are there different kinds of freedom, some of which deserve our allegiance more than others? Most of us have heard the cynical jibe about the poor man who, in a free society, is 'free' to dine at the Ritz (there being no law to prevent him). On the philosophical plane, this jibe is resolved into some such abstract question as: Is freedom subordinate to equality in the sense that, without an equal or at any rate 'just' distribution of resources, the mere absence of restraint is of little value to the majority? Politicians sometimes draw a distinction between 'freedoms to' or 'freedoms of', on the one hand (freedoms to criticise, freedom of speech etc), and 'freedoms from', on the other (freedom from hunger, freedom from want etc). Sir Isaiah Berlin has suggested that political philosophy should draw a distinction between negative and positive liberty. The former regards absence of constraint on human desires as an intrinsic value, the latter has the truly free man as an ideal, the realisation of which justifies coercion. He rejects positive liberty, on the ground that there is no such coherent ideal as the truly free man. The 18th-century philosopher, Rousseau, on the other hand, held that men could be 'forced to be free'; and Marxists believe that only after the alienating effects of capitalism have been forcibly removed can there be any true freedom. Many reject a sharp dichotomy between freedom, in the sense of absence of constraint, and freedom, in the sense of coerced self-realisation. Is not lack of education, for example, a form of coercion, so that people must be compelled to achieve that degree of self-realisation which education provides in order to be negatively free from the constraints which being uneducated entails? In this respect, liberals commonly amalgamate 'human rights' and 'fundamental freedoms', as the European Convention does: the moral status of the human individual entails that he ought to be afforded certain goods (sometimes, even against his will), and that constraints of some kinds ought not to be applied to him.

A conclusion about what it means (if anything) to be 'truly free' would, no doubt, affect one's attitudes to law as to the rest of life. To make the topic of freedom manageable for jurisprudential purposes, however, I shall postpone consideration of the relative value of freedom and other goods until the discussion of theories of justice in chapter 20, below; and deal here with the narrower question of what justifies legal restraints on negative liberty. If unmerited suffering is an evil, and if laws have some deterrent effect, it is not difficult to defend laws which prohibit murder, rape, assault, theft or fraud. But should the law restrict a man's liberty in respect of actions which harm no one else, either on the ground that he is too foolish to be the judge of his own interests, or on the ground that the action is intrinsically immoral? A negative answer to this question has been associated since the middle of the 19th century with the famous 'harm principle' of John Stuart Mill. In his *Essay on Liberty*, first published in 1859, Mill wrote:

'The object of this Essay is to assert one very simple principle, as entitled to govern absolutely the dealings of society with the individual in the way of compulsion and control, whether the means used be physical force in the form of legal penalties, or the moral coercion of public opinion. That principle is, that the sole end for which mankind are warranted, individually or collectively, in interfering with the liberty of action of any of their number, is self-protection. That the only purpose for which power can be rightfully exercised over any member of a civilised community, against his will, is to prevent harm to others. His own good, either physical or moral, is not a sufficient warrant.'[1]

Mill was an avowed utilitarian. For him, therefore, legislation and other institutional constraints could be justified only if they on balance promoted general happiness. He, like many other liberal utilitarians, never made clear the relationship of the value of liberty to the overall utilitarian principle which is supposed to be the test of all value (see chapter 4, above). Is freedom merely instrumental, good because its exercise will in fact promote general welfare? Or does the harm principle provide an extra-utilitarian basis for valuation, to be assumed before a utilitarian calculation of pleasures and pains is to be made? If the former is correct, it is open to other utilitarians to take issue on the facts – doing what I like won't make me and others happy. If the latter is correct, my free choice of action has a special plus value, and the pain associated with others' mere disapproval of what I do (as distinct from proven harm to them) has a nil value. But then these special valuations do not come from the utilitarian happiness principle itself.

Another famous Victorian utilitarian, Sir James FitzJames Stephen, wrote an attack on Mill, in *Liberty, Equality, Fraternity*, first published in 1873. Stephen denied that there were good utilitarian grounds for defending liberty as such – it all depended on what a person was at liberty to do. Further, no clear line could be drawn between acts which harmed others and acts which harmed only oneself. The punishment of 'the grosser forms of vice' was a proper object of legislation, as it would not be felt as a restraint by the vast majority, but would, on the contrary, satisfy feelings of hatred towards the vicious and provide proper substitutes for disorganised revenge.

The citation of Mill's harm principle given above shows that he was opposed to sanctions on self-regarding actions, whether emanating from the law or from other social institutions and arrangements. If what you do harms no one but yourself, not only should you not be subject to legal

1   *On Liberty in Utilitarianism, Liberty and Representative Government* pp 72-73.

restraint, but you ought not to lose your place in an institution of higher education or your job. He can thus be seen as the apostle of what came to be known in the 1960s as 'the permissive society'. Whether he would actually have liked it is largely a matter of biographical speculation. Certainly, some advocates of permissiveness would reject two exceptions which Mill admitted to his principle. He thought that restraints, going beyond protection of others, were justified in the case of children, and in the case of primitive peoples. Today, much legislation in the area of sexual behaviour is seen by its critics as enforcing 'middle class' or 'bourgeois' or 'religious' morality on people who do not share it. But for any Victorian, there may not have seemed to be much incompatibility between such legislation and the harm principle. Those who promoted legislation raising the age of consent in 1875, or making incest for the first time criminal in 1907, believed that these measures were desirable to protect people, and it would probably have astonished them to be told that they were enemies of liberty.

'Permissive society' is, of course, a misleading label for what has emerged in Britain over the past three decades. In fact, more and more legal restrictions have been placed on what people are allowed to do. Breathalyser laws, laws prohibiting incitement to racial hatred, bans on commercial surrogacy, laws prohibiting the dumping of dangerous waste, all restrict people's freedom of action. The laws which supporters or critics of the 'permissive society' seem to have in mind are laws about homosexuality, obscenity, pornography, easier divorce, abortion, and so on. Some would bring within the same compass proposed changes in the law relating to voluntary euthanasia and the destruction of deformed infants.

The precise bearing of Mill's harm principle on all such laws is controversial. But a more fundamental controversy concerns the issue of the enforcement of morality. If society is entitled to use the law to uphold conventional moral standards, then Mill's principle is at least partially false; for then the enforcement of morality can be seen as a distinct warrant for punishment. Interest in this question received an enormous boost in 1957 from the Report of the Committee On Homosexual Offences and Prostitution, under the chairmanship of Sir John Wolfenden. The report includes some general observations which look Mill-like, and were undoubtedly influenced by the Mill libertarian tradition.

'[The function of the criminal law] is to preserve public order and decency, to protect the citizen from what is offensive and injurious, and to provide sufficient safeguards against exploitation and corruption of others, particularly those who are specially vulnerable because they are young, weak in body or mind, inexperienced, or in a state of special physical, official or economic dependence.' (para 13)

'Unless a deliberate attempt is to be made by society, acting through the agency of the law, to equate the sphere of crime with that of sin, there must remain a realm of private morality and immorality which is, in brief and crude terms, not the law's business.' (para 61)

The opposite view, that the law should prohibit conduct simply because it is immoral, has an ancient pedigree. Plato in his *Laws* stated that the lawgiver 'shall lay down what things are evil and bad, and what things are noble and good'. The *Book of Common Prayer* calls for 'the punishment of wickedness and vice'.

The Wolfenden Committee made two recommendations which were eventually embodied in legislation. The first was that, while prostitution itself should not be punishable, soliciting on the streets by prostitutes should be punished more effectively than hitherto. Soliciting caused 'offence' and so should be rigorously dealt with. Prostitution in private harmed no one apart from the participants. The second recommendation was that homosexual acts between consenting adults in private should no longer be a criminal offence. The harm principle, as understood by the committee, warrants punishing actions which involve 'corruption' or 'exploitation'. Hence, homosexual acts with persons under 21, and living off the earnings of prostitutes, were to continue to be offences. The age of consent for heterosexual intercourse is 16. If the committee favoured neutrality over sexual preferences, why did it stipulate a higher age for homosexual acts? (It has since been reduced to 18.) If society should pass no moral judgment about the sex industry, should there not be a system of licensed brothels, with provisions for safe working conditions and remedies for unfair dismissal?

The harm principle has also influenced the definition of obscenity in the Obscene Publications Act of 1959, as pertaining to publications liable to corrupt persons into whose hands they may fall. There may be conventional moral standards according to which certain things just are 'obscene', but (consistently with the harm principle) legal prohibition requires one to prove that someone or other is likely to be damaged – and, as critics of the law have pointed out, it is ticklish business to produce witnesses who will say: 'Whereas I was pure, since reading this I've become corrupted and depraved'.

The Wolfenden Committee's contention, that conflict with morality is not enough to warrant legal prohibition, was challenged in 1959 by Lord Devlin. In his Hamlyn lecture on 'The Enforcement of Morals', he put forward the view that society has a right to punish any kind of act which, in the opinion of the man in the jury-box ('the right-minded man'), is grossly immoral; there is no need for proof that the act in question harms assignable individuals or groups. First, he mounted an attack on the Wolfenden Committee Report in particular, and the harm principle in general; and, secondly, he advanced an argument, in terms of social cohesion, why it is justifiable to enforce society's morality by law. On both counts, he has been strongly criticised by a number of writers, especially H. L. A. Hart; and the Devlin/Hart controversy has become a standard jurisprudential topic.

Devlin argues that what is 'indecent' or 'offensive', or what amounts to 'exploitation' or 'corruption', in Wolfenden terms, can, in many contexts, only be understood if we use the measure of society's morality. Further, he challenges those who advocate the harm principle to say why the following offences should (if they should) stay on the books: bigamy, bestiality, incest, living off immoral earnings; and to deal with the law's refusal to allow consent as a defence to homicide or serious assault.

The interrelation of harm, consent and changing public moral standards raises intricate issues. Do we prohibit duelling because, whatever the participants may believe, we are sure that it is morally wrong? Or is it to prevent the 'harm' of public disorder (which was the ground given in the 19th century for outlawing prize fights)? What about private fist fights? It is likely that the same Victorian consensus, which condemned ranges of sexual behaviour now seen as perfectly acceptable, would have been astonished to be told that it was morally wrong for adult males to engage in a private fair fight. The hero of Charles Dickens's novel, *David Copperfield*, took them for granted. Yet the English Court of Appeal has ruled that such conduct is criminal.[2] At the same time professional boxing is tolerated.

That was the state of the law when the House of Lords recently had to decide on the criminality of homosexual sado-masochistic behaviour in *R v Brown*.[3] A group of adult males engaged in acts of genital torture, some of which caused minor blood-letting. There was no permanent injury and no medical treatment was needed. All involved were willing and enthusiastic participants for their mutual sexual gratification. They made the mistake of recording the scenes on videos for circulation within the group, which accidentally fell into the hands of the police. The perpetrators were convicted of two crimes under the Offences Against the Person Act 1861: assault occasioning actual bodily harm, and wounding. Two questions were canvassed. (1) Should the House of Lords overrule previous Court of Appeal authority and declare that the consent of a 'victim' is a defence to anything short of serious injury? (2) If the law should continue

---

2   *Re A-G's Reference (No 6 of 1980)* [1981] QB 715.
3   [1994] 1 AC 212.

to deny the defence of consent to all bodily harms going beyond the transient and trifling, should the existing list of exceptions (surgery, sport, chastisement, ritual circumcision and tattooing) be extended so as to include one which would cover the facts of the case? The House upheld the convictions by a majority of three to two. The majority all answered the above questions 'no'. In answering the second question, they rejected the relevance of the principle of privacy in relation to sexual behaviour and decided instead that it was in society's interest to prevent the spread of a cult of sado-masochism. Of the dissenting judges, Lord Slynne answered 'yes' to the first question so that the privacy point did not arise; whereas Lord Mustill considered it undesirable to lay down any general rule about harm and consent and founded an affirmative answer to the second question squarely on the principle that people should be free to engage in private sexual behaviour even if what they did disgusted public opinion.

What about minors? Mill believed that minors could be required to refrain from certain actions for their own good. If that includes 'moral' as well as 'physical' good, as the notions of 'corruption' and 'exploitation' in criminal law evidently suppose, then, at least in the context of education, society's conventional moral opinions will be 'enforced'. If the exception were taken to exclude 'moral good', educators must abstain from biassing children's minds, one way or the other, as to the morality or immorality of behaviour. Some believe that this is indeed the right approach to questions of sexual preference or sexual promiscuity. It is not for the state, through its employees, to engage in partisan indoctrination over questions of moral belief. Should such restraint be universalised? Should teachers be instructed not to indoctrinate their pupils into believing that racist docrines are false?

Hart's reply to Devlin produced two important qualifications on the harm principle. First, he disagreed with Mill that an adult's self-inflicted harm is no warrant for legal intervention. Hart was opposed to 'legal moralism', to the view that general agreement among the members of society that conduct is immoral is a ground for legal prohibition. But he favoured 'paternalism', the view that society may prevent people from doing themselves physical harm. Paternalism (he argued) justified the criminal law in refusing the defence of consent to homicide and assault. Whereas Mill believed that a man's own good, physical or moral, did not warrant interference, Hart believed that his physical good does.

It is not clear how far paternalism of this sort is to be taken. Does it justify legislation restricting the taking by adults of excessive drink, harmful drugs, or driving without seat-belts? Some would argue that restrictions of this sort can be supported by reference to the harm principle without any need to resort to paternalism. If I get myself injured in a duel, or through drink or drugs or driving without a seat-belt, do I not harm others in that I impose costs on society's medical services and perhaps deprive my dependants of support and the taxman of revenue? 'No man is an island', as John Donne told us. But, on that basis, might not the law prohibit dangerous sports, like pot-holing or mountaineering? If Mill is wrong, and a man's physical well-being is a ground on which society may restrict his liberty – either for Hartian paternalist reasons or on the no-man-an-island argument – no doubt libertarians would insist that the harm must be great in relation to the restriction on liberty involved before interference is justified. Is it practical or desirable to disregard, in this equation, whether the physical harm is self-inflicted in morally neutral or immoral ways?

Hart's second qualification to the harm principle concerns the definition of 'harm' itself, and imports a distinction between offence through public spectacle and offence through knowledge. Hart said that punishment of bigamy can be justified on the ground that, as a public act, it causes offence to religious sentiments; but that, in deciding whether any act inflicts 'harm', we must disregard the distress suffered by X through knowing that Y is doing what X regards as immoral. This is an exclusion to be made as a prior step to any utilitarian balancing. It is justified, seemingly, on distinct libertarian grounds, and is not derived from the principle of utility itself:

> '[A] right to be protected from the distress which is inseparable from the bare knowledge that others are acting in ways you think wrong, cannot be acknowledged by anyone who recognises individual liberty as a value ... If distress incident to the belief that others are doing wrong is harm, so also is the distress incident to the belief that others are doing what you do not want them to do. To punish people for causing this form of distress would be tantamount to punishing them simply because others object to what they do; and the only liberty which could coexist with this extension of the utilitarian principle is liberty to do those things to which no-one seriously objects.'[4]

In 1979 the report of the committee on obscenity and film censorship, chaired by Professor Bernard Williams, expressly adopted Mill's harm principle (as modified by Hart) and endorsed Hart's criticism of Devlin. In particular, it approved Hart's distinction between offence-through-knowledge and offence-through-witnessing: private display and circulation even of 'hard porn' should not be the subject of legal intervention, whereas its display in public parts of shops could legitimately be restricted. To the argument that adults employed in producing pornography were 'corrupted' or 'exploited', the committee answered that this was not a matter as to which society should second-guess those who had voluntarily consented

4   *Law, Liberty and Morality* pp 46-47.

to take part (although it did draw a line at live sex shows). It discounted as inconclusive evidence purporting to demonstrate a causal connection between porn-consumption and sexual violence. To the more general contention about 'cultural pollution', it averred that we could not be sure what would be best for society in the long run so we had better opt for maximum liberty of experimentation in sexual matters.

Ronald Dworkin criticises the report, not for its conclusions, but for its procedure. Balancing harms is (he says) too shaky a basis for preserving liberty in this area. It would be open to others to contend that 'harms' discounted by the Williams committee should be given a decisive role. Instead, legislative non-intervention should be premised on the right of every individual to 'moral independence'. Such a right should, like other rights (see chapter 14, below), 'trump' the achievement of social goals. It should be respected even if it could be shown that society's total welfare would be increased were it denied. It should not be restricted for any reason grounded in the belief that the life-style of porn-consumers is morally inferior to other life-styles.

The Williams committee's approach has been condemned, in the other direction, by some strands of feminist opinion. As we shall see in chapter 20, some feminists take issue with the whole idea of seeing topics such as pornography in terms of liberal-individualist rights. Some also deny that restrictions are only to be admitted if harm to assignable individuals can be proved. Whether or not there is a direct causal link between porn-consumption and rape, porn is itself a degradation and an affront to women.

Mill advanced the harm principle as a banner of individual liberty, but it appears to leave many questions unanswered: What is to count as harm? How is harm to be proved? In what circumstances is society in a paternalist relationship to the individual so that he may rightly be protected from himself? Furthermore, it cannot deal with fundamental issues such as who is to count as a person capable of suffering relevant harm. If the foetus or the deformed infant counts as a person, then depriving him of life involves the same kind of harm (loss of future satisfactions) as does painless homicide to any other human being. Consequently abortion and infanticide should be prohibited, unless that harm is out-weighed by the suffering caused to a woman who is forced to endure an unwanted pregnancy or to share a world with a deformed offspring. If they do not count as persons, their destruction is no 'harm' to them; but we still have to decide whether distress to fathers, as well as mothers, is a relevant harm. If it is not, abortion on demand and humane infanticide (on the mother's sole say-so) appear not to infringe the harm principle.

Is there any other basis on which someone who values individual liberty can draw the limits which such a belief ought to impose upon legal intervention? In his essay on 'The Enforcement of Morals', Devlin advanced what Basil Mitchell has called the 'social cohesion' argument.

Devlin argued that one of the essential elements of a society is a shared morality. Different societies have different moralities, and there is no way in which the legislature can or need choose between them. As it happens, he said, our own society's shared morality is derived from Christianity, even if Christian belief as such is no longer prevalent. If a society's shared morality is weakened, this has a tendency to lead to the destruction of the society itself. Even if an act which is wrong by the society's morality is committed in private and harms no one in the way of offence-to-decency, corruption or exploitation, its very practice weakens the shared morality and so may lead to a weakening of society. Individual freedom of choice is an important value, but it is outweighed by the overriding right of society to survive. No society can be expected to make provision for its own dissolution. Just as treason is punishable because it threatens society's existence, irrespective of the private moral opinions of the traitor; so, Devlin argues, society is entitled to punish any act which, according to popular opinion, is grossly immoral.

Devlin's view is that our society's morality is historically derived from Christianity; but he does not suggest that the way to discover whether any act is immoral is to consult Christian opinion. Indeed, it would be difficult for anyone engaged in rebutting Wolfenden-type programmes to make any such suggestion, since there has been no consensus among leading church figures about the morality or immorality of such matters as homosexuality or obscenity. Devlin himself seems highly suspicious of intellectuals as having any special right to speak on moral issues, whether they are churchmen or not. The Christian nature of society's morality is now beside the point. It should be enforced now, not because it is or was Christian, but because it is (so Devlin supposed) the shared morality of the majority. Hence, the person whose moral opinion is to be consulted is the man in the jury-box. In this respect, Devlin's views march in line with those of many other English judges. Since 1962, the courts have recognised an offence of 'conspiring to corrupt public morals', which gives an important role to jury moral opinion;[5] and the courts have held that the concept of 'dishonesty', employed by the Theft Act 1968, is not a legal term of art but something which the jury is to test by its own moral standards.[6]

'[T]he moral judgment of society must be something about which any 12 men or women drawn at random might after discussion be expected to be unanimous ... No society can do without intolerance, indignation and disgust; they are the forces behind the moral law, and indeed it can be argued that if they or something like them are

5   *Shaw v DPP* [1962] AC 20; *Knuller (Publishing, Printing and Promotions) Ltd v DPP* [1973] AC 435.
6   *R v Feely* [1973] QB 530; *R v Ghosh* [1982] QB 1053.

not present, the feelings of society cannot be weighty enough to deprive the individual of freedom of choice.'[7]

Devlin does not suggest that all popular morality is to be enforced. An act must be sufficiently grave as to be likely to cause a jury intolerance, indignation and disgust. Even then there may be grounds which make legal intervention undesirable. The law should be concerned with the minimum necessary for the preservation of society. There must always be a gap between the criminal and the moral law. The practical difficulty of enforcing any law must be taken into account and, as far as possible, privacy is to be respected. Despite the apparent drift of his original lecture, Devlin has since indicated that he is not in favour of punishing homosexual acts between consenting adults in private.

Dworkin argues that, even on the assumption that a society is entitled to enforce the moral opinions of the majority of its members, Devlin's test for what counts as a moral opinion is 'shocking and wrong'. We must, Dworkin claims, distinguish opinions which are supported by moral reasons from opinions based on 'prejudice', 'aversion', or 'rationalisations' (implausible propositions of fact). The conscientious legislator may take account of the former, even if the reasons are controversial, so long as they are sincerely and consistently invoked; but he must ignore the latter. It then becomes a question whether what someone claims to be her 'moral opinion' can be dismissed by her opponent as mere prejudice, aversion or rationalisation.

Take the topic of childless couples accepting the services of a surrogate mother to provide them with a baby. It might be difficult to condemn such a practice simply on the basis of Mill's harm principle. One could not interfere with the decisions of the adults who take part in the arrangement without substituting society's decision for their own choice about what is in their interests. Could the practice be said to 'harm' the child? That would mean that one's attention was focused on a person not yet in existence for whom one takes the decision that he or she would be better off never being born than to come into being as the result of a surrogacy agreement. The Surrogacy Arrangements Act 1985 criminalised commercial agencies which promote surrogacy arrangements. There are two ways of interpreting this event. Either it gave effect, in Devlinesque fashion, to popular revulsion about 'baby-selling' or 'rent-a-womb' transactions. Or it gave effect to the majority's opinion as to the balance of moral reasons. The latter interpretation may be supported by the fact that the enactment was preceeded by the report of the committee of inquiry into 'human fertilisation and embryology', chaired by Baroness Warnock.

7   *The Enforcement of Morals* pp 15, 17.

The foreword to the Warnock report is somewhat ambivalent about the distinction between 'feelings' and 'moral reasons'. It warns that 'moral indignation or accute uneasiness may often take the place of argument' (para 2). On the other hand, it rejects a strict utilitarian approach on the ground that the sort of moral questions with which the committee was concerned were 'by definition, questions that involve not only calculation of consequences but also strong sentiments with regard to the nature of the proposed activities themselves' (para 4). 'The question must ultimately be what kind of society can we praise and admire' (para 8).

The procedure actually adopted by the committee was to report arguments and sentiments presented to it by those it consulted, for or against any proposal, and then to announce its conclusion and recommendation. On this basis it concluded that artificial insemination, in vitro fertilisation, egg and embryo donations and (in the view of the majority) experimentation on human embryos should be permitted subject to a system of licensing and regulation; but that (in the view of the majority) surrogacy agencies, whether commercial or non-profit-making, should be brought within the scope of the criminal law. The ban should include even non-commercial agencies because, however willing the participants and however desirable the consequences, that people should treat others as means to their own ends in this way 'must also be liable to moral objections' (ch 8 para 17).

In Dworkin's terms, do you suppose that such 'moral objections' are based on moral reasons, or on prejudice, aversion and rationalisation? Or is Dworkin's distinction itself a philosopher's trick designed to rule arguments one disagrees with off-side?

Hart's criticism of Devlin's social cohesion argument is twofold. First, he denies that a society need have a shared morality in Devlin's sense. Hart believes that there is a morality which every society must have and indeed must embody in law. This is his 'minimum content of natural law' discussed in chapter 2, above. Every society must have rules restricting violence, theft and deception. This morality is common to all societies, although its detailed implementation varies. Apart from this minimum, a society need have no shared morality peculiar to itself. Our own society is pluralistic, especially in relation to sexual morality. Secondly, Hart argues, even supposing a society does have a shared morality peculiar to itself, there is no good reason to believe that its preservation is necessary to the survival of the society. The fact that people differ from the majority of their fellow citizens on matters of personal morality does not in any way indicate that they are likely to be less loyal citizens. Furthermore, moral experiment – the permitting of activities which the majority now regard as immoral – is positively beneficial. It is always possible that the majority may be wrong, and they will be able to make more informed judgments if they can see other people behaving in 'deviant' ways.

The debate raises some issues of fact; and also some issues about our perception of social bonding, which involve a subtle interplay between the facts we know and the conceptions of society we have. Is it the case that our society has a shared morality about certain kinds of activities such as surrogacy arrangements, incest, or bestiality? If the answer is no, then Hart seems to be right in his contention that not every society need have its own distinctive shared morality. Presumably, Hart would not deny that some societies have distinctive moralities of this sort, that some Muslim societies, for example, have a distinctive morality about the consumption of alcohol, and some Hindu societies a distinctive morality about killing cows.

If a society does have a shared and distinctive morality, does allowing deviant behaviour, as compared with repressing it by law, tend to the society's 'dissolution'? One can see that it might lead to a social change, in that one will have a society which is seen to be more diversified than would be one in which deviations were suppressed; and this would make changes in social behaviour possible in an open way. Those Arab countries which imprison European visitors who flout the local laws against drink could cite Devlin in support of what they do. The distinctively Muslim nature of their societies would be threatened if they tolerated such activities on the part of non-believers. Hart's answer would be that, if you define 'society' in terms of all its current morality, of course there is a 'change' if you tolerate deviation and the deviants persuade the majority. But that is not necessarily bad. It is not the same thing as a breakdown in society, a destruction or dissolution of it, so that Devlin's analogy with treason is inapposite. In the name of freedom, the western drinkers should be tolerated.

The crux of the disagreement about social cohesion turns on whether one believes in social contamination from laxness in one kind of standard to laxness in others. Does not enforcing conventional morals tend to laxness about paying taxes, to more shoplifting, to a general disregard for the claims which society makes upon us? It is common enough to hear complaints about 'decay in standards', in which all these things are bracketed together. No doubt, an apologist for prohibition laws in a Muslim state, or an apologist for restrictive legislation about sexual behaviour in a non-western country, would agree with this bracketing together, when he deplores 'western decadence'. Hart says that it is implicit in Devlin's social cohesion argument that we 'swallow our morality whole': relax part of it, and the rest is weakened. Whereas, he says, morality is not a 'seamless web'; we can reject part of it and adhere just as strongly to the rest. This is no more than an unproven assertion about human psychology and social bonding; and Devlin's view is an unproven counter-assertion. The disagreement is paralleled by one kind of disagreement about a duty to obey the law: between those who say that the moral man is free to decide in the case of each legal obligation whether it morally binds him, and those who say that, if we allow freedom to pick and choose, wrong choices will be made as well as good (see chapter 16, below).

Faced with such disagreements, one can only rely on such experience as one has, and on imaginative guesses about the nature of man and of societies. Imagine two neighbouring states, in both of which the overwhelming majority agree that eating pork is morally wrong, in both of which theft is punishable under the criminal law, but, whereas in Millhart land, eating pork is visited with no sanction, in Devlin land it is subject to a criminal fine. Says the Millhart parent, or schoolteacher, or university professor: 'Both eating pork and shoplifting are wrong, but we don't punish the former because it does no one (other than the actor) any harm. Harm is what matters when it comes to punishment. That is so because we believe in freedom.' Says his Devlin land equivalent: 'We punish all serious transgressions of morality, pork-eating and shoplifting included. Once allow people to think they have a right to choose, save where harm is involved, and who is to say that someone might not take the view that shoplifting does no 'harm'? Freedom is very well, but standards must be upheld.' Who is right?

Bibliography

Bayles M. D. 'Criminal Paternalism' in Pennock and Chapman (eds) *The Limits of Law* (1974)

Berlin I. 'Two Concepts of Liberty' in Miller (ed) *Liberty* (1991)

Devlin P. *The Enforcement of Morals* (1965)

Dworkin G. 'Paternalism' in Laslett and Fishkin (eds) *Philosophy, Politics and Society* (5th series, 1979)

Dworkin R. M *Taking Rights Seriously* (revised edn, 1978) ch 10
  –   *A Matter of Principle* (1985) ch 16

Feinberg J. *Harmless Wrongdoing* (1990)

Gavison R. *Issues in Contemporary Legal Philosophy* (1987), pt 3

George R. P. *Making Men Moral* (1993)

Hart H. L. A. *Law, Liberty and Morality* (1963)
  –   *Essays in Jurisprudence and Philosophy* (1983) ch 11

Hittinger R. 'The Hart/Devlin Debate Revisited' (1990) 35 Am J Jur 47

Hughes G. B. J. 'Morals and the Criminal Law' in Summers (ed) *Essays in Legal Philosophy* (1968)

Itzin C. (ed) *Pornography: Women, Violence and Civil Liberties* (1992)

MacCallum G. C. 'Negative and Positive Freedom' in Laslett, Runciman and Skinner (eds) *Philosophy, Politics and Society* (4th series, 1972)

Mill J. S. *On Liberty* in *Utilitarianism, Liberty, Representative Government* (1960)

Mitchell B. *Law, Morality, and Religion in a Secular Society* (1967)

Regan D. B. 'Justifications for Paternalism' in Pennock and Chapman (eds) *The Limits of Law* (1974)

Samek R. A. 'The Enforcement of Morals: a Basic Re- examination in its Historical Setting' (1971) 49 Can Bar Rev 188

Sartorius R. E. 'The Enforcement of Morality' (1972) 81 Yale LJ 891

Stephen J. F. *Liberty, Equality, Fraternity* (2nd edn, 1874)

Taylor C. 'What's Wrong with Negative Liberty?' in Ryan (ed) *The Idea of Freedom* (1979)

Warnock Committee: Report of the Committee of Inquiry into Human Fertilisation and Embryology (Cmnd 9314 (1984))

Williams Committee: Report of the Committee on Obscenity and Film Censorship (Cmnd 7772 (1979))

Wolfenden Committee: Report of the Committee on Homosexual Offences and Prostitution (Cmnd 247 (1957))

11 The morality of law and the rule of law

'Legality' and 'the rule of law' are parts of the currency of political debate. To say of a country that its officials observe legality, or that the rule of law is maintained, are expressions of approval. The mere word 'law' has an honorific ring. How is that to be squared with the positivist contention that law is one thing, good law another? Positivists like Hart, Kelsen and Austin tell us that a legal system exists if rules (norms, general commands) are effectively enforced. By that reckoning, there seems to be 'law' and 'legality' in racist and tyrannical regimes. Yet, in chapter 6, above, we noted the distress produced among commentators on the Rhodesian rebellion when Kelsen's theory seemed to lead to the conclusion that it had introduced a new legal system. Some people deny that there was legality or the rule of law in pre-democratic South Africa, pointing to provisions which allowed for detention without trial and alleging that no legal restraints were applied to the police. Others made the same accusation against the Soviet Union, instancing sham political trials in which constitutional safeguards were ignored, and the abuse of psychiatric medicine for the purpose of detaining political opponents. In the United Kingdom, governmental measures are from time to time criticised in the name of 'the rule of law' such as retrospective legislation in the field of taxation and immigration control, and selective withdrawal of subsidies by a government seeking to enforce pay policy.

Where an official acts contrary to some formally valid legal rule, a positivist account enables us to say that he is acting illegally. Nothing in positivist definitions commits us to saying that his action is morally wrong. Whether there is a moral duty to obey the law is controversial (see chapter 16, below). The question here is whether we can give some non-positivist account of law which will make sense of political criticisms not based on breach of formally valid provisions, but which yet appeal to 'legality' or 'the rule of law'. Such an account would show how 'law' itself has some necessary moral qualities.

One way of attacking positivism is to deny (as Dworkin does) that law is just a system of rules (see chapter 14, below). But that will not yield conclusions like: 'Nazi law was not "law" at all.' Another way is to adopt the higher-law view of some exponents of natural law, that any rule which contradicts natural law is a nullity (see chapter 2, above). This was the approach adopted in some of the post-war trials of Nazi supporters by German courts. But it requires a belief in higher law which not all share. Lon Fuller (1902-1978) suggested a third method of attacking positivism. He accepts that law is a system of rules and he does not ask us to believe in higher law.

His strategy is to fasten on the concept of 'purpose'. He uses it in three ways. First, we cannot know what any rule is unless we know what it was intended to achieve:

'We must in other words be sufficiently capable of putting ourselves in the position of those who drafted a rule to know what they thought "ought to be". It is in the light of this "ought" that we must decide what the rule "is".'[1]

Secondly, we cannot understand what a system of rules is if we try to comprehend it as a brute social fact. Instead, we must view it as a purposive enterprise: 'The enterprise of subjecting human conduct to the governance of rules.'[2] So conceived, we will appreciate that it cannot exist unless it has certain moral qualities.

Thirdly, it should be recognised that the definition of law is itself purposive. Positivists have usually purported to define merely to clarify terms. Often, however, there are concealed definitional purposes, such as promoting the ideals of peace and good order. Legal philosophy should, Fuller argues, deliberately define law so as to assist good legal enterprises:

'No one more than [the legal philosopher] runs the risk of forgetting what he is trying to do ... Though there are no doubt many permissible ways of defining the function of legal philosophy, I think the most useful is that which conceives of it as attempting to give a profitable and satisfying direction to the application of human energies in the law.'[3]

1   (1958) 71 Harv L Rev 630 at 666.
2   *The Morality of Law* pp 53, 74, 91, 106.
3   *The Law in Quest of Itself* p 2.

This third use of the concept of purpose raises the most fundamental of the questions in the positivist/non-positivist debate. Should we strive for two pictures, one of what law is, another of what law ought to be? Or do we want one picture only, in which moral colours can be shaded in? That depends on what one makes of all the theories and issues discussed in this book.

The first use of the concept of purpose raises issues about the nature of legal reasoning. Fuller accuses Hart of a 'pointer theory of meaning', since he seems to suggest that there are cases where rules (conceived as the meaning of words) clearly apply. The truth, argues Fuller, is that we can never apply a rule without attention to its purpose. Whether deductive reasoning is ever possible, and (when it is not) whether it is 'purpose' or some other criterion which guides decisions, are matters discussed in chapters 12 and 15, below. Even supposing Fuller is right, however, and that no rule can be understood or applied without reference to its purpose, it is not clear that this bridges the is/ought gulf in any way a positivist would wish to deny. The positivist view is that what the law ought to be, all things considered, is a different question from what the law is. We may have no doubt what the purpose of a rule is, while maintaining that the law ought to contain no such rule.

Fuller's most important contribution to jurisprudence turns on the second use of the concept of purpose. It is his claim that law, as a purposive enterprise, necessarily fulfils certain moral requirements. He lists eight principles of what he terms 'the inner morality of law', or 'principles of legality', or 'procedural natural law'. These are the requirements of generality, promulgation, non-retroactivity, clarity, non-contradiction, possibility of compliance, constancy through time, and congruence between official action and declared rule.

These requirements are contingently necessary if law is to work, given the definition of law as an 'enterprise of subjecting human conduct to the governance of rules'. First, some generality is essential because there must be rules. Second, the enterprise could not be forwarded without promulgation. Third, retroactivity would normally be pointless, especially in the sphere of criminal law, because of the brutal absurdity of today commanding someone to do something yesterday. Fuller denies, however, that laws imposing taxes on gains made at an earlier date are objectionable on the score of retroactivity, since their object is to raise revenue, to command payment now, not to control past conduct. He concedes also that judge-made retroactive law can be justified. All legal systems seek to govern conduct. Some also have a side-purpose of settling disputes and hence employ courts. In the latter, it may be necessary to allow courts retroactively to change rules. Here, the dispute-settlement function prevails over the conduct-governance function.

Fourth, rules, to achieve their object, must be clear – although they may incorporate standards whose content can be determined by reference to community and commercial mores (such as 'good faith', 'due care' or 'fairness'). Fifth, the requirement of non-contradiction has, Fuller says, nothing to do with the principles of logic. There is nothing contrary to logic in making a man do something and then punishing him for it. Non-contradiction, as a requirement of the law enterprise, outlaws incompatible provisions which, in the context of governing conduct by rules, could not together 'make sense'. Sixth, commanding the impossible is clearly inconsistent with the enterprise. This does not mean, however, that strict liability is never justified; for it can be viewed either as a tax on conduct, or as a way of directing people to adopt even higher standards of care than ordinary negligence rules require. Seventh, very frequent changes in the law must diminish the effectiveness of the enterprise.

Eighth, 'congruence between official action and declared rule' is a requirement upon which Fuller lays much stress, but which he does not define very clearly. It seems to mean two things: first, officials must themselves comply with rules which impose duties on them so that lawlessness by the police is an infringement of the requirement; secondly, law officers must require of citizens only that they (the citizens) observe rules imposing duties on them – so that the requirement is infringed when rules are misinterpreted.

Fuller demonstrates, by means of a parable about an incompetent king, that a system which failed totally by reference to any one of these criteria would not be 'law' at all. On the other hand, all legal systems fail by some of the criteria to some extent. They are not – except perhaps the publicity requirement – the subject of 'the morality of duty', but of 'the morality of aspiration'. That is, these principles of legality set ideals of excellence. They may, indeed, conflict. Fuller says that retroactivity may sometimes be justified in order to correct other failings, for instance, where a law was not properly publicised or could not in practice have been obeyed.

Total failure would mean that no law exists. Gross failure means that law exists only in a rudimentary form. This was the case in Nazi Germany, owing to the enactment of retrospective legislation to legalise government outrages, and the frequent reliance on secret legislation. To the extent that a governmental apparatus does not observe the internal morality of law, it is not true law.

Some of Fuller's critics take issue with him for making the existence of law a matter of degree, arguing that it does not make sense to say that a legal system relatively exists. If Fuller's criteria are applied, this issue might be thought to be merely verbal: does it matter whether we say that, by these criteria, a legal system is partially in operation, or that the legal system in operation is partially defective? On the other hand, there do appear to be contexts in which it is important to give a yes/no answer to the question: Is there (or was there) a legal system in existence? Day-to-day descriptive legal science may have to presuppose an answer to it – for example, when a lawyer is giving advice about 'the law' now in force in a territory, or when a comparative lawyer is seeking to show how bad the laws of country X are compared to those of country Y. The needs of descriptive legal science are, of course, the basis of positivist definitions of law. Even in the context of law-politics, we may need a yes/no answer. Fuller himself wished to deny that, in the context of an evil system, we have to choose between a duty to obey the law and other moral claims, and he was anxious to support the German courts who refused to recognise immoral Nazi laws. Would it not have been better, then, if he had stipulated, not relative existence, but a cut-off point? He could have said that a sufficiently gross departure from the principles of the internal morality of law means that no legal system exists, so that the usual moral claims of 'law' disappear, and courts passing judgment after the event can act on the basis that there was no 'legality'.

A more important criticism levelled at Fuller is that his criteria are not 'moral' at all. Granted that some compliance with them is necessary for law to work, no amount of compliance guarantees that the system has moral worth. Evil laws would be no less evil merely because they were general, well publicised, prospective, clear, consistent, capable of performance, permanent, and strictly upheld. Conversely, no failing by reference to Fuller's criteria is, his critics claim, in itself morally wrong. Fuller gives as an example of laws not meeting the clarity requirement those South African laws which discriminated against non-whites by reference to imprecise notions of racial classification. What about American laws which discriminate in favour of blacks? Those who consider the South African discrimination laws to be bad and the American reverse discrimination laws to be good do so by reference to moral considerations unconnected with any lack of clarity which, if it exists, is the same for both. All that Fuller has done is to set out criteria which must be met for a legal system to be effective. You might as well speak, argues Hart, of criteria for successful poisoning as the 'morality of poisoning'.[4]

Two issues must be distinguished. First, in so far as Fuller's eight 'principles of legality' are instrumental, are they necessarily an instrument of something good? Secondly, do they represent non-instrumental values? So far as the first question is concerned, Fuller argues, by reference to evidence of practices in tyrannical regimes, that bad aims are not achieved through the use of his principles. Tyrants do not find it expedient to make public their evil aims through the medium of promulgated general rules which are then consistently enforced; good rules are left on the books, but

4   (1965) 78 Harv L Rev 1281.

ignored by officials. His critics reply that, although this may often be true, there is no necessary connection. In pre-democratic South Africa, there were racist laws which were public and generally adhered to by officials; and they were no less objectionable for that. A lot here turns on what one makes of 'necessary' connection. Fuller has not established any logical, instrumental connection between his principles and substantive moral criteria; but if one's survey of the world's regimes suggests that evil aims are generally better advanced where principles of legality are infringed, one may conclude that insisting on these principles has a tendency towards achieving good.

The second issue raises the question of the inherent, as distinct from instrumental, value of the principles of legality; and that depends on the political value one ascribes to the rule-of-law ideal. In the revised edition of *The Morality of Law*, Fuller adds a new chapter in which he replies to his critics. Drawing on interactional social theory, he claims that they have misunderstood the nature of law, in that they have confused it with 'managerial direction'. Positivists, he says, think of law as a 'one-way projection of authority'. (Compare Raz's authority theory of law discussed in chapter 9, above.) An interactional view of law, on the other hand, reveals that it is a co-operative enterprise between legislator and citizen, each with reciprocal expectations, each with a role conceived in terms of 'the rule of law'. The confusion between law and managerial direction occurs because analogues of five of the principles of legality are relevant to efficient managerial control. A managerial authority must promulgate his wishes to his subordinates, and they must be reasonably clear, free from contradiction, possible of execution, and not changed so often as to frustrate the efforts of the subordinate to act on them. The requirements of generality and official congruence, however, are not essential to managerial control, and the issue of non-retroactivity will not arise. There is no need for a managerial authority to limit his own actions by reference to general rules, whereas the specific morality of their role does impose this limitation on lawful governments. It is this role-limitation which explains why retrospective legislation is sometimes resorted to; it provides a means of making what the government has already done conform to general rules. We may have more or less effective systems of managerial direction. Such systems approach more or less to 'legality' depending on how much they observe the inner morality of law, including the two crucial rule-of-law requirements, that prescriptions should be general, and that official action itself conforms to general prescriptions:

'[T]he existence of a relatively stable reciprocity of expectations between law-giver and subject is part of the very idea of a functioning legal order ... Though the principles of legality are in large measure interdependent, in distinguishing law from managerial direction the key principle is that I have described as "congruence between official action and declared rule".

Surely the very essence of the Rule of Law is that in acting upon the citizen ... a government will faithfully apply rules previously declared as those to be followed by the citizen and as being determinative of his rights and duties. If the Rule of Law does not mean this, it means nothing. Applying rules faithfully implies, in turn, that rules will take the form of general declarations; ... Law furnishes a base line for self-directed action, not a detailed set of instructions for accomplishing specific objectives.

The twin principles of generality and of faithful adherence by government to its own declared rules cannot be viewed as offering mere counsels of expediency.'[5]

Does this building in of the rule-of-law ideal into the definition of a legal system provide a satisfactory answer to our initial questions about some concept of law which would be serviceable in the language of political controversy? That depends, first, or whether one thinks that Fuller has provided an adequate characterisation of the rule of law; and, second, on how one sets this ideal alongside other political ideals. As to the first question, Fuller's list of principles does not include two things which some might think essential to the rule of law, namely, the need for independent courts, and the need for some monopolisation of force within a territory. Fuller indicates that the concept of a legal system is not to be so limited. He regards rules of non-state bodies, like schools and clubs, as legal systems. Such bodies plainly do not seek to monopolise force, and they need not employ courts. There is a common association between the ideas of 'the rule of law' or 'legality' and what in America is called 'due process' and in England 'the rules of natural justice'. Fuller says that where courts are used as a means for enforcing congruence between official action and declared rule, due process is a useful instrument. Others might claim that independent courts observing due process is of the essence of the rule of law.

What is the political value of the rule-of-law ideal? This stark question is one which Fuller does not confront. When not employed to condemn systems like the Nazis', Fuller's main use for his principles of legality is by way of recommending more sensitive legal craftsmanship. In *Anatomy of the Law*, he seeks to show that there are 'made' and 'implicit' elements (though in different degrees) in four forms of legal enterprise: enacted law, adjudicative law, law made by contracts, and customary law. All these forms of legal enterprise have their place, and those who handle them will do so better if they are conscious of both made and implicit elements. The

5   *The morality of law* pp 209-210.

main function of the principles of legality is to show what is implicit in enacted law.

The literature of political and social theory contains many answers to our stark question (see chapters 19 and 20, below). Here I shall cite three, which cross the political spectrum from right to left. On your right, you have the views of F. A. Hayek. He associates the rule-of-law ideal with an individualistic conception of liberty:

'Nothing distinguishes more clearly conditions in a free country from those in a country under arbitrary government than the observance in the former of the great principles known as the rule of law. Stripped of all technicalities this means that government in all its actions is bound by rules fixed and announced beforehand – rules which make it possible to foresee with fair certainty how the authority will use its coercive powers in given circumstances, and to plan one's individual affairs on the basis of this knowledge.'[6]

Hayek draws a distinction, similar to Fuller's, between law proper and the rules of an organisation. Law proper consists of 'rules of just conduct' which first evolved as custom and later became articulated by judges. They are typically represented by what is called 'lawyers' law', or 'private law' (including criminal law). They impose negative restraints upon people, only so far as necessary to preserve each man's free domain of life, limb and property. The ideal method of articulating such rules is exemplified by common law judges, before everything began to be ruined by Benthamite legal positivism.

Eighteenth century judges were, Hayek claims, aware that rules of just conduct evolve to meet evolutionary needs of society, and that their job was to declare them. They employed proper criteria of consistency, and not fallacious notions of purposive social engineering. The rule-of-law ideal requires that legislatures too must only lay down rules modelled on those of private law, that is, general rules of just conduct. The legislature has authority to amend existing judge-declared rules where, owing to fossilisation or change of economic background, they no longer reflect community standards of corrective justice. But it has no authority to make selective redistributions of resources in the interests of particular groups. Overall social planning can be shown to be based on misconceptions of the nature of science and a failure to appreciate the inevitable limits on human knowledge. The idea that such planning could be achieved through the medium of 'law' is the fault of the legal positivists. They confused the rules of governmental organisations ('public law'), with the rules of just conduct by calling both 'law'. They consequently failed to realise that true

6   *The Road to Serfdom* p 54.

law grows and is not made; and they failed to appreciate that the rule of
law requires that governmental managerial functions must not detract from
the maintenance of general rules of just conduct:

> 'Thus it came about that government assemblies, whose chief
> activities were of the kind which ought to be limited by law, became
> able to command whatever they pleased simply by calling their
> commands "laws".'[7]

In the early 1970s I attended a lecture at the London School of
Economics given by Professor Hayek, which had been advertised as 'The
Destruction of Liberalism by Logical Positivism'. Many philosophers
came only to hear, to their dismay, an announcement that there had been
an error in the notice: it should have read 'Legal' not 'Logical' Positivism.

Both Fuller and Hayek condemn legal positivism for its failure to
incorporate the rule-of-law ideal into the concept of law. But they differ
about what that ideal entails. For Fuller, it is co-operation between
government and governed in producing and implementing governance by
rules. For Hayek, it consists of abstention from creating new rules, other
than by analogous extension of those rules which have grown up.

For an approach representing the political centre, we may turn to J. N.
Shklar. She announces her commitment to liberal toleration, to a
recognition that there is no consensus about morals and politics in society
and to belief that we ought not to try to produce one. She seeks to expose
the preoccupation of lawyers with 'legalism', the view that ethical conduct
is a matter of rule-following. She claims that 'justice', the policy of
legalism, should be recognised for what it is: one particular 'ideology',
that is, one kind of political preference. Lawyers, she believes, do not
appreciate that governing conduct by rules is merely one kind of political
policy. Legal rules are devices for compromising conflicts in society, and
are to be compared with other political devices:

> 'Direct bargaining, splitting the difference, direct coercion, or
> propaganda not only compete with legalism, they also provide the
> conditions within which it exists socially.'[8]

She argues that, in some contexts (such as international relations), harm
may be done by insisting on legalism. She seeks to show that, in the trials
of war criminals at Nuremburg and Tokyo, there was a pretence of legalism
which was mere sham, since there were no pre-existing rules. It would
have been more frank to recognise these trials as the elimination of

7   *Rules and Order* p 130.
8   *Legalism* pp 105-106.

enemies, justified on political grounds. Nevertheless, although she begins by announcing that she is going to be controversial and to put legalism in its place, she seems to conclude that, from a liberal standpoint, legalism has a lot to be said for it:

> 'On the political level it is thus the manipulative state that is the real rival of the legalistic state, and the policy of inducement, whether by propaganda or by terror and related pressures, competes with the policy of legalism.'[9]

On the left stands R. M. Unger (who, as we saw in chapter 8, above, is a standard-bearer of the critical legal studies movement). For him the rule-of-law ideal is a failed attempt to legitimate domination in 'liberal' societies where the consensus of customary law has broken down, and no single individual or group is accorded the right to impose its will through bureaucratic law. The attempt fails because domination persists and is perceived as illegitimate:

> 'Thus, the very assumptions of the rule of law ideal appear to be falsified by the reality of life in liberal society. But, curiously, the reasons for the failure of this attempt to ensure the impersonality of power are the same as those that inspired the effort in the first place: the existence of a relatively open, partial rank order, and the accompanying disintegration of a self-legitimating consensus. The factors that make the search necessary also make its success impossible. The state, a supposedly neutral overseer of social conflict, is forever caught up in the antagonism of private interests and made the tool of one faction or another. Thus, in seeking to discipline and to justify the exercise of power, men are condemned to pursue an objective they are forbidden to reach. And this repeated disappointment accentuates still further the gap between the vision of the ideal and the experience of actuality.'[10]

Unger makes Marxist assumptions about society being comprised of antagonistic groups rather than competing individuals and about the psychology of alienation and domination. But he does not share the Marxist-historicist view that any particular outcome from our present impasse is inevitable. What he thinks would be desirable is a spiralling back to a new form of customary law. If real inequalities were eliminated, we might regain spontaneous conceptions of the rules of group life, without loss of freedom or loss of the ability to criticise current practices.

9   *Legalism* p 120.
10   *Law in Modern Society* p 181.

Thus, according to Hayek, the welfare state stands condemned by reference to the rule-of law ideal – or at least, all measures of social amelioration not formulated on the model of the rules of private law. According to Shklar, the ideal is merely a political device, to be considered along with others, for dealing with the permanent and desirable pluralism of a tolerant society; and it compares well with manipulative devices used in intolerant societies. For Unger, the ideal is a failed experiment; it masks, but can never hide, intolerable domination.

If one believes that some conception of the rule of law represents a political ideal worth pursuing, then one may praise or blame regimes and measures in terms of their 'legality'. To avoid misunderstanding, however, some way must be found for distinguishing such legal political critiques from employment of 'legality' in that other sense stressed by positivists, where it signifies merely that conduct accords with some formally valid rule. Which sense of 'legality' should we have in mind when we define law?

The answer may be that there is no single definition of 'law' or 'legal system' which will meet all our needs. The practising lawyer who merely provides information about 'the law' may mean no more than the rules in force at the time, and may use the words 'legal' and 'legality' solely with this conception in mind. But the political assessor who attributes 'legality' or 'the rule of law' to a system of law may presuppose a system which consists, not of rules, but of a complex of institutions. If that is right, Fuller's eight criteria are misleading in so far as they suggest that the inner morality of law is an attribute of rules. It is an attribute of institutions. Legislatures and courts fail to comply with the rule of law *if they operate with* rules which are not general, well publicised, prospective, clear, consistent, possible of performance, permanent, and strictly upheld. Reading the contents of a country's legal rules will often not help very much if we are asked to decide whether the rule of law flourishes there. Such a perusal cannot tell us whether the rules are strictly upheld; and information about institutional practices may convince us that the generality, clarity etc of the rules is mere window-dressing. Perhaps then positivists and Fuller passed each other in the dark without really colliding; for the former were concerned with law as the subject matter of descriptive legal science, and Fuller with law as a complex of political institutions.

Bibliography

Dworkin R. M. 'Philosophy, Morality and Law: Observations Prompted by Professor Fuller's Novel Claim' (1965) 113 U Pa L Rev 668
Friedmann W. *Law in a Changing Society* (2nd edn, 1972) ch 15
Fuller L. L. *The Law in Quest of Itself* (1940)

- 'Positivism and Fidelity to Law: a Reply to Professor Hart' (1958) 71 Harv L Rev 593
- *The Morality of Law* (revised edn, 1969)
- *Anatomy of the Law* (1971)

Hart H. L. A. 'Positivism and the Separation of Law and Morals' (1958) 71 Harv L Rev 593 (reprinted in *Essays in Jurisprudence and Philosophy* ch 2)
- 'Fuller's *The Morality of Law*' (1965) 78 Harv L Rev 1281 (reprinted in *Essays in Jurisprudence and Philosophy* ch 16)

Hayek F. A. *The Road to Serfdom* (1946) ch 6
- *The Constitution of Liberty* (1960) Pt 2
- *Law, Legislation and Liberty* vol I, *Rules and Order* (1973) chs 4-6

Jones H. W. 'The Rule of Law and the Welfare State' (1958) 58 Colum L Rev 143

Lyons D. *Ethics and the Rule of Law* (1984) ch 7
- *Moral Aspects of Legal Theory* ch 1

Marsh N. S. 'The Rule of Law as a Supra-national Concept' in Guest (ed) *Oxford Essays in Jurisprudence* (1961)

Murray J. E. et al 'The Morality of Law (a Symposium)' (1965) 10 Vill L Rev 631

Rawls J. *A Theory of Justice* (1972) pp 235-243

Raz J. *Ethics in the Public Domain* ch 16

Samek R. A. *The Legal Point of View* (1974) ch 10

Sartorius R. E. *Individual Conduct and Social Norms* (1975) ch 9

Shklar J. N. *Legalism* (1974)

Summers R. S. *Lon L Fuller* (1984)

Unger R. M. *Law in Modern Society* (1976) pp 66-68, 166-242

12 Statutory interpretation

The American jurist, J. C. Gray, was very fond of quoting the following words of Bishop Benjamin Hoadly, contained in a sermon delivered before the King in 1717:

> 'Nay, whoever hath an absolute authority to interpret any written or spoken laws, it is he who is truly the Law-giver to all intents and purposes, and not the person who first wrote or spoke them.'[1]

But that cannot be right, can it? Surely the judges are limited in their decisions by statutes, else why do we bother with parliaments and elections?

How should statutes be interpreted? This question has often been posed, but there has been no agreement about what sort of question it is. Is it a question of positive law? If so, one would expect to find the answer in one of the usual sources – a written constitution, a statute, or case law; and one would expect the answer to differ from one legal system to another. In some ways, this is true. English principles of statutory interpretation are often contrasted with those in the United States or in continental countries. On the other hand, there seems to be something about rules of interpretation which makes them not like other legal rules. For one thing they have to be formulated in terms of concepts which cannot be elucidated like other legal concepts. One comes across intractable notions like 'meaning', 'purpose' and 'legislative intent'. Such concepts might have a universal sense, the same for all legal systems. On the assumption that they do, juristic writers have treated statutory interpretation as a trans-systemic topic. But then again, critics call for reform in methods of

1   Gray *The Nature and Sources of the Law* pp 125, 172

statutory interpretation, suggesting that the needs which the law is supposed to serve could be better served by improved techniques or, more fundamentally, that our polity would be improved if our approach to interpretation embodied a rather different match between legislative and judicial power. Thus, the subject of statutory interpretation has something to do with particular canons, which differ from one system to another; something to do with universal concepts, which indicate that these canons have a special status different from that of ordinary legal rules; and something to do with improvable techniques, or alterable constitutional arrangements.

The English canons of interpretation are to be found in the decisions of the courts and are therefore part of English common law. They are notoriously difficult to formulate, for two reasons. First, one does not find with them, as with other settled common law rules, a match between a rule and a *ratio decidendi* of a case or a series of *rationes decidendi*. For the most part, judicial formulations of these canons are *obiter dicta*. Secondly, the *dicta* are often obscure and sometimes conflicting. The best one can do is to postulate formulations supported by the greatest possible weight of *dicta*. Such *dicta* invoke the 'ordinary' or 'natural' or 'plain' meaning of words, the 'absurd', 'inconvenient' or 'unreasonable' consequences of particular interpretations, and the 'purpose', 'object' or 'underlying scheme' of legislation. The first controversial issue is: how do canons of interpretation interrelate these matters of meaning, consequences and purpose? The traditional view has been that there are three rules: the literal (or plain meaning) rule, the golden rule, and the mischief rule. Willis argued that these were distinct rules and that a court invokes 'whichever of the rules produces a result which satisfies its sense of justice in the case before it'.[2] Similarly, Llewellyn claimed that canons of statutory construction 'hunt in pairs'.[3]

There have been innumerable statements by English judges over the past two centuries to the effect that, if the meaning of the words of a statute is plain, their job is simply to give effect to that plain meaning. One of the most frequently cited is that of Tindal CJ, when advising the House of Lords on the *Sussex Peerage Claim*:

> 'My Lords, the only rule for the construction of Acts of Parliament is, that they should be construed according to the intent of the Parliament which passed the Act. If the words of the statute are in themselves precise and unambiguous, then no more can be necessary than to expound those words in their natural and ordinary sense. The

---

2   (1938) 16 Can Bar Rev 1, 16.
3   (1950) 3 Vand L Rev 395.

words themselves alone do, in such a case, best declare the intention of the lawgiver.'[4]

This is a statement of the 'literal rule'. Other judicial pronouncements, however, indicate that even when words are clear, they should not be given effect if this will produce a result so outrageous that the legislature cannot have intended it. In the words of Lord Blackburn in *River Wright Comrs v Adamson*:

> 'I believe that it is not disputed that what Lord Wensleydale used to call the golden rule is right, viz, that we are to take the whole statute together, and construe it altogether, giving the words their ordinary signification, unless when so applied they produce an inconsistency, or an absurdity or inconvenience so great as to convince the court that the intention could not have been to use them in their ordinary signification, and to justify the court in putting on them some other signification, which, though less proper, is one which the court thinks the words will bear.'[5]

Both the literal and the golden rules emphasise fidelity to the legislature's words, although the latter makes some allowance for consequences. There was a time in English legal history when judges were far less preoccupied with the words of enactments. In the 16th century, 'purpose' was much more to the fore. The classic formulation of the mischief rule appears in the resolutions of the barons of the Exchequer in *Heydon's* case:

> 'And it was resolved by them, that for the sure and true interpretation of all statutes in general (be they penal or beneficial, restrictive or enlarging of the common law), four things are to be discerned and considered -
>
>   1st: What was the common law before the making of the Act.
>   2nd: What was the mischief and defect for which the common law did not provide.
>   3rd: What remedy the Parliament hath resolved and appointed to cure the disease of the Commonwealth. And
>   4th: The true reason of the remedy; and then the office of all the Judges is always to make such construction as shall suppress the mischief, and advance the remedy, and to suppress subtle inventions and evasions for continuance of the mischief, and *pro privato*

4   (1844) 11 Cl & Fin 85 at 143.
5   (1877) 2 App Cas 743 at 764-765.

commodo, and to add force and life to the cure and remedy, according to the true intent of the makers of the Act, *pro bono publico*.'[6]

Even in the 19th century, when fidelity to the written word was at its height, one comes across *dicta* which indicate that plain meaning falls, not merely before bad consequences, but also before achievement of legislative purpose. For example, Alderson B said in *A-G v Lockwood*:

> 'The rule of law, I take it, upon the construction of all statutes ... is whether they be penal or remedial, to construe them according to the plain, literal, and grammatical meaning of the words in which they are expressed, unless that construction leads to a plain and clear contradiction of the apparent purpose of the Act, or to some palpable and evident absurdity.'[7]

Twenty years ago Sir Rupert Cross attacked the traditional trilogy. He pointed to the stress which modern judges lay on 'context' in determining what the natural meaning of statutory language is. 'Context' includes the object of the legislation. Therefore, it is not a case of, first catch your plain meaning and then drop it in favour of consequences or purpose. Purpose and meaning are taken on board together in determining whether we have a plain case. If we do, we may still defer to consequences; provided we can find some secondary meaning. He recommended the following reformulations of the old rules:

> '(1) The judge must give effect to the ordinary or, where appropriate, the technical meaning of words in the general context of the statute; he must also determine the extent of general words with reference to that context.
> (2) If the judge considers that the application of the words in their ordinary sense would produce an absurd result which cannot reasonably be supposed to have been the intention of the legislature, he may apply them in any secondary meaning which they are capable of bearing.'[8]

The courts may look at the whole of the enacting part of the statute in which the provision is contained. In construing it and other statutes 'in pari materia', they must apply rules of grammar and, unless some contrary intention appears, they must give any word or phrase the meaning laid

---

6   (1584) 3 Co Rep 7a.
7   (1842) 9 M & W 378 at 398.
8   *Statutory Interpretation* (1976) p 43. The editors of the current edition repeat these rules in slightly different terms: Cross *Statutory Interpretation* (3rd edn) p 49.

down in the Interpretation Act 1978. They may give weight to three maxims of linguistic convention. The *eiusdem generis* rule indicates that a word of general scope following particular words standing for members of a class is to be construed as referring only to members of that class. The House of Lords has ruled that the 'class' must contain at least two members.[9] The *noscitur a sociis* maxim allows the meaning of any word to be known from words surrounding it. The maxim *expressio unius est exclusio alterius* permits one to infer that, where one of a natural collectivity of items is expressly mentioned, the legislature must have intended not to include the rest. The courts may look at the rest of the law, and take judicial notice of any facts of common knowledge when the statute was enacted. To resolve an 'ambiguity', they may look at the statute's long title, the preamble (if any), and its cross-headings and side-notes.

There are as well various presumptions of legislative intent, although their scope and strength is often unclear. They include presumptions against wide construction of penal legislation, against the imposition of criminal liability without fault, against changes in fixed rights, against deprivation of property without compensation, and against the conferral on officials of arbitrary discretion. There is also sometimes said to be a presumption against change in the common law, though, in so far as this goes beyond the presumptions just mentioned, it may mean no more than that the courts will employ established common law and equitable doctrines as guides to determine all doubtful legal issues. In interpreting both statutes and rules of common law, the courts have from time to time invoked the Bill of Rights of 1688 and, although the European Convention on Human Rights and Fundamental Freedoms has not been incorporated into English law, its provisions are frequently cited as persuasive authority.

Conventions and presumptions of this sort need have no counterparts in other jurisdictions. Any system which requires judges to interpret legislation must, however, address issues of meaning, purpose and consequences. What sense could be given to a constitutional injunction which read: 'The judges, in construing statutes, shall take no account of the meaning of words, or of conjectures as to the purpose of the enactment, or of the consequences of different constructions'?

On the basis of their comparative survey of nine countries, Neil MacCormick and Robert Summers suggest that arguments based on the ordinary meaning of words are a universal feature of statutory interpretation. Indeed, if there were no such thing as ordinary meaning, how does one explain the thousands of instances in daily life when enacted rules appear to be understood and applied by those to whom they are addressed? There are conventions shared by the speakers of a particular language without which all communication, including regulative

9   *Quazi v Quazi* [1980] AC 744.

communication, would be impossible. The recording of these changing conventions is the business of dictionary-compilers, and dictionaries are frequently invoked by judges. The conventions may relate to what the 'normal' speaker of a language may be expected to share with other members of her linguistic group; or they may be the conventions of a specialist sub-group, as when words are said to have a 'technical' signification.

On the other hand, the plain meaning of a provision 'in context' may not be successfully unearthed simply by taking each word, individually, and giving to it its dictionary meaning. Consider the following hoary old joke. A notice reads: 'Dogs must be carried on the escalator'. Jones stands fuming with vexation at the top of the escalator for half an hour until a friend comes along and asks him what the trouble is, and he replies: 'I'm waiting for a dog!' Note that Jones has not misunderstood any particular word contained in the notice. He has misinterpreted the obvious purpose of the directive. The story would never happen in real life – that is why it is a joke – because there is as complete a consensus about the purpose of that kind of regulation as there is about usage of particular words. Both are based on contingent conventions. It could have been the case that the English language had developed in such a way that the word ordinarily used to indicate the furry animal which barks was 'cat'. One could imagine a society in which dog-worship was such an entrenched cultural phenomenon that persons not carrying dogs would be excluded from public facilities. Legislative communication, in plain cases, takes place against a background of shared conventions about both linguistic usage and purposes of particular kinds of regulation. In that sense, as Fuller argued (see chapter 11, above), the meaning of words may be said to be dependent on how their author intends and knows they will be understood.

Notice, however, that, in the fanciful dog-carrying scenario, Jones's friend needs no special information about the persons who erected the notice or the circumstances which led them to do so in order to conclude that Jones has misunderstood the purpose of the directive. He is informed by what one might call 'bare context', that is, common knowledge about semantics and the point of familiar kinds of regulation. In real-life disputed questions of interpretation, 'context' may be more or less richly conceived. Sometimes, judges disagree about the 'ordinary', 'literal' or 'plain' meaning of legislative texts precisely because they differ as to the kinds and the significance of context which ought to be taken into account. English judges today generally proclaim that they espouse a 'purposive' approach to statutory interpretation, in contrast with one of 'strict', 'literal' or 'mechanical' construction. This appears to mean that one should pay more attention to non-linguistic facets of context than used to be done. For many practitioners, it is simply not possible to announce anything more precise. Lord Wilberforce said that statutory interpretation 'is what is nowadays popularly called a non-subject. I do not think that law reform can really grapple with it. It is a matter for educating the judges and practitioners and hoping that the work is better done.'[10]

This leaves hanging in the air the question of what it is that judges and practitioners are to be educated in, and the criteria by which one would know that 'the work is better done'. Lord Wilberforce seems to assume that interpretation is an arcane art, something that comes with worldly wisdom and experience.

Other judicial pronouncements pose isssues of statutory interpretation, alternatively, as questions of legal technique or of constitutional propriety. Witness the disagreement about gap-filling between Lord Denning and Lord Simonds in *Magor and St Mellons Rural District Council v Newport Corpn*. In the Court of Appeal Denning LJ said:

> 'We sit here to find out the intention of Parliament and of Ministers and carry it out, and we do this better by filling in the gaps and making sense of the enactment than by opening it up to destructive analysis.'[11]

This proposition was repudiated by Lord Simonds in the House of Lords:

> 'The duty of the court is to interpret the words that the legislature has used; those words may be ambiguous, but, even if they are, the power and duty of the court to travel outside them on a voyage of discovery are strictly limited.'[12]

He spoke of filling in gaps in a statute as a 'naked usurpation of the legislative function under the thin disguise of interpretation.'[13]

What, in principle, should we expect our judges to take notice of when 'bare context' leaves them a choice? It seems to be generally agreed that they should look sideways, to the rest of the statute and, where relevant, to the rest of the law. Beyond that, should they take a purely forward-looking approach, assess which interpretation would have best consequences, all things considered, and on that basis construct a legislative purpose? (In so doing they might have to adopt, one way or another, a choice between those conventionalist and realist approaches to questions of moral truth discussed in chapter 2, above.) Or should they look backwards and seek the minds of those who promoted the legislation and defer to their legislative purpose? Both practice and theory hover

10   277 HL Official Report (5th series) col 1254.
11   [1950] 2 All ER 1226 at 1236.
12   [1952] AC 189 at 191.
13   Ibid at 191.

between these poles just because there is no consensus as to the vexed question of what is meant by 'legislative intention'.

It is by no means clear what is meant when we speak of an individual as having an intention. A strict behaviourist would insist that this is no more than a figure of speech derived from judgments wherein we assess people's conduct in terms of adverbs like 'intentionally' or 'deliberately'. Let us assume, however, that the contrary dualistic position (uniformly assumed by systems of criminal law) is correct: apart from what people do, they may also have states of mind, including intentions. Then, it has frequently been objected, the expression 'legislative intention' cannot refer to some psychological state of affairs. Quite apart from the minority who vote against a measure, what possible reason would there be for supposing that the majority, often a fluctuating group at different stages of a bill's enactment, shared some common mental experience? Rupert Cross concluded that 'the intention of parliament' is 'not so much a description as a linguistic convenience'.[14]

The question then arises: for what is the conception convenient? Furthermore, if one took the view that courts ought to interpret ambiguous legislation as to them seemed best, why persist in this misleading intentionalist terminology?

There are various purposes which employment of 'legislative intention' might be thought to serve. It might signify only that, so far as statutory language is clear, it constitutes an authoritative source of law superior to judge-made law. Secondly, it might signify the assumption that any statute is to be read as a coherent and consistent whole, as though it were the product of a single, rational mind. Thirdly, it might indeed express a commitment to allow biographical information about what those involved in the legislative process actually had in mind a controlling role in the interpretation of statutes.

In support of the first view, one could argue that deference to enacted language is what is meant, and all that is meant, by giving effect to the legislature's intention – that language sets bounds within which judges reach their own conclusions as to how the language should be read. As Lord Reid said:

> 'We often say that we are looking for the intention of Parliament, but that is not quite accurate. We are seeking the meaning of the words which Parliament used. We are seeking not what Parliament meant but the true meaning of what they said.'[15]

---

14 *Statutory Interpretation* (1st edn) p 36.
15 *Black-Clawson International Ltd v Papierwerke Waldhorf-Aschaffenburg AG* [1975] AC 591 at 613.

Occasionally, however, courts add to, or subtract from, the language of statutes precisely on the ground that to do otherwise would have absurd consequences and therefore cannot have been what parliament intended. In one case, a statute made it an offence to obstruct members of the forces 'in the vicinity of' defence establishments. The defendant engaged in obstructive conduct within the perimeter of an airfield. He contended that he could not be said to be in its vicinity, since he was actually in it. The court held that the words 'in or' should be read in before the words 'in the vicinity of'.[16] In another case, a statute made it an offence for unlicensed sex establishments to provide entertainments 'which are not unlawful'. The defendant contended that he was not caught by this provision, since his entertainments were unlawful (constituting crimes of public indecency). The House of Lords held that the quoted words were the result of incompetent draftsmanship and should be treated as surplusage.[17]

Such cases may be invoked in support of the second understanding of 'legislative intention'. Parliament cannot be supposed to lay down two provisions which no rational person, whatever his objectives, could wish to be simultaneously observed. That would constitute the vice of incoherence. No-one could think it desirable to ban obstructions outside, but not inside, defence establishments (although anyone might, coherently, want both, or neither, banned). No-one would insist that sex establishments must obtain licences if they practice lawful entertainments, but that they should be excused if the entertainments transcend the bounds of the criminal law. No legislature ever supposes it requisite to enact: 'The provisions of this statute shall be read in such a way as to avoid logical contradiction or incoherence'. (In chapter 15, below, we consider whether non-contradiction and coherence are implicit in legal reasoning more generally.) If that were the only purpose served by the conception, then 'legislative intention' would serve only as a constructive metaphor to found the court's commitment to reading the statute as a whole.

On the third view, judges invoke 'legislative intention' because they take seriously the need to look backwards at the history of the legislative process which resulted in an enactment. They may do so either to determine the general objective of the act or even to decide what meaning to attribute to some particular term or phrase. The analogy with the intention of individuals is significant either if there are good grounds for supposing that the majority of those who voted for a measure had some objective or meaning in mind (the majoritarian model), or if there are reasons to conclude that a question of objective or meaning was delegated to some individual or committee (the agency model). Nothing about the concept

16   *Adler v George* [1964] 2 QB 7.
17   *McMonagle v Westminster City Council* [1990] 1 All ER 993.

prevents it from being employed in these ways. Whether it is so used depends on the judicial conventions prevalent in any particular jurisdiction.

In its report on statutory interpretation, the Law Commission expressed the view that if legislative intention 'is looked upon as a common agreement on the purposes of an enactment and a general understanding of the kind of situation at which it is aimed, to deny the existence of a legislative intention is to deny the existence of a legislative function.'[18] In the 1970s the question was raised whether legislation which conferred immunity on trade unions in respect of acts done 'in furtherance of a trade dispute' could apply to secondary picketing. The Court of Appeal ruled that parliament could not have intended the immunity to be so wide. The House of Lords reversed the Court of Appeal, holding that the parliament which passsed the legislation – that is, the Labour Party majority of that parliament – might well have taken the view that trade unions could be relied on not to abuse their immunity.[19]

It is well established in English law that government White Papers and the reports of law reform bodies may be taken into account when statutes are construed as evidence of the 'mischief' to which legislative reform was directed. References are also frequently made to the intention of the draftsman. The agency model of legislative intention has been given a further boost by the recent departure of the House of Lords, in *Pepper v Hart*[20], from the rule to which it had previously adhered which exluded citations of parliamentary proceedings as an aid to interpretation. The speeches of their Lordships also exhibit a familiar ambivalence over the notion of 'plain' or 'ordinary' meaning.

The case concerned income tax payable by masters at a private school in respect of reduced fees charged for the education of their sons at the school. The relevant legislation provided that the cost of such benefits should be assessable to tax and defined the cost of the benefit as 'the amount of any expense incurred in or in connection with its provision'. The Revenue contended that these words required the benefit to be calculated on an average cost basis, that is by dividing the total cost of running the school by the number of pupils. The taxpayers submitted that it should be calculated on a marginal cost basis, that is by taking into account the extra expense incurred by the school in admitting their sons, which would obviously be much lower. When the appeal first came before the House of Lords the majority favoured reading the statutory language as importing average cost; but it was drawn to their attention that the report of parliamentary proceedings in *Hansard* showed that the very question

18 Law Com No 21, para 55.
19 *Express Newspapers Ltd v Macshane* [1980] 1 All ER 65; *Duport Steels Ltd v Sirs* [1980] 1 All ER 529.
20 [1993] AC 593.

of how the words would apply to schoolmasters in these circumstances had been raised, and that the Financial Secretary to the Treasury, during the committee stage of the bill, had made it clear that they imported only a marginal cost assessment, and that nothing further had been said about the matter before the Finance Bill was voted on. Accordingly, a special panel of seven Law Lords was convened to enable argument to be presented about whether the rule excluding reference to parliamentary proceedings (repeatedly affirmed in previous decisions of the House) should now be modified, so bringing English practice into line with that which prevailed in other common law jurisdictions. On that rehearing six out of the seven agreed that the rule should be changed and that the statements of the Financial Secretary were admissible evidence of parliament's intention. Accordingly, they found for the taxpayers even though most of them adhered to the view that, without this evidence, a 'natural' reading of the language, read in the context of the rest of the statute, would have entailed a decision for the Revenue.

Lord Mackay L. C. alone dissented from the view that the exclusionary rule should be modified (while allowing the taxpayers' appeal on what he took to be the most natural reading of the statutory language). He did so on the ground of increased litigation costs if counsel arguing points of interpretation had always to search *Hansard* just in case there might be relevant evidence of parliament's intention. (As Lord Chancellor, he was also the government minister one of whose primary concerns has been reduction in soaring expense incurred by litigants.) That had been the sole ground on which the Law Commission had also supported the exclusionary rule. Neither the Law Commission nor Lord Mackay denied that parliamentary proceedings might be relevant evidence of parliament's intention.

The other six members of the House maintained that the experience of other jurisdictions did not suggest that practical objections of this sort were so serious, that modern techniques of electronic retrieval made *Hansard* more readily available to advisers, that the principle of giving effect to the 'true intention' of the legislature conformed to the 'purposive approach' to the construction of statutes, and that the modification they proposed would mean that it would be necessary to consult *Hansard* only in exceptional cases. The modified rule they laid down was this. Reference to parliamentary materials should be permitted where (a) the legislation is ambiguous or obscure or the literal meaning leads to an absurdity; (b) the material relied on consists of statements by a minister or other promoter of the bill which led to the enactment of the legislation, together if necessary with such other parliamentary material as is needed to understand such statements and their effect; (c) the statements relied on are clear. They seemed to have assumed that these restrictions would make citations of *Hansard* rare. If so, they were mistaken. *Pepper v Hart* has been invoked on many occasions in the past four years.

The principle justifying the relaxation of the previous exclusionary rule was bluntly stated by Lord Browne-Wilkinson, speaking for the majority, as follows:

'The court cannot attach a meaning to words which they cannot bear, but if the words are capable of bearing more than one meaning why should not Parliament's true intention be enforced rather than thwarted?'[21]

He continued:

'The question then arises whether it is right to attribute to Parliament as a whole the same intention as that repeatedly voiced by the Financial Secretary. In my judgment it is.'[22]

It is to be noted that Lord Browne-Wilkinson both found that the 'literal meaning' of the words was as contended for by the revenue so that (without referring to *Hansard*) the case would have had to be decided against the taxpayers, but also that the words were 'ambiguous or obscure' in that they were capable of bearing two meanings (the reference to *Hansard* decisively showing that parliament intended the one favourable to the taxpayers). That was because he and four of his colleagues understood the 'literal', 'primary', or 'plain' meaning of the provision by taking into account, as relevant 'context', only the rest of the statute and were not willing to give weight to other considerations, such as the possible 'unfairness' which might result if employees' in-house benefits were always taxed on an average cost basis.

Statutory interpretation, in England as elsewhere, is the subject of evolving and ill-defined judicial conventions which, one way or another, ring the changes on conceptions of meaning, legislative intention and 'context'. There is a widespread view that there are outer limits fixed by the boundary of the possible meanings of legislated words – although even that, as we have seen, does not prevent English courts from reading words in or out in exceptional cases where coherent construction is thought to require it. Meaning itself, I have suggested, is dependent both on linguistic conventions and on conventions about obvious purposes of particular kinds of regulation. Perhaps the outer boundary coincides with what I have called 'bare context'. More detailed contextual information of various kinds may

21 Ibid at p 635.
22 Ibid at p 642.

be thought to entail a 'plain' or 'literal' reading. The modern approach is said to be 'purposive' rather than one of 'strict construction'; but it is far from clear whether that means merely that the court takes a wider view of 'context', or that the court itself constructs the 'purpose' which it thinks best, or that the 'purpose' of the legislature is a function of that which persons involved in the legislative process had in mind. The Lords in *Pepper v Hart* understood 'purposive' in this latter sense. But perhaps more typical is a recent decision in which it had to be decided whether storing digital images on a computer connected to the internet amounted to possession of copies of indecent photographs of children 'with a view to their being distributed or shown'. The defendant argued that it did not, since the technology was unknown when the relevant legislation was passed. The Court of Appeal upheld his conviction saying, both, that it was not necessary to go beyond the statutory language in order to discover 'the intention of Parliament', and that it approved the 'purposive approach' taken by the trial judge.[23]

At any rate sometimes 'legislative intention' has a relatively close analogy to the ordinary sense of 'intention', in that the courts defer to what some flesh-and-blood person or group actually sought to achieve or even to the meaning such persons intended words to bear.

As we shall see in chapter 14, below, much legal and social theory has nowadays taken an 'interpretive turn' most particularly the rights thesis of Ronald Dworkin. In that context, 'interpretation' has a quite different sense from that given to it by lawyers in relation to statutory interpretation. Nevertheless, such theorising purports to subsume, along with other features of the understanding and application of law such as precedent and constitutional adjudication, all the mix of issues reviewed in the present chapter.

Bibliography

Bennion F. *Statutory Interpretation* (2nd edn, 1992)
Bix B. *Law, Language and Legal Determinacy* (1993) ch 3
Cross R. *Statutory Interpretation* (3rd edn by John Bell and Sir George Engle, 1995)
Dickerson F. R. *The Interpretation and Application of Statutes* (1975)
Driedger E. A. *The Construction of Statutes* (2nd edn, 1983)
Endicott T. 'Linguistic Indeterminacy' (1996) 16 OJLS 667
Eskridge W. *Dynamic Statutory Interpretation* (1994)
Evans J. *Statutory Interpretation: Problems of Communication* (1988)
Frankfurter F. 'Some Reflections on the Reading of Statutes' (1947) 47 Colum L Rev 527

---

23   *R v Fellows* (1996) Times, 3 October.

Hurst J. W. *Dealing with Statutes* (1982)

Kress K. 'Legal Indeterminacy' (1989) 77 Calif L Rev 283

Landis J. 'A Note on Statutory Interpretation' (1930) 43 Harv L Rev 886

Law Commission *The Interpretation of Statutes* (Law Com. No 21 (1969))

Llewellyn K. N. 'Remarks on the Theory of Appellate Decision' (1950) 3 Vand L Rev 395

MacCullum G. C. 'Legislative Intent' in Summers (ed) *Essays in Legal Philosophy* (1968)

MacCormick D. N. and Summers R. S. *Interpreting Statutes: A Comparative Survey (1991)*

Marmor A. *Interpretation and Legal Theory* (1992) ch 8

Marmor A. (ed) *Law and Interpretation* (1995) pt 3

Paton G. W. *A Textbook of Jurisprudence* (4th edn, 1972) ch 9

Payne J. J. 'The Intention of the Legislature in the Interpretation of Statutes' (1956) CLP 96

Radin M. 'Statutory Interpretation' (1930) 43 Harv L Rev 863

Schauer F. (ed) *Law and Language* (1993) pt 3

Summers R. S. and Marshall G. 'The Argument From Ordinary Meaning in Statutory Interpretation' (1992) 43 NILQ 213

Willis J. 'Statutory Interpretation in a Nutshell' (1938) 16 Can Bar Rev 1

13 Precedent

In all modern legal systems, judicial precedents are relevant information for anyone seeking to find the law. It is a peculiarity of common law systems that a ruling of a superior court in a single case may be deferred to as the sole source for a legal proposition. Furthermore, there have emerged precedent rules in accordance with which the *ratio decidendi* (reason for deciding) of a superior court must be applied by courts lower in a judicial hierarchy; and even a final appellate court will not depart from a prior decision of its own without giving reasons why the earlier ruling was mistaken or has become outdated.

Contrast the attitude of the European Court of Justice to its own decisions. It has been urged by Mr Advocate-General Lagrange that the court should accept the strict French view of *Res Judicata*, according to which no decision of any court can have regulatory effect for anyone who was not a party to the litigation.[1] In consequence, while a line of cases may be partially constitutive of the law, the court may simply ignore a single decision of its own whose ruling it now disapproves: 'better for a court to interpret the law, the purpose for which it is set up, than to interpret its own decisions'.[2]

This chapter will explore some of the conceptual and constitutional problems associated with common law conceptions of precedent, taking English law as an example.

---

1   *Case 28/62 Da Costa en Schaake v Nederlandse Belasting Administratie* (1963) ECR 31 at 40-46.
2   Ibid at p 44.

1   Precedent rules and the common law

Precedent rules may be divided into those whose operation depends on a strict distinction between *ratio decidendi* and *obiter dicta* (statements by the way) and more general practice rules not dependent on this distinction. The former answer the question: which courts bind which (within a particular judicial hierarchy)?

In England, the House of Lords is not bound by its own decisions, though it will not depart from them merely because they are 'wrong'. All inferior courts and tribunals are bound by decisions of the House of Lords. The Court of Appeal is bound by its own decisions, with certain exceptions mentioned below. All courts below the Court of Appeal are bound by its decisions. Divisional courts, when hearing appeals from magistrates' courts by way of case stated, are bound by their own decisions, with the same exceptions as those applicable to the Court of Appeal; and inferior courts and tribunals are bound by decisions of divisional courts. Judges of the High Court are not strictly bound by each other's decisions, but will not depart from them unless convinced that they were mistaken; and divisional courts exercising merely supervisory (as distinct from appellate) jurisdiction are nowadays regarded as being in the same position vis a vis their own prior decisions as judges of the High Court. In relation to all these rules, 'decision' refers to the *ratio decidendi* of a case. Where there is more than one *ratio decidendi*, each is binding.

Precedent rules evolve, and are sometimes the subject of dramatic change. In the 19th century the House of Lords came to regard itself as absolutely bound by its own past decisions. This rule was finally confirmed by the decision in *London Tramways v London County Council*[3]. In 1966 the law lords issued a joint 'Practice Statement' sweeping this rule aside. It read as follows:

> 'Their lordships regard the use of precedent as an indispensable foundation upon which to decide what is the law and its application to individual cases. It provides at least some degree of certainty upon which individuals can rely in the conduct of their affairs, as well as a basis for orderly development of legal rules.
>
> Their lordships nevertheless recognise that too rigid adherence to precedent may lead to injustice in a particular case and also unduly restrict the proper development of the law. They propose therefore to modify their present practice and, while treating former decisions of this House as normally binding, to depart from a previous decision when it appears right to do so.
>
> In this connection they will bear in mind the danger of disturbing retrospectively the basis on which contracts, settlements of property

---

3   [1898] AC 375.

and fiscal arrangements have been entered into and also the especial need for certainty as to the criminal law.

This announcement is not intended to affect the use of precedent elsewhere than in this House.'[4]

When the House issues a ruling which changes what was previously considered to be settled law, it may be difficult to determine whether it does so by virtue of its practice statement power. To be certain that it does, it must appear that their Lordships recognise that the law prior to its present decision had the authority of a *ratio decidendi* of the House which, up to this moment, was binding on all inferior courts; and that the House now lays down that the proposition founded on that earlier *ratio decidendi* is no longer to be treated as part of English law. Take the decision in *Pepper v Hart* (discussed at the end of the last chapter), where the House modified the rule excluding citation of parliamentary materials in interpreting statutes. Important *dicta* in previous decisions of the House were disavowed, but the Practice Statement was not specifically invoked in their Lordships' speeches. On this basis I would suggest that, to date, there have been only nine instances in which the House of Lords has unequivocally exercised its new power.[5] The decisions relate to important questions of criminal, tort, commercial, tax, immigration and remedial law. They cover questions of common law and of statutory construction. The age of decisions overruled or 'departed from' ranges from 80 years to one year. Predictions by some commentators that the Practice Statement would make little practical difference have been falsified.

On the other hand, it has frequently been re-asserted that the House will not depart from a decision merely because the present panel considers it to be 'wrong'. Factors cited in this connection include the possibility that people have justifiably relied on the impugned decision in arranging their affairs; that parliament has enacted legislation on the assumption that the law was as stated in the earlier case; or that the issue is moot (that is, on the facts of the instant case, it would make no difference to the outcome whether the impugned ruling were part of the law or not). But the most important consideration concerns no new reasons. The arguments in the earlier case may not have considered all the implications of the proposition there affirmed, or overlooked some important principle of constitutional or common law or the significance of a law reform proposal

4　[1966] 3 All ER 77.
5　*The Johanna Oldendorff* [1974] AC 479; *Miliangos v George Frank (Textiles) Ltd* [1976] AC 443; *Dick v Burgh of Falkirk* [1976] SLTR 21; *Vestey v IRC* [1980] AC 1148; *R v Secretary of State for the Home Department, ex p Khawaja* [1984] AC 74; *R v Shivpuri* [1987] AC 1; *R v Howe* [1987] AC 417; *Murphy v Brentwood District Council* [1991] 1 AC 398; *Westdeutsche Landesbank Girozentrale v Islington London Borough Council* [1996] AC 669.

which preceeded legislation. There may have been some material change in circumstances relevant to the issue in question (such as alteration in the fluctuation of exchange rates). Or there was a failure to advert to undesirable consequences which subsequent experience has brought to light. But if all the reasons now in play are the same as those considered in the case under review, then the earlier decision was 'wrong' in the sense that the judges on the former occasion balanced the reasons in a way which the present court would not have done. In that event, were the present panel to overrule the earlier decision, why should not a third panel revert to the impressionistic assessment of reasons reached in the first case? The primary objection to overruling a decision merely because it was 'wrong' (in the sense of misbalancing a particular set of reasons) is finality. In the words of Lord Wilberforce, spoken in a decision in 1977 where the House was asked to depart from a decision on a question of tax law which had been ruled against the taxpayer in 1966 by a three to two majority of the House:

> 'My Lords, two points are clear. (1) Although counsel for the taxpayer developed his argument with freshness and vigour, it became clear that there was no contention advanced or which could be advanced by him which was not before this House in 1966 ... (2) There has been no change of circumstance ... such as would call for or justify a review of the 1966 decision ...
>
> There is therefore nothing left to the taxpayer but to contend, as it frankly does, that the 1966 decision is wrong. This contention means, when interpreted, that three or more of your Lordships ought to take the view which appealed then to the minority.
>
> My Lords, in my firm opinion, the 1966 Practice Statement was never intended to allow and should not be considered to allow such a course. Nothing could be more undesirable, in fact, than to permit litigants, after a decision has been given by this House with all appearance of finality, to return to this House in the hope that a differently constituted committee might be persuaded to take the view which its predecessors rejected. True that the earlier decision was by a majority: I say nothing as to its correctness or as to the validity of the reasoning by which it was supported. That there were two eminently possible views is shown by the support for each by at any rate two members of the House. But doubtful issues have to be resolved and the law knows no better way of resolving them than by the considered majority opinion of the ultimate tribunal. It requires much more than doubts as to the correctness of such opinion to justify departing from it.'[6]

6   *Fitzleet Estates Ltd v Cherry* [1977] 3 All ER 996 at 999.

No-new-reasons is not, however, an absolute constraint on overruling. An ultimate appellate court may take the view that 'finality' is less important than its duty to give effect to what it sees to be the correct answer to some fundamental moral principle. In *Lynch v DPP for Northern Ireland*[7] the House of Lords (departing from the traditional common law) ruled that the defence of duress might sometimes be invoked on a charge of murder. Twelve years later in *R v Howe*[8] the House overruled that decision. They did so primarily on the ground that the traditional common law view (that no-one could plead such a defence as an excuse for killing an innocent person) was morally sound, or at least could not be shown to be wrong. (Compare the discussion of 'moral truth' in chapter 2, above.)

Similarly, in common law jurisdictions with written constitutions final appellate courts may hold that 'wrongness' is all that is needed to justify overruling their own decisions. Finality falls before their obligation to expound the 'true' interpretation of the constitution. In the United States, it seems, constitutional 'verity' is the overriding consideration, as when the Supreme Court ruled that requiring school-children to salute the flag was unconstitutional and overruled a three-year-old decision of its own to the contrary.[9] In an important Australian constitutional case, involving the respective rights of the states and of the federal Commonwealth, judges were divided as to whether (in deciding to overrule) finality was more important than the duty to declare a judge's perception of constitutional truth.[10]

Is there any sound reason for holding that intermediate appellate courts should be bound by their own decisions to any greater extent than final appellate courts are? Most academic commentators on the position of the English Court of Appeal have answered that question in the negative. Where there is extant an erroneous Court of Appeal ruling it would (they maintain) save the trouble and expense of an appeal to the House of Lords if the Court of Appeal could itself overrule it. The contrary view, which was vigorously re-asserted by the House of Lords in *Davis v Johnson*[11], is that finality would be gravely threatened if the Court of Appeal were not strictly bound by its own decisions. Since the Court of Appeal sits in panels of only three (sometimes only two[12]), it could easily happen that a point might be ruled one way in case A, another in case B, and the view accepted

7   [1975] AC 653.
8   [1987] AC 417.
9   *West Virginia State Board of Education v Barnette* 319 US 624 (1943) at 640 *per* Jackson J, delivering the majority opinion.
10 *Queensland v The Commonwealth* [1978] 139 CLR 585.
11 [1979] AC 264.
12 It has now been settled that Court of Appeal rulings are equally authoritative whether issued by a court of three or of two judges: *Langley v North West Water Authority* [1991] 3 All ER 610.

in case A be re-instated in case C, and so on. Accordingly, in *Davis v Johnson* the House of Lords insisted that the only exceptions to the rule that the Court of Appeal is bound by its own decisions are the three enunciated by Lord Greene MR in *Young v Bristol Aeroplane Co Ltd*[13]: first, where there are two conflicting decisions of the Court of Appeal; second, where a decision of the Court of Appeal cannot stand with a decision of the House of Lords; third, where a decision of the Court of Appeal was made *per incuriam*.

This formula is repeated frequently. However, the second exception has been extended to instances in which a prior decision of the House of Lords was 'misunderstood' in an earlier Court of Appeal case; and the *per incuriam* exception has been said to include, not merely instances where some relevant authority was overlooked, but also 'rare and exceptional' cases in which a decision of the Court of Appeal involved a 'manifest slip or error'. There are, furthermore, occasional invocations of exceptions other than the three listed in *Young*'s case.[14]

It is much more difficult to formulate precedent rules which do not depend, for their direct operation, upon the distinction between *ratio decidendi* and *obiter dicta*. They are connected with the elusive notion of 'the common law'. The case law of any particular jurisdiction may be regarded as settled by a weight of judicial *dicta* and juristic writings, even though one cannot point to a binding *ratio decidendi* of the local ultimate court. On the other hand, the common law 'evolves' and its content varies from one jurisdiction to another, so that one might expect there to be as many common laws as there are common law jurisdictions. Yet, I suggest, there are five elements which contribute to a supra-jurisdictional conception of the common law.

First, it is accepted that the final appellate court of any common law jurisdiction has a power, by a single ruling, to change what was previously supposed to be settled case law. Opinions persistently fluctuate, however, about when it is proper to exercise this power.

Secondly, whatever divergence there may be in the substantive rules and principles, there are common conceptual building bricks. These include an array of estates and interests in land, the hazy classification of obligations into contractual, tortious, fiduciary and restitutionary, a limited conception of juristic personality, the institution of the trust, and the division between legal and equitable remedies and between legal and beneficial ownership.

Thirdly, each jurisdiction accepts a corpus of written sources as the basis of doctrinal reasoning. That was not always so. There was a time when 'the common law' was constituted by a consensus of opinion among

13 [1944] KB 718.
14 See Cross and Harris *Precedent in English Law* (4th edn) pp 143-56.

a tiny coterie of professional lawyers in London. That notion has long since disappeared. Nowadays each jurisdiction has a distinct tradition which shapes the persuasive authority to be accorded common law sources. At the root of each tradition are institutional writers like Coke, Hale and Blackstone and the early concept-forming English decisions. These sources are today largely submerged by recent local authorities. In common law jurisdictions in the United States pre-eminence is given to decisions within the particular jurisdiction and those in other American jurisdictions and the various collations by commentators in restatements of the law. Modern English decisions still constitute a large portion of accepted sources in commonwealth jurisdictions and, until very recently, some judges (in England and elsewhere) adhered to the view that uniformity within commonwealth common law countries was desirable for its own sake. The demise of this 'imperial' conception of the common law has been hastened by the abolition, in most jurisdictions, of the right to appeal to the Privy Council. In English courts, including the House of Lords, citation is frequently made of decisions from all common law jurisdictions, commonwealth and American.

Fourthly, there is the idea of 'policy'. Superior courts should adapt the common law in the light of changing social conditions. 'Local circumstances' are invoked as a ground for diversity of approach. Sometimes this refers to perceived differences in social life. More often, it signals that judicial impressions about the best balance to be struck between competing interests may differ, and local judges ought to have the last say.

Finally, the formative period of the common law exhibited a largely individualistic conception of man's place in society. Most common law rules and principles concern the relations of the individual to the state (his rights and liberties), or the duties and responsibilities between one person and another. As to the former, one of the complaints against the British imperial government contained in the American Declaration of Independence of 1776 was that it had flouted common law liberties – in particular, it had failed to impose the common law on the recently conquered territory in Quebec. Common law constitutional rights and liberties provide the basis for judicial control of the executive and, by virtue of the presumptions of legislative intention mentioned in the last chapter, they constrain the style even of sovereign legislation. In the words of Lord Simon of Glaisdale: 'Since the common law, as so often, favours the freedom of the individual, the rules enjoining strict construction of a penal statute or of a provision in derogation of liberty ... merely re-inforce the presumption against change in the common law.'[15] The practical significance of this constitutional side of the common law diminishes in

15   *Tzu Tsai Cheng v Governor of Pentonville Prison* [1973] AC 931 at 954.

importance once its values are embodied in bills of rights with a status superior to legislation; and, even in the United Kingdom, citations of the European Convention of Human Rights now compete with those of common law presumptions.

Individualistic notions of duty and responsibility are constantly revised in all common law jurisdictions. In the words of Lord Diplock: 'The common law would not have survived in any of those countries which have adopted it, if it did not reflect the changing norms of the particular society of which it is the basic legal system. ... Despite the unifying effect of that inheritance upon the concept of man's legal duty to his neighbour, it does not follow that the development of the social norms in each of the inheritor countries has been identical or will become so.'[16]

In chapter 20, below, we shall consider the recent 'communitarian' attack on individualist (liberal) conceptions of justice. It should be pointed out, however, that, although individualism can be seen as its primary touchstone, the notion of the 'common law' is sufficiently flexible to incorporate what might be called 'communitarian' values. As we saw in chapter 10, above, courts may restrict individual liberty in the light of their own views of shared social morality. A more unusual instance of community-centred reasoning by a common law court is represented by the decision of the Australian High Court in the *Mabo* case.[17] The court held that justice, and therefore Australian common law, required that aboriginal groups in possession of land at the date of European settlement be recognised as communal owners of their land. The court swept aside all the case law which had assumed that title to land in Australia could derive only from legislation or Crown grant.

What precedent rules emerge from these fluid conceptions of 'the common law'? If counsel cites the opinion of any court, whether from a common law jurisdiction or not, one would not expect a judge to retort: 'I don't wish to hear that! Kindly shut the book!' If, however, the citation is from a common law jurisdiction, it represents an instance of what the cited court thought could be done with the power, and within the conceptual constraints, of common law adjudication. Hence it is a model which may be followed and so constitutes 'persuasive' authority. A judge should not dismiss *in limine* any pronoucement by any court on the question at hand; but there is a positive obligation to give more weight to a common law ruling, not because common law judges are especially learned or foresighted, but because they are working within the same (constitutionally and conceptually variable) version of the rule of law. Of course, all that may change as our legal system becomes more and more integrated within that of the European Union.

16 *Cassell and Co Ltd v Broome* [1972] AC 1027 at 1127.
17 *Mabo v State of Queensland (No 2)* [1992] 175 CLR 1.

What weight the court should give to judicial statements (not being binding *rationes decidendi*) is said to depend on many factors: the position in the judicial hierarchy of the judge whose statement it is; the individual reputation of the judge; the number of judges who concurred with what was said, if the court was an appellate court; whether the point was properly argued; how relevant it was to the issue upon which the case turned that is, how far it fell short of being *ratio*; whether it was in line with other judicial statements in other cases. The circumstances vary from *dicta* unanimously approved, after elaborate argument, in the House of Lords (which because of some peculiarity of the litigation were not strictly necessary to the decision), to an off-the-cuff and totally *obiter* observation of a judge at first instance.

When is case law so settled that not even the House of Lords can (or, at any rate, should) alter it? It is generally assumed that there are such areas, but notoriously difficult to formulate criteria for recognising them.

Apart from the longevity of a particular rule, principle or classification, three factors may be taken into account: justified reliance on it; its interconnection with other parts of the law; and limitations on the ability of judges, as distinct from the legislature, to consider all the issues involved in changing the law.

The House of Lords recently reviewed the centuries-old common law principle that a contract to confer exclusive possession of land for an indefinite period cannot constitute a lease. In the view of the majority of their Lordships, no reason had been or could be advanced in favour of this conceptual dogma. Nevertheless, they declined to expunge it solely on the ground that parties to transactions might have relied on it.[18]

Another recent case[19] concerned the rule that a child between the ages of 10 and 14 is presumed '*doli incapax*' – as well as proving that the child intentionally committed some act prohibited by the criminal law, the prosecution must lead evidence sufficient to establish (beyond reasonable doubt) that the child knew that what he was doing was seriously wrong (not just 'naughty'). The rule goes back to the era when criminal convictions entailed draconian consequences. The Divisional Court held the rule to be outdated and that it should no longer be regarded as good law. The House of Lords reversed the Divisional Court and upheld the *doli incapax* rule, while recognising that its application might entail anomalies and even absurdities. They did so because parliament had frequently enacted legislation in this general area without altering the rule; and a change in a fundamental doctrine of this kind might not cohere with the rest of the law so as to provide finality and certainty.

---

18   *Prudential Assurance Co Ltd v London Residuary Body* [1992] 2 AC 386.
19   *C v DPP* [1996] 1 AC 1.

The third of the factors mentioned above raises the issue of 'justiciability'. Are there questions of policy which judges are not equipped to settle? Some House of Lords' decisions suggest that there are. For example, in *Morgans v Launchbury*[20] the House held that it was not for the courts to develop the common law of torts in such a way as to make the owner of a family car vicariously responsible for the negligent driving of other members of the family or their guests. This step should not be taken because its full impact, especially in the field of accident insurance, could only be assessed after wide-ranging enquiries had been carried out and judges were not equipped to make them. Nevertheless, if their Lordships are faced with a question where they have no doubt as to the morally sound answer, they will not wait for parliament. Since the 17th century it had been accepted as a rule of English common law that a husband could not be guilty of raping his wife. Some exceptions were introduced earlier in this century, and five years ago the House of Lords unanimously abolished the rule.[21] They had no doubt that the marital rape exemption was now completely out of line with contemporary opinion as well as with their own view of justice.

2 The status of precedent rules

Rules governing the authority of precedents are not contained in statutes and, in common law jurisdictions with written constitutions, they are not generally set out in the constitution. In one sense, therefore, they are rules of the common law. On the other hand, they do not deal directly with the rights and obligations of citizens, but with the law-declaring or law-creating powers of judges. In that sense, they are constitutional rules. They have evolved, and are evolving, as judicial practices change; so they are also rules of judicial practice or judicial custom. Which label one gives to them may affect one's view as to whether, and by what means, they can be changed.

The logical status and constitutional propriety of the 1966 Practice Statement have been the subject of controversy among academic commentators. As to logic, it has been claimed that the statement, like the ruling in the *London Tramways* case, suffers from the vice of self-reference. Both were 'decisions' of the House of Lords purporting to lay down that decisions of the House are or are not binding. Sir Rupert Cross rebutted this allegation. He pointed out that it was premised on the false assumption that statements about rules of precedent constitute, as well as refer to, *rationes decidendi*. Once it is recognised that the distinction between *ratio* and *obiter dicta* does not apply to such statements, it can

---

20 [1973] AC 127.
21 *R v R* [1992] AC 599.

be seen that they are not 'decisions' in the same sense that *rationes decidendi* laying down substantive rules of law are 'decisions'.[22] Precedent rules confer authority on the *rationes decidendi* of various courts; but they derive their own authority from a judicial practice which transcends the outcome of particular cases. To the extent that this practice is settled, they are conceived of as imposing obligations which are as peremptory as any other legal obligations; and in that sense they constitute rules of law. However, they dwell at a higher level than ordinary rules of substantive case law whose authenticity they control. There is consequently no problem of self-reference.

The constitutional propriety of the Practice Statement presents more difficulty. Cross asked rhetorically: 'But can there be any doubt that it owes its validity to the inherent power of any court to regulate its own practice?'[23] Yet, as we have seen in the case of the English Court of Appeal, a judicial custom may emerge which denies to a particular court the unilateral power to change rules governing the circumstances in which it is bound by its own decisions. The word 'practice' may be misleading here. There is no doubt that any superior court may from time to time issue 'practice directions' concerning procedural steps to be taken in litigation before that court. It does not follow, merely because precedent rules derive from judicial 'practice', that they also embody a similar freedom.

Precedent rules, like anything else deriving from a tradition, may evolve. The English rules have changed over the centuries and on many points of detail they are constantly subject to modification. Whenever a judge is faced with some debatable feature of the rules, he may express a view about what the tradition requires, having regard to past instances reported in the cases and his conception of the underlying purpose of the rule in question. Such a pronouncement, if it subsequently meets with general approval by other judges, may have the effect of crystallising a particular rule or exception. Lord Greene's pronouncement in *Young v Bristol Aeroplane Co Ltd* is an example. It is another thing if judges claim overtly to bring about, at a stroke, a change in rules which have hitherto been treated as settled.

There would appear to be two plausible views of the 'constitutionality' of what was done in 1966. They diverge on a historical understanding of how judges and other lawyers conceived of the tradition at that time. On one view, it was accepted that the House of Lords was bound by its own decisions only until such time as the House should, by some appropriate announcement, change the rule – that is, the practice then accepted

---

22 'The House of Lords and the Rules of Precedent', in Hacker and Raz (eds) *Law, Morality, and Society*.
23 Ibid p 157.

included a power in the House to bring about the change. The second view is that in 1966 the rule was so firmly rooted that it could only be changed by legislation – there was no power in the House itself to alter it. On the former view, the Practice Statement constituted an exercise of an enduring constitutional power which might be invoked again in the future by the House of Lords to abolish or introduce other precedent rules. On the latter view, the Practice Statement was issued without constitutional authority and so amounted to a technical 'revolution' analogous to what Kelsen described as a change in basic norm (see chapter 6, above).

A similar mixture of conceptual and constitutional issues may be involved whenever one looks back to some constitutional turning-point introduced by judicial initiative, such as the announcement by the US Supreme Court nearly 200 years ago that it had power to rule legislation unconstitutional.[24]

Of more perennial concern to the status of precedent rules is the problem of identifying *rationes decidendi*. Unless there is some procedure whereby the binding part of a decision can be isolated, what is the point of having rules about which courts bind which? Much of the difficulty stems from the interrelation of the words in the judge's opinion and the facts of the case as criteria for identifying the *ratio*. It is frequently asserted that the judge's words are not the rule of the case. A judgment is not to be treated like a statute. It is permissible for a later judge – one who is notionally 'bound' by the decision of the earlier judge – to reformulate the rule for which the earlier case is authority in his (the later judge's) words. He will be justified in doing that if the formulation appearing in the earlier judgment was not based on the facts of the case. This is an inherent limitation on any doctrine of *stare decisis*. No precedential system could contemplate that a judge, however elevated in the court hierarchy, could say: 'I conclude this issue of labour law as follows ... and while I'm at it, I lay down the following general rule for the law of wills ...'. On the other hand, there would be no point in having precedent rules which required courts to follow earlier cases only when the facts are identical to those of the present case. The facts are never literally 'the same'. Apart from this tension between judicial words and reported facts, many other difficulties have been noted. How does one identify the *ratio decidendi* of an appellate court when judges who concur in the result differ as to their reasons? How does one account for the practice of seeking the *ratio decidendi* of a particular case, in the light of prior and subsequent cases? Should one elucidate what the judge was saying by reference to other evidence one has about that particular judge's views? Does it matter if the judge's statement was not strictly necessary to his decision, in the

---

24 *Marbury v Madison* 32 1 Cranch 137 (1803).

sense that there are grounds for thinking the same order would have been made without it?

Problems such as these were among the considerations which influenced the American realists in their sceptical approach towards legal rules in general (see chapter 8, above). However, against all these difficulties must be set the fact that judges frequently announce themselves to be bound by previous decisions, sometimes with regret. Are these all instances of self-delusion?

The views of two writers illustrate a 'stick to the facts' approach, on the one hand, and a 'stick to the reasons' approach on the other. A. L. Goodhart suggested that the *ratio decidendi* of a case is to be found by adding the facts which the judge treated as material to the conclusion he drew: where material facts A, B and C obtain, a defendant is liable. This provides a rule which a later judge can apply and, given a lower status in the judicial hierarchy, is bound to apply in any case in which the same material facts, and no other material facts, occur. Goodhart says that the facts of person, time, place, kind and amount are, on their face, 'immaterial'. This suggests that his 'material facts' are different in kind from brute facts, being generalisations from them – like the 'fact' that the defendant could have foreseen damage to the plaintiff. Being this sort of generalisation, they can recur. Further, Goodhart states that potentially material facts are not to be treated as such by the later judge if the earlier judge regarded them as immaterial. In finding the *ratio decidendi*, he is to have regard only to those facts which the earlier judge expressly or impliedly treated as material. In the event of a decision comprising several judgments the *ratio decidendi* is given by adding all the facts treated as material in all the majority judgments to the conclusion.

Rupert Cross offered the following definition:

'The *ratio decidendi* of a case is any rule of law expressly or impliedly treated by the judge as a necessary step in reaching his conclusion, having regard to the line of reasoning adopted by him, or a necessary part of his direction to the jury.'[25]

Cross's definition is not apt to meet those cases where no reasons are given or can be implied (which are few), nor those appellate cases where there is no majority agreement on reasons (which are all too frequent). On the other hand, Goodhart's test may be thought inappropriate in those appellate cases where all concur in the result, a majority concur in reasons, but a minority give different reasons; why should we then, as his test requires, add up all the facts which majority and minority treated as material in order to get our rule? More importantly, Goodhart's test may

25   Cross and Harris *Precedent in English Law* (4th edn) p 72.

be difficult to apply even to a single judgment when the 'facts' treated by the judge as material can be characterised in different ways – for example, at different levels of generality. If we say the facts are to be characterised just as the judge described them, are we not back to citing his reasons as *ratio*? How do we know that the fact treated as material in *Donoghue v Stevenson*[26] was not a decomposed snail in a ginger beer bottle, rather than a potentially harmful product, unless we look at the underlying reasoning of the decision?

The general objection to both these approaches to the identification of *rationes decidendi* is that they do not adequately deal with the time-honoured common law technique of 'distinguishing'. A judge may say of an earlier decision, binding within the hierarchy, that what was said there does not bind him since the case is distinguishable on its facts. By this he may mean either that the true *ratio* of the earlier case is narrower than the earlier judge's statement; or, where the statement imposed some limiting condition which the present judge wishes to discard, that the true *ratio* is wider than the earlier statement. Since all agree that the words of the earlier judge are not to be treated like the words of a legislature, this distinguishing process appears to be unstoppable by any definition of *ratio decidendi*. The later judge can always say that, notwithstanding his language, the earlier judge did not really intend certain facts to be treated as material; or that the reasons which the judge really treated as a necessary step in reaching his conclusion are not properly expressed in the language he chose to employ.

If judges can always distinguish, should we regard the so-called 'rules of precedent' as not normative at all, but mere descriptions of practices in which judges purport to follow decisions? Or should we say that the obligations which the rules impose are real, but not quite what they appear to be on their surface? Perhaps what a judge has to do in regard to a binding decision is to find some rule for which the case is authority and, having found it, see whether it applies to his case – an obligation, that is, to follow or distinguish. If that is right, then there is only a difference of degree between what judges, under a system of strict *stare decisis*, are required to do in relation to decisions above them in the hierarchy, and what the doctrine of precedent requires common law judges to do in relation to all court decisions. In both cases, the judge must listen to what the earlier judge said; in both, he must give some weight, which may include working out why the earlier judge said what he did. But under strict *stare decisis*, he must go further and formulate some rule for which the earlier case is authority. That rule may be based on the case in isolation, or it may take into account treatment of the case in subsequent decisions. It is of no consequence whether we use the expression *ratio decidendi* to stand for

26   [1932] AC 562.

the rule attributed to a case read on its own, or the rule for which, given subsequent legal development, the case is now authority.

If, however, the obligation is merely to formulate some rule (follow or distinguish), how does that account for judges being bound *malgré soi*? Perhaps there are limits to the plausibly acceptable rules for which a case can be said to stand; and when a judge follows reluctantly, what he means is that, although a certain rule formulation is (all things considered) undesirable, he cannot think of any better rule for which the binding case could be said to stand.

Another perennial problem about the status of precedent rules is the extent to which they empower judges to change the law with retroactive effect; and, if so, whether this constitutes unjust treatment both of the parties to the litigation and of those who have ordered their affairs on the faith of an overruled precedent. One suggested solution is for the courts (or at any rate the House of Lords) to assume a power of prospective overruling. The court would apply the old precedent in the instant case, but would announce that, for the future, a new rule is going to be followed. If precedent rules are mere 'practice rules', perhaps the law lords could issue a new practice statement introducing the device. If they are conceived of as 'common law' rules, then persuasive authority for adopting prospective overruling can be provided from another common law jurisdiction. In the United States, the technique has been employed in recent years, especially where a court has wanted to introduce a new rule nullifying exercises of administrative power without upsetting arrangements previously made by virtue of such power, or a new rule nullifying procedures in criminal prosecutions where it has not wished all past convictions obtained by such procedures to be upset.

The argument for introducing prospective overruling is that the courts would then be more free to make new law without deleterious effects on those who have relied on the old law. There are many arguments against. If the new rule was totally prospective, litigants would have no incentive to argue for it since it would not affect the outcome of their case. If the new rule were made partially prospective – for example if it were applied to the present case but not to past transactions which were not the subject of the current litigation – where precisely is the cut-off point to be? Should the new rule apply to other litigation which has been commenced but not yet reached resolution? A more fundamental objection is one based on formal justice. If the court decides that such and such a rule is the correct rule, how can it be just to apply it to rights and duties of parties in the future but not to the present parties? Whether judges 'declare' or 'create' the law, like cases should be treated alike.

When the House of Lords abolished the marital rape exemption, husbands convicted of rape or attempted rape argued before the European Court of Human Rights that the decision was a violation of Article 7(1) of the Human Rights Convention: 'No one shall be held guilty of any criminal offence on account of any act or omission which did not constitute a criminal offence under national or international law at the time when it was committed'. Not surprisingly, their application was unanimously dismissed.[27] It was held that progressive development of the criminal law through judicial law-making was a well entrenched and necessary part of the tradition of the United Kingdom and of other Convention states.

There are two aspects of the doctrine of precedent which can be cited in favour, not so much of a change in our precedent rules, but of overall codification of the common law. First, one of the unarticulated assumptions of common law jurisidictions is, as we have seen, that all precedents must be considered. The burden might be diminished if we made a fresh start with a code. Second, since *rationes decidendi* cannot be unambiguously identified, the law would be made more determinate if embodied in a code. These were among the considerations which led Bentham to condemn the common law and advocate codification, and they have been voiced again by enthusiastic supporters of the injunction laid upon the Law Commissions by s 3 of the Law Commissions Act 1965, to 'take and keep under review all the law with a view to its systematic development and reform, including in particular the codification of such law'. The opposite view is that, while particular reforms and even codifications of particular areas may be desirable, the common law as a whole is best left to evolutionary development, the doctrine of precedent providing the right balance between certainty and flexibility.

General questions about certainty, flexibility, judicial activism or restraint, and specific questions about the merits of prospective overruling and codification, require us to examine assumptions about the nature of legal reasoning in general, about the proper interaction between statutory interpretation and the evolution of case law, and whether or not there is an ideal model of what settling legal issues ought to be like. To these questions we turn in the next two chapters.

Bibliography

Cross R. 'The House of Lords and the Rules of Precedent' in Hacker and Raz (eds) *Law, Morality, and Society* (1977)
–   'The Ratio Decidendi of a Plurality of Speeches in the House of Lords' (1977) 93 LQR 378
Cross R. and Harris J. W. *Precedent in English Law* (4th edn, 1991)
Douglas W. O 'Stare Decisis' (1949) 49 Colum L Rev 735
Fitzgerald P. J. *Salmond on Jurisprudence* (12th edn, 1966) ch 5
Fuller L. L. *Anatomy of the Law* (1971) pp. 120-156

27   *S W v UK, C R v UK* (1995) Times, 5 December.

Goldstein L. 'Four Alleged Paradoxes in Legal Reasoning' (1979) 38 CLJ
    373
Goldstein L. (ed) *Precedent in Law* (1987)
Goodhart A. L. 'Determining the Ratio Decidendi of a Case' in Goodhart
    Essays in Jurisprudence and the Common Law (1931)
  –   'Precedent in English and Continental Law' (1934) 50 LQR 40
Hahlo H. R. 'Codifying the Common Law: Protracted Gestation' (1975)
    38 MLR 23
Harris J. W. 'Towards Principles of Overruling – When Should a Final
    Court of Appeal Second Guess?' (1990) 10 OJLS 135
  –   'The Privy Council and the Common Law' (1990) 106 LQR 574
Hicks J. C. 'The Liar Paradox in Legal Reasoning' (1971) 29 CLJ 275
Lyons D. *Moral Aspects of Legal Theory* (1991) ch 5
MacCormick D. N. 'Can Stare Decisis be Abolished?' (1966) Jur Rev 196
Marshall G. 'Justiciability' in Guest (ed) *Oxford Essays in Jurisprudence*
    (1961)
Nicol A. G. L. 'Prospective Overruling: a New Device for English Courts'
    (1976) 39 MLR 542
Perry S. R. 'Judicial Obligation, Precedent and the Common Law' (1987)
    7 OJLS 215
Radin M. 'Case Law and Stare Decisis: Concerning Prajudizienrecht in
    Amerika' (1933) 33 Colum L Rev 199
Raz J. *The Authority of Law* (1979) ch 10
Rickett C. E. F. 'Precedent in the Court of Appeal' (1980) 43 MLR 136
Sartorius R. E. 'The Doctrine of Precedent and the Problem of Relevance'
    (1967) 53 ARSP 343
Simpson A. W. B. 'The Ratio Decidendi of a Case and the Doctrine of
    Binding Precedent' in Guest (ed) *Oxford Essays in Jurisprudence*
    (1961)
  –   'The Common Law and Legal Theory' in Simpson (ed) *Oxford
    Essays in Jurisprudence* (2nd series, 1973)
Stone J. *Precedent and Law* (1985)

14 Dworkin's rights thesis

We have seen that, according to positivist accounts of the nature of law, 'what the law is' is always potentially different from 'what the law ought to be'. The opposite contention of natural lawyers appeared easily dismissed by reference to professional practice. When lawyers give information about the law, or apply the law, they often complain about its contents; they show no readiness to trace its validity back to a moral basis. If asked to justify an assertion about the law, they cite authority, not reason; precedents and statutes, not treatises about justice or the good life.

On the other hand, listen to a professor of law being interviewed on radio or television about the law on some controversial aspect of industrial relations or racial discrimination. You may find it difficult to draw a line dividing those sentences in which he says what the law is, from those in which he says what it ought to be: 'The Act says ... and it's clear that Parliament must have intended ... after all, the reactions of the TUC make it plain how absurd it would be if any other view were taken ... so my answer to your question is, yes, the law does require that ...'.

Furthermore, as we saw in the last chapter, precedents are regarded as authority for rules, yet no one has been able to devise a logically watertight procedure for deriving any rule from any case. Judges justify holding that a rule formulated in one way is the correct proposition for which an earlier case stands as authority, by reasons which look rather like arguments about what the law ought to be: 'I cannot accept counsel's contention. It seems to me incredible to suppose that Doodle J had the sort of situation I am confronted with in mind when he said ... and that accordingly his language must be read in a narrower sense. To my mind, the law laid down in *Alph v Bloggs* is as follows: ...'.

Controversial cases, then, and perhaps most cases turning on the interpretation of judge-made law, challenge the positivist claim about 'is' and 'ought' in law. On the other hand, it seems implausible to say that the law is always what it ought to be, that all law is good law; for are there not countless instances where what the law requires is only too clear to its vocal critics? Sometimes, what the law is has a clear answer by reference to authority, and then many may claim that it is bad and ought to be changed. But sometimes the law is uncertain, and disputants will argue for what it is on the basis of what it ought to be.

One solution to the problem is the cynical solution of the realists and the critical legal studies movement, discussed in chapter 8, above. But as we saw, their kind of cynicism is ultimately stultifying of conventional legal argument and legal reform. If the law is simply anything the judge cares to say it is, how is an advocate supposed to argue, and a judge justify, any decision? And what is the point of Parliament laying down new rules about anything, if they do not have a clear range of application?

If there is clear law and argued law, and neither is a sham, the clear law can be good or bad, but the argued law appears to be law only if its goodness is accepted. How are we to understand the relation between the two? Does the one deserve more political allegiance than the other? Do judges apply the one and choose the other? If judges do choose the law in controversial cases, is that something democrats can accept? If they do not choose the law in such cases, how do they find it?

Professor R. M. Dworkin seeks to answer such questions by means of his rights thesis. Discovery of law in all cases requires 'constructive interpretation', that is the morally soundest statements about the rights of citizens which will fit the legal materials. Law does not consist of the prescriptions which the authorities have laid down; it consists of the best politics which will fit such prescriptions. Law is not something we give information about. It is something we argue about.

1   The interpretive turn

Dworkin's anti-positivist theory has evolved in three phases. He began by mounting an attack on 'The Model of Rules'.[1] Taking Hart as an exemplary target, Dworkin denounced the idea that law consists of a system of rules whose legal status is settled by their 'pedigree' and which authorise judges to exercise discretion in all cases which they do not regulate. That was a distorted picture of law because it overlooked non-rule standards – 'principles' and 'policies'. Principles were especially important because of the role they played in judicial reasoning. Judges invoke them when the law is controversial. They do not announce that, since a question is not clearly covered by some rule, they have the power to decide what the law ought to be – that is, to exercise 'discretion' in a

1   *Taking Rights Seriously* chs 2 and 3.

strong sense. (He recognised that they have discretion in two 'weak' senses: their decisions settle the case; and they must apply their own judgments in reaching their conclusions.) Furthermore, such principles are regarded as 'legal', in part, because of their substantive moral and political content. They are not treated as parts of the law merely by virtue of some master test, such as Hart's rule of recognition. There is, in consequence, no line to be drawn (as the positivists supposed) between law and morality.

At this phase, Dworkin also maintained that principles differ from rules in logical type. Whereas rules apply in an all-or-nothing fashion (either they are valid and dispose of the question, or they are invalid and contribute nothing), principles have a dimension of 'weight'. A principle will be taken into account, but may be overridden by other considerations. If it is overridden, it still survives as a principle.

In the postscript to the second edition of *The Concept of Law*, Hart acknowledges that he should have given more attention to principles; but he insists that their membership of a legal system can be tested by a master rule ('pedigree'), so that they do not threaten the distinction between law and morality. (As we saw in chapter 9, above, Hart espoused 'soft positivism' – the law might, but need not, incorporate substantive moral standards.) Hart also denies that principles differ from rules in logical type. The difference is one of degree: rules, if valid, have more conclusive force than principles do; but either standard may be overridden.

Dworkin's later writings do not repeat his initial claim that principles differ from rules by virtue of the weight/validity distinction. It is not his view that the law consists of discrete, individuated standards, among which 'rules' and 'principles' are distinguishable types. He now speaks of 'arguments of principle', that is, propositions of political morality which affirm the existence of rights. His insistence that judges do not exercise a discretion to create law whenever issues are not regulated by valid rules is, however, a persistent feature of his attack on positivism. He expressed this view most dramatically in an essay in which he challenged the popular belief that there could be difficult legal questions as to which there is 'No Right Answer'.[2]

The second phase of Dworkin's attack on positivism appeared in his essay on 'Hard Cases'.[3] There he introduced the reader to a super-human judge named Hercules. Hercules would not merely take non-rule standards, including ones derived from substantive morality, into account when occasion required. He would construct a political theory which best justifies the entire body of law and, in its light, he would produce the right answer to any case coming before him, however 'hard' it might seem. Hercules's approach to the law is holistic. His theory encompasses the

2   Reprinted in *A Matter of Principle* ch 5. See also *Taking Rights Seriously* ch 13.
3   Reprinted in *Taking Rights Seriously* ch 4.

constitution, statutes and case law of his jurisdiction. He interprets all this material in the light of the best politics. In reaching any particular decision, he moves to and fro between the extant legal materials and arguments of political morality until he achieves an appropriate 'fit' which will settle the question whether the plaintiff does or does not have a right to win.

The third phase is represented by Dworkin's book *Law's Empire*, and subsequent essays. This work subsumes Hercules's holism under a more general idea of 'constructive interpretation'. Lawyers commonly speak of 'interpretation' when they have in mind a search for the intention of some authority which enacted a text, such as a statute or a constitution, or the intentions of parties to a contract or of testators or people who make settlements of property. This 'speaker's meaning' concept of interpretation is not what Dworkin has in mind. He suggests that, in the case of various social practices and in art and literature, we bring to bear an interpretive attitude. We take the data – the obvious instances of the practice, an artistic work or a literary text – and we advance a conception of it which makes it the best exemplar of the genre to which it belongs. The same is true with law. There are institutions and precepts which, by common consent, are part of law. Those are identifiable at the 'pre-interpretive' stage. Then we develop a theory which shows these elements in their best light, the 'interpretive' stage. After that we can, at the 'post-interpretive' stage, settle whatever concrete legal questions may crop up.

In *Law's Empire*, Hercules re-appears as the exemplary judge who has the super-human skill required to push this process through. Furthermore, it is Hercules's approach to hard cases which is the pivotal support for Dworkin's claim that law exhibits the interpretive attitude. Of course, no real judges are Herculeses. Nevertheless, Dworkin contends, they exhibit, piecemeal and imperfectly, the interpretive attitude upon which the legal theorist must build. As Dworkin says in *Law's Empire*: 'In the end all my arguments are hostage to each reader's sense of what does and can happen in court.'[4]

2   Interpretation and legal theory

According to Dworkin, law is interpretive through and through. We are to adopt an interpretive attitude whether we are reaching concrete conclusions about the outcome of a particular case, as judges have to do; or whether we are asserting more general propositions of law, as a legal text-writer might; or whether, at the level of theory, we are advancing claims about the nature of law. At each level, we bring political convictions to bear on the relevant data. It follows that legal theory (claims about the nature of law) must always be politically committed. There is no room

4   *Law's Empire* p 15.

for alleged value-free theorising of the kinds professedly set forth by Bentham, Austin, Kelsen or Hart.

Theory must represent the materials identified at the pre-interpretive stage in their best light. They are all concerned with state coercion. Portraying them at their best means advancing arguments which will show such coercion to be justified. Hence, the concept of law refers to justified coercion: 'Law insists that force not be used or withheld ... except as licensed or required by individual rights and responsibilities flowing from past political decisions about when collective force is justified.'[5] Different theories diverge according to the political grounds they invoke for justifying coercion – that is, they advance different conceptions of the concept of law.[6] The best general theory of law is that which is superior to all others taking into account the two axes of all constructive interpretation, namely, fit with the data, and political merit.

Dworkin poses three alternative answers to the question: How is state coercion to be justified? (that is, three competing conceptions or theories of law): 'conventionalism', 'legal pragmatism', and 'law as integrity'.

According to conventionalism (Dworkin says) a community's legal institutions include clear social conventions in accordance with which rules are promulgated demarcating the circumstances in which force will or will not be applied to individuals or groups. They have only to consult these conventions, which are plain matters of fact, and they can confidently rely on their expectations not being disappointed. Such an interpretation, argues Dworkin, both fails to fit the facts and is morally unacceptable. The truth is that there are countless occasions where there are no hard social-conventional facts delimiting law's scope; and when this is the case, conventionalists can supply no just ground for depriving people of their liberty or property.

Legal pragmatism, as Dworkin describes it, holds that state force cannot be justified at all by reference to the practices identified at the pre-interpretive stage. Since law means justified coercion, the pragmatist concludes that there is no law. He may nonetheless pretend that particular provisions yield legal rights on pragmatic grounds. Doing that, in particular contexts, may forward some political project which he favours. Dworkin considers that there is more to be said, on the dimension of political morality, for pragmatism than for conventionalism. Nevertheless, it is woefully unsuccessful as to fit. Judges and other lawyers who affirm legal rights are not pretending.

Dworkin's portrayal of legal pragmatism is his reworking of American legal realism. He regards realist views as respectable, although ultimately

---

5   Op cit p 93.
6   Dworkin's distinction between concept and conception is adopted from Rawls, who in turn took it from Hart: see Rawls *A Theory of Justice* p 5 n 1.

mistaken. However, he treats the critical legal studies movement with scorn. A good pragmatist, says Dworkin, is one who has conned the legal materials with care to see whether any acceptable political justification underlies them and concluded that it does not. Crits, by contrast, reach their negative conclusions without doing the work. They take a 'quick route' by a blanket condemnation of liberal theories.[7] Dworkin is here unfair to many Crits who, as was pointed out in chapter 8, above, immerse themselves in legal details as much as other lawyers do. It is true that they come to the task with preconceptions against finding justifiable orderings of inter-personal relations; but they suppose they have good reasons for doing that. They consider our political practices irredeemably bad. Dworkin thinks that, working from within the system, something justifiable can be constructed.

'Law as integrity' is Dworkin's favoured constructive interpretation of the concept of law, that is the best legal theory. Coercion is justified if the personified community exhibits that virtue which, in an individual, we recognise as integrity. We may disagree with a man's opinions; but if we see that he has a well-thought-out system of values which he applies consistently, we grant that he has integrity. Analogously, we attribute the whole of the law in force at any point of time to the personified community, and ask which scheme of values would represent it as treating its citizens in a consistent fashion. We may find that parts of the extant legal materials cannot be captured by such an approach, and these will need to be set aside as 'mistakes'. Our aspiration in arriving at propositions of law is, however, that of displaying the constitution, all unrepealed statutes and all non-repudiated precedents as a consistent and coherent scheme of just coercion.

Law-as-integrity (Dworkin claims) fits legal practice better than legal pragmatism because it explains why past political decisions, embodied in legal enactments or case law, are regarded as proper grounds for applying collective force. It wins over conventionalism, on the score of fit, because it accounts for legal controversy. When judges and other lawyers dispute the validity of some abstract or concrete proposition of law, it cannot be that they disagree about the applicable social conventions. It must be because they advance competing arguments for showing that one proposition or another would, given the rest of the law, show the community's treatment of all its citizens in the best light. In other words, we should conceive of law as the best politics which will fit the legal materials.

What, then, is the best politics? In answering that question Dworkin invokes the value of fraternity. Citizens appropriately share a sense of responsibility for what is done in their name. This entails that they suppose that community institutions are trying to extend concern and respect to

7   *Law's Empire* p 274.

all on a basis of equality; and it is this attributed endeavour which alone makes community force into legitimate coercion, that is 'law'. Consequently, law-as-integrity is, on the scale of political morality, at least a viable competitor with legal pragmatism and much superior to conventionalism. Law-as-integrity affirms a universal abstract right of each member of any community to be treated with equal concern and respect and, within particular communities, subsumes under this fundamental right a particular constellation of abstract and concrete right-affirming principles, that which best fits the (non-mistaken) legal enactments:

> 'A community of principle ... can claim the authority of a genuine associative community and can therefore claim moral legitimacy – that its collective decisions are matters of obligation and not bare power – in the name of fraternity. ...
> If we can understand our practices as appropriate to the model of principle, we can support the legitimacy of our institutions, and the political obligations they assume, as a matter of fraternity, and we should therefore strive to improve our institutions in that direction.'[8]

How should we assess 'law as integrity' as a general theory of law? Dworkin has been attacked both by those who are prepared to take 'the interpretive turn' and by those who reject it. Suppose we allow that social practices, like law, cannot simply be described but must be interpreted to be understood, why should we suppose that interpretation of any enterprise necessarily involves showing it in the best light? So argues Andrei Marmor.[9] Stanley Fish goes further. He, like Dworkin, makes much of the analogy between law and literary criticism and, like Dworkin, insists on the importance for both of 'interpretive communities'. Yet despite these shared starting-points, each writer treats the other's views with derision.

Fish condemns Dworkin on two counts. First, Dworkin supposes that interpretations must fit the (legal or literary) text. Statutory interpretation is constrained by the plain meaning of the words in which statutes are expressed.[10] Evolution of the common law is controlled by earlier cases in the way a contributor to a chain novel would be obliged to make his piece consistent with the chapters written by previous participants in the chain.[11] There is however, Fish argues, no such thing as a text 'out there'. All meaning derives from the interpretive community.

8   Op cit pp 214-5.
9   Marmor *Interpretation and Legal Theory* pp 51-57.
10   *Law's Empire* pp 338-40.
11   Op cit pp 228-38.

Fish's second criticism is directed not merely at Dworkin, but at all those who suppose that there can be 'theory' 'that is attached to (in the sense of being derived from) no particular field of activity, but is of sufficient generality to be thought of as a constraint on (and explanation of) all fields of activity.'[12] The supposition is that one can stand back from the beliefs of a community and advance higher level arguments about them in the pursuit of some programme of enlightenment or reform. Members of the critical legal studies movement, marxists and adherents of feminist jurisprudence are all, according to Fish, guilty (like Dworkin) of this false 'theory hope'. Its fallacy consists in the invention of a 'theorist' without any beliefs of his own who can articulate metaphysical propositions in terms of which all beliefs can be tested. There is and could be no such person. We are (says Fish) all prisoners of the beliefs we happen to have. All we can do by way of argument is to engage in rhetorical proclamation of our own beliefs and thereby, if we are lucky, subvert other people's beliefs. Fish calls for the death of 'theory':

> 'One simply cannot tell in advance what will work a change in someone's views; and the range of possible change-producing agencies extends far beyond argumentation to include family crises, altered financial circumstances, serious illness, professional disappointment, boredom, and so on ad infinitum.'[13]

Fish may have a point in so far as he fires a shot across the bows of anyone who supposes he can describe the 'ideology', or the 'false consciousness', of others from a scientific, ideology-free perspective of his own. However, his general characterisation of theory is, as Dworkin and others have argued, a straw creation of Fish's own making. Of course, a Dworkinian interpreter will bring beliefs and value-commitments to his work. We may contest them all, but it would be banal simply to react: 'Ah well, you are just a member of an interpretive community comprised of like-minded American, egalitarian liberals.'

As to the first Fishian criticism, I suggest that the analogy with literature is a distraction legal theory could well do without. Suppose Fish is right (and Dworkin wrong) and that a Shakespeare play is not a cookery book only because the community of readers are of one mind about the matter – no constraint emanates from the text itself. We ought not to infer that propositions of law are true by virtue only of an interpretive community of lawyers who agree about 'justice', which is what Fish maintains. 'Justice' is not something about which there is a simple consensus among lawyers or anyone else, in the way that you can find common agreement

12   Fish *Doing What Comes Naturally* p 14.
13   Op cit p 461.

about the type to which a piece of writing belongs. On the other hand, all lawyers suppose that, among other things, the canonical meaning of legal materials enters into the grounds of true legal propositions. Income tax rates are whatever they are, not because of an interpretive community which is convinced that such and such is the just rate, but because (justly or otherwise) the legislature has so laid it down. (See the discussion of 'bare context' in chapter 12, above.)

Why, in any case, should we take the interpretive turn at the level of theory? Dworkin's recognition that constructive interpretation must fit institutions and prescripts identified at the pre-interpretive stage lays him open to another kind of criticism. Why should not positivists argue for a value-free theory of law, one which sets out the general characteristics of the social phenomenon called 'law' which have to be identified before any interpretation begins? In his postscript Hart suggests that there is nothing incompatible with a justificatory theory, like Dworkin's, and his own value-free theory.

Dworkin acknowledges that a sociologist might advance theories 'about' law – about the working of legal institutions. He argues, nevertheless, that there could be no value-free theories 'of' law – that is, theories which seek to explain the meaning of legal propositions, or of claims about legal rights, legal duties, or legal validity. The legal positivists purport to provide such value-free theories. But Dworkin considers that he has them over a barrel. Legal-positivist claims must, he says, amount to one of two things: assertions about words, or conventionalism. They may be denying the need for the interpretive attitude because they say that we know what law is simply by attending to the way in which people use the word 'law' – Dworkin calls this 'the semantic sting'. But that would mean that when people disagree about the law on any topic they are disagreeing about questions of linguistic usage. That would be such a silly view that Dworkin charitably recasts legal positivists as theorists who do take up the interpretive attitude, but the wrong one – conventionalism.

Dworkin's semantic-sting characterisation of positivism is bizarre. None of the positivists we have discussed rested their case on the ground that the word 'law' is used in only one sense. Austin, as we saw in chapter 3, above, was well aware that this word had several senses and gave his reasons for restricting 'laws properly so called' to general commands. Kelsen took one meaning of 'law', where it refers to a system of coercive rules, and advanced grounds for erecting a theory upon it. Hart, in the postscript, rightly maintains that he was never a purveyor of the semantic sting.

Hart goes on to deny that his theory is conventionalist. He does not share even Dworkin's starting-point – that the concept of law refers to coercion. (Kelsen did – see chapter 6, above. But for Kelsen, law is organised coercion, not justified coercion; so that he too does not take the interpretive turn.) Hart points out that, as an avowed 'soft' positivist, he does not claim that citizens can always discover the law as plain matter of fact. (It is Raz, the 'hard' positivist, who says that law is constituted exclusively of social facts; but these facts might not be 'plain', because they could involve difficult, but still empirical, questions about complex conventions – see chapter 9, above.)

Most importantly, Hart denies that positivists like himself set out to show law in its best light. They seek to provide general information about social institutions and to explain how claims concerning validity, obligations, rights and so forth figure within such institutions. We need, Hart maintains, a clear understanding of these matters as a precursor to evaluative theories. In fact, he says, law has various functions, such as providing standards of criticism and guides to action; but we can convey these truths without committing ourselves, one way or the other, as to whether these are valuable functions, let alone as to whether the coercive measures brought in to supplement these functions are just.

The strongest card which Dworkin repeatedly plays against the positivists relates to controversy. Lawyers who know all the facts about enactment and adoption of rules disagree about what the law requires. Therefore, judgments of political value must enter systematically into propositions of law. A theory must explain what it is that the lawyers are ultimately disagreeing about. At the most abstract level, there must be disagreements about law's point. If he is ever to contribute to the solution of concrete disputes, the theorist must take sides on that fundamental question. 'Jurisprudence is the general part of adjudication, silent prologue to any decision at law.'[14]

The positivists' strongest card is that, outside the courts, lawyers can convey information about law without apparently committing themselves on questions of political morality – they may even describe the laws of past, foreign or unjust legal systems. Dworkin answers this point, but his response is equivocal. He suggests that a judge dispensing decisions within an unjust legal system might do one of two things. He could apply *the* concept of law (justified coercion) and take the pragmatist position: there is no law because the materials identified at the pre-interpretive stage cannot be justified, but it is worthwhile to 'lie' and pretend that someone has a legal right. That might be the judge's personal moral duty. Alternatively, although the system as a whole cannot be justified, the particular transaction before the court might be one which merits enforcement because it reflects settled expectations; and hence the judge might apply, to that field of transactions alone, a conventionalist conception of law (which would mean that he could affirm legal rights without lying). The fact that law-as-integrity may not represent the best constructive

14   *Law's Empire* p 90.

interpretation in such systems is, Dworkin maintains, no reason for denying it the status of a general theory of law.[15]

We have seen that Austin supposed his theory to apply only to 'mature' systems, and Hart took as his archetype the law of the modern state. Are we to assume that 'law as integrity' is a legal theory applicable only to systems which pass some threshold of justice? If so, how many such are there in the modern world? Dworkin does not say.

3   Interpretation and adjudication

Any lawyer who asserts a proposition of law must, according to Dworkin, presuppose a theory of law – some conception of the point of legal practice, seen in its best light. The super-judge, Hercules, works out the right conception – law as integrity. He will accept the truth of the rights thesis: the community, through its coercive enactments, respects the fundamental right of all citizens to equal concern and respect. Armed with that starting-point, he will interpret the legal materials, so far as he can, in such a way that they can be seen to yield general and concrete rights in a consistent and coherent fashion. He will have reached 'law as integrity' at the interpretive stage; and can then proceed to the post-interpretive stage.

In any case which comes before him, Hercules will take into account both the dimension of 'fit' and the moral 'substantive' dimension. Since he is, by definition, endowed with super-human wisdom, Hercules could announce the just outcome every time; but doing that might not respect 'fit'. He might conclude that the extant enactments and case law are witness to a conception of the rights people have which is imperfect, but which nevertheless displays integrity in that the rights it confers are accorded equally to all. If so, he has discovered 'the law'. Often enough, however, cases will be 'hard' because the materials may be read as supporting different conclusions about the concrete rights of the parties. The substantive dimension then comes in. However, substantive considerations may in turn point Hercules back to 'fit'. Perhaps, of three views about a particular legal question, X is superior to Y, and Y to Z, in terms of political morality. However, whereas X will not fit the legal materials, both Y and Z do fit. Then the law is Y.

Dworkin uses 'hard cases' to show the falsity of positivism and the inadequacy of conventionalism. Nevertheless, as he makes clear in *Law's Empire*, law-as-integrity requires the substantive dimension to be taken into account in every case. Cases are relatively easy just because the constraint of fit makes prolonged investigation of the substantive dimension unnecessary. Whatever the morally right view may be about

---

15   Dworkin *Law's Empire* pp 101-8; 'A Reply' in Cohen (ed) *Ronald Dworkin and Contemporary Jurisprudence* at pp 254-60.

traffic law, only the particular speed limit which the legislature has laid down will pass the test of 'fit'.[16]

The substantive dimension concerns issues of political morality. In *Law's Empire* Dworkin splits it into three components: 'justice', 'fairness', and 'procedural due process'. These elements may pull different ways, and Hercules must take them all into account (along with fit) before reaching the right answer.

'Justice' refers to those rights and policy-goals which the ideal legislator, committed to equal concern and respect, would lay down. Hercules can discover what these are because he is a moral objectivist.

Dworkin, stepping into Hercules's shoes, has contended for various familiar 'liberal' positions – women have rights to choose abortions; white candidates have no rights not to be discriminated against by educational programmes of reverse discrimination; and, in the context of pornography and unusual sexual lifestyles, everyone has a right to moral independence (see chapter 10, above). More generally, Dworkin has argued for moral objectivism by deploying two of the strategies discussed in chapter 2, above. The first is 'deep conventionalist'. Equal concern and respect is foundational to our public culture. Anyone who announces that some kinds of people are inherently sub-human can be ignored. Secondly, he uses what I called the 'wheelbarrow' argument against 'external' sceptics. An external sceptic might say: 'I abhor genocide and ethnic cleansing; but these are just my opinions. No-one can prove that these opinions are true, within some supra-scientific realm of truth.' Dworkin's response is 'so what!' It is the external sceptic who has needlessly wheeled in the metaphysical realm in which no moral truths exist. If we debate questions of literary criticism, morals or law, we talk as though there were objective answers and that is all the 'objectivism' we need.[17] Dworkin rules the external sceptic offside; but he allows that a person may properly adopt 'internal' scepticism. He might conclude that the available arguments on some question of morals or law are inconclusive. If so, he is conceding the possibility of objective answers, while denying that they can be found in the particular context.

By 'procedural due process' Dworkin means the moral requirement to abide by previously announced legislative choices if people have relied on them. Hercules might conclude that, on balance, justice requires that an earlier precedent be overruled; but that, since people have understandably organised their affairs on its basis, it would be wrong to upset their expectations. The politically best outcome might then (all things

16   *Law's Empire* pp 353-4.
17   *Law's Empire* pp 80-83; *A Matter of Principle* pp.137-45, 171-77; 'A Reply' in Cohen (ed) *Ronald Dworkin and Contemporary Jurisprudence* at pp 275-88.

considered) be not to overrule.[18] (Finality, it seems, should not, as such, stand in the way of overruling a 'bad' precedent – compare the discussion of this topic in chapter 13, above.)

'Fairness' is a problematic element of the substantive dimension. In day-to-day speech the adjectives 'fair' and 'just' are used more or less interchangeably. A philosophical usage has grown up by which an outcome is 'fair' if it was arrived at by a process in which all those concerned had a proper say – Rawls speaks of 'justice as fairness' in this sense. Dworkin begins with 'fair' in this sense; but, in the context of Herculean adjudication, 'fair' becomes synonymous with 'supported by majority opinion'. Thus, 'justice' diverges from 'fairness' if an ideal scheme of rights comes down one way, popular opinion another. 'Fairness' is especially important in the context of statutory interpretation, since it licenses Hercules to pay attention to contemporary views of what a statute means in preference to inferences to be drawn from its legislative history. Consequently, Dworkin tells us, the televised address of an important politician may be a more important guide to statutory interpretation than the fine print of a committee report.[19] (Compare our discussion of legislative history as evidence of the legislature's intention in chapter 12, above.) Similarly, 'fairness' justifies Hercules in deferring to current opinions about how a constitution should be understood rather than the concrete intentions of those who drafted or ratified the constitution.[20]

Hercules weighs the three elements of the substantive dimension against one another (if they conflict) and finds the optimal political solution which will fit the legal materials. In the case of constitutions and of statutes which he has no authority to set aside, 'fit' constrains him within the outer limits of the meaning which their words will bear (the assumption condemned by Fish). However, on many important questions of American constitutional law, this is no severe shackle on Hercules, thanks to the broad terminology of the amendments contained in the Bill of Rights. The same would be true in the United Kingdom were the European Convention on Human Rights enacted into our law. Indeed, it is for that reason that people who distrust the politics of real judges oppose that development.

Though bound by the words, Hercules may regard particular constitutional or statutory items as 'embedded mistakes'. He will accept that he must give effect to them so far as their intrinsic meaning extends; but he can ignore them in formulating his general scheme of justified rights.[21]

---

18 *Law's Empire* pp 400-403.
19 Op cit pp 348-50.
20 Op cit pp 363-65.
21 *Taking Rights Seriously* pp 118-23.

The dimension of fit applies to precedents in the following way. If Hercules sits in a superior court, he may expunge any objectionable precedent from the materials his ruling must fit, unless procedural due process stands in the way and is not outweighed by considerations of justice or fairness. As to those precedents which Hercules is not empowered to, or ought not to, overrule, some he may treat as embedded mistakes. He will confine them to their 'enactment force', the narrowest possible construction of their *rationes decidendi*. Precedents which are neither overruled nor treated as embedded mistakes will be accorded 'gravitational force'. Hercules will assume that they reflect some background right and hence, in conventional lawyers' parlance, 'reason from them by analogy'.[22]

Furthermore, Hercules treats 'fit' holistically. If he is faced with a novel question of tort law, like whether a person not at the scene of an accident has a concrete right to recover damages for nervous shock, he may find that the (non-disavowed) precedents on that topic could be read either way. That may require him to consider related branches of the law to see whether the community has committed itself to some background right from which the concrete right would follow. Ultimately, he may need to consult all the law now in force:

'The law may not be a seamless web; but the plaintiff is entitled to ask Hercules to treat it as if it were. ... He must construct a scheme of abstract and concrete principles that provides a coherent justification for all common law precedents and, so far as these are to be justified on principle, constitutional and statutory provisions as well.'[23]

No wonder Hercules is, by definition, super-human. But does that matter? Real judges may aspire to imitate him so far as they can. Critics of Dworkin suggest that, if they do, they may become too political; and we don't want to be ruled by the politics of the judiciary. How much constraint does 'fit' actually impose? Since Hercules may dismiss legal materials as mistakes, would a toehold of fit be enough (at least where the moral dimension points clearly in one direction)? Are real judges supposed to reflect equally, so far as in them lies, each feature of the Herculean enterprise – holism, mistake-elimination, determinations about what true justice requires, conclusions about contemporary moral standards ('fairness'), and the restraints of procedural due process? Is the whole picture too grandiose to cope with the day-to-day intersticial choices which real judges have to make?

---

22   Ibid.
23   *Taking Rights Seriously* pp 116-17.

A deal of critical attention has focused on the distinction insisted on by Dworkin between arguments of principle and arguments of policy:

'Arguments of policy justify a political decision by showing that the decision advances or protects some collective goal of the community as a whole. The argument in favor of a subsidy for aircraft manufacturers, that the subsidy will protect national defense, is an argument of policy. Arguments of principle justify a political decision by showing that the decision respects or secures some individual or group right. The argument in favor of anti-discrimination statutes, that a minority has a right to equal respect and concern, is an argument of principle.'[24]

Principles are propositions that describe rights. Policies are propositions that describe goals. A right differs from a community goal in several important respects. First, its specification calls for an opportunity or resource or liberty to be accorded to particular individuals or groups. Secondly, a 'right' must have a certain 'threshold weight' against collective goals in general. Dworkin contends that one would not be speaking consistently if one agreed that people have a right to free speech, but also took the view that any balance of community welfare would justify abrogating free speech. Thirdly, law-as-integrity requires that rights be distributed consistently; whereas it does not prevent a community goal from being attained by unequal distribution of benefits and burdens. For example, the goal of boosting declining industries may be forwarded by subsidising some manufacturers and not others; whereas if they had a right to subsidy, political responsibility would require each to be accorded the same. In matters of principle, there is a requirement of 'articulate consistency', which does not have the same force in matters of policy.

It is the contention of the rights thesis that judicial reasoning takes place against a background of assumptions about rights. Whatever the legal question, the judge must finally decide whether the plaintiff has a concrete right to win, and that in turn depends on judgments about the moral and political background rights of the parties. If the judge is interpreting a statute, he will have to consider policy to the extent that he finds a policy in the legislation; but his interpretation will be guided by the assumption that, in pursuit of its policy, the legislature was conferring or taking away rights. In the context of the criminal law, the judge will ask himself whether the accused has or has not a right to be acquitted. He will not ask himself whether the state has a right to a conviction. (Why there should be this asymmetry of rights in the context of the criminal law is something Dworkin never explains.) In civil cases in which case law alone is applied,

24 Op cit p 82.

the judge will consider nothing but principles. He will decide which of the parties has the stronger right. In these cases, he will take no account of community goals.

It might be inferred, for example, that if consistent application of arguments of principle yields the conclusion that a plaintiff has a right to recover damages for negligent medical treatment, the judge should not be swayed by 'policy' considerations which suggest that such claims lead to wasteful expenditure on defensive medicine; or that if there is a background right to recover for forseeably-caused nervous shock, the judge must ignore the 'floodgates' argument (that a finding for the plaintiff might encourage speculative and time-consuming litigation). In *Law's Empire*[25] Dworkin singles out for approval the speech of Lord Scarman in a nervous shock case, which may itself have been influenced by Dworkin's principle/policy distinction. Lord Scarman said:

> 'The distinguishing feature of the common law is this judicial development and formation of principle. ... And, if principle inexorably requires a decision which entails a degree of policy risk, the court's function is to adjudicate according to principle, leaving policy curtailment to the judgment of parliament.... [T]he policy issue as to where to draw the line is not justiciable.'[26]

It is to be noted, however, that in the same case Lord Edmund-Davies said:

> 'In my judgment, the proposition that "the policy issue ... is not justiciable" is as novel as it is startling. So novel is it in relation to this appeal that it was never mentioned during the hearing before your Lordships. And it is startling because in my respectful judgment it runs counter to well-established and wholly acceptable law.'[27]

Critics of Dworkin have urged that judicial decisions in hard cases are often dictated by policy considerations. In areas such as the law of nuisance, for example, courts take account of the benefit to the community of certain kinds of activities before ruling that they must not take place; and in the context of disclosure of documents in civil litigation, or of reasons for certain kinds of administrative decisions, courts listen to arguments of public policy against disclosure, and are sometimes swayed by them.

Had the primary thrust of the rights thesis been prescriptive – a call for a change in existing judicial practices – Dworkin might have urged

---

25 *Law's Empire* p 28.
26 *Mcloughlin v O'Brian* [1983] 1 AC 410 at 430-31.
27 Ibid at p 427.

that these are instances where the courts do that which a proper regard for rights should lead them not to do: they sacrifice the rights of the individual in the interest of the community. But in fact Dworkin insists that his thesis is not revolutionary in that way. In all the instances mentioned by critics, he claims that there are no counter-examples to the rights thesis. What the courts are really doing is weighing the rights of some claimants against the rights of others. If they go wrong, it is not because they take into account arguments of policy rather than principles; it is because, in weighing the rights described by various principles, they misunderstand or misbalance particular rights.

If a judge's decision appears, on its face, to be based on considerations of public policy, it ought really to be understood, Dworkin argues, as an appeal to the rights of individual members of the public. In support of this contention, he advances the conception of the 'substitutability' of arguments of principle and arguments of policy. If a judge refers to economic public policy or community welfare, one can interpret what he says as statements about the political rights of each and every individual member of the community:

'If a judge appeals to public safety or the scarcity of some vital resource, for example, as a ground for limiting some abstract right, then his appeal might be understood as an appeal to the competing rights of those whose security will be sacrificed, or whose just share of that resource will be threatened if the abstract right is made concrete.'[28]

If substitutability of this kind is always possible, is there any point in the distinction? Dworkin insists that policy arguments would have the same force as arguments of principle only in the case of a judge who (mistakenly) adopted a purely consequentialist conception of rights – one who supposed that the only rights we have are those emanating from that rule which, all things considered, ought to be part of the law.[29] Even such a judge would be deciding on principle. To find a copper-bottomed counter-example to the descriptive aspect of Dworkin's thesis one would, it seems, have to find a case in which a judge proclaimed: 'I find for the plaintiff although I do not think that he has any right to win.' If that is correct, the descriptive thesis is true but trivial. Could there be work for the prescriptive claim – that judges ought to decide by principle and not policy – in that it would condemn the purely consequentialist judge on the ground that he deploys the wrong conception of 'rights'? Not much, it seems, because Dworkin

28   *Taking Rights Seriously* p 100.
29   *Taking Rights Seriously* pp 297-327; 'A Reply' in Cohen (ed) *Ronald Dworkin and Contemporary Jurisprudence* at pp 263-68.

doubts whether there are any such judges. So we return to the question: when a judge takes consequences into account, why is it important, as Dworkin supposes it is, that (whatever terminology the judge employs) we should understand his argument as based on principle and not policy? What is all the fuss about?

Perhaps the argument has psychological implications. If judges who appeal to the public good appreciated that they were really invoking the rights of each and every member of the community, they would make less mistakes in weighing rights. That might be so because expressions like 'public interest' or 'welfare of the community' carry more psychological punch than they substantively deserve.

However this may be, the main thrust of Dworkin's substitution programme has nothing to do with changing judicial practices. His ground for insisting that we ought to understand reasoning in hard cases as reasoning about rights rather than reasoning about policy is one of political philosophy. If we do so understand it, it is then much easier to justify the settlement of controversies by non-elected judges.

One who supports a democratic theory, which calls for compromises between individual and group demands to be settled by elected representatives, has to face the problem that many important controversies are settled by adjudication. This problem is especially acute in the United States, where political issues of the greatest importance are determined by the Supreme Court. But in the United Kingdom also, highly contentious political questions are, at least temporarily, settled by the superior courts. Many of those opposed to the introduction of a bill of rights into this country express doubts about the justiciability of political questions. How can it be right that a handful of non-elected men should impose their political judgments on the rest of us?

Dworkin's answer is that they don't. It may look as though they are deciding the sort of policy issues which political parties are at odds about, but really they are making determinations about existing individual rights.

One's assessment of Dworkin's contention (that arguments of principle underlie adjudication) must therefore be based, not on the evidence of decided cases, but on a judgment of political philosophy. Does looking at decisions in this light better justify the ways of the law to men than if one takes the alternative view that, in some cases, *faute de mieux*, judges do what normally we like political representatives to do?

Dworkin says that the supposed originality of judges in hard cases appears less objectionable if we regard them as deciding on principle, for two reasons. First, if they are considering the rights of individuals rather than the welfare of the community, then it does not matter so much that they lack the means of assessing the total impact on the community of decisions which politicians are supposed to have – no letters from pressure groups, constituency meetings, and so on. Secondly, if a judicial decision were thought of as based on public policy, then it would create a new duty imposed retrospectively, and therefore unfairly, on one of the parties to the litigation; whereas, if his decision is generated by principle, a judge discovers that the plaintiff already has a right against the defendant so that what is enforced is an existing corresponding duty of the defendant.

The first argument appears to have little force in the context of the substitutability programme. For if we are to understand references to public policy as references to all the rights of the individual members of the public, what difference does this make to the desirability of maximum information? Surely, mailbags and public meetings are just as useful for assessing public rights as for assessing public good? Of course, if the rights thesis were a critique and not a description of judicial practices, the argument might be thought to have some bite. It would demand of judges that they minimise, as far as possible, those excursions into public policy which they now make, since they are not equipped to determine such matters. But Dworkinian substitution means that in such cases judges are already deciding on principle.

As to the second argument, how can a decision in a hard case not create duties retrospectively? Because, says Dworkin, it is part of the responsibility incident to the office of a judge to make only such decisions as he can justify within a political theory that also justifies all the rest of the law. No enactment may cover the point in hand, but a consistent arrangement of all the moral and political assumptions which underlie other parts of the law will give the answer. From the point of view of the losing party, however, may not a decision in a hard case seem no less retrospective whether it is reached Hercules's way or whether it is based on judicial assessments of policy?

4   Right answers and judicial legislation

Most legal positivists assert that available legal sources will sometimes yield no determinate solution to a legal question and that therefore there is no uniquely correct answer and the judge is obliged to exercise a law-creating discretion. This point is sometimes made by speaking of 'gaps' in the law, as Joseph Raz does. Hart preferred the terminology of 'penumbra'. Kelsen deprecated talk of 'gaps' because he suspected it of being employed when, in reality, the law was clear enough, but some critic considered it unjust.

Dworkin mounted an attack on the view that, just because there is no right answer in hard cases, judges must exercise a law-creating discretion. His position may therefore be described with a double negative – the 'no-no-right-answer' thesis. However, he combines this offensive with indications about how right answers might actually be discovered even in hard cases. This constitutes a more substantial contribution to a theory of adjudication and I shall therefore, from now on, drop the double negative and characterise Dworkin's position as the 'right-answer thesis'.

Blackstone took the view that judges merely declare the law, and was ridiculed by Bentham and Austin and by positivist writers ever since, for so holding. Is it not plain that much law has been judge-made? Bentham hoped that law-making by judges might be eliminated by adequate codification. Subsequent positivists, however, have contended that, in view of the inevitable imprecision of statutory language, judges are bound to legislate, at least 'intersticially'. This may have unfortunate implications for democratic political theory, but facts must be faced. Perhaps something can be done to mitigate the inevitable retroactivity of judicial legislation by instituting the practice of prospective overruling, discussed in the last chapter.

Dworkin contends that there is no clash with democratic theory in existing practices, and no retrospective judicial law-making to mitigate. This is so because, he says, judges do not exercise a law-creating discretion. The answer to controversial questions of law may be difficult to find, and the judge may get it wrong; but, in principle, there is always a right answer.

Dworkin appeals, in support of his right-answer thesis, to the 'phenomenology' of legal practice – to what judges and other lawyers say about the grounds they have for claiming the truth of legal propositions. They give competing reasons for settling the matter one way or the other. They do not speak as if reasons had run out and there is nothing left for it but that a judge should toss a mental coin:

> 'In the entrenchment clause dispute, for example, the one proposition that is common ground amongst the disputants is that the matter is not one in which judges are free to exercise discretion. Those who think that Parliament does have power to bind its successors believe that judges have no right to recognise a subsequent attempt at repeal. Those who believe that Parliament does not have this power believe that judges have a duty to recognise the subsequent repealer. It is true that some judges might be uncertain. But they are uncertain about their duties, not certain that they have none.'[30]

There are two ways of interpreting Dworkin's right-answer thesis. One view builds on the analogies he draws between rendering judgments on questions of law and judging in any other institutional context. Perhaps all that Dworkin meant was that, if someone takes on the role of judge – in a beauty contest, in a flower show, or in awarding a prize for the best advertising jingle – he commits himself to finding a winner. He cannot

30 *Taking Rights Seriously* pp 63-4.

keep the job and insist that there is nothing to choose between the competitors. He just must find some reasons for reaching a decision, even if he cannot articulate them publicly. Stephen Guest, in supporting Dworkin against his critics, adopts this interpretation of his 'no-no-right answer' thesis.[31]

If that is all Dworkin meant, the whole question sinks into triviality. We have a knock-down phenomenological argument. No judge, either of a beauty contest or of a law-suit, ever announces: 'Stop the show! There is nothing to choose between the contestants!' On this view, the right-answer thesis would be directed against an empty set: situations in which a person is and is not judging. There would be right answers to questions of law whether the judge reasoned like Hercules or decided every case on the basis of policy, or in any other way.

There are certainly passages in Dworkin's writings, and oral comments he has made at seminars in Oxford, which support this interpretation. On the other hand, Dworkin acknowledges that there are issues where the law explicitly invests judges with 'strong' discretion – for example, as to adjournment dates or the precise length of sentences.[32] Why was this concession required? Judges do not say: 'There is no way of deciding whether to send the prisoner down for 15 or 16 months, so I'll toss for it!' Should one not, in accordance with the first interpretation, attribute to them the view that there is a right answer to the question?

The second interpretation of Dworkin's right-answer thesis asserts, not merely that judges do not proclaim that reasons have run out, but also that, as to substantive questions of law, reasons hardly ever do run out. That explains why, in matters of sentencing, it makes sense to speak of strong discretion – a judge might not be able to give a distinct reason for opting for 15 rather than 16 months. It would be compatible with the 'phenomenological' observation that, over procedural and ancillary questions, judges themselves speak, in so many words, of 'no right answers' – as the House of Lords has done in connection with the exercise of discretion in child-custody cases.[33] On this view, whereas procedural and sentencing problems may be under-determined by all available reasons, there is no parallel indeterminacy when it comes to matters of substantive law.

If hard social facts were the only grounds on which propositions of law could be claimed to be true or false then, Dworkin concedes, there would be situations in which there was no right answer but only 'gaps' to be filled by the exercise of discretion. If, however, we expand the truth-grounds of legal propositions in Herculean fashion, we will find that, in modern legal

31 Guest *Ronald Dworkin* pp 146-7.
32 *A Matter of Principle* p 122.
33 *G v G* [1985] 2 All ER 225.

systems, there are sufficient reasons to settle virtually any question of substantive law. Hercules, when he reaches a post-interpretive legal conclusion, takes account of 'moral facts'. Even for Hercules, it is conceivable that reasons of justice, fairness, procedural due process and 'fit' might be in exact equipoise.[34] That is, however, so unlikely that legal practice does, and should, assume that a right answer is always to be found. Real-life lawyers disagree about the law, but that is because one side or the other has failed to discover the right answer; and even those who have got it right will not have articulated all the reasons Hercules could.

Dworkin is aware that someone viewing legal practice from the outside might not accept that all the reasons which were, or could have been, canvassed in a case are sufficient to settle the matter. Such an observer can be put aside, along with those who espouse external scepticism on questions of political morality. If you join the practice of law, you emulate Hercules (always imperfectly, of course). Theoretical puzzles, like that about whether legal questions have right answers, must be viewed from an insider perspective. [35]

Dworkin appeals in support of his argument to the fact that legal concepts are generally dispositive in a yes/no fashion. Either a contract is valid or it is not. Either the accused was guilty of a crime or he was not. Such concepts leave no room for a middle ground: 'Valid if the judge so chooses'; 'guilty, if the court opts to read the law one way rather than another'. To this argument it may be answered that, from the point of view of practitioners advising clients, the quoted expressions may be just the terms in which they represent the law: 'Given the conflicting authorities, your contract is valid (you are guilty), depending which way the court chooses to read them.'

Dworkin's stronger argument for the right-answer thesis is this. Even when the House of Lords is split three to two, none of their Lordships announces: 'there is nothing to choose between counsels' admirable arguments. I am rendering a judgment because I have to, but I can give no reasons in its support.' They always talk as if the balance of reasons comes down one way or the other. Nevertheless, read their speeches with care and you may find occasions on which they say something like: 'To my mind ...'; or 'As a matter of impression ...'. Are these not ways of acknowledging that the balance of reasons is tilted, not by some clinching second-order reason which shows (say) that the reasons advanced for the plaintiff are outweighed by those for the defendant, let alone an invocation of a Herculean holistic interpretation; but rather that the judge is adding to the reasons a process of irreducibly subjective assessment?

---

34 *Taking Rights Seriously* pp 285-7; *A Matter of Principle* pp 143-5.
35 *Law's Empire* pp 13-14.

Even if, with Dworkin, we dismiss external moral scepticism and the outsider view of legal practice, it does not follow that there will always be sufficient reasons to settle every hard legal question. Herculean 'weighing' may be a misleading metaphor. The arguments of fit, justice, fairness and due process are not like weights on a pair of scales, which might just possibly (but almost certainly will not) balance exactly. They are qualitatively different kinds of reasons. Must this not be so even for Hercules? He will know that solutions X and Y each have a degree of fit; and he may conclude that one of them is a mite more just, but a little less fair or conformable to procedural due process, than the other. His brother judge, Hercules\2, could reach the same conclusions. Yet they might render different judgments about the best (all things considered) constructive interpretation. If that is possible, at the end of the day discretion cannot be eliminated.

Would such a conclusion amount to a recognition of 'judicial legislation'? Positivists generally suppose that judges 'legislate' intersticially; but not, of course, that they have a legislator's carte blanche freedom to create new law. Dworkin himself recognises that judicial decisions may change the law in two contexts. It may be that the correct solution to a hard case is X, that a superior court mistakenly pronounces Y, and that thereafter the ruling so affects the balance of 'fit', or raises new considerations of procedural due process, that the answer to the legal question has become Y. Secondly, when the superior court reaches the right answer, its ruling provides a firmer ground, in terms of fit, for future judges so that the answer to the legal question is now less open to debate. Nevertheless, if Dworkin is right in claiming that civil cases at common law should not be decided by reference to policy (and assuming that 'substitutability' does not make the principle/policy distinction illusory), he allows for less 'judicial legislation' than some positivists might. (Compare the discussion of consequentialist reasoning in the next chapter.)

The most important issue subsumed within the question 'Do and should judges legislate?' is political and constitutional. Members of any free society disagree about how governments should treat their citizens – about how resources should be allocated, about appropriate controls on the executive, about when state force should be applied. Positivists suppose that, unavoidably, such matters are sometimes decided by judges according to their own (the judges') personal political opinions. (They may insist that judges should defer, whenever possible, to specific information about the intentions of the promulgators of legislation; that is, adopt (what Dworkin rejects) a 'speaker's meaning' model of interpretation.) The thrust of Dworkin's theory is that, whenever the materials can be read in different ways, judges should not (and do not) simply give effect to their personal views. Instead, they have a responsibility to apply their convictions about what the morality to which the community is committed should be

understood to entail. So long as these convictions 'fit' the legal materials,
they reveal what the law is. The process is law-discovery, not legislation.
For Dworkin's critics, this is a smokescreen behind which judges can
impose their personal moral and political choices.

Bibliography

Bodenheimer E. 'Hart, Dworkin and the Problem of Judicial Lawmaking
    Discretion' (1977) 11 Ga L Rev 1143
Cohen M. (ed) *Ronald Dworkin and Contemporary Jurisprudence* (1984)
Dworkin R. M. *Taking Rights Seriously* (2nd edn, 1978)
    –   *A Matter of Principle* (1985)
    –   *Law's Empire* (1986)
    –   'Pragmatism, Right Answers and True Banality' in Brint and
        Weaver (eds) *Pragmatism in Law and Society* (1991)
    –   'Gaps in the Law' in Amselek and MacCormick (eds) –
        Controversies About Law's Ontology (1991)
Dyzenhaus D. *Hard Cases in Wicked Legal Systems: South African Law
    in the Perspective of Legal Philosophy* (1991)
Finnis J. 'On Reason and Authority in Law's Empire' (1987) Ls Rev 357
Fish S. *Doing What Comes Naturally* (1989)
Greenawalt K. 'Discretion in Judicial Decision' (1975) 75 Col L Rev 359
Guest S. *Ronald Dworkin* (1992)
Hart H. L. A. *The Concept of Law* (2nd edn, 1994) Postscript
Hunt A. (ed) *Reading Dworkin Critically* (1992)
Marmor A. *Interpretation and Legal Theory* (1992) chs 3 and 4
Marmor A. (ed) *Law and Interpretation* (1995) pts 1 and 2
Moore M. 'The Interpretive Turn in Modern Theory: a Turn for the
    Worse?' (1989) 41 Stan L Rev 871
Raz J. 'Dworkin: a New Link in the Chain' (1986) 74 Calif L Rev 1103
Simmonds N. E. 'Imperial Visions and Mundane Practices' (1987) 46 CLJ
    465
Waluchow W. J. *Inclusive Legal Positivism* (1994) chs 6 and 7

15 Legal reasoning

'You're talking like a lawyer!' is sometimes a commendation, sometimes a sneer. Whichever it is, it does seem to be generally assumed that lawyers have a special way of talking and reasoning. Their professional preoccupation with statutes, regulations, precedents, court ways and (in some jurisdictions) constitutions leads them into thinking about problems in a peculiar way. Some critics call for change in legal styles of thought. Lawyers should be less 'mechanical', less conservative, more attuned to social needs. Both to understand what it is, and to decide whether it should be changed, we ought to see if we can pick out the crucial differentiating characteristics of this legal reasoning.

The first thing we might try to get clear is what is supposed to be the function of legal reasoning: what does it aim to achieve? That might be thought to vary depending on which sort of lawyer you are talking about. Books on legal reasoning in common law jurisdictions concentrate on judges, whose published opinions contain masses of reasoning. In civil law jurisdictions, they focus more on the writings of jurists; both because their works – 'la doctrine' – are regarded as important evidence of what the law is, and because court judgments are much less elaborate in their ratiocinations. But perhaps we should think about those lawyers who advise clients – solicitors and barristers. The function of their reasoning might be thought to be prediction – as the American realists claimed (see chapter 8, above). They give reasons for thinking that the other side is (or is not) likely to sue, defend or settle a claim; and reasons for thinking that a particular judge would (or would not) be likely to decide in your favour. Then there is the reasoning of advocates. They seek to persuade the court to make awards, render verdicts or issue orders. C. H. Perelman has argued that persuasion, rather than justification, is the overall function of legal reasoning. T. D. Perry contends that, in the legal as in the moral context, persuading an audience to accept your view is what 'justification' means. Most writers, however, have assumed that the object of legal reasoning is 'justification' in the more familiar sense of supporting the right answer. A lawyer gives his reasons for thinking that such and such a course of conduct or decision is legally justified – whatever its other merits.

Justification must be at least the ostensible purpose of judges' reasons. They are not in the business of predicting or persuading. Legal textwriters may go in for some prediction and persuasion, but do they not predominantly engage in giving reasons why something should be considered the 'correct', 'best', 'most justified' legal solution? They differ from advocates in that they are supposed to consider all sides of the question, whereas advocates 'submit' that the correct legal solution is the one which favours their clients. But in making such submissions, advocates marshall reasons which are of the same sort as those which judges and textwriters deploy by way of justification. Advisers, too, must have some regard to justificatory reasoning, at least if they take the view that what justifies a decision as legally sound has some effect upon the decisions judges are likely to render, and upon litigants' decisions to sue, defend or settle. In the succeeding discussion, I shall assume that justification is the primary function of legal reasoning, upon which the functions of prediction and persuasion are parasitic; but that view is certainly controversial.

Having got that far, it is still a debatable question whether lawyers' justifying reasons differ from other people's. As we saw in chapter 8, members of the critical legal studies movement have attacked the perpetuation of the myth of 'legal formalism', according to which there is a special kind of intellectual endeavour known as 'legal reasoning' which is distinct from open-ended political controversy. Positivist legal theorists generally suppose that 'formalism' is warranted, at least in very clear cases: if a statute or regulation makes conduct illegal beyond any dispute, then a lawyer, who is practised in looking up the relevant text, tells you that it is unlawful. But in the unclear cases, where what is at issue is what the correct legal solution ought to be, are special sorts of argument available to legal reasoning? Kelsen thought not.

He repudiated any attempt by legal science to produce solutions going beyond the reproduction of valid norms (see chapter 6, above).

If that is right, what should textwriters do? 'Here is the law, and here are my politics. So far as the law is not cast iron clear, I will give nothing but political reasons as to the proper legal solution.' There would then be no difference between the sorts of reason advanced by a reformer who says that the clear law should be changed, and those advanced in arguing that a doubtful point should be decided in a certain way.

As things are, textwriters make use of special legal justificatory arguments in doubtful cases – the purpose of the statute, consistency with other parts of the law, and so on. Just compare the different sorts of criticism in case notes in legal journals with those in comments on new statutes. Counsel arguing before our judges – whatever their private suspicions – do not make use of the clincher: 'Hell, man, aren't you a conservative?' At the end of the day, perhaps we should dismiss legal reasoning as an illusion or a smokescreen, but we had better first try to understand what sort of animal it is.

In recent years, English judges have not been shy in committing to print their own conceptions of the judicial process. We learn from these writings that they are generally aware of a tension between legal certainty and legal adaptability, between the requirement of fidelity to law and the value of judicial creativity. They recognise that they sometimes have to make choices (even on politically sensitive questions), but they take it for granted that they do not have a complete free hand. They appeal to an ill-defined sense of craftsmanship rather than to an overall view of what counts as 'legal reasoning'.

It is far from easy to get a comprehensive view of the subject. Most writers who have discussed legal reasoning have either concentrated on the form as distinct from the substance of justificatory arguments, or else dealt with only part of the subject. Two forms of argument, the deductive and the inductive, have generally been considered inapposite characterisations of legal argument. Some take the view that deductive argument – from major and minor premises to a logically necessary conclusion – is inappropriate even in clear cases. This may be asserted on the general ground that deductive arguments only hold true of factual propositions not of norms; or on the more specific ground that even the clearest rule may be held not to apply to a case where that would frustrate the purpose of the law or produce absurd consequences, and the decision whether this is so or not cannot be dictated by logic. On the other hand, reasoning in clear cases seems very close to deductive reasoning – here is a speed-limit rule applying to all car drivers, I am a car driver, so it applies to me. Even in unclear cases, it can be contended that the form of the argument is deductive, since what is at issue is which of competing rulings should be adopted, granted that the winner will be applied deductively in all cases of the present type – although here our major concern will be with the substantive arguments which dictate choice among the rulings.

In view of what was said in chapter 13 about judges being required at least to listen to all precedents, it might be argued that case law reasoning is inductive – arrival at propositions from survey of data. Such a view has been generally rejected. Judges may produce rulings which, they think, cover the majority of *dicta*, but they do not have to account for them all. It is not even bad legal reasoning to suggest that a few important authorities outweigh a mass of less important ones.

R. A. Wasserstrom and D. H. Hodgson have debated the question of how, in principle, adjudication should proceed, but only in areas not covered by statute law, and primarily with reference to the respective merits of a rule-utilitarian and a precedential approach. Wasserstrom examines reasoning by reference to precedents, and finds it wanting. Given the quantity of precedents and the inexhaustible possibilities of distinguishing them, there can be no certainty about judicial decisions; and, in so far as judges can and do stick to precedents, their decisions are likely to be ill-adapted to social change. For the most part judges produce the decision which would (if universalised) have best consequences, so the best course would be to drop precedential reasoning and instead adopt a 'two-level decision procedure' analogous to rule-utilitarianism (see chapter 4, above). The judge should first ask himself what rule governing this sort of case would, if generally applied, have best consequences; and then make that rule the basis of his decision. Hodgson replies that the adoption of such a procedure would lead to greater uncertainty than we have with our present system of common law justification. There would be no certainty about judicial decisions because everyone would know that, although judge X had rendered a decision required by a rule which he (X) thought would have best consequences, future judges would not necessarily apply judge X's rule. They would, following the same two-level procedure, ask again which rule would have best consequences. The result, Hodgson argues, is that the adoption of this rule-utilitarian approach, in substitution for reliance on precedents, would, paradoxically, have greater disutility than what we do now.

What we need is a view which synthesises form and substance, and comprehends all the varieties of argument regarded as relevant to settling a question of law. In my book, *Law and Legal Science*, I endeavoured to list the different sorts of substantive reason which, disregarding the form, were employed as justifications for legal decisions. I called these the 'will', 'natural meaning', 'doctrine' and 'utility' models of rationality. The former covers those situations in which genuine reference is made to what some agent in the legislative process, or some individual judge, actually had in mind when laying down a rule. The second covers those cases in which the fact that a word appearing in a rule has natural meaning X is a justifying reason. The third embraces all those situations in which some maxim – whether rule, principle, policy, classification or whatever – comprised in a historic legal system is supposed to justify a decision. The fourth covers situations in which the perceived consequences of a decision are determinative. I suggested that the mix and prioritising of these models varied from one jurisdiction to another.

In his *Legal Reasoning and Legal Theory*, Neil MacCormick sets out to provide a theory of legal reasoning which is both explanatory and normative. It both explains what reasons judges use in justification of their decisions – at any rate, English and Scottish judges – and contends that these are the reasons they ought to use.

MacCormick demonstrates at length how purely deductive reasoning is possible in justification of a judicial decision in law, using as an example the decision of Lewis J in *Daniels and Daniels v R. White and Sons and Tarbard.*[1] A publican (Mrs Tarbard), who sold to Mr Daniels a bottle of R. White's lemonade which turned out to contain carbolic acid, was held liable as a 'seller by description' of goods which were not of 'merchantable quality', within the terms of s 14 (2) of the Sale of Goods Act 1893 (as authoritatively interpreted in prior cases). In such cases, the major premise is an indisputable rule of the legal system, the minor premise consists of proven facts, and the conclusion is the holding; the decision is therefore justified purely by deduction plus the normative assumptions which warrant acceptance of the system's rule of recognition.

In most cases where there is litigation on a question of law, however, such deductive justification is not possible. These MacCormick distributes under three heads: problems of 'relevancy', problems of 'interpretation', and problems of 'classification'. A problem of relevancy arises when it is open to dispute what legal rule is relevant to the issue. The typical case is a dispute arising in the area of case law, as in *Donoghue v Stevenson*[2] where the majority of the House of Lords thought that there was, and the minority thought there was not, a rule of law imposing a duty of care on manufacturers vis-à-vis consumers. A problem of interpretation arises when the words of a statute are ambiguous, and the court has to choose between two interpretations. For example, in *Ealing LBC v Race Relations Board*,[3] the majority of the House of Lords held that a statutory rule prohibiting discrimination on the ground of 'national origin' did not apply to discrimination on the ground of legal nationality, so that the council was not acting unlawfully when it limited its housing list to British subjects. A problem of classification arises where the court has to decide whether the facts admitted or proved do or do not come within a factual category stipulated in a rule. For example, in *MacLennan v MacLennan*,[4] Lord Wheatley held that artificial insemination was not classifiable as 'adultery'.

MacCormick argues that problems of interpretation and of classification are, in truth, logically equivalent, since both involve choice between two competing rulings. They are distinguished only for institutional reasons, having to do with the distinction between questions of law and questions of fact. A problem is treated as one of classification rather than interpretation, and therefore a question of fact rather than law, in situations where appeal to higher courts is limited to questions of law and it is felt that this particular question ought to be settled by the lower court; or where

1 [1938] 4 All ER 258.
2 [1932] AC 562.
3 [1972] AC 342.
4 [1958] SC 105.

an issue is one as to which, it is felt, future cases should not be hampered by precedent – which they will not be if the issue is regarded as one of fact.

Reasoning in relation to these three sorts of problems is, MacCormick argues, limited as to form by the requirements of formal justice, and as to substance by the requirements of consistency and coherence. Within these limits, the reasoning is consequentialist; save that no ruling, however desirable its consequences, is legally permitted unless it is authorised by legal principle or is analogous to an existing legal rule.

The limitation of formal justice means that no decision may be given which cannot be universalised. As Kant and R. M. Hare argue for ethics, so MacCormick argues for law. It is formally irrational to say X is the right solution in circumstances Y, unless you accept that there is a class of Xs which will always be right for the class of Ys. That does not mean that rules can have no exceptions. Where there is an exception, there is something present besides Y. MacCormick makes it clear that what is formally essential is universalisability, not generalisation. So far as formal justice is concerned, one could support the holding in *Donoghue v Stevenson* by a universal rule to the effect that all manufacturers of ginger beer are liable to residents of Paisley who suffer foreseeable damage from decomposed snails in the manufacturers' bottles.

The requirement of consistency means that, in deciding whether a certain rule is legally relevant (that is, whether that particular rule formulation can be said to be part of the law), or in choosing between two rules each of which is permitted by different interpretations of a statute or by different classifications of facts, no rule can be accepted which contradicts any other rule in the system. 'The system' here means all the rules valid by reference to criteria of recognition *at the time when the decision is made* – what I have called a 'momentary legal system'. I suggested in my book that legal science constructs the 'present law' of any jurisdiction by reference to four logical principles, those of exclusion, subsumption, derogation and non-contradiction. The first requires the law to be identified by reference to a finite set of sources. The second indicates that rules originating in an inferior source must be subsumed under rules originating in superior sources. The third stipulates a priority among rules depending on a ranking of sources. The fourth insists that any other contradiction must be eliminated. It should be stressed that the view for which I and MacCormick argue – that it is part of legal reasoning to eliminate logical conflicts between rules – is by no means universally admitted. As we saw in chapter 6, Kelsen once adhered to this view but changed his mind about it in his last writings. I contend that, in reaching a conclusion about what the law is, judges and other lawyers presuppose that seeming logical contradictions must, one way or another, be eliminated. For example, the House of Lords has ruled that, if lower courts are faced with two inconsistent decisions of the House, they must follow the later one, and there is no need to invoke the Practice Statement overruling power discussed in chapter 13, above.[5] Whether or not a system embodies the maxim *lex posterior derogat priori*, legal reasoning universally assumes that the present law does not impose on judges and citizens a duty and also no duty covering the same act-situation on the same occasion.

MacCormick's requirement of coherence means that, even where there is no question of logical contradiction, the legal reasoner should not put forward a ruling which cannot be coherently sustained in conjunction with other rules in the system. Rules requiring different coloured cars to observe different speed limits would not be logically inconsistent, but would be incoherent since no set of evaluations could justify them. If a proposed ruling promotes value X, by indicating that a certain pattern of behaviour or a certain state of affairs is desirable, and it would not make sense to pursue value X while also pursuing values embodied in other rules of law, then it is irrational (MacCormick argues) to adopt the proposed ruling. The concept of coherence involves attributing rational purpose to the law, rather than regarding it as a wilderness of single instances. In *Donoghue v Stevenson*, Lord Atkin said: 'In English law there must be, and is, some general conception of relations giving rise to a duty of care of which the particular cases found in the books are but instances.' He then went on to formulate his famous 'neighbour principle': the duty is owed to persons whom you can reasonably foresee would be likely to be injured by your careless acts or omissions.[6]

So long as a proposed ruling is consistent and coherent with the rest of the system, it is, according to MacCormick, legally permitted if authorised by principle or analogy, and legally justified if it would have better consequences than any other similarly authorised ruling. He rejects Dworkin's definition of principles as propositions describing rights. Principles are, he says, 'relatively general norms which are conceived of as 'rationalizing' rules or sets of rules'.[7] A legal principle, in the view of the person putting it forward as a principle, explains and justifies existing legal rules. It authorises any new ruling which it would also explain and justify.

As well as having this authorising function, a principle may, through regular explicit application by the courts, acquire great presumptive weight in its own right. But it never fully justifies a decision. Only consequences do that. For example, Lord Atkin's neighbour principle explained and justified rulings in earlier cases, and also the ruling about manufacturers'

---

5   *Moodie v IRC* [1993] 2 All ER 49.
6   [1932] AC 562 at 580.
7   *Legal Reasoning and Legal Theory* p 232.

liability in *Donoghue v Stevenson* itself. It has since been used to authorise many other new rulings in the law of negligence. But it does not require them. Its persuasive force may be overriden by consequentialist arguments, as happened in *Rondel v Worsley*.[8] There the House of Lords held that there would be unacceptable consequences for the administration of justice if barristers were liable for the foreseeable harm resulting from negligent conduct of litigation.

A ruling is authorised by analogy, MacCormick says, if there is an existing legal rule or principle of the form: 'if P then Q', if the proposed ruling stipulates: 'if P/1 then Q', and if P/1 is similar to P. For example, the situation of a salvor putting himself in danger to save property is similar to that of a rescuer putting himself in danger to prevent injury; so if there already exists a legal rule entitling the rescuer to recover damages from the person responsible for the danger, the court is authorised (though not obliged) to announce a similar rule for salvors. The limits of analogical reasoning are set by the requirement that P, the operative facts of the rule or principle with which analogy is drawn, must be stated with reasonable specificity; otherwise one could find vaguely-worded pronouncements in the books, analogical application of which would justify anything.

MacCormick contends that, within the limits set by the requirements of formal justice, consistency and coherence, and within the range authorised by principle and analogy, legal reasoning is essentially consequentialist. In most problems of relevancy, interpretation and classification, more than one decision may be formally just (universalisable into a ruling), and more than one ruling consistent and coherent with the rest of the law and authorised by principle or analogy. When this is so, the perceived consequences of alternative rulings are what do (and what ought to) justify judicial decisions. In this sense, MacCormick says, his theory is a variety of ideal rule-utilitarianism. But he prefers the label 'consequentialist' to 'utilitarian', because he is anxious to stress that there is no Benthamite objective scale for measuring good and bad consequences *inter se*. His view on this point should be contrasted with the theory of the economic analysis of law that, in common law contexts at least, the underlying logic of consequentialist reasoning is related to an objective scale (see chapter 4, above).

MacCormick distinguishes consequences of three sorts. First, there are considerations of corrective justice – 'for every wrong there ought to be a remedy'. Second, there are considerations of 'common sense' – a judicial expression which boils down (he says) to perceptions of community moral standards. Third, there are considerations of public policy. The latter include both direct public interest in bringing about changed behaviour, and also questions of convenience or expediency such as the desirability

8   [1968] 1 AC 191.

of having a clear rule or the floodgates argument – 'allow this claim, and the courts will be flooded out with litigation'. A particular decision may be shown to be irrational, if the foreseen consequences were premised upon incorrect facts. But there comes a point at which the consequences may be agreed and yet honest men still differ as to the rulings that are justified. At this stage, the choice is irreducibly subjective. For that reason, MacCormick disagrees with Dworkin's views on discretion.

It is with Dworkin's 'rights thesis' (discussed in the last chapter) that MacCormick's elegant theory of legal reasoning is primarily to be compared. Which of them is right about discretion and 'right answers'? Should consequentialist arguments be understood (as Dworkin maintains) in terms of their distributive effects on individuals – that is, as concerning 'rights'? Does the fact that 'principles' enter into legal reasoning mean, as Dworkin urges, that no positivistic pedigree test of what counts as 'law' is possible, so that no line can be drawn between legal and moral argument? Or is MacCormick right in maintaining that legal principles are, indirectly, identifiable by reference to Hart's rule of recognition, in that they are always parasitic on the rules they underpin and justify?

Supposing two lawyers contend for different principles, each of which, according to its proponent, underlies the same body of rules, and neither of which has yet been blessed with judicial recognition. Dworkin would say that that principle is a 'legal' one which follows from the best political theory, having regard to institutional fit and moral truth. I have myself argued that neither would be 'legal', since principles acquire the status of legality only once they are accepted as part of the tradition of a body of officials. It is not clear how MacCormick would deal with this problem. On the one hand, he tells us that legal principles explain and justify legal rules, which suggests that both candidates are already legal principles. On the other hand, he speaks of drawing analogies from 'existing principles', which suggests that some kind of authoritative formulation is necessary before a norm 'exists' as a legal principle.

MacCormick expresses disagreement with the House of Lords' decision in the *Ealing Borough* case. He thinks that the minority were right to prefer the principle underlying the Race Relations Act – that discrimination in general is undesirable – to the common law principle which influenced the majority – that freedom of action is to be upheld unless curtailed by clear statutory language. He does not, however, deal with the more general question: should judges always prefer legislative analogy to common law analogy? Presumably, this sort of general issue would be fitted into the 'political theory' which Dworkin attributes to his super-human judge.

Ninety years ago, Roscoe Pound listed four ways in which courts might deal with legislative innovation: (1) reason from it by analogy in preference to analogies based on judge-made rules, on the ground that it is a later and more direct expression of the will of a superior authority; (2) reason from it by analogy, but regard it as of equal authority with judge-made rules; (3) refuse to reason from it by analogy, but nevertheless give it a liberal interpretation to cover the whole field it was intended to encompass; (4) refuse to reason from it by analogy, and insist on giving it a narrow interpretation limited to cases which it covers expressly. Pound said the fourth approach represented the orthodox common law attitude, but that there was a tendency towards the third; and that the course of legal development should lead to the second and eventually the first.[9] There are occasional instances of the second approach;[10] but certainly, we have not yet reached the first approach, and some would argue that considerations of stability tell against it. If all arguments from common law principles are to give way before analogical extensions of legislation promoted by the parliamentary majority of the day, what price legal continuity?

Other questions may be raised about MacCormick's theory of legal reasoning. He says that no line can be drawn between easy and hard cases, yet maintains that there are situations in which strict deduction is possible. Why should not the limits of deduction constitute the line? Is he right about deductive justification? In his example of the *Daniels* case, he says that the judge rightly dismissed out of hand counsel's submission that the sale of the bottle of lemonade was not a 'sale by description'. But could not Lewis J have concluded, faithful to the requirements of universalisability and consistency, that this category did not apply to sales by sellers who had no means of verifying the quality of goods? That might have led to incoherence with the rest of the law; and probably strict liability in contract has good consequences. But such coherence and consequentialist arguments are not dictated by logic. One might even wonder whether the very fact that an issue is litigated as to the law demonstrates that it is not one as to which indisputable deductive logic gives only one answer.

In *Law and Legal Science*, I suggested that deductions in law are never formally valid, but that legal reasoning is for all practical purposes deductive when all that is needed to make it watertight is the exclusion of ludicrous purposive interpretations. (Compare the discussion of 'bare context' in chapter 12, above.) Since Lewis J was sympathetic to the seller it might be argued that he should have at least tried to discover whether some purposively coherent explanation of existing statute and case law might be given which would let her off. A possible litigated instance where no such endeavour was warranted (so that the decision was, for all practical purposes, deductive) is the Canadian case of *R v Liggetts-Finlay Drug Stores Ltd*.[11] There a byelaw directed that 'all drug shops shall be closed at 10pm on each and every day of the week'. The Appellate Division of

---

9　(1908) 21 Harv L Rev 383.
10　Cross and Harris *Precedent in English law* (4th edn) pp 174-77.
11　[1919] 3 WW R 1025.

the Supreme Court of Alberta rejected peremptorily the contention that there was no infringement if a drug shop closed at 10pm and opened a few minutes later.

As a statement of the interrelationship between what I call 'legal models of rationality', MacCormick's theory may be considered as on the whole descriptively accurate, so far as the reasoning of UK judges is concerned. But his theory is intended to be normative as well as explanatory and, on the normative side, some may regard it as complacent. He accepts that doctrine-model reasoning should limit utility-model reasoning. Analogy with existing rules, or conformity with principles underlying existing rules, should restrain the proposed rulings which are candidates for consequentialist comparison. That is required, MacCormick argues, by the need to do 'justice according to law'. Judges should not make new rulings, however desirable in terms of corrective justice, community morality and public policy, unless they are authorised by analogy or existing principle. It might be argued that 'justice according to law' is satisfied so long as new rulings are consistent and coherent with the rest of the system. In *Malone v Metropolitan Police Comr*,[12] Megarry VC held that telephone tapping is not a legal wrong. Supposing he had laid down a new rule of tort law to the effect that a citizen may sue those who tap his telephone, unless the defendants are specifically authorised by statute or statutory instrument, and had justified this new rule by enunciating a new legal principle that 'privacy is to be respected'. That principle would not, I think, be incoherent with other principles underlying existing legal rules, but the new ruling would not be authorised by any such principle. Would such an innovation overstep the conception of 'doing justice according to law' which we wish to defend? That must depend on our appraisal of the proper constitutional distribution of power between legislature and judiciary, and the conception we have of the rule of law – does it exclude decisions justified by wholly innovative judicial rulings? For Dworkin, coherence (institutional 'fit') is all that is needed, so long as the new principle reflects a 'background' moral right.

MacCormick appears to regard the 'natural meaning' model of rationality as merely an aspect of the 'will' model, and consequently he accepts uncritically the view that there should always be a presumption in favour of plain meaning.

> 'Whether or not all the members of the legislature have the least idea of the contents of clauses of Bills, the least unsuccessful way of securing that the will of elected legislators will prevail will be to take the words enacted by them at their face value and so far as possible apply them in accordance with their plain meaning.'[13]

12 [1979] Ch 344.
13 *Legal Reasoning and Legal Theory* p 204.

The presumption in favour of plain meaning may be justified, not because of assumptions about Parliament's intention, but because giving effect to it avoids judges entering into politically controversial questions – that is, it supports the objectivity of the rule of law. On the other hand, it may be condemned as arbitrary ('mechanical', 'legalistic'). These are important normative issues about legal reasoning which MacCormick's failure to recognise the natural-meaning model as a distinct model of legal reasoning prevents him from investigating.

MacCormick also accepts uncritically the view that speculations about legislative intent never permit you to go beyond some meaning which statutory words can bear. Utility and doctrine can prevail over plain meaning, but never over possible meaning:

'There is a justified presumption in favour of applying statutes in accordance with their more obvious meanings, but provided there are other *possible* meanings the presumption can be displaced by good arguments from consequences and/or from legal principles.'[14]

But supposing we are confident that the legislature did intend something which the words it ineptly chose cannot achieve? In *IRC v Hinchy*, a statute provided that a person making an incorrect tax return shall forfeit the sum of £20 'and treble the tax which he ought to be charged under this Act'. The taxpayer in his return slightly understated some interest he had received. The House of Lords held unanimously that the wording of the Act left them no alternative but to award a penalty of treble the whole tax payable on his year's income, not just treble the underpaid tax. Lord Reid said that, since the words were not capable of a more limited construction, 'we must apply them as they stand, however unreasonable and unjust the consequences, and however strongly we may suspect that this was not the real intention of Parliament.'[15]

To an English or Scottish lawyer, this approach may once have seemed acceptable. How could legal reasoning justify giving an enactment a meaning which the words *cannot bear*? But that, as the House of Lords has since stressed, is a parochial view. In *R v Henn*[16] convictions for importing obscene articles were challenged by reference to the Treaty of Rome. The Court of Appeal refused to refer to the European Court of Justice the question whether an absolute prohibition on importation could be a 'quantitative restriction on imports between member states' contrary to Article 30 because it was plain that the words could not bear that meaning. The House of Lords referred the question, expecting (and getting)

14   Op cit p 213.
15   [1960] AC 748 at 767.
16   [1982] AC 850.

from the court the answer that absolute prohibitions were 'quantitative restrictions'. As Lord Diplock pointed out, the European Court seeks to give effect to the spirit rather than the letter of the treaties, sometimes indeed to an English judge it might seem to the exclusion of the letter. (Convictions were none the less upheld as the UK legislation came within the 'public morality' exception in Article 36.)

Because of his uncritical assumption that words in the statute are the only evidence of legislative intent, MacCormick does not address those questions about statutory interpretation discussed in chapter 12, above, which involve the interrelated issues of meaning, purpose and consequences. For the same reason, broader questions are neglected. What is the proper relationship between will-model reasoning and the utility and doctrine models? Should speculation as to legislative purpose be considered a ground for authorising new rules, distinct from principle and analogy? Was Pound right when he argued that principles introduced by legislation should not merely be used as a basis for analogical reasoning in the way common law principles are, but should (in deference to their democratic origin) be given priority over common law principles?

Bibliography

Alexy R. *A Theory of Legal Argumentation* (1989)

Atiyah P. S. 'Common Law and Statute Law' (1985) 48 MLR 1

Atiyah P. S. and Summers R. S. *Form and Substance in Anglo-American Law* (1987)

Burton S. *Judging in Good Faith* (1993)

Cardozo B.*The Nature of the Judicial Process* (1921)

Cross R. and Harris J. W. *Precedent in English Law* (4th edn, 1991) pp 173-77, 186-207

Devlin P. 'Judges and Lawmakers' (1976) 39 MLR 1

Eckhoff T. 'Guiding Standards in Legal Reasoning' (1976) 29 CLP 205

Edmund-Davies Lord 'Judicial Activism' (1975) 28 CLP 1

Friedmann W. *Legal Theory* (5th edn. 1967) ch 32

Fuller L. L .'The Forms and Limits of Adjudication' (1978) 92 Harv L Rev 353

George R. P. (ed) *Natural Law Theory* (1992) chs 6, 11 and 12

Golding M. P. 'Principled Decision-Making and the Supreme Court' in Summers (ed) *Essays in Legal Philosophy* (1968)

Gottlieb G. *The Logic of Choice* (1968)

Guest A. G. 'Logic in the Law' in Guest (ed) *Oxford Essays in Jurisprudence* (1961)

Harris J. W. *Law and Legal Science* (1979) ch 5

Hodgson D. H. *Consequences of Utilitarianism* (1967)

Hook S. (ed) *Law and Philosophy* (1964) Pt 3

e

Jensen O. C. *The Nature of Legal Argument* (1957)

Lee S. *Judging Judges* (1989)

Levi E. H. *An Introduction to Legal Reasoning* (1948)

MacCormick D. N. *Legal Reasoning and Legal Theory* (1978)

Perelman C. H. *Justice, Law and Argument* (1980)

Perry T. D. *Moral Reasoning and Truth* (1976) pp 75-112, 196-216

Pound R. 'Common Law and Legislation' (1907) 21 Harv L Rev 383

Reid Lord 'The Judge as Law Maker' (1972) 12 JSPTL 22

Sartorius R. E. *Individual Conduct and Social Norms* (1975) ch 10

Schauer F. *Playing by the Rules* (1991)

Shuman S. I. 'Justification of Judicial Decisions' (1971) 59 Calif L Rev 723

Stoljar S. J. 'The Logical Status of a Legal Principle' (1953) 20 U Chi L Rev 181

Stone J. *Legal System and Lawyers' Reasonings* (1964) chs 6-8

Wasserstrom R. A. *The Judicial Decision* (1961)

16 The duty to obey the law

Is there a moral duty to obey the law? Most public men say there is. In the history of speculative thought, adherents of widely different social perspectives have said that there is. Socrates went to his unjust execution proclaiming such a duty. St Paul, writing to the Christians at Rome, affirmed a religious obligation to obey the secular law. St Thomas Aquinas states that human law ought to be obeyed unless it contravened natural law, and even then it was generally right to obey 'to avoid scandal'. Bentham, who rejected natural law and advocated that all law should be subject to criticism by reference to the standard of utility, recommended the following maxim: 'Obey punctually, censor freely.'

The House of Lords, in upholding an order requiring a journalist to disclose the source of his information, was unimpressed by the argument that he, as a matter of conscience, considered that his obligation to keep his promise not to disclose outweighed his duty to obey the law. Such a doctrine would, in their Lordships' view, directly undermine the rule of law and is completely unacceptable in a democratic society.[1] The European Court of Human Rights has since ruled that the order violated the journalist's right to freedom of expression which is protected by Article 10 of the European Convention of Human Rights.[2] But, of course, that court did not rule that breaking the law for conscience sake is a human right. It upheld what it took to be a legal right under the Convention. One court may decide that another court has misinterpreted the law, without questioning that 'the law' (properly interpreted) should always be obeyed.

Yet, if you look around you, you find people of impeccable character who break the law and see nothing morally objectionable in so doing. An

---

1 *X Ltd v Morgan-Grampian Ltd* [1991] AC 1.
2 *Goodwin v UK* Case 16 1994/463, (1996) Times, 18 March.

acquaintance of mine tells me that he drives to work every day in excess of the speed limit; it does no one any harm, and he'd never be on time if he did not. People I know, of the highest respectability, enter into informal transactions with builders and decorators on a cash basis, so as to avoid the value added tax which they are legally obliged to pay, and see nothing wrong with it. And, of course, radical critics of our political and legal institutions see nothing morally objectionable in breaking the law; it may be 'imprudent', but never 'wrong', to defy the establishment by flouting its laws. On the other hand, the same critics will be heard condemning official acts, or the actions of employers, on the specific ground that what they do is 'illegal' and therefore 'wrong'.

If someone affirms that there is a moral duty to obey the law, or implies that there is by the nature of the criticisms he makes of others, but at the same time breaks the law and sees nothing wrong with it, is he a hypocrite? Some believers in the duty might say this, or, more charitably, that he has made a mistake about the moral position in his own case which reflection and discussion might correct. If he dwells on the advantages which we all derive from legal institutions, he will come to understand the importance of co-operation and setting a good example. In this way moral education will at last lead him to realise that it is wrong (and not just illegal) to break traffic and tax laws.

But nowadays there are writers who take an opposite view. Our good citizen – be he supporter of the establishment or radical critic – is not mistaken when he says that there is nothing wrong with breaking the law. There is nothing wrong with it – not, at least, just because the law is broken. The only mistake lies in the belief that there is ever any moral duty to obey the law as such. The root cause of this mistake is a failure, so it is argued, to distinguish the act from its legal quality. Of course, there are good moral reasons against many acts which also happen to be illegal – like murder or theft – but it is not because they are illegal that we are morally obliged to abstain from them.

To assert that there is a moral duty to obey the law means affirming that there are moral grounds why one ought to perform any act which the law prescribes or abstain from any act which the law prohibits. Affirming this proposition leaves open the question whether the duty is absolute or qualified in some way. There are probably few people who would support the duty in its absolute form – that is, assert that the moral reasons for obeying the law could never be outweighed by moral reasons pointing towards disobedience. It is implausible to attribute to Socrates or St Paul the view that an ordinance of the state flatly contrary to one's religious duty should be complied with. St Thomas was explicit on the point. Democratic politicians would allow that it might be right to disobey the laws of undemocratic regimes, and probably also that protest against unjust laws of democratic regimes can sometimes legitimately include some kinds of lawbreaking. So the real issue is whether there is or is not a prima facie duty to obey.

If I have in my left hand a book of Jubbjubb etiquette – something totally unknown to you – and in my right hand a book of your country's law, and I announce that I am going to open each at random, will you allow that there are moral reasons indicating obedience to whatever comes out of my right hand which plainly do not obtain in the case of the left-hand book? Or is your conscience equipoised between the two books – that is, until you hear the prescription read out, there is no way of knowing whether there will be moral reasons to comply? And remember: the question is not just one of probabilities. You might allow that, given your previous acquaintance with English law, there is more than a 50:50 chance that something required by it is something which there are moral grounds for performing. That is not enough. For one to be able to affirm that a prima facie moral duty to obey English law exists, one must be satisfied that, whatever comes out of the English law book, there are reasons (stateable in advance) why it is morally right to comply – albeit that, once the prescription is known, other moral reasons may tell against.

The present discussion must be distinguished from the topic dealt with at the end of chapter 9, above – that is, law's alleged normativity. We saw that there are a variety of positions from which it is asserted that a conceptual connection exists between 'legal' and 'ought to be obeyed', only some of which would clothe 'true law' with full-blooded moral status. Such conceptual claims, even if sound, contribute nothing to the moral dilemmas of daily life with which we are here concerned. In the case of tax and traffic laws, the citizen may have no difficulty in recognising what the law is, but still be perturbed about the moral question of compliance. Can critical morality furnish an extra-legal platform on which a distinct duty, directed towards the law, can be stood? Four concepts have been invoked – gratitude, promise-keeping, fairness, and the promotion of the common good. Of course, one could deny ultimate moral status to any one (or all) of these concepts and so raise the discussion to the abstract level of alleged bases of 'moral truth' (see chapter 2, above). It is fashionable, however, to proceed as follows: granted, *arguendo*, that such concepts have objective standing within an acceptable critical morality, does a prima facie moral duty to obey the law follow?

The appeal to gratitude is conservative or romantic. Your country and its laws have conferred great benefits on you. The least you can do is to obey all its laws, unless some good ground for not doing so can be shown. As to this, it may be argued in reply that the concept of gratitude, as ordinarily understood, does not carry us so far. One may be grateful to one's parents, and obligations of many kinds may be said to flow from such gratitude – but not the obligation to do everything they tell you to do, nor even to give reasons why you should not do what they say. Even supposing one accepts that there is a prima facie duty to obey a benevolent parent – that is, to comply with her directions unless some countervailing reason exists – the relationship to legal authorities is different. Gratitude to them, if such there be, is more like the gratitude we owe to a friend who has conferred a favour in the course of a co-operative relationship. Certainly, we should do as much for him, but there is no question of taking his orders even as a prima facie moral guide.

The argument from promise-keeping is as old as the concept of the social contract, which for something over 300 years has been toted about in political philosophy. Men who enter into a political compact with a government promise obedience in exchange for protection and other benefits – figuratively speaking. Anyone receiving the benefits commits himself to this social contract, and so impliedly promises obedience. Variants of this argument allege that anyone who takes part in democratic processes, for instance by voting, impliedly promises to obey the law. Granted that promise-keeping, in the absence of good reasons to the contrary, is morally required, it follows that obedience to the law is morally required.

The most sophisticated version of the social contract in modern political philosophy is contained in John Rawls's theory of justice, discussed in chapter 20, below. As we shall see, Rawls argues that a society is just if it is governed by principles which people would have agreed to in a state of ignorance about their particular position in society. Where a society is just or nearly just by this test there is, he says, a 'natural duty' of all citizens to support and further just institutions. This natural duty includes doing what is required of one by society's institutions, including the law. The duty exists independently of any actual promise to obey because, behind the veil of ignorance about their own situation, people would have agreed to it. So long as the basic structure of society is reasonably just, the duty extends to obeying unjust particular laws – provided they do not exceed certain limits of injustice, such as by making unjust demands only of a particular group or by denying basic liberties. When these limits are exceeded, conscientious refusal to obey the particular law is justified; and, in the case of blatant injustice, 'civil disobedience' of it or other laws may be warranted. Civil disobedience is a public, non-violent act aimed at bringing about a change in the law or the policies of the government. Unlike 'conscientious refusal', civil disobedience may warrant breaking laws which are not themselves unjust in order to draw attention to those which are.

Opponents of such lines of argument usually point to the simple 'fact' that receiving benefits, or voting, or getting the social set-up you would have agreed to in advance of knowledge of your position, are not equivalent to promising to obey. If you join a club and promise to observe the rules, you are acting wrongly, prima facie, if you break them. But a state organised under law is not like a club. We have no choice about belonging.

In this context, there may be a difference between ordinary citizens and persons exercising official roles. If we accept that nothing a citizen does, and nothing that happens to him, is equivalent to a promise to obey the law, we might wish to distinguish the case of someone taking up a position as a judge or a minister or a town councillor or a policeman. Perhaps, given the nature of their legally-defined roles, taking up office is for them equivalent to a promise to obey all the laws – or, at any rate, all the laws directed to them in their official capacity. Rawls argues that, quite apart from the natural duty of citizens to obey the laws of a reasonably just society, officials have a special 'obligation' to do so. All obligations arise from the 'principle of fairness', which is a distinct principle to which people would have agreed from behind the veil of ignorance:

> '[T]his principle holds that a person is under an obligation to do his part as specified by the rules of an institution whenever he has voluntarily accepted the benefits of the scheme or has taken advantage of the opportunities it offers to advance his interests, provided that this institution is just or fair.'[3]

Some may find a principle of fairness of this sort acceptable, independently of the contractarian basis Rawls offers for it, and might wish to extend it to all citizens. For them, 'fairness' would be a moral ground for the duty to obey the law, distinct from promise-keeping. Society may not be like a club in the sense of an association people join voluntarily, but it could be argued that a comparatively beneficent state has other qualities of non-political associations: it confers benefits and, in order to do so, imposes burdens. Those who support the closed shop in industry – that is, compulsory union membership for all employees – often do so on the ground that it would be unfair if people took the benefits of higher wages and improved conditions negotiated by the union without paying subscriptions. The argument is not that they ought to pay because they have promised to, but that they ought to promise to pay because it would be unfair if they did not. Similarly, some would argue, you ought not to take the benefit of a well-managed traffic system, or the benefits derived from tax expenditure, without submitting to the laws. You have a duty to obey the law, not because of anything you owe the government, but because of something you owe your fellow citizens. If they all comply and you benefit, it is unfair if you benefit without complying.

To this argument, various sorts of answers are possible. An anarchist would deny that the legal institutions confer any benefit at all. Those who

3   *A Theory of Justice* p 342.

regard the state's institutions (at least in a democracy) as on the whole beneficial, counter the argument of fairness by pointing out that it cannot apply where submitting to a legal restraint in fact does no one any good. If I am driving along a deserted road, how can it be unfair in me to exceed the speed limit, even if I know that other people have regularly observed it? What one makes of this sort of example depends on how typical one thinks it is. If it is commonly the case that occasions of law-compliance benefit no one, then the analogy with the 'fairness' implications of day-to-day co-operative transactions breaks down. If, on the other hand, one supposes that compliance with the law usually confers some benefit, even if the benefit is not immediately obvious to the actor, then one can make out a case for saying that fairness requires that you obey the law (whatever it is) unless on the particular facts its total uselessness is made evident.

You have to be satisfied of two things before a prima facie duty to obey the law can be said to be founded on the moral concept of fairness: first, that laws have generally beneficial effects; second, that most other people obey, so that you would be taking an unfair advantage if you do not. Just as, in the closed shop case, for the fairness argument to be appropriate – and there too, as with the law, it might be outweighed – you have to be satisfied, first, that the union does confer benefits, and second, that all other employees (or the great majority) are paying their subscriptions. It is rumoured that there are industries in which theft of material by workers, or misappropriation of resources for private purposes by managers, is so common that such conduct is no longer thought of as 'wrong'. If that is true, it might well be that someone whose conventional law-breaking actions are challenged on moral grounds would say: 'But everybody does it'. That would amount to a denial of any duty based on fairness.

Notice, however, that the fairness argument for a moral obligation to obey the law (unlike the consequentialist arguments we are about to consider) does not require showing that compliance on the particular occasion will do anyone any good. Suppose a ban on using garden hose-pipes is instituted when there is a water shortage. The ban applies to 1000 households. 999 comply, which has the effect of saving sufficient water even if the thousandth citizen uses as much water as he likes. It would still be 'unfair' for him to disregard the ban, even if (indeed, especially if) he knew that his neighbours would continue to observe it.

Perhaps the commonest justification for the duty to obey the law is appeal to the public good. If people break the law, the collective welfare of society is diminished: therefore, we are morally obliged to obey. In the parlance of moral philosophy, such arguments are called 'utilitarian', and their soundness is often challenged. It is not difficult for critics of the argument to think of examples where (on the face of it) total welfare would be diminished rather than increased by obedience to law. The law requires everyone to declare every item of income in his tax return. Supposing a man has received a small payment from a friend for performing some minor service, such as mowing a lawn or decorating a house. (Suppose also that he knows that most people do not declare such income, so that no argument of fairness would be relevant.) How is the public good affected if he breaks the law by omitting this item from his tax return? If he did comply, a little more tax would be collected from him by the authorities, and incremental benefits flowing from expenditure of state revenue would accrue. But against that would have to be set the disadvantage to himself and his family of having to forego the money collected – this, like all consequences to individuals, is a relevant consideration for the purpose of a utilitarian calculus in a way in which it is not for a fairness argument. He might claim that the loss to him and his family would outweigh any trivial benefit to others; and he could certainly make out this claim if he could show that the increase in administration costs required by collecting the extra sum would actually swallow up the addition to the state's revenue.

Those defending a utilitarian basis for the duty to obey the law may challenge this sort of hypothetical case on the ground that it naively limits those consequences which have to be taken into account. In particular, it ignores the effects of bad example. Even if my lawbreaking directly does more good than harm, indirectly the reverse may be true because, following this example, others may break the law in circumstances where manifest harm is done, or I myself, on other occasions, may follow my own bad example with bad effects on the public good. *Ex hypothesi*, the man concealing the extra income will not produce bad consequences by way of bad example in the particular context of tax evasion, because I have assumed that he knows that most other people already cheat in this way. But his impressionable children, for instance, may get the idea that you need not obey the law where your own resulting loss will be greater than any tangible benefit to others. Dad will have explained that point when filling in his tax return last night, and so today they will shoplift from large stores, calculating (perhaps mistakenly) that their gains will be greater than the losses to the company which owns the store. (If they were familiar with the terminology of theoretical economics, they would base such a view on 'marginal utility'. They would point out that, given their comparative poverty and the comparative wealth of the company, the next pound gained by them has more value than the next pound lost by the company.)

The argument from bad example attempts to justify the duty to obey the law on the basis of what is known as 'act-utilitarianism'. An act is morally wrong if it will have worse consequences than some other act open to the actor on the occasion. The argument suggests that an act of lawbreaking is wrong by this test because its consequences include imitation in the way of further law-breaking, and some of the further acts of law-breaking will have bad consequences. Its plausibility depends on one's assessment of the generalisability of the effects of 'law-breaking' as a class of activities. If one takes the view that breaking some kinds of laws in no way leads, through bad example, to breaking other kinds of laws, this argument cannot found a duty to obey the law as such.

Sometimes consequentialist arguments for a duty to obey the law are stated in a particular form which makes it easy for the moral philosopher to shoot them down, as when someone says: 'You shouldn't evade your taxes, for what would happen if everybody did it?' To this the moral philosopher can answer that the wrongness of an action can never be established merely by pointing out that, if everyone did it, the consequences would be bad: if everyone caught the 9am train to Paddington tomorrow, there would be chaos; but that does not show that my catching it is in any way morally questionable. This misses the difficult but crucially important question, which is whether law-breaking is potentially imitative behaviour, in a way which train-catching is not. The argument should not be stated: 'What if everyone did it?' but: 'Other people will do it if you do.' This is an empirical proposition, whose truth cannot be tested in the philosopher's armchair. Is it in fact plausible?

Everyone would agree that some acts of law-breaking have bad effects on the collective welfare (whether through imitation of bad examples or otherwise), and that some do not – like the lone car driver exceeding the speed limit on the deserted road. It could be argued that everything turns on the particular situation, so that, before I open the law book, there is no way of knowing whether it will be right or wrong to obey any particular prescription; therefore, there is no prima facie duty to obey the law as such. To this it might be answered that, in many cases, it will be impracticable for the actor to assess the consequences of obedience or disobedience, that the consequences of disobedience are usually worse than the consequences of obedience, and that therefore one ought to obey the law (whatever it says) unless the consequences of doing so can be proved to be harmful. One's judgment on the question must turn on one's impression of whether consequences of law-breaking are or are not easily assessable at the moment when the issue of obedience or disobedience arises.

The other typical form of utilitarian argument is 'rule-utilitarianism': an action is right if required by a rule, where general observance of the rule would have best consequences. The difficulty with this kind of argument in the particular context of obedience to law is that it is hard to exhaust all possible formulations of rules about obedience in order to compare their respective consequences. Clearly, a rule that one should always obey will have better consequences than a rule that one should always disobey – the latter rule would be too onerous even for the most dedicated rebel, for one could not move about without being morally obliged constantly to smash things, hit people and break contracts. However, a rule requiring one to obey (with certain exceptions) would probably have better consequences than a rule requiring one always to obey. The problem is to formulate all the exceptions. They would presumably relate to occasions on which law-breaking did no harm, either directly, or indirectly through setting bad examples. In other words, on the issue of obeying the law, there are no considerations relevant to rule-utilitarianism which are not involved in a discussion of act-utilitarianism. The important points concern the actual consequences of obedience or disobedience to different kinds of laws, whether influence through bad example is a plausible source of consequences, and whether assessment of consequences is likely to be so impracticable that one ought to assume a moral presumption in favour of obeying the law.

Bibliography

Boardman W. S. 'Coordination and the Moral Obligation to Obey the Law' (1987) Ethics 546

Christie G. A. 'On the Moral Obligation to Obey the Law' (1990) Duke LJ 1311

Dworkin R. M. *Taking Rights Seriously* (revised edn, 1978) ch 8

Fortas A. *Discerning Dissent and Civil Disobedience* (1968)

Gans C. *Philosophical Anarchism and Political Disobedience* (1992)

Gavison R. (ed) *Issues in Contemporary Legal Philsophy* (1987) ch 4

Green L. *The Authority of the State* (1990) chs 8 and 9

Greenawalt K. 'The Natural Duty to Obey the Law' (1985) 84 Mich L Rev 1
  – *Conflicts of Law and Morality* (1989)

Hart H. L. A. 'Are There Any Natural Rights?' in Quinton (ed) *Political Philosophy* (1967)

Hook S. (ed) *Law and Philosophy* (1964) Pt 1

Hurd H. M. 'Challenging Authority' (1991) 100 Yale LJ 1611

Pennock J. R. and Chapman J. W. (eds) *Political and Legal Obligation* (1970)

Perry M. *Morality, Politics, and Law* (1988)

Pitkin H. 'Obligation and Consent' in Laslett, Runciman and Skinner (eds) *Philosophy, Politics and Society* (4th series, 1972)

Puna N. W. 'Civil Disobedience: an Analysis and Rationale' (1968) 43 NY U L Rev 651

Rawls J. *A Theory of Justice* (1972) pp 350-356, 363-391

Raz J. *The Authority of Law* (1979) Pt 4

Sartorius R. E. *Individual Conduct and Social Norms* (1975) ch 6

Singer P. *Democracy and Disobedience* (1973)

Smith M. B. E. 'Is There a Prima Facie Obligation to Obey the Law?' (1973) 82 Yale LJ 950

Symposia
    (1981) 67 Virginia Law Review
    (1884) Georgia Law Review
    (1985) 62 Southern California Law Review.
Walzer M. *Obligations* (1970) chs 2, 6, 8-10
Wasserstrom R. A. 'The Obligation to Obey the Law' in Summers (ed)
    Essays in Legal Philosophy (1968)
Zwiebach B. *Civility and Disobedience* (1975)

17 The historical school and non-state law

Jurisprudential controversies about the nature of law commonly assume, expressly or tacitly, that the law we are talking about is the law of the modern state. Is that not perhaps too parochial? Should we not be careful to ensure that our conception of law is wide enough to encompass the 'law' under which man lived before the modern state evolved, as well as the 'primitive law' of non-state communities? Besides these, are there not other systems of non-state 'law' for which our conception must account, such as the laws of churches, universities, clubs and, above all, public international law and other supra-state international legal orders?

The literature of jurisprudence speaks of a movement of thought among legal theorists of the 19th century as the 'historical school'. The members of this school, like the legal positivists, rejected natural law, but not for the same reasons. They agreed with the positivists that law was not discoverable by abstract reason, but they did not accept that it was the product of deliberate choice. Law was the outcome of historical processes, and could only be understood in their light.

Membership of this school is usually said to include German 'romantic' writers, like C. von Savigny (1779-1861), on the one hand, and Sir Henry Maine (1822-1888), on the other. In fact, Savigny and Maine had little in common, beyond the view that history matters in our understanding of what law now is. There is, of course, nothing unusual in those who agree that we should learn lessons from the past finding that they have quite different views of the lessons it teaches.

The central tenet of the German romantic school was that law resides in the spirit of the people, the *volksgeist*. It was an error to suppose that a legislator stood above the community and imposed his will. He was an organ of the people, giving effect to its intuitions. This entailed that law both did and should vary from one country to another, since different peoples had different spirits. The romantics resisted – ultimately without success – the move towards codification on the model of the *Code Napoleon*. For them, the idea of a code based rationalistically upon universal features of human nature contradicted the lesson of history, that a people's law resides in its own peculiar customs. Their treatises are seldom cited today in connection with the problems which preoccupy modern jurisprudence, such as the controversy between positivist and non-positivist conceptions of law, the nature of legal reasoning, the relations between law and morals, the proper attitude for citizens to take to the law's claims and the respective roles of legislature and judiciary. But two of their underlying contentions still matter. First, if they were right, then both 'higher law' theorists and Benthamite utilitarians are wrong when they claim that good law is everywhere the same; and comparative lawyers should not assume that legal systems can learn from each other. Secondly, they provide one reason for revering customary law. As we shall see in chapter 19, below, there are social theorists who value customary law because it contributes to 'community'. The historical romantics valued it because it expresses national uniqueness.

The romanticism of the German historical school should be contrasted with the idealist historicism of G. W. F. Hegel (1770-1831). The romantics were backward-looking, seeking the true roots of a people's law. Hegelian idealism is forward-looking. For Hegel, 'World Spirit' worked itself out through a series of historical evolutionary phases. It comprehended the 'moment' of abstract right (centred on the idea of freedom) within the 'moments' of morality and concrete ethical life. The modern state, once shorn of archaic encumbrances, would be the culmination of this process. As we shall see in chapter 19, this prophetic historicism was taken over and given a materialist interpretation in Marxist theory.

Many of the romantics stressed specifically Germanic features of the law. Savigny, however, was both a historical romantic and a Romanist. He traced the historical unfolding of German law back to its sources in the *Corpus Juris* of Justinian. Many critics see this as a paradox. If the universal source of law is custom, why focus our interest upon those Roman texts which continental lawyers had received in displacement of local custom? Savigny's answer is that jurists are another organ of popular consciousness, alongside the legislature. In expounding legal science, they are articulating the *volksgeist*.

A less dramatic version of this seeming paradox, and its alleged resolution, infuses debates about the value of the common law. It is less dramatic, because England never experienced a wholesale reception of a foreign system, requiring to be explained or explained away. (It may be otherwise with former parts of the British Empire which have received segments of the common law in displacement of earlier law.) The common law is sometimes referred to – for instance, by Blackstone – as the general custom of the realm. A romantic outlook contrasts legislation with the common law: whereas the former is produced by the parliamentary majority of the moment, the latter has evolved from the peculiar genius of the English people. On the other hand, its content can be discovered only by what Coke called 'the artificial reason of the law'. Thus, the common law is at once the product of the people and a technical achievement of lawyers. For a Bentham, this is a confidence trick. For an English Savignyan, there is no contradiction. Law is not, or should not be, what rationalistic bureaucrats conceive to be for our good. It should express the people's peculiar intuitions and needs; and, in so far as law must deal with technical matters on which overt consciousness is silent, the proper agent for the spirit of the people is legal science.

For Sir Henry Maine, the significance of history was the light it shed, not so much upon the nature of law, as upon its content. It was a mistake, he urged, to take the legal provisions in force at any time and to explain them in terms of some rationally coherent set of aims and functions. The law always contains deposits of institutions, principles and distinctions which reflect ideas of earlier ages. We may think we have wills and testaments because of the function they serve, in allowing people to determine how their property is to be distributed on death. The truth is that we have wills because we inherited this device from Rome, and historical research reveals that the Romans originally saw them as conveyances to heirs. Like the fiction of adoption, these conveyances had as their object the continuance of the family, not satisfaction of property control from the grave. The principle of primogeniture was usually explained in feudal-functional terms – it kept the land together and so was a source of strength. But that, argued Maine, was only part of the story. Why was this particular device chosen? The answer, he suggests – with rather more speculation than evidence – was that the Germanic tribes who invaded the Roman empire carried with them memories of an ancient form of family government in which continuity was preserved through single chieftain heads. An idea which was, in its distant origins, concerned with devolution of responsibilities was thereafter impressed with Roman conceptions of absolute property. Maine noted the difficulty Blackstone had experienced in rationalising the common law rule which prohibited brothers of the half blood from inheriting on intestacy. The explanation, he said, lay in an ancient conception of property devolving on death only to agnatic male kin. This would exclude sons of a common mother.

Whatever the truth of these particular contentions, no one today would quarrel with Maine's historical method as applied to particular provisions. Pollock, Maitland, Holmes, Pound and many others have demonstrated that a law which now serves one purpose arose originally to meet quite another. It is on the level of historical generalisation that Maine has come in for most criticism. In this regard, he put forward hypotheses about legal forms and the social forces producing legal change, as well as about content. As to form he appears to suggest a six-fold developmental thesis. In the infancy of law, there were kingly judgments supposed to be divinely inspired. Next comes custom. This is followed by the age of codes, like the 12 tables of ancient Rome. These three stages, Maine believed, were common to all the Indo-European races. Thereafter, some peoples, like those of India, cease to evolve new legal forms, whereas the 'progressive' peoples, like the Romans and the English, proceeded to three further stages: fictions, equity, and legislation. The social forces behind this development concern the emergence from an archaic type of society in which communities are based solely on kinship, through larger units consisting of collections of familial groups, to the modern state where community is founded on territorial contiguity.

It is not clear how rigidly sequential Maine supposed his six stages to be. He stresses that the earliest communities, of which we have any knowledge, regarded themselves as descended from a common stock even though they were aware that strangers had been introduced through the 'fiction' of adoption. This suggests that fictions need not come after codes. In any event, his six-fold classification of forms is difficult to accept without qualification. Homeric texts are not an adequate basis for suggesting that royal judgments precede the development of custom. The invention of writing did lead to codification in ancient Mesopotamia, but apparently not in ancient Egypt. As to the later stages, the remarkable parallel between 'fictional' devices employed by the Roman jurisconsults and by common law courts, and between the establishment of a supplementary 'equitable' body of rules by the Praetorian edict and by English chancellors, has often been drawn. Are we entitled to regard this as a symptom of 'progress'?

On the level of legal content, Maine asserts that in early law most of a man's obligations were fixed from birth by his status. Through many gradual stages, and despite the law of any one time being encumbered with inherited archaic notions, modern law comes to regard a man's free choice as the chief source of his obligations. His most often quoted generalisation runs:

'All the forms of Status taken notice of in the Law of Persons were derived from, and to some extent are still coloured by, the powers and privileges anciently residing in the Family. If then we employ Status, agreeably with the usage of the best writers, to signify these personal conditions only, and avoid applying the term to such conditions as are the immediate or remote result of agreement, we may say that the movement of the progressive societies has hitherto been a movement from *Status to Contract*.'[1]

---

1   *Ancient Law* pp 181-182.

Critics of this formula have pointed out that, since Maine's day, the law has tended to attach rights and obligations much more to status than to contract: witness the statutory protected tenancy, which supervenes when a contractual tenancy is terminated; and the right not to be unfairly dismissed from employment even when the employer is not in breach of contract. To this it may be answered that Maine did say 'hitherto'. He may have been a believer in progress, but there is little indication that he believed in historical inevitability. Another type of criticism accuses him of paying too much attention to the form of the law, at least in his analysis of modern law. He had been at pains to suggest that ancient provisions were dictated by belief in kinship community, and how this was fostered by the fiction of adoption. Might it not be said that the contract of employment of his own day was a similar 'fiction', in that it stressed obligations flowing from free consent whereas economic reality and class status denied any true freedom?

Maine was no antiquarian, examining the past for its own sake. He believed that historical research could expose modern error. He argued that the belief in natural law had arisen historically from confusions in Roman thought. The *Ius Gentium*, which had been devised to deal with disputes involving foreign residents in Rome, had been worked out on the basis of elements common to Italian tribes. Later, under the influence of Greek philosophy, it had come to be identified with *naturalis ratio*. In particular, *occupatio*, as a means of acquiring property, was just one of the provisions of the *Ius Gentium*. Political philosophers who alleged that, in the state of nature, individuals made things their own by occupying what was previously owned by no one, were anti-historical. All the evidence pointed to common ownership as the oldest proprietary institution, and to long possession of what had belonged to another as the typical title. Similarly, social compact theories were anti-historical, since the very notion that men could acquire obligations by agreement alone was a late development.

It is a controversial question whether historical information of this sort has a bearing on theories of justice which rely on a 'notional' state of nature or a 'notional' contract. As we shall see in chapter 20, below, Rawls's contractarian theory of justice requires no assumptions about any real contract. On the other hand, Nozick's entitlement theory of justice is avowedly historical, requiring that all 'just' property-holdings should be derived from an original proprietor whose acquisition was just. Can that be squared with Maine's contention that private titles arise from trespass on the common domain? So far as natural law is concerned, does the fact that the Romans appealed to it to meet a certain historical contingency prove that it does not exist?

Nor was Maine a romantic. Legal forms and codes of thought of the past should be investigated, but not necessarily revered. Natural law theory had served a good turn, with its insistence on symmetry and generality, but we moderns could do without it. Fictions had been an intelligent device for combining necessary change with respect for the written word, but they could not be supported today. Maine objected to Bentham's lack of historical perspective, but he had no objection to proposals for codification based on rational calculation of needs. He rejected Blackstone's view that the common law was custom; it was, he said, just another, rather unwieldy form of written law.

As Paolo Grossi has shown, the publication of Maine's *Ancient Law* fuelled a debate among 19th century continental theorists between the proponents and opponents of 'primitive communism'. If private property was unknown to our forebears, might not that lend support to claims that it is a dispensable institution? In fact, anthropological and ethnographic studies in the 20th century reveal such a variety of property arrangements within primitive societies that any generalisations about historical priority must probably be rejected. Lawrence Becker, having reviewed this literature, concludes:

'Every attempt I have made is refuted by a counter-example actually observed in the field. The data indicate that, although property rights exist everywhere, what is necessary about them is just that some exist. It appears that many specific systems of ownership are compatible with any set of environmental conditions and social structures.'[2]

Maine is perhaps most respected today for the impetus he gave to the study of contemporary primitive law. He applauded Montesquieu (1689-1755) for having the right idea about explaining laws in terms of social forces, but complained at his lack of empirical research. Montesquieu's *L'Esprit des Lois* contained 'guesses' about the effect on the laws of different peoples of such matters as climate and racial characteristics. The thing to do (Maine said) was to look carefully at the records of ancient peoples, and also to investigate surviving communities still in a primitive stage of development. For Maine, the major source of information of this latter sort were the village communities of India. Since his time, anthropological research has accumulated information about a wide variety of pre-state communities. Generally, what Maine said about the importance of kinship groups and the absence of wholly executory contracts has been borne out. Not surprisingly, however, the content of the laws of primitive communities has been found to exhibit enormous variation.

What should the jurist ask of the anthropologist? Does the anthropologist have any obligation to deliver? The anthropologist

---

2   'The Moral Basis of Property Rights' in Pennock and Chapman (eds) *Property: Nomos xxii* at p 200.

investigates his chosen community in all its facets of life. Should he be hamstrung by a search for 'law'? Those who advocate the introduction of mechanisms for alternative dispute resolution into modern societies, which bypass conventional courts and tribunals, may (although they clearly need not) buttress their arguments by anthropological and ethnographic information about how things are managed within small face-to-face communities. It might be thought to be a terminological question of little import whether the analogies invoked are said to be instances of 'non-law' or of a different kind of 'law'.

Perhaps the jurist can derive generalisations from the detailed information provided by anthropological research, about the contents of primitive law, or about the nature of primitive 'legal' institutions, or about the functions served by 'law' in primitive societies. We saw in chapter 2, above, that Hart was able to deduce a 'minimum content of natural law' from certain 'truisms' about man – a society must have rules restricting force, theft and deception. Being 'necessary', such rules should appear in all societies, past, present and to come. It does, indeed, appear that there are such rules in all primitive societies; but there is no question of uniform provisions about these things. Homicide rules vary greatly. Because of their harsh conditions of life, Eskimo law not merely permits, but requires suicide and senillicide in certain circumstances. 'Property', and so theft, exists everywhere in some form; but private property in land is rare, and modern conceptions of ownership – in the sense of an exclusive and unlimited right to do what one likes with one's own – is often absent (there may not even be a word for it). Although deception of some sort is proscribed, the law will not – as Maine pointed out – concern itself with all the forms of dishonesty which sophisticated institutions make possible.

Apart from filling in the details in Hart's list, does anthropological evidence add anything? Are there other types of rules which, though not necessary for all societies at all times, are universally found in primitive societies? E. A. Hoebel concludes from a survey of a wide variety of primitive societies that the one assumption of overwhelming importance underlying all primitive legal systems is the postulation of magico-religious forces as being superior to men; but there is no consistency as to whether magico-religious practices are permitted, required, or prohibited as the crime of 'sorcery'. He also says that primitive societies generally recognise the social inferiority of women and the relative exclusiveness of marital rights; but again, details vary. If Hoebel and Hart are right, early societies have rules 'about' the supernatural, sexual relations, violence, property and deceit; but developed societies could drop the first two.

The institutions employed in primitive legal systems vary also. The survey reported by R. D. Schwartz and J. S. Miller shows that they may use mediation, police and counsel, or some or none of these. They may even have 'courts', as does the Lozi society investigated by M. Gluckman.

Perhaps more illuminating generalisations will be discovered if we concentrate on functions, rather than content or institutions. Hoebel lists four functions which, he maintains, are served by the law of primitive man: defining relationships among the members of society; taming naked force and directing it to the maintenance of order; the disposition of trouble cases; and the redefinition of relationships as the conditions of life change. These may be contrasted with the wider range of functions which modern law is supposed to serve (see chapter 18, below). In connection with the fourth function, Hoebel criticises Maine's assumption about the static nature of customary law. It will be recalled that Hart, too, spoke of the static character of rules (owing to absence of rules of change) as one of the 'defects' of a 'pre-legal' society (see chapter 9, above). As we shall see in chapter 19, the social theorists 'ideal type' of a customary society is one in which there is no perceived tension between what is practised and what is thought right, and no selfconscious creation of rules. It seems, however, that in many non-state societies people may recognise that a rule with a certain content exists and at the same time withhold moral approval from it; and may indeed, on occasion, make deliberate changes in their rules.

'Custom' is sometimes regarded as a separable topic in jurisprudence or legal theory, parallel to precedent or statutory interpretation. Such treatment is not to be recommended. Lawyers describing the contents of a modern legal system support their statements by reference to sources, one of which may be 'custom'. It is usually low down in the ranking of sources. English courts sometimes give effect to local customs, or to commercial customs. One is considering 'custom' in a quite different sense when it is urged that constitutional practices rest on custom. Then custom is not just another source, but the basis upon which some or all sources are fitted together. The most fundamental tenets of the UK constitution are, in this sense, 'customary'. Even where the constitution is written, it does not necessarily dictate the relationship between judge-made law and legislative enactments, nor indeed the criteria for the recognition of judge-made law. In the United States, for example, these vital matters rest on the practices of the courts and other officials. As we saw in chapters 12 and 13, above, canons of statutory interpretation and rules of precedent involve mixed questions of particular practices and analytic issues. Thirdly, as we saw in the discussion of Savigny's theory at the beginning of this chapter, 'custom' may be employed as an approbative juristic classification, as a 'hurrah' word. Then law is seen to be good so far as it truly reflects custom. Fourthly, when social theorists compare whole systems, describing some as systems of written law and others as systems of customary law, the topic of 'custom' is raised in yet another light. Finally, 'custom' may be appealed to as a ground for modifying the concept of law itself. To this issue we now turn.

A special battery of jurisprudential problems has been raised by attempts to include primitive law and public international law within, or exclude them from, an overall conception of law. Austin excluded them by defining law as the command of the sovereign (see chapter 3, above). Kelsen included them, by terming a victim's relatives (and states) 'organs'; and blood revenge (and war and reprisals) 'sanctions' (see chapter 6, above). One view is that, so long as we have appraised our systems rightly and are aware of all the similarities and differences, how we choose to employ the label 'law' is a matter of small importance. What can be said on the other side? One ground for holding that labels do matter is frankly pedagogic: only if primitive law and international law are called 'law' will they get included within courses of instruction for law students. I doubt whether anyone recommending an inclusive concept would rest his case on this argument alone.

So far as primitive 'law' is concerned, the arguments for an inclusive concept of law are of two, totally incompatible, kinds. The first holds that if we bring to bear on primitive societies some conception of law derived from our own society, we will learn more about them. The converse of this is that, if we mould a conception of law broad enough to encompass the ways in which primitive peoples themselves see their own social arrangements, we will learn more about ourselves. The first ('labels matter') line of argument calls for a discriminating concept of law to be used for slicing up the undifferentiated normative arrangements of primitive societies. Primitive communities generally have no specialist vocabulary for distinguishing legal from non-legal rules in the way we do. As observers of them, we can bring out some crucial feature of their social life by applying some distinguishing characteristic of 'law'. For B. Malinowski, this distinguishing characteristic was reciprocity:

> 'The rules of law stand out from the rest in that they are felt and regarded as the obligations of one person and the rightful claims of another. They are sanctioned not by a mere psychological motive, but by a definite social machinery of binding force based as we know, upon mutual dependence, and realised in the equivalent arrangement of reciprocal services.'[3]

P. Bohannan criticises Malinowski's reciprocity criterion as being too undiscriminating between customary norms as a whole and law in particular. We should instead define law in terms of institutionalised customary norms. In the same vein, M. Gluckman isolated Lozi 'law' from Lozi custom and morality by reference to recognition by the judges. Of course, institutional criteria will not be of much assistance where the

3   *Crime and Custom in Savage Society* p 55.

society in question lacks law-applying institutions. L. Pospisil suggests that primitive law can be isolated by reference to a cluster of differentiating criteria, such as authority, universality, the sense of obligation and sanctions. Depending on the extent to which these criteria were met in the disposal of disputes, the solution should be regarded as more or less 'legal'. Hoebel takes coercive enforcement to be the sole badge of law:

> 'A social norm is legal if its neglect or infraction is regularly met, in threat or in fact, by the application of physical force by an individual or group possessing the socially recognized privilege of so acting.'[4]

Many anthropologists find that they can do their work perfectly well without any such discriminating concept of law. If the people being studied did not distinguish law from other customary norms, why should the observer? Indeed, insisting on fitting their rules into our preconceived pigeon-holes, with all our inappropriate conceptual paraphanalia, may be distinctly unhelpful.

If the question were simply whether a concept of law helps or hinders the understanding of primitive communities, the issue would be entirely internal to anthropology. Nothing relevant to the concept of law appropriate to modern states could turn on it. At this point, however, we turn to the second and converse ('labels matter') argument. The argument runs: not only should we not try to distinguish legal from other social rules when studying primitive societies, it is a mistake to do so in our own society. This is a view which, as we shall see in chapter 18, is advocated by Ehrlich's sociology of law. The contention now under consideration regards the existence of primitive law as providing ammunition for the 'living law' approach. The call of the primitive is added to the call of the social.

M. Barkun argues that our 'common sense' notion of law is too professionally oriented. We need a conception of law which would apply to primitive law and to international law. Such a wider conception would provide us with a better picture of state law. He suggests that we should view law as a 'set of interrelated symbols', a 'means of conceptualising and managing the social environment':

> 'The loci of power, the ties that persons and groups have with one another, the forces that deter and that attract decision-makers – all these are the "underground" questions of legal analysis ... If "legal

4   *The Law of Primitive Man* p 28.

system" is not limited to the parochial confines of courtrooms and law offices, it is – in the end – merely a product of its society.'[5]

I suggest the following exemplary proof as a test for the strength of this argument:

Demonstrandum: Social rules governing English family life are 'laws':

(1) Any definition of law which cannot be applied, without distorting the subject, to primitive societies is parochial and unacceptable.

(2) Any definition of law which distinguishes among social rules (by reference to source, sanction, courts or any other criterion) results in distortion when applied to primitive societies.

(3) Any definition of law which distinguishes among social rules is parochial and unacceptable.

(4) All social rules are laws.

(5) Social rules governing English family life are laws. QED

Are you convinced?

International law, like primitive law, differs from state law in not possessing a legislature, and in the non-central significance of sanctions and courts. Both may suffer distortion if definitions of law emphasising these features are applied to them. On the other hand, there is not the same distortion when state-law concepts, like right, duty, delict and property are applied. It may be true of many primitive societies that these words have no counterpart in the local language; but those who deal in international law have derived their vocabulary from municipal law contexts. Moreover, there are professional and normative arguments for calling international law 'law' which do not apply to primitive law.

International tribunals and government advisers have to use some term to distinguish the rules they wish to appeal to from other rules, such as those of 'comity' or 'policy'. They have to do that because 'legality', to put it at its lowest, plays a distinctive role in diplomatic exchange. Whereas, if some primitive societies successfully settle disputes without a clear-cut legal/non-legal distinction, why should they change? Colonial governments or their successors may wish to introduce the distinction with its accompanying battery of specifically legal concepts, but then that will bring the 'primitive law', in its undifferentiated condition, to an end.

---

5   *Law Without Sanctions* p 44. For a similar argument see Ehrlich (1922) 36 Harv L Rev 130; and Roberts *Order and Dispute*.

Sensitivity on the part of such governments towards primitive communities arguably requires that alien legal conceptions should not be imposed upon them. That was recognised by the High Court of Australia when it ruled that the 'radical title' to land acquired by the Crown on settlement was burdened with the 'native title' of any aboriginal group which occupied a distinct portion of territory.[6] It was not necessary to show that, internally, the members of such a group viewed their relationship to the land as an ownership interest of the sort known to modern legal systems. All questions about the rights of individual members were to be determined, as questions of fact, by reference to the particular evolving tradition of the group.

Special normative claims also cluster round the law-label issue in the context of international law, which are not relevant to primitive law. They are connected with the rule-of-law ideal. One common reaction to international law is disappointment and frustration. Why should we call it 'law' when it does not bring us peace? The assumption is that law's supreme claim to respect is its shield against the chaos which Hobbes depicted in the state of nature where 'the life of man is solitary, poor, nasty, brutish and short'. To this it is answered that international law serves many of the other functions for which we value law – dispute-mediation, co-ordination of plans, and so forth. Further, it is argued, teach our leaders and their servants to think of international law as 'law', and the world will be a better place. Many of the arguments which we considered in chapter 11, above, for the view that 'principles of legality' have to be observed for law to work apply equally to international law. The same, as we saw, can be said of other non-state systems which do not have the special virtue of bringing peace, such as the 'laws' of churches, universities and clubs.

If we believe that there is a moral duty to obey the law – or at any rate that officials are so obligated (see chapter 16, above) – we may wish to argue that the same applies to international law. On the other hand, we may take the view that this crucial aspect of the rule-of-law ideal – compliance with declared rules by officials – has value only in the municipal context. When, in 1968, Sir Harold Wilson ordered the bombing of the stranded oil tanker, the *Torrey Canyon*, he justified the action as essential to prevent disastrous pollution, and indicated that the question of its international legality was a minor matter. When, in 1979, President Giscard D'Estaing justified breach of the law of the European Economic Community in relation to importing British lamb, he appealed to urgent French interests. Neither man would have advocated breaking municipal law in pursuit of government policy, would they?

6   *Mabo v State of Queensland (No 2)* [1992] 175 CLR 1.

Bibliography

Allen C. K. *Law in the Making* (7th edn, 1964) pp 87-129

Barkun M. *Law Without Sanctions* (1968)

Becker L. C. 'The Moral Basis of Property Rights' in Pennock and Chapman (eds) *Property: Nomos xxii* (1980)

Bohannan P. 'The Differing Realms of the Law' (1965) 67 Am Anth 33

Burrow J. W. *Evolution and Society* (1970) ch 5

Campbell A. H. 'International Law and the Student of Jurisprudence' (1950) 35 GST 113

Carter J. C. *Law: its Origin, Growth and Function* (1907)

Diamond A. S. *Primitive Law, Past and Present* (2nd edn, 1971)

Ehrlich E. 'The Sociology of Law' (1922) 36 Harv L Rev 130

Freeman M. D. A. *Lloyd's Introduction to Jurisprudence* (6th edn, 1994) ch 10

Friedmann W. *Legal Theory* (5th edn, 1967) chs 18-19

Fuller L. L. *Anatomy of the Law* (1971) pp 71-82

Gluckman M. *The Judicial Process Among the Barotse of Northern Rhodesia* (2nd edn, (1967)

Grossi P. *An Alternative to Private Property: Collective Property in the Juridical Consciousness of the Nineteenth Century* (1981)

Hegel G. W. F. *Elements of the Philosophy of Right* (1991, trans Nisbet)

Hoebel E. A. *The Law of Primitive Man* (1954)

Jones J. W. *Historical Introduction to the Theory of Law* (1956) ch 2

Kantorowicz H. U. 'Savigny and the Historical School of Law' (1937) 53 LQR 326

Llewellyn K. N. and Hoebel E. A. *The Cheyenne Way* (1941)

MacCormack G. 'Professor Gluckman's Contribution to Legal Theory' (1976) Jur Rev 229

Maine H. J. S. *Ancient Law* (Pollock edn, 1930)

Malinowski B. *Crime and Custom in Savage Society* (1932)

Patterson E. W. 'Historical and Revolutionary Theories of Law' (1951) 51 Colum L Rev 681

Pospisil L. *Anthropology of Law* (1971)

Pound R. 'Law in Books and Law in Action' (1910) Am L Rev 12

Roberts S. *Order and Dispute* (1979)

Robson W. A. 'Sir Henry Maine To-day' in Jennings (ed) *Modern Theories of Law* (1933)

Savigny F. C. von *On the Vocation of our Age for Legislation and Jurisprudence* (2nd edn, Hayward trans, 1831)
– *System of the Modern Roman Law* (Rattigan trans, 1884) ss 7-16

Schapera I. 'Malinowski's Theories of Law' in Firth (ed) *Man and Culture* (1957)

Schwarz R. D. and Miller J. S. 'Legal Evolution and Societal Complexity''
    in Schwarz and Skolnick (eds) *Society and the Legal Order* (1970)
Walton F. P. 'The Historical School of Jurisprudence and Transplantation
    of Law' (1927) 9 JCL (3rd series) 183
Williams G. L. 'International Law and the Controversy Concerning the
    Word "Law"' in Laslett (ed) *Philosophy, Politics and Society* (1956)

18 Sociological jurisprudence

'Law is a social phenomenon.' That is the universal cry of progressive
law schools. But what precisely does it mean? Against what view of law
is it directed? To what new vision is it a banner? The sociological approach
to law is generally contrasted with the analytic. Yet analytical jurists
purport to convey sociological information. Austin tells us that in every
political society there is some sovereign person or body who receives
habitual obedience and renders it to none. Kelsen says that in all societies
lawyers make systematic descriptions of norms which are by and large
effectively enforced. Hart explains what sorts of practices and attitudes
are involved when a society lives by rules – and, indeed, describes his book
as 'an essay in descriptive sociology'. Would any of these authors, if
pressed to give a yes/no answer, deny that law is a social phenomenon?

The quarrel of sociological jurists with the analytical school is not so
much that the latter's sociological assumptions are wrong – for after all,
they disagreed with each other. It is the use they made of concepts drawn
from the law itself in setting down information about society. There was
too much talk about legal rights, duties, powers, property, persons and so
forth. We should instead employ societal concepts, like interest, function,
role, group and class. This will enable us to make the crucial break with
the professional lawyer's view of law.

'Legal sociology' is a burgeoning research enterprise. As its
practitioners are the first to admit, however, there is as yet little agreement
about its proper subject matter. Just as general jurisprudence embraces
debates about the nature of 'law' when it is the subject of legal science –
what do lawyers mean by 'law'? – so sociological jurisprudence should
concern itself with 'law' as the subject of legal sociology – what do
sociologists of law mean by 'law'?

As things are, works proclaiming their concern with the social aspects of law lie across a spectrum from the law-out-to-society end to the society-into-law end. At the nearer end, the researcher takes legal materials or legal institutions – identified by a legal-positivist criterion – and asks what are their social implications, effects or causes. He might find, for instance, that some rule of contract law to be found in the books has precious little influence on the way businessmen actually arrange their affairs; or that the moral implications of 'fault' in the law of tort do not correlate with community attitudes; or that statutory rights to welfare benefits or to legal aid are taken up more by some social classes than by others; or that an attempt to compromise a clash between certain interest groups is the historical explanation for the passing of a certain Act; or that what directs the exercise by the Lord Chancellor of his powers to nominate judges is an old-boy network. Detailed studies of this kind are commonly called 'socio-legal research', and generalisations from them 'sociological jurisprudence'. Yet such research turns out not to presuppose any concept of law different from that investigated in analytical jurisprudence. It requires that we identify 'law' just as lawyers do; but then we move out to society. Nonetheless, accurate generalisations which this 'moving out' provides might supplement or correct the sort of sociological information which analytical jurists supply.

The writers dealt with in the next two sections, on interests and functions, have been close to this end of the spectrum. So too, in practice, has most of the research carried out in the name of 'realism'. At the mid-point of the spectrum comes the view that we need to set alongside a conception of law as something contained in books a quite different conception of law, as a spontaneous social product. To this we turn in the third section, under the heading of 'living law'. At the further end of the spectrum, there are social theorists for whom conceptions of law must be subsumed under conceptions of society. For them, you cannot define law without a social theory which defines society. Some of these writers are discussed in the next chapter. Speculations from the mid-point to the further end of the spectrum are often termed 'the sociology of law', in contrast to 'sociological jurisprudence'. But there exists no uniformity in the use of such expressions.

Controversies within theoretical sociology have to be taken on board. In particular, should a sociological study of law be value-free and 'positivistic', as D. Black argues? Or should it – as writers like P. Selznick and P. Nonet maintain – elucidate the working of the law in terms of social ideals? ('Positivism', for sociologists, is not the same thing as 'positivism' for legal theorists; it refers to the view that social phenomena can be causally explained, as natural phenomena are causally explained in the natural sciences.) Legal sociology also has its own peculiar methodological problems. Should our focus be the behaviour patterns of governmental officials, or wider behaviour patterns? Or should it be, not behaviour at all, but abstract legal rules and principles?

Further, there is a strand in contemporary social theorising which threatens any methodology of applied research. It insists that we cannot relate discourse, including legal discourse, to anything 'out there' because it is discourse itself which constructs social phenomena. Taken to its extreme, this approach yields the conclusion that law, from a sociological point of view, is a self-contained system of communication. There is no question of measuring law's effectiveness against anything external to itself, let alone asking whether it serves (externally conceived) values. The only legal 'facts' are those which the law itself constructs; and the law has nothing to say about anything outside itself. That is the conclusion reached by Niklas Luhmann in his autopoietic analysis of law – the term 'autopoiesis', borrowed from biology, refers to a self-contained organism which generates and regenerates in isolation from other organisms. There seems to be no way in which the value of this approach can be tested in its own terms, since presumably all meta-theoretical discourse is also self-referential. You make an act of faith in favour of autopoieses and hence reject all other sociology of law; or you refuse to do so and proceed with the rest of this and the next chapter.

1   Social interests

The phrase 'sociological jurisprudence' is most often associated with the work of the prolific American jurist, Roscoe Pound (1870-1964). He gave this label to the new approach to legal studies which, he said, was the culmination of the legal philosophy of the past. In 1912, he set down a six-point programme for sociological jurists. First, study of the actual effects of legal institutions and legal doctrines. Second, sociological study in preparation for legislation – particularly, the effects of comparative legislation. Third, study of the means of making legal rules effective: 'The life of the law is in its enforcement.' Fourth, a 'sociological legal history', which would consider what effects legal doctrines had had in the past. Fifth, advocacy of reasonable and just solutions of individual cases, too often sacrificed in the name of certainty. Sixth, making effort more effective in achieving the purpose of law.[1]

This mixture of rather vague methodological and normative precepts is all too typical of Pound's writings. His work comprises a massive survey of legal philosophy, researches into legal history and discourses on particular legal problems. It is collated in the five volumes of his *Jurisprudence*, published in 1959, but the principal themes were laid down in the early years of the century. He can be regarded as an advocate for

1   (1912) 25 Harv L Rev 489 at 514-516.

socio-legal studies, although researchers in this field are unlikely to derive much nourishment from his writing. They are interested in problems like devising efficient questionnaires and statistical techniques, not in the comparative history of juristic speculation. So far as his own contribution to theory is concerned, the focal points for Pound are 'legal interests' and 'jural postulates', ideas which he derived respectively from R. von Jhering and J. Kohler.

The sociological jurist should engage in a survey of 'social interests', that is, of those 'claims or demands or desires' which have pressed or are pressing for legal recognition. He should distinguish 'individual interests', which are asserted in the title of individual life; 'public interests', which are asserted in the title of politically organised society; and 'social interests', which are asserted in the title of social life. It is a matter of controversy whether Pound conceived of these three types as different entities or as different levels of generality for the same entity. At any rate, he indicates that, when we are considering whether some interest ought to be preferred to some other, they must be weighed on the same plane (generally the social plane). Our appraisal will be distorted if we conceive of a clash as one between an individual interest and a social interest. Consequently, individual interests should be subsumed under broader social interests for the purposes of comparative evaluation. Social interests include: first, general security in safety, health, peace and public order, acquisitions, and transactions; second, security of social institutions – family, religious, political, and economic; third, general morals; fourth, conservation of social resources; fifth, general progress – economic, political, and cultural; sixth ('and most important'), the social interest in individual life – that each individual be able to live a human life according to the standards of the society.[2]

Thus, the sociological jurist, unlike the traditional legal scientist, is not to engage in logical reconstruction of the meaning expressed by legal texts, but is to survey and classify social interests to which those texts do, or should, give effect. But his source of information about claims, demands and desires is still lawbook-bound. The most he looks at, apart from statutes and reported judgments, are claims which the courts have rejected, and possibly proposals for legislative reform. Pound rejects the idea of a Benthamite felicific calculus – a survey of all human needs measured by an objective scale. In his early writings, he accepted the 'pragmatic' philosophy of William James. James had said: 'Everything which is demanded is by that fact a good.'[3]

Pound's pragmatic jurisprudence equates justice with quietening those who are banging on the gates. We should not attempt an all-embracing

2   (1943-44) 57 Harv L Rev 1-39.
3   *The Will to Believe* (1897) p 205.

blueprint for legal reform. We should record the demands which people have made or are making on the law, and achieve the best balance we can. 'Social engineering' consists in giving effect to as much as possible of such claims. Where there are irreducible value-conflicts, we can rely on the 'trained intuition' of the judge. Later, Pound extended the concept of social interest to include 'desires' as well as 'claims' and 'demands'; and he expressed misgivings about pragmatism. Perhaps we should take account of reasonable expectations which no one has articulated, and not give countenance to unreasonable claims. But he never achieved a theory of justice by which such decisions could be measured:

> 'I have come to feel that instead of putting the task of law, as William James did, in terms of satisfying as much as we can of the total of human demands, we do better to speak of providing as much as we may of the total of men's reasonable expectations in life in civilised society with the minimum of friction and waste.'[4]

Where the legal technician cannot accommodate interests, there is no objective way of resolving conflicts. There are, however, 'jural postulates' by which new interests may be tested. These are 'presuppositions' of legal reasoning. They involve what men must be able to assume 'in civilised society' – no intentional aggression by others; beneficial control over what they acquire under the existing social and economic order; good faith in dealings; due care not to injure; control over dangerous activities. These jural postulates are similar to Dworkin's 'background rights' (see chapter 14, above), except that, for Pound, their sole basis is what Dworkin calls institutional 'fit'. There is no question of testing them against objective morality.

Pound formulates a jural postulate by generalising some value protected by the existing law. He then tells us that entirely novel claims are to be judged by reference to jural postulates. This suggests that creative legal reasoning must be incremental: new claims will be recognised only if claims of that sort are already recognised. On the other hand, Pound takes note of the fact that jural postulates change, that they are relative to stages in social evolution. In 1942, he recorded the emergence of new jural postulates, relating to job security, enterprise liability and social insurance.[5]

Pound's pragmatism and relativism resemble much work-a-day discussion of law reform. You set out the law as it is. You note suggestions for change in dissenting judgments and law reform committees, and consider whether they are incompatible with some underlying principle of the system ('jural postulate'). You put competing considerations in

4   (1954) 68 Harv L Rev 19.
5   *Social Control through Law* (1942).

different pans of the scales. And you do your best to give as much satisfaction as possible, having regard to all technical limitations. If one is sceptical about theories of justice, or about the desirability of wholesale change, then perhaps this will do. But if law reform is to be piecemeal, relativist and pragmatic, is there any point in broad-scale classifications of interests and jural postulates? Why not employ detailed socio-legal research to problems one by one, as they arise? Pound believed that his theory was of practical value in relation both to problems of 'law reform', and to the sorts of problems of 'legal reasoning' discussed in chapter 15, above. Was he right in either respect? If not, should we draw the conclusion that 'sociological jurisprudence' means the death of theory altogether?

2   The functions and limits of law

Sociological jurisprudence is sometimes referred to as 'functional'. In a broad sense, all legal theories make assumptions about 'functions'. As we saw in chapter 6, Kelsen's pure theory of law assumes that all legal systems tend to a monopoly of violence. We may think of 'function' as an overall legal goal, or as an attribute of particular legal rules. On the most abstract plane, some would claim that the function of law is to keep the peace, to stop us from killing or injuring each other: or to prevent 'free riders' from taking unfair advantage of the rest of us by not playing their part in schemes of social co-operation; or to resolve disputes between individuals; or to provide a balance between the claims upon social resources of different interest groups; or to impose on society the interests of a ruling class; or some combination of some or all of these. On the plane of individual rules, we may suggest that particular kinds of rules have typical social functions. We saw in chapter 9 that Hart gives as a reason for distinguishing power-conferring rules from duty-imposing rules that not to do so would distort their social function.

R. S. Summers has argued that abstract and particularistic functional analyses can be reconciled if we distinguish the overall functions of law from the 'technique element'. In Summers and Howard's *Law: its Nature, Functions and Limits,* he applies this distinction to modern American law. The book contains a comprehensive survey of the social functions which legal institutions 'help' to serve. They help: (1) to promote human health and a healthy environment; (2) to reinforce the family and protect private life; (3) to keep community peace; (4) to protect basic freedoms; (5) to secure equality of opportunity; (6) to recognise and order private ownership; (7) to exercise surveillance and control over persons in power, including lawyers. The authors see all these functions as subserving the ultimate end of individual self-realisation – a concept much stressed by Pound who derived it from the Neo-Hegelianism of Kohler. Like Pound, their legal critique is in terms of 'social engineering'; but they clarify the relation between means and ends. The seven functions of law are served by five legal 'modes' ('instrumentalities', 'techniques'): (1) the grievance remedial instrument; (2) the penal instrument; (3) the administrative regulatory instrument; (4) the government benefit-conferral instrument; (5) the private arrangement facilitating instrument.

Various combinations of these instrumentalities are used to further the law's functions. For instance, in furthering a healthy environment, the grievance remedial mode comes in by allowing actions for certain kinds of deleterious nuisance, negligence or breach of treatment or insurance contracts; there are penal prohibitions; conduct bearing on health is subjected to administrative regulation and licensing; benefits are conferred through revenue law and health-care law; and private arrangements relating to health are facilitated by contract law and charity law. Summers and Howard invite the reader to consider whether particular legal instruments are efficiently employed towards achieving the social goals. They stress the fact that each instrumentality is a 'process', involving the co-operation of legislators, administrators, law-enforcement officers, lawyers, private citizens and courts; and they draw attention to 'process values', similar to the principles of legality mentioned in chapter 11, above. They suggest that the nature of these processes imposes inherent limits on the extent to which law can further its functions. For example, the penal mode should not be employed where conduct cannot be effectively policed. Prohibition was an instance of an abuse of this instrument. And there are limits flowing from the fact that excessive zeal in fulfilling one function may derogate from another. Providing uniform education (through the benefit-conferral technique) in the interests of the function of securing equality of opportunity might derogate from the function of securing basic freedoms, as when it takes away a parent's right to choose schools.

Such a survey of the functions of law has the merit of providing much more sociological information than does the standard analytic approach. It avoids certain kinds of distortions. The authors stress that law is not just about rights, duties, powers and sanctions. The mass of modern law devoted to what they call the administrative regulatory and benefit-conferral modes makes that clear. They might have added that their analysis (if accurate) also falsifies Hart's assumption that it is possible to 'individuate' laws by reference to social function. Not only is it not true that one type of law corresponds with one legal function; it is not even the case that one type of law corresponds with one legal technique. 'Power-conferring' rules have their place in the private arrangement facilitating instrument, but they crop up in other instruments as well.

Nevertheless, this functional survey is still at the near end of the sociological jurisprudence spectrum. Summers and Howard make clear that law 'helps' to achieve the seven goals, that there are other co-ordinating 'non-legal' factors – psychological, moral, political, economic, religious and so on. The law then is a distinct means of social control, and it is assumed that one identifies it by reference to legal-positivistic criteria. It consists of legal rules and legal institutions.

It may be objected that the entire picture is artificial, that the law has been cut to fit clothes it does not deserve to wear. Seven desirable end-points are conceived. Then swathes are hacked through legal materials to find those that appear to tend in a desired direction. Anything that tells against the achievement of some end is called a 'non-legal factor'. For example, in the context of securing equality of opportunity, 'the rule of law' is exemplified by reference to law relating to welfare, education and restrictions on discrimination; while the non-legal factors are said to include wealth, athletic ability, economics and considerations of justice and utility. Might one not stand the picture on its head and say that the law helps to secure inequality of opportunity, in that it facilitates arrangements which confer privileges on the wealthy and the well-endowed; but it is hampered in its unequalising function by a multiplicity of social and economic forces?

There are two problems for the idea of 'function of law'. First, by 'function', do we mean simply 'effects' or 'intended effects'; and if the latter, whose intention is crucial? Secondly, which segments of legal material shall we select before attributing to them any 'function'? It seems likely that the select-and-collect procedure we apply will be illuminated by normative presuppositions we ourselves bring to the task. A radical social critic who engages in legal-functional analysis will make different segmental selections out of the law from those made by Summers and Howard; and no doubt will read the effects differently.

The expression 'the limits of law' appears to be even more ambiguous. Sometimes it is used as a label for the positivist thesis that there are criteria of validity by reference to which legal standards can be distinguished from non-legal ones. More often, it has to do with limits on what the law can (or ought to try to) achieve – as in the essays contained in Pennock and Chapman (eds) *The Limits of Law*. Some issues relate to alleged ethical limitations, such as the questions whether the law should be employed to enforce popular morality or paternalistically to save people from harming themselves (discussed in chapter 10, above); or whether coercion should be exercised according to a retributive principle, or according to an analogy with medical treatment, or merely for community self-defence (discussed in chapter 5, above). Issues may, however, be viewed instrumentally. Granted that a certain goal is desirable, nevertheless 'You can't make people good by legislation'.

Illuminating generalisations seem hard to come by. Ingrained attitudes may frustrate an enterprise of law reform; or law may have an 'educative' role. Some kinds of behaviour cannot be effectively policed; but which these are is not static, given developments in data collection, bugging, telephone tapping and the like. Perhaps all limits on law's effectiveness should be seen as ultimately ethical rather than instrumental: there are things the law could achieve, but only by unacceptedly intrusive means. Measuring the effectiveness of law raises obvious methodological problems connected with sampling technique and statistical correlation, but also difficult conceptual problems. How do we identify 'the law' before assessing its effects? Is it a system of rules or a pattern of official behaviour or a process conceived in terms of 'governmental' functions? If it is rules, should we individuate them into different types before measuring their effectiveness? And do we determine effectiveness by reference to outward compliance, conscious obedience, or achievement of goals?

If there are any necessary limits to what the law can achieve, they must flow either from our conception of man or from our conception of law. The former is the basis of what Hart calls 'the minimum content of natural law' (see chapter 2, above). The latter underlies Fuller's 'inner morality of law' (see chapter 11, above). If man's altruism is ineradicably limited, the law cannot make it unlimited. If the law is necessarily something that operates through rules, then its contributions to social organisation are limited by the requirements of formal justice (rule justice); and it cannot achieve the sort of individuated justice which requires every problem to be treated exclusively on its merits.

3 The living law

Supposing we take the view that the effects normally attributed to the law are really brought about by spontaneously generated social norms. Business is carried on, family life and education fostered, anti-social violence kept within bounds, all because of the effective operation of rules; but the rules in question have no necessary relation to the rules in the law books. We might then conclude that law is socially unimportant; or we might change our view of what law is. The latter is the course recommended by Eugen Ehrlich (1862-1919).

Pound indicated that there was a distinction between 'the law in books' and 'the law in action', but he paid little detailed attention to the latter. Ehrlich, on the other hand, was preoccupied with what he called 'the living law'. He believed that social associations have an 'inner order' which is the true determinant of action. He does not recommend that book law should be ignored. It contains 'norms for decision' addressed to officials and may well affect what they do. Individual citizens, however, follow the 'living law', the spontaneous norms of the social associations to which they belong. It is the business of juristic science to press for alterations in the norms for decision so as to bring them into line with the living law:

'The inner order of the associations of human beings is not only the original but also down to the present time the basic form of law. The legal proposition not only comes into being at a much later time but is largely derived from the inner order of the associations.'[6]

That social groups may have customary rules is true. Why should we call them 'law'? Two arguments are implicit in Ehrlich's writings. The first is the analogy with primitive 'law' mentioned in the last chapter. The second is the more important. Lawyers are supposed to be people who convey chunks of useful rule-information. What is the good of them reading rules out of books, when social life actually goes by other rules?

Suppose a trainee manager comes to a factory and is told to bone up on some relevant law. The traditionalist would refer him to the Factory Acts, where it would say that certain kinds of machine should be fenced. The Ehrlichian 'living' lawyer would tell him, say, that, in the life of this factory those machines are not to be fenced, but on the other hand there is a very rigid 'law' about tea-breaks. In *Law and Legal Science* I argue that, since legal science is supposed to be useful precisely because it informs one of the rules officials will apply consistently with the values of legality and constitutionality, there is no special point in calling anything but the first sort of information 'law'. That is not to say that the Ehrlichian information should not also be passed on to our trainee. He ought to be told that the machinery-fencing law is a dead letter in this factory – a significant legal-sociological detail. And he ought to know about the tea-breaks, even though, *pace* Ehrlich, they have nothing to do with the law. The fact that the established practice is not to fence machines, or that it is to take tea-breaks at fixed hours, may be given as a reason for altering existing regulations, or existing labour contracts, respectively. But there may be arguments against such changes; and the debate should not be pre-empted by saying that, because these things are already the subject of group practices, they are already 'law'.

Ehrlich was conscious of this kind of criticism, and the following was his response:

'The question as to the difference between the legal and the non-legal norm is a question not of social science but of social psychology. The various classes of norms release various overtones of feeling, and we react to the transgression of different norms with different feelings. Compare the feeling of revolt that follows a violation of law with the indignation at a violation of a law of morality, with the feeling of disgust occasioned by an indecency, of the disapproval of tactlessness, and ridiculousness of an offense against etiquette, and lastly with the critical feeling of superiority

6   *Fundamental Principles of the Sociology of Law* pp 37-38.

with which a votary of fashion looks down upon those who have not attained the heights which he has scaled.'[7]

A variant of the 'living law' approach sometimes appears in attitudinal socio-legal research. Whereas Anglo-American studies in legal sociology tend to be oriented either to behavioural or to effectiveness surveys – that is, they assess the behaviour patterns of officials, or consider whether particular legal measures achieve their objectives – continental scholars appear to regard the 'sociology of law' as a discipline which inquires whether norms have been 'internalised', and whether there is a match between book law and internalised norms. Adam Podgorecki insists that such research requires a conception of law which is wider than the traditional one. This is so because there may be 'legal sentiments' or 'legal attitudes' which do not correlate with formal law. The existence of such sentiments is established if people answering questionnaires indicate that they believe conduct ought to be punished. They may evince such an attitude towards conduct which is not formally proscribed.[8]

That attitudinal research, like behaviour research, is a proper activity for legal sociology may readily be accepted. I have suggested that book-law rules ('pure-norm rules') should be compared with internalised rules ('rule-ideas') as well as with behavioural patterns ('rule-situations').[9] It is not clear to me that any non-traditional conception of law is required by such research. On the contrary, living law notions can result in useful information being presented in tendentious terms. One of Podgorecki's colleagues, B. Kutchinsky, summarises the results of research into the attitudes of criminals towards penalisation of conduct in the following words:

'Contrary to expectations criminals apparently do not have criminal attitudes – they are, at best, slightly more tolerant towards crimes than non-criminals.'[10]

Kutchinsky uses 'criminal attitude' as the opposite to 'legal attitude'. If your view about whether conduct should be punished coincides with that of the majority, you have a legal attitude. If it does not, you have a criminal attitude.

In my submission, no new conception of law is required by socio-legal research. It remains for consideration whether different conceptions of law are needed for more fundamental social critiques, a topic dealt with in the next chapter.

7   Op cit p 165.
8   Podgorecki *et al Knowledge and Opinion about Law* pp 65ff.
9   *Law and Legal Science* ch 6.
10   *Knowledge and Opinion about Law* p 118.

Bibliography

Black D. 'The Boundaries of Legal Sociology' (1972) 81 Yale LJ 1086
 –   *The Behaviour of Law* (1976)
Cotterrell R. *The Sociology of Law* (2nd edn, 1992)
Gibbs J. P. 'Definitions of Law and Empirical Questions' (1968) 2 LS Rev 429
Harris J.W. *Law and Legal Science* (1979) Ss. 12,23
Hunt A. *The Sociological Movement in Law* (1978) ch 6
Luhmann N. 'Operational Closure and Structural Coupling – the Differentiation of the Legal System' (1992) 13 Card L Rev 1419
MacCormick D. N. 'Challenging Sociological Definitions' (1977) 4 Br J L Soc 87
Nonet P. 'For Jurisprudential Sociology' (1976) 10 LS Rev 525
Selznick P. 'The Sociology of Law' in Merton, Broom and Cottrell (eds) *Sociology To-day: Problems and Perspectives* (1959)
Teubner G. 'How the Law Thinks' (1989) 23 LS Rev 728

Social interests

Braybrooke E. K. 'The sociological jurisprudence of Roscoe Pound' in Sawer (ed) *Studies in the Sociology of Law* (1961)
Hunt A. *The Sociological Movement in Law* (1978) ch 2
Lepaulle P. 'The Function of Comparative Law with a Critique of Sociological Jurisprudence' (1921-22) 35 Harv L Rev 838
Morris H. 'Dean Pound's Jurisprudence' in Summers (ed) *More Essays in Legal Philosophy* (1971)
Patterson E. W. 'Pound's Theory of Social Interests' in Sayre (ed) *Interpretations of Modern Legal Philosophies* (1947)
Pound R. 'The Scope and Purpose of Sociological Jurisprudence' (1911) 24 Harv L Rev 591; (1912) 25 Harv L Rev 140, 489
 –   *Social Control Through Law* (1942)
 –   'A Survey of Social Interests' (1943-44) Harv L Rev 1
 –   'The Role of Will in Law' (1954) 68 Harv L Rev 19
 –   *Jurisprudence* (1959) vol iii, chs 14-15
Stone J. *Human Law and Human Justice* (1965) ch 9

The functions and limits of law

Allott A. *The Limits of Law* (1980)
Cowan T. A. 'Law Without Force' (1971) 59 Calif L Rev 683
Galanter M. 'Why the Haves come out Ahead: Speculations on the Limits of Legal Change' (1974) 9 LS Rev 95, 347
Honoré A. M. *Making Law Bind* (1987) ch 4

Pennock J. R. and Chapman J. W. (eds) *The Limits of Law* (1974)
Pound R. 'The Limits of Effective Legal Action' (1917) IJE 27
Raz J. *The Authority of Law* (1979) ch 9
Summers R. S. 'The Technique Element in Law' (1971) 59 Calif L Rev 732
–   'Naive Instrumentalism and the Law' in Hacker and Raz (eds) *Law, Morality, and Society* (1977)
Summers and Howard *Law: its Nature, Functions and Limits* (2nd edn, 1972)

The living law

Ehrlich E. *Fundamental Principles of the Sociology of Law* (Moll trans, 1936)
Fuller L. L. *Anatomy of the Law* (1971) pp. 64-71
Lucas J . R. 'The Phenomenon of Law' in Hacker and Raz (eds) *Law, Morality and Society* (1977)
Nelken D. 'Law in Action or Living Law' (1984) 4 LS 157
Partridge P. H. 'Ehrlich's Sociology of Law' in Sawer (ed) *Studies in the Sociology of Law* (1961)
Podgorecki A. et al *Knowledge and Opinion about Law* (1971)

19 Law, social theory and Marxist jurisprudence

Our starting-point at the beginning of the last chapter was the aphorism that 'law is a social phenomenon'. We then discussed various ways of looking at society from the point of view of law. Might it not be better to try to explain the aphorism by first asking what we mean by 'social'? What is the bond that holds men together in societies and social groups? What part, if any, does the law play in the social bond? Such questions have been raised in the history of political and social philosophy from the time of the ancient Greeks. But towards the end of the last century, they came to be subsumed under what was conceived of as a new kind of discipline, that of 'social theory'. Political philosophers had generally not distinguished the questions as to what it was that did, and what it was that ought to, hold men together; and they had usually framed their answers in terms of a supra-historical conception of human nature. Social theorists sought to demarcate a value-free 'sociology'. Man was to be conceived, not as an entity in terms of which the justice of social arrangements could be measured, but as the product of forces which determined his relations with others. The social bond was different, and consequently the perceptions of the individual were different, depending on the stage of historical development of society. In particular, the society of contemporary western capitalism was unique. Light would be shed on the legal institutions of this unique development if we viewed it against an overview of how different kinds of society produce, or correspond with, different kinds of law.

1 Law and social theory

Two of the most important progenitors of social theory, Durkheim and Weber, made just this claim – that different kinds of society correlate with different kinds of law. Emile Durkheim (1858-1917) distinguished primitive from modern societies. The former were characterised by 'mechanical', the latter by 'organic', social solidarity. Primitive societies were held together by shared values. The collective conscience of the group constituted the reality of society. In modern societies, in contrast, economic specialisation had led to role-differentiation. The collective conscience was weakened to the extent that role values had emerged. Society was held together by the complex interrelation of roles. Durkheim insisted on a 'scientific' methodology, on establishing the social by reference to externally observable phenomena: and nothing could be harder evidence of a society's collective values than its law:

'Since law reproduces the principal forms of social solidarity, we have only to classify the different types of law to find therefrom the different types of social solidarity which correspond to it.'[1]

The proof of the two types of social solidarity lay in the manifest existence of two kinds of law, distinguishable by their content. Primitive society had 'repressive' law in which sanctions were prescribed for violations of the collective conscience. Modern society had 'restitutive' law, which provided, through civil remedy, for the restitution of the balance between society's components.

Max Weber (1864-1920) provided more complex typologies and society/law correlations. He spoke of the social bond in terms, not of solidarity, but of legitimate domination. In different historical settings, people had accepted the right of others to control their lives for one of three kinds of reason: the charismatic qualities of a leader; the traditional sanctity of an office; or the fact that power was mediated via an impersonal law. Alongside this typology of authorities, he set a four-fold classification of laws distinguished by the kind of rationality they exhibited. Law is substantively irrational where every case is decided on its merits by the judge's intuition. Law is formally irrational where decisions turn on some test beyond human control, such as an oracle or an ordeal. Law is substantively rational whenever a legal question is subsumed under that rule which would, on religious, moral, economic or social grounds, be the best to adopt. Law is formally rational where answers are derived from the extant body of legal doctrine. All these classifications refer to 'ideal' types. In real-world societies, one should expect to find elements of different kinds of legal rationality or irrationality and of authority structures. Nevertheless, the unique society of the modern West was characterised by allegiance to the law itself, and that required that its law have a formally rational nature.

1   *The Division of Labour in Society* p 68.

There are, Weber maintains, important sub-divisions within formal rationality, depending on the legal *honoratiores* who control it. First, it may be casuistic. Casuistry ('cautelary jurisprudence') insists that the ruling in a case must be based on precedent or analogy with some earlier ruling. Casuistry may be more or less empirical or conceptual, depending on whether precedential or analogical cogency is mediated through factual similarities or through the intrinsic meaning of concepts deployed in the earlier ruling. Secondly, professional legal rationality may reach the higher form in which it is 'logically formal'. Then concepts are subsumed, in accordance with their intrinsic meaning, under highly abstract propositions, forming a consistent and 'gapless' juristic system from which answers to all legal questions may be deduced. Casuistic formality was the hallmark of jurisdictions in which evolution of law was in the hands of practitioners, as was the case in common law systems. Logically formal rationality was the speciality of those continental jurisdictions where legal development had been controlled by university-trained bureaucrats. Formal reasoning, of one kind or the other, was 'immanent' in 'lawyers' law'. 'This is just as true of the English law which we glorify so much today, as it has been of the ancient Roman jurists or of the methods of modern continental legal thought.'[2]

Logically formal rationality entailed a high degree of predictability and hence served the needs of capitalist entrepreneurs. Nevertheless, Weber rejected simple economic determinism. His historicism is multi-causal. In continental Europe, the need of capitalists for predictability had combined with the need of princely bureaucracies for organisational planning and professorial control over legal education to produce logically formal rationality. Capitalism alone did not bring it about, as the English counter-example demonstrated:

> '[I]t may indeed be said that England achieved capitalistic supremacy among the nations not because but rather in spite of its judicial system.'[3]

The literature of theoretical sociology devoted to critical examination of Durkheim and Weber is vast. For the most part, however, it has not centred on their views about law. Cultural anthropologists have chewed over what Durkheim had to say about the repressive nature of primitive law, generally rejecting it. So far as modern societies are concerned, the sociology of Talcot Parsons gives a special place to the court system as a sub-system within the total political order, whose specialist function is to integrate society. This theme is developed by H. C. Bredemeier in his *Law*

2   *Law in Economy and Society* p 308.
3   Op cit p 231.

as an Integrative Mechanism. Such 'consensus' models of the role of law are commonly contrasted with 'conflict' models, which see the law as a means for influential groups or, in the case of Marxist jurisprudence, for a ruling class, to impose their interests on the rest of society.

On a more prosaic level, Weber's typology of forms of legal rationality can be invoked to distinguish different elements to be found in judicial reasoning. Judges sometimes deploy what is called 'policy' ('substantive rationality'). Alternatively, they invoke doctrine, sometimes 'casuistically', or else by appealing to over-arching legal categories in the way of 'logically formal' rationality. I have employed Weber's typology in the context of developments in English land and tort law.[4]

Different typologies of law may be set up in critical reaction, not merely to these 'classics', but encompassing also the political and social philosophy which preceded them. Two recent authors, F. A. Hayek and R. M. Unger, have attempted to do this. In chapter 11, above, their views on 'the rule of law' were contrasted.

Hayek distinguishes two kinds of social order, 'grown order', and 'made order'. The former consists of the reciprocal expectations which spontaneously arise between men and which make social life possible. The purpose served by the 'rules' – that is, regularities in expected behaviour – which constitute such an order need not be known to those who observe them. A made order consists of a completely different kind of 'rules', namely purposive prescriptions laid down to establish an organisation and to further its aims. A different kind of 'law' corresponds to each kind of social order. To the order of reciprocal expectations corresponds 'rules of just conduct'. These are abstract, negative rules, restraining individuals from invading the free domain of others. Such law originally grew up as customary law. But this was not necessarily the sort of customary law which legal anthropologists investigate. Its rules existed as regularities of behaviour and expectation long before they were consciously articulated as the basis of tribal mediation or enforcement:

'Although man never existed without laws that he obeyed, he did, of course, exist for hundreds of thousands of years without laws he "knew" in the sense that he was able to articulate them.'[5]

Rules of just conduct came to be articulated in the settlement of disputes. Eventually, this task becomes the specialist activity of lawyers. Their role is, in case of doubt, to find what the rules are by a test of consistency with all other rules of just conduct. Although rules are inevitably modified in

4   Harris 'Legal Doctrine and Interests in Land' in Eekelaar and Bell (eds) *Oxford Essays in Jurisprudence* (3rd series, 1987); 'Murphy Makes it Eight' (1991) 11 OJLS 416.

5   *Rules and Order* p 43.

the process of articulation, only aiming at consistency rather than a purposive creation can produce legal rules which serve the underlying social order of reciprocal expectations. The common law system of precedent provides the best institutional background for this process:

> 'It seems that the constant necessity of articulating rules in order to distinguish between the relevant and the accidental in the precedents which guide him, produces in the common law judge a capacity for discovering general principles rarely acquired by a judge who operates with a supposedly complete catalogue of applicable rules before him.'[6]

To made social orders corresponds another kind of 'law', namely the rules for the organisation of government. As mentioned in chapter 11, Hayek sees a deplorable tendency for such organisational law to replace the rules of just conduct, owing to the legal positivist heresy that all law is made law. This tendency is exacerbated by attempts to enforce the 'mirage' of a welfarist conception of 'social justice' (see chapter 20, below). The likely outcome is totalitarianism.

Unger presents a similar match between forms of social life and types of law:

> 'A society's law constitutes the chief bond between its culture and its organization; it is the external manifestation of the embeddedness of the former in the latter.'[7]

But where Hayek offers two types of law, Unger offers three. This he does to account, in society/law correlation terms, for a cultural phenomenon which he believes in and which Hayek denies: an ineradicable sense of unjustified hierarchy, of illegitimate personal domination, as a pervasive attribute of the psychology of modern man in liberal market societies. Unger's three types of law are customary law, which corresponds to tribal society; bureaucratic law, which is public and positive and corresponds to aristocratic society; and the 'legal order' of liberal society. The legal order has two further characteristics, besides being 'public' and 'positive'. It is 'general' and 'autonomous'. It is autonomous as to substance in that its norms are not restatements of non-legal norms; as to the institutions which administer it; as to its methodology, in that it incorporates a special manner of legal justification; and as to occupational specialisation of those who staff it. It arose uniquely in the West because of the conjunction of two necessary conditions: political compromise

6   *Rules and Order* p 87.
7   *Law in Modern Society* p 250.

between three interest groups – the nobles, the merchants, and the princes and their bureaucratic staffs; and the belief in a higher law, which made the articulation of the compromise take the particular form of the rule of law.

So far the analysis is not far different from Weber's. But Unger goes on to assert that the legal order did not and could not produce a sense of legitimate domination. The ideology of the rule of law is doomed to failure because the reality of subjection by dominant groups forces itself on people's consciousness. Whereas Hayek sees lawyers' law as the continuation of customary law, both being concerned with rules of just conduct, Unger regards feelings of unjustified hierarchy as the inevitable sequel to the loss of unreflective legitimacy which is characteristic of customary law. Law is not properly customary law if people have critical feelings about it. (As mentioned in chapter 17, above, some writers on 'primitive law' have stressed that members of a tribal society sometimes do both acknowledge and criticise customs. But Unger deals in 'ideal types' with which actual societies need only partly correspond.)

Unger, like Hayek, sees the modern law of the West as 'post-liberal'. The legal order has been modified by the introduction of welfare law, which is neither general nor autonomous, and by state corporatist law (incorporating the 'living law' of associations), which is neither public nor positive. Unger compares post-liberal society with two other kinds of modern society, neither of which (he says) have solved the dialectic between the experience of personal dependence and the ideal of community. In traditionalistic society, like that of modern Japan, some aspects of the Western legal order have been superimposed upon the customary rank system and industrial bureaucratic law. In revolutionary socialist societies, there is a pervasive tension between the customary law of autonomous organisations and a vast amount of ruthlessly enforced bureaucratic law. The only way out for modern man, in Unger's view, is a reversion to a new kind of customary law of independent groups, which could restore a sense of legitimacy without destroying the possibility of free critical appraisal. (In chapter 8, we discussed Unger's prescriptions for 'super liberalism', which he commends as the ultimate social goal for the critical legal studies movement.) Thus, both Hayek and Unger cry 'back to customary law'. But they mean quite different things by it: for Hayek, it is lawyers' law; for Unger, the living law of equalised associations.

The models of society and of law offered by these various theorists are all what Weber called 'ideal types'. They are mental constructions designed to illuminate complex over-arching elements in human history. They do not purport to be precise descriptions. Whether giving a central place to law is necessary to an understanding of the general problem of human social bonding is a question for social theory – just as it is arguable, as we saw in chapter 17, whether rules of a primitive society can usefully be treated as 'law' is a question internal to anthropology. For jurisprudence, the question is whether the typologies of law which emerge from these social theorists are informative about law.

Is Durkheim's contention about an evolutionary shift from repressive to restitutive law an accurate generalisation about the content of law? How do the contrasting commendations made by Weber of the rationality of conceptual deduction, or by Hayek of the compatibility-through-general principle of the common law, compare with other discussions of legal rationality not based on a social-theoretical superstructure, such as those mentioned in chapters 14 and 15, above? The historical explanations of different legal systems offered by social theorists should be compared with those offered by the historical school and by Marxist jurisprudence. At the very least, social theorising of this kind goes beyond traditional jurisprudence by its attempt to specify the social and political setting of the lawyer's role. Is it his business to forward social solidarity, the implication drawn by L. Duguit from Durkheim's sociology? Is he the natural and creditable ally of rational bureaucratic government, as Weber suggests, or is that, as Hayek would have it, a perversion of his true role (as declarer of the community's rules of just conduct)? Or is Unger right, and the lawyer, when asked for the bread of impartial justice, offers only the stone of class-supremacist legality?

2   Marxist jurisprudence

Of the new breed of social theorists who broke away from the tradition of classical political philosophy in the 19th century, one writer has acquired a certain notoriety. If the reader of this book is new to social theory, he may not have heard of Durkheim or Weber, but I would lay very long odds that he has heard of Marx. 'Marxist theory' refers to any body of social thought which claims to be based on the writings of Karl Marx (1818-1883), and of Friedrich Engels (1820-1895). Prior to the collapse of communist governments in the Soviet Union and Eastern Europe in 1989, half the world was ruled by governments who claimed that these writings were uniquely 'scientific' and ought to be the basis for all governmental action, including the operation of legal institutions. Elsewhere some analysts of society express a commitment to these writings in a way in which commentators do not concede authoritative allegiance to other texts, except for the religious. These are reasons enough for jurisprudence to concern itself with what these writers had to say about law.

However, unlike the theorists discussed earlier in this chapter, Marx and Engels did not give law any centrality in their analysis of the social bond. None of their voluminous works contains a separate treatment of law. In the preface to *Contribution to Critique of Political Economy* (1859), Marx drew a famous distinction between the base and the superstructure of social relations. The base consisted of the relations between members of society and the means of production. This economic base had a determining effect over all forms of social intercourse. Religion, philosophy, aesthetics and law were all but part of the superstructure resting on it. That being so, one might argue, so long as one has correctly appraised the relations of production existing at any particular historical period, one would be able to state all that really matters about the law of that period. A separate theory of law might suggest, what Marx and Engels denied, that law (an element of the superstructure) could have a separate history, that it was something with its own autonomy.

On the other hand, there are lengthy passages in their writings about law, now collected in M. Cain and A. Hunt *Marx and Engels on Law*. Is it possible (should one try) to build a distinct theory of law on these extracts? In this chapter, I shall merely draw attention to three aspects of Marxist theory which seem to have important jurisprudential implications, whether or not a distinct Marxist theory of law can be constructed: Marxist economism; Marxist critique of law in capitalist society; and Marxist prophetic historicism.

According to Marx and Engels, it is a fallacy to suppose that the content of law depends on 'will', on the arbitrary choice of a legislature. The relations of production control what the legislature can and does lay down. In primitive clan society, production of the means of life was spontaneously ordered on a communal basis. Since man emerged from this primitive stage, there has been class division: always a ruling class and one or more oppressed classes. These classes are defined in terms of relations of production, replacing one another as the mechanics of production have changed. In this way society has evolved from clan society, through slave-owning society and feudalism, to modern capitalist society. The law, like other instrumentalities of the state, does express the will of the ruling class at different historical epochs; but what they will is ultimately dependent on their class interests, themselves dictated by their definitional involvement in the means of production. Relations of production are thus the economic basis of law.

Marxist economism should be sharply contrasted with the 'economic analysis of law' discussed in chapter 4, above. That view takes as the unit of value the satisfaction of wants, as evidenced by willingness to pay. The Marxist unit of value is productive work. So, for example, if you contract with me that you will do work and I will pay you a wage, according to the classical economists satisfactions are, prima facie, maximised: the work must be of more value to me than anything else I could have done with the money, or else I would not have hired you for that amount; and the money must be of more value to you than anything else you could have achieved with your time and effort, or else you would have done that other thing. According to Marxist economics, however, the relevant units are the thing you produced with your work and the products of labour-power stored up in my money. If you are a member of an exploited class and I an exploiter, we can be sure that what you have produced has cost more labour-power than the control over others' labour-power which the money will give you. The surplus I expropriate. In a capitalist society, the ruling class (the bourgeoisie) are in just this relationship to the exploited class (the proletariat). The latter produce goods with their labour; the former take the goods and give the proletariat only so much as is necessary for them to maintain bare existence. The surplus value of the workers' labour is expropriated by the capitalists.

It is far from clear how specific Marx and Engels believed the determination of law by relations of production to be. Their comments on historical legislative events suggest that not every statute can be read off as directly caused by some shift in relations of production. Marx discusses legislation in England from the end of the middle ages up to the 19th century, and argues that much of it did assist the rising bourgeoisie, by driving the poor from the land so as to provide a ready army of exploitable proletariat. But he also mentions the early legislation which tried, ineffectually, to prevent enclosure. Perhaps the point is, not that each legislative choice is directly motivated by the interests of the ruling class, but that the economic basis of class interests will filter out and render ineffective all laws which are not.

One of the problems raised in discussion of Marxist theory is whether the economic base can be distinguished, logically, from the superstructure. G. A. Cohen has argued that it can, if we conceive of it as comprised of 'power' relations from which all normative terms are excluded. Stephen Lukes has countered by pointing out that, apart from the terminology of obligation, a norm-free description of the base would have to eliminate all references to roles (slave, owner, worker, employer and so on); and that this is a hopeless project. Hugh Collins has suggested that, even were it possible to render the economic base without using law-like terminology (something which Marx himself never attempted), one would still have to explain the mechanism whereby that base translates itself into customary or legal norms. He suggests that crude economic determinism is not required by Marxist legal theory. Law can be adequately portrayed as an instrument of class oppression by fastening on to the particular interpretation given by Marxists to the concept of 'ideology'.

'Ideology' is a term employed by social theorists in various ways. Roughly, it refers to a system of beliefs about values and the facts of the world. It is more abstract than the brute facts of psychology to which the Scandinavian realists appealed in their reduction of law to internalised rules (see chapter 8 above). On the other hand, it is less abstract than the analysis proffered by adherents of 'structuralism' such as the anthropologist Levi-Strauss, according to which all thought is mediated via a complex of binary oppositions – 'cooked'/'raw', 'insider'/'outsider', 'right'/'wrong'.

'Ideology' is an interpretive tool whereby the social theorist can explain the filtering of power and the demarcation of roles within a society, without teasing out mechanistic causal connections, by pointing to the belief-sets of social actors. It is certainly true that we are all the subjects of socialisation which includes taken-for-granted assumptions about values and facts. It is, however, controversial whether the theorist himself can look down upon the ideologies of those he investigates from a 'scientific' vantage point (which does not merely reflect his own ideology). (See the discussion of Stanley Fish's condemnation of 'theory hope' in chapter 14, above.)

The most prevalent version of Marxist economism today contends that the dominant class maintains its position by foisting its own ideology, its beliefs about 'the natural' form of economic relations, on those it oppresses. Law is an important facet of this ideology. It is in the interests of the oppressors that so-called 'free' bargains, property-ownership, civil wrong-doing and crime should be conceived of as permanent features of social interaction; and they succeed in bemusing the oppressed into thinking in the same way. The preservation of this ideological hegemony requires that the law has an appearance of objectivity. That explains why some parts of it seem to be in conflict with the interests of capitalists – such as environmental law, welfare law, consumer-protection law and laws limiting landlords' rights or the rights of employers. These are minor sacrifices on the part of the ruling class, compared with the great boon of perpetuating among the oppressed the superstition that the law operates for the benefit of all.

What about the fact that the same laws sometimes stay on the books after some Marxist-significant economic change, or the fact that different societies at the same stage of economic development have (on the face of it) different laws? It seems clear that Marx and Engels did not suppose that every detail need have an economic explanation, and Engels at least indicates that the law may react on its economic base – may, to some extent, warp or temporarily halt the inexorable march of the relations of production. The Austrian Marxist, K. Renner (1870-1950), elaborated a theory according to which the functions of law may change, consistently with economic determination, although the form remains the same – feudal Europe employed the same Roman law concept of ownership as does capitalist Europe, but it now serves as the vehicle for capitalists to give orders to workmen, whereas in feudal law the duty of feudal inferiors to obey their lords was explicitly laid down. The Russian Marxist, E. B. Pashukanis (1891-1937), produced a more abstract theory, showing that the form of law is essentially capitalist, so that 'law' as such reached its highest flowering in capitalist society – it is of the essence of a juridical interpretation of human effort that it regards what a man does as an exchangeable commodity, not as something intrinsic to his personality.

The critique of capitalist society which bulks so large in Marxist theory is both moral and functional-economic. Marx claimed that his theory was scientific, that it showed how changes in the material world in the modes of production, inevitably produced the evolution into class society in general, and changes from one form of class society to another in particular. But this alleged objectivity was not divorced from ethical comment. The capitalists were both historically inevitable and ruthlessly cruel. The coercive machinery of the state, including all law, was used to further their class interests. Furthermore, – and this was a crucial plank in Marx's explanation of how the circulation of commodities could bring about an increase in wealth – every service contract is necessarily a transfer of the ownership of labour-power from employee to employer. The worker places his labour-power at the disposal of a buyer for a definite period of time by 'handing it over to the buyer for him to consume'.[8] Lawyers usually suppose that the obligations of an employee or of an independent contractor depend on the terms of their contracts. It is central to Marx's analysis that every kind of service contract *must* be a conveyance. The purchaser is as free to make any use of the seller's physical and mental capabilities as he would be free, as owner, to do what he pleased with any chattel he had purchased.

In the upshot, by direct coercion and by enforcement of these transfers of ownership of labour-power, law was employed to reduce workers to the minimum of subsistence so that profits could be maximised. The capitalist economic system had achieved an enormous increase in total human wealth; but, in late capitalism, it was now hindering a much greater output which would only come when the proletariat took over the means of production.

Modern Marxists accept this critique of 19th-century capitalism, and believe that it is applicable, with modifications, to the modern world. They differ about proper Marxist practice in relation to law. Some approve agitations for changes in the law as part of class struggle. The Marxist historian, E. P. Thompson, has gone so far as to claim that, even in the 18th century when penal legislation crudely and overtly promoted the interests of the ruling elite, the under-classes received some benefit from the fact that oppression was mediated through law rather than naked force; and that, more generally, the values of the rule of law (as described in chapter 11, above) are an 'unqualified good'. Other Marxists insist that the rule-of-law ideal must constantly be exposed as an oppressive ideological smokescreen, and that law reform campaigns will only serve to bolster it. Denigration and defiance of all law is the better road to achieving that consciousness among workers wherein they will understand where their true class interests lie and the achievement of which, Marx had said, was a pre-condition for social revolution.

Marx's prophetism was the tail-piece of his historicism. Marxist theory explains social evolution in terms of inexorable forces. Hegel saw historical development in terms of ideas – a 'dialectic' involving a thesis, its opposite (an antithesis), and the resolution in a synthesis. Marx and Engels envisaged historical forces operating on the material plane – so that the dialectic consisted of a struggle between classes, producing a revolutionary synthesis. The bourgeois revolution had been the outcome of the struggle between the ruling feudal class and classes opposed to it. They prophesied that the next revolution would occur when the forces of production unleashed by capitalism could no longer be kept within the bounds of bourgeois domination, when the proletariat would throw off its chains and seize the means of production for itself. The result of this revolution would be that the proletariat, the overwhelming majority of the population, would itself become the ruling class for a time. But at the end of a transition period, the 'dictatorship of the proletariat' would be succeeded by a society in which all classes had been abolished and 'communism' would be achieved. At this final stage there would be no classes, no domination, no exploitation, and hence no coercion.

What about 'law' after the revolution? Here one must distinguish the views of theorists writing in countries which, in this century, have sought to implement the prophecy from the opinions of contemporary western Marxists. Engels had said that the state would 'wither away'. According to Lenin, Engels did not mean that the bourgeois state would wither away. That was to be entirely smashed by the revolution. The proletariat, under the leadership of the communist party, would then establish a proletarian state and it was that state which would wither away, once its enemies had been crushed. Lenin was writing in 1917 and Pashukanis, writing in 1924, claimed that the law to be used during the transition period was bourgeois law – there could be no other sort. That view was subsequently repudiated and a novel concept evolved, that of 'socialist legality'. Law is needed as an instrument for constructing the new society. In different communist countries, at varying stages of political development, either the first or the second of the words in 'socialist legality' has been stressed. Sometimes it is insisted that our legality is 'socialist', that is, that it has nothing to do with the bourgeois concept of the rule of law. Consequently, informal tribunals may undertake re-educating tasks in which they need not stick within the letter of the law. At other times it is urged that socialist administration insists on 'legality', that is, the strict observance of the law by citizenry and even party officials.

Earlier in this century some Western Marxists were prepared to accept the authenticity of the self-proclaimed 'Marxist' revolutions. The predominant view among them today is that they were aberrations. Hence, the practices and the demise of communist regimes is irrelevant so far as the veracity of Marxist prophecies are concerned. Indeed, the classical Marxist texts contain the scantiest information about what, if any, law will continue after the final stage of communism has come to pass; and Marxist theorists generally regard it as unprofitable to speculate about the matter. The thing to do is to apply Marxist critique to the societies we have now.

It seems clear that at least two things are to be expected of the envisioned Marxist future. Human nature will be transformed, or returned to its primitive 'unalienated', condition – once the institutions of class oppression have been done away with. Each person will see himself, not as the isolated, right-bearing individual which bourgeois justice focuses upon, but as an integral member of a community. Its life will be his life. Secondly, modern technology, once released from the shackles of capitalist constraint, will produce abundantly enough to meet all the needs of the transformed humanity; and productive work will become a pleasure. Lenin foretold that people would then spontaneously observe the 'elementary rules of social life' – which might be a sort of 'law' – and that should there be isolated infractions they would be dealt with by spontaneous reactions, not coercive institutions.

The most attractive description of this future society was written a hundred years ago by William Morris in *News from Nowhere*, before there was any need to explain away the dark shadows cast by 20th century experience of 'Marxist' experiments. In *Nowhere* there will be no civil or criminal law, no individual or group ownership of dwellings or chattels, no courts, no police, no government, no co-ordination of activity through publicly announced rules. Its inhabitants provide for all their own and each other's needs by spontaneous labour in which they engage for the love of the thing. There are rare homicides, occasioned by sexual jealousy; and these produce nothing but sympathetic concern for the repentant slayer. For the most part, their lives brim with good will and cheerful, uncoerced work.

The final Marxist vision has, as yet, no counterpart in history. Nor, if western Marxists are to be believed, has there yet occurred a successful proletarian revolution of the kind Marx predicted to be imminent. None of us knows the future fate of humanity.

Bibliography

Law and social theory

Albrow M. 'Legal Positivism and Bourgeois Materialism – Max Weber's View of the Sociology of Law' (1975) 2 Br J L Soc 14
Andreski S. L. 'Understanding, Action and Law in Max Weber' in Podgorecki and Whelan (eds) *Sociological Approaches to Law* (1981)

Aubert V (ed) *Sociology of Law* (1969) Pt I

Bredemeier H. C. 'Law as an Integrative Mechanism' in Evan (ed) *Law and Sociology* (1962)

Chambliss W. and Seidman R. *Law, Order and Power* (2nd edn, 1982)

Clarke M. 'Durkheim's Sociology of Law' (1976) 3 Br J L Soc 246

Cotterrell R. B. M. 'Durkheim on Legal Development and Social Solidarity' (1977) 4 Br J L Soc 241

Duguit L. 'Objective Law' (Grandgent and Gifford trans) (1920) 20 Colum L Rev 817, (1921) 21 Colum L Rev 17, 126, 242

Durkheim E. *The Division of Labor in Society* (Simpson trans, 1964)

Grace C. and Wilkinson P. *Sociological Inquiry and Legal Phenomena* (1978)

Hayek F. A. *Law, Legislation and Liberty: vol 1 Rules and Order* (1973)

Hunt A. *The Sociological Movement in Law* (1978) chs 4-5

Kronman A. T. *Max Weber* (1983)

Lukes S. and Scull A. *Durkheim and the Law* (1983)

Morris C. 'Law, Reason and Sociology' (1958-59) 107 U Pa L Rev 310

Parsons T. 'The Law and Social Control' in Evan (ed) *Law and Sociology* (1962)

Schwarzenberger G. 'The Three Types of Law' (1949) 2 CLP 103

Stoljar S. D. 'Weber's Sociology of Law' in Sawer (ed) *Studies in the Sociology of Law* (1961)

Trubeck D. 'Toward a Social Theory of Law: an Essay on the Study of Law and Development' (1972) 82 Yale LJ 1
–   'Max Weber on Law and the Rise of Capitalism' (1972) 3 Wis LR 720

Unger R. M. *Law in Modern Society* (1976)

Weber M. *On Law in Economy and Society* (Rheinstein edn, Shils trans, 1954)

Marxist jurisprudence

Bankowski Z. and Mungham G. *Images of Law* (1976)

Beirne P. and Quinney R. (eds) *Marxism and Law* (1982)

Cain M. and Hunt A. *Marx and Engels on Law* (1979)

Cohen G. A. *Karl Marx's Theory of History: a Defence* (1978)

Collins H. *Marxism and the Law* (1982)

Engels F. *Socialism Utopian and Scientific* in *The Essential Left* (1968)

Harris J. W. 'A Structuralist Theory of Law: an Agnostic View' in Podgorecki and Whelan (eds) *Sociological Approaches to Law* (1981)
–   *Property and Justice* (1996) pp 191-97, 256-58, 264-70, 362-66.

Heath A. 'The Principle of Exchange as a Basis for the Study of Law' in Podgorecki and Whelan op cit

Hunt A. 'Marxism and the Analysis of Law' in Podgorecki and Whelan op cit

Hurst P. *Law, Socialism and Democracy* (1986)

Kamenka E. and Tay A. E. 'Socialism, Anarchism and Law' in Kamenka, Brown and Tay (eds) *Law and Society* (1978)

Kinsey R. 'Marxism and the Law: Preliminary Analyses' (1978) 5 Br J L Soc 202

Lapenna I. *State and Law: Soviet and Yugoslav Theory* (1964)

Lenin V I. *The State and Revolution* in *The Essential Left* (1968)

Levi-Strauss C. *Structural Anthropology* (1963)

Li V H. 'The Role of Law in Communist China' (1970) China Q 66

Lubman S. 'Mao and Mediation: Politics and Dispute Resolution in Communist China' (1967) 55 Calif L Rev 1284

Lukes S. 'Can the Base be Distinguished from the Superstructure' in Miller and Siedentop (eds) *The Nature of Political Theory* (1983)

Marx K. H. and Engels F. *The Manifesto of the Communist Party* in *The Essential Left* (1968)

Marx K. H. *Capital* volume 1 (Fowkes trans, 1990)

Morris W. *News From Nowhere and Other Essays* (1993)

Pashukanis E.B. *Law and Marxism: a General Theory* (Einhorn trans, 1978)

Renner K. *The Institutions of Private Law and Their Social Functions* (Kahn-Freund (ed), Schwarzschild trans, 1949)

Robson P. 'Renner Revisited' in Attwooll (ed) *Perspectives in Jurisprudence* (1977)

Rudden B. 'Law and Ideology in the Soviet Union' (1978) 31 CLP 189

Sugarman D. (ed) *Legality, Ideology and the State* (1983)

Sypnowich C. *The Concept of Socialist Law* (1990)

Thompson E. P. *Whigs and Hunters* (1975)

20 Justice: liberal, communitarian and feminist

1 Justice and law

Men have talked about justice for as long as they have talked about law. The scope of justice is, however, wider. A man may be just or unjust in his dealings with his family or his friends. For legal philosophy, we are interested only in couplings of assertions about justice with those about law. Three sorts should be distinguished. Justice may be claimed to be something inherent in law, or law may be contrasted with justice, or justice may be a measure for testing law.

If law is a system of rules, then some aspects of 'procedural' and of 'formal' justice may be inherent to it. If a rule stipulates that all motorists exceeding a speed limit shall be fined, but those exacting fines take no (or insufficient) steps to find out whether people have fulfilled the condition of the rule, then both procedural justice is violated and, it may be, the rule becomes an empty formula which does not deserve the designation 'legal'. If, during a period of political turbulence, a revolutionary 'court' selects victims for execution on an ad hoc basis, without announcing any universalisable criteria for distinguishing those subject to punishment from those not, it violates formal justice and may, for that reason, be said not to be operating under any system of law. Questions of procedural and formal justice are comprised within the concept of the rule of law, discussed in chapter 11, above. It should be borne in mind, however, that they are only part of that doctrine. If a revolutionary court announces that all those who voted for an ousted regime are to be shot, and takes diligent steps in each case to find out whether or not a person had so voted, it meets the requirements of both formal and procedural justice; but it still might be claimed to be violating the rule of law, because of the opposition between that doctrine and totally retroactive rules.

Questions of procedural and formal justice also overlap with the topic of legal reasoning, discussed in chapter 15, above. Legal reasoning, whatever it comprises, is supposed to exclude personal bias. If a judge were to announce: 'The evidence about the defendant's negligence is inconclusive, but I shall find against him because I don't like his type', his decision could be described as procedurally unjust – it would not lack formal justice if he laid down that all people of this 'type' should, in similar circumstances, be held negligent. It is controversial, as we have seen, to what standards a judge should appeal in deciding a case not clearly covered by a valid legal rule; but it may be that the reasons he gives must at least be 'universalisable' so that his reasoning is circumscribed by the requirements of formal justice. If that is true, then it would be 'unjust' in a judge to say: 'For the following reasons I find that this manufacturer should pay damages, but I do not lay down that any other manufacturer, to whom the reasons would equally apply, should also be liable.' If formal justice is a requirement of legal reasoning, it raises problems in the context of 'prospective overruling', as we saw in chapter 13, above.

The second of the three distinctions to which I referred concerns an alleged contrast between 'law' and 'justice'. From Aristotle onwards, it has been a controversial question whether all law must be contrasted with one's sense of 'justice' or 'equity'. Is it the case that legal rules, however good in themselves (however 'just' in terms of the third distinction), may nonetheless lead to injustice in particular cases? If that is so, it is because the features of some situations in which individuals confront the law are so unique that they cannot be captured by any rule (including any universalisable exception to any rule), but can be captured by this particular sense of justice. We know what solution would be just in all the circumstances of the case, but we cannot frame any rule which would stipulate this solution. If we can frame such a rule but the existing legal rules do not include it, then we are making a point falling under the third distinction: we are saying that the existing rules are unjust and should be replaced by our new rule. We are then using justice as a measure for the law. In terms of the second distinction, the allegation is that no rule can do justice. The conception of justice appealed to is intuitive. I know that it would be unjust to hold this party liable, although I cannot give reasons which could be generalised and form the basis of a new rule or a new exception.

In *An Introduction to the Philosophy of Law*, Roscoe Pound argued that 'executive justice' has to be reconciled with 'justice according to law' by giving proper allowance to individualisation. The former, he says, relies on 'trained intuition', and is particularly important where judgment has to be passed on human conduct and moral issues, less important in the area of property and commercial law. He lists seven agencies for giving effect to executive justice, to be found in Anglo-American legal systems: discretion in the application of equitable remedies; general standards, like reasonableness; jury general verdicts; judicial latitude in finding the law; penal treatment; informal methods of judicial administration in petty courts; and administrative tribunals.

These are curious bed-fellows. The fourth (judicial latitude in finding the law) deserves special attention. If the more extreme of the American realists are right, judges always have latitude, and all they can ever do is to administer intuitive 'executive justice'. This being so, as Frank argued, the way forward is for judges to be as forthcoming as possible about the factors which guide their intuitions, and to give up the pretence of rule-bound decisions, of 'justice according to law' (see chapter 8, above). On Pound's own view, however, judges have latitude in finding the law only sometimes. When they do, why should their decisions be guided by individualising 'executive justice'? If judges exercise 'discretion' in finding the law, they may balance competing considerations in an intuitive way, but the considerations weighed may still be general in nature rather than the individual circumstances of the parties.

As to the first, second and fifth of Pound's agencies (discretionary remedies, general standards, and sentencing), individual circumstances are often stressed, but usually in a principled way. That is, judges giving reasons in such contexts do not normally indicate that they are reasons which can have no bearing on any other case. So far as that is true, principled reasoning appeals to rule-like standards, to 'justice according to law'.

Perhaps jury general verdicts are the best illustration of what Pound intends by 'executive justice'. If Lord Devlin's view of the sovereignty of the jury is correct no one may question the jury's right to render an acquittal verdict, however clear the law and however strong the prosecution evidence. This suggests that the jury is entitled to give preference to its own view of the justice of the case as against justice according to law.

For the most part, when people speak of the law and of justice together, they are not concerned with any alleged inherent justice of law, nor with any alleged inherent contrast between law and justice, but with my third distinction – justice as the measure of law's virtue. If a court applies a legal rule conscientiously according to its terms or, in an unclear case, justifies its decision by reference to accepted standards of legal reasoning, it may do justice according to law; but the outcome may still be unjust because the rules or other legal standards are themselves unjust. What is then invoked is some conception of moral truth, 'conventional' or 'real', in the senses discussed in chapter 2, above. As we saw there, from the perspective of natural law doctrine, a law so found to be unjust might be stigmatised as not law at all, or as lacking the quality to bind in conscience which is possessed by law when it is just. For legal positivists, it would be equally 'law' whether just or unjust; but its injustice would be a reason for calling for reform and perhaps for civil disobedience.

When justice is used as the measure of the law, the assumption is that the law either does or could be made to conform to justice. 'Justice' in this context stands for a substantive moral criterion. The law ought to allocate rights, duties or resources in a certain way, and if it does not it is unjust.

Two senses in which law may be condemned for flouting substantive justice should be distinguished. They concern 'remedial' (or 'commutative') justice, on the one hand, and 'distributive' (or 'social') justice, on the other. By the first measure, law is just if it affords remedies for, and only for, all true wrongs by one man to another; and if it attaches the just, and no more than the just, retribution to crime. It is the law's sole business to lay down what Hayek calls 'rules of just conduct' (see chapter 19, above).

Substantive remedial justice is sometimes what is meant by a judge who appeals to 'justice' as a ground for laying down some new rule. It is assumed that such and such conduct is obviously a wrong, and such and such redress obviously the right remedy. For example, in *Pickett v British Rail Engineering Ltd,*[1] the House of Lords laid down a new ruling, that damages for an injury which had shortened a person's life should include the earnings which would have accrued to him during the 'lost years'. The primary justification for the decision – which overruled earlier authorities – was stated to be that this new rule would accord with the ordinary man's expectations about claims against tortfeasors, and was for that reason 'just'.

Those debating the merits of a proposed bill, or criticising legislation, in terms of 'justice' may, however, have a quite different conception of substantive justice in mind. The justice of the law is dependent on how it, along with other social arrangements, allocates all the good things of life – such as wealth, power, and liberty. The distributive justice appealed to in the case of tax, welfare or planning law is 'social justice' rather than 'remedial justice'.

It is possible to be sceptical about all conceptions of substantive justice. Alf Ross writes:

'To invoke justice is the same thing as banging on the table: an emotional expression which turns one's demand into an absolute postulate. That is no proper way to mutual understanding. It is

1   [1980] AC 136.

impossible to have a rational discussion with a man who mobilises "justice", because he says nothing that can be argued for or against. His words are persuasion, not argument. The ideology of justice leads to implacability and conflict, since on the one hand it incites to the belief that one's demand is not merely the expression of a certain interest in conflict with opposing interests, but that it possesses a higher, absolute validity; and on the other hand it precludes all rational argument and discussion of a settlement.'[2]

But if that is right, what is the criterion for 'rational discussion'? Law may be applauded or condemned when it criminalises consensual masochism.[3] Its failure to provide a remedy when journalists invade privacy[4] may be deplored or welcomed. The distribution of resources embodied in law may be said to pass, or to fail, tests of desert, need, incentive or equality. Do we simply announce whose interests would be furthered, and whose prejudiced, by a change in the law and leave it at that? Such abnegation of controversy might be 'rational', but it would not be 'argument'. If we suppose that the reasons we advance for or against changing the law carry moral force within the political community to which we belong, then we are judging the law by some moral criteria or other (whether we are objectivists, conventionalists, relativists, utilitarians or anti-utilitarians, positivists or believers in natural law, or whatever). The moral criteria we marshal in political controversy about the law's merit or demerit could do with a name; and the traditional label is 'justice'.

2 Liberal individualism

In chapter 2 I mentioned popular invocations of the value of 'tolerance'. That is taken to be a hallmark of liberalism. Furthermore, liberal political philosophies are generally thought of as 'individualistic'. They assume that a just society is one composed of free and equal individuals, each permitted to pursue his or her own view of the good life (so far as that does not interfere with other people's life-plans). Government should be neutral. It should not seek to impose any particular conception of human flourishing. Liberals generally assent to some version of Mill's harm principle, discussed in chapter 10. Beyond that, there is much for liberals to disagree about, as they ring the changes on conceptions of individual autonomy and equality. As we saw in chapter 14, Ronald Dworkin supposes that the underlying value is equality, upon which can be founded rights against other citizens and against the government. For Joseph Raz,

2 *On Law and Justice* pp 274-5.
3 *R v Brown* [1994] 1 AC 212.
4 *Kaye v Robertson* [1991] FSR 62.

on the other hand, the basic value is freedom, which is to be positively promoted, if need be, by government intervention:

> 'One of the main goals of government authority … is to ensure for all persons an equal ability to pursue in their lives and promote in their societies any ideal of the good of their choosing.'[5]

In the next two sections, we examine critics of liberalism from a conservative communitarian standpoint and from a radical feminist critique. Each of these positions challenges the notion of the independent individual as the starting-point for conceptions of remedial or distributive justice. In this section, I draw attention to a major division within liberalism, which turns on the implications of autonomy for resource-distribution: egalitarian liberalism, and libertarian liberalism. The most discussed exemplars of each variety are represented by books written in the 1970s, respectively, by John Rawls and Robert Nozick.

The problem is this. If you suppose that autonomy includes freedom to accumulate resources without limit, then the rich will, in the outcome, have the ability to pursue life-plans which is denied to the poor, so where is the equality? On the other hand, if you insist that resources be equally divided, how can anyone pursue an autonomous life? Taking equality of resources literally would seem incompatible with all the independence associated with private ownership, including freedom to choose between goods and services by spending or saving money. 150 years ago Pierre Joseph Proudhon (whom no-one would accuse of being a liberal) argued that, in principle, society encompasses men the world over (but not women).[6] Augmentation in wealth arises, differences in talent or capacity notwithstanding, only from social co-operation, and hence should be divided in arithmetically equal shares between all who work. Property entails the power of individuals to assert exclusive and permanent rights to unequal shares of assets and the increase to be derived from them. Therefore, 'Property is theft'.[7]

If one favours an egalitarian approach to resource-distribution but wishes to retain individual (liberal) autonomy, how is the circle to be squared? In *A Theory of Justice*, Rawls adopts a refined version of the contractarianism espoused by 17th and 18th century political philosophers.

He asks his reader to do two things. First, he must reflect on what it is about people's judgments of justice which gives them either authenticity or else the appearance of self-interested special pleading. He should

---

5 *The Morality of Freedom* p 115.
6 Proudhon *What is Property?* (Kelley and Smith trans.) pp 165, 176-7, 178, 186.
7 Op cit pp 13, 14, 16, 33, 184.

construct an imaginary situation in which people are making judgments about society from the outside, without personal bias, and consider what such neutral outsiders would decide. The principles they would choose, having been arrived at by a fair procedure, constitute 'justice as fairness'. Secondly, the reader must match the principles which would be chosen in this way against his own considered judgments of justice. He may find that what his imaginary outsiders would choose does not gell with the considered judgments he is accustomed to make. If that is so, then either he should modify his considered judgments, or else he should go back to the construction and see whether it was defective in some way. In the end, Rawls hopes, the reader will reach a position of 'reflective equilibrium', in which his own considered judgments cohere with principles which the neutral outsiders would choose.

The constructive situation is called by Rawls the 'original position'. It consists of a congress of people, each representing a social class. They are placed behind a 'veil of ignorance'. They have only general information about human psychology and the laws of science. They do not know to which social class they are going to belong, nor even at what stage of development their society stands. They choose, by unanimous agreement, the principles which will regulate whatever society they belong to. In making this choice, they are guided only by rational self-interest. Each knows that he will have a plan of life (his own conception of the good), but he does not know what it will be. They will therefore agree to social principles which will give them the best chance of achieving each his life plan, whatever that may turn out to be. Since these are, by definition, principles which people would choose without taking into account special interests, they are objectively just.

Rawls concludes that the principles which the people in the original position choose are two in number:

> '*First Principle.* Each person is to have an equal right to the most extensive total system of equal basic liberties compatible with a similar system of liberty for all. *Second Principle.* Social and economic inequalities are to be arranged so that they are both: (a) to the greatest benefit of the least advantaged, consistent with the just savings principle, and (b) attached to offices and positions open to all under conditions of fair equality of opportunity.'[8]

Rawls does not specify the 'system of equal basic liberties' precisely. He indicates that it includes political liberties (the right to vote and to be eligible for public office, freedom of speech and of assembly, liberty of conscience and freedom of thought); freedom of the person; the right to

8   *A Theory of Justice* p 302.

hold personal property; and freedom from arbitrary arrest and seizure, as defined by the concept of the rule of law. By their first principle, the people in the original position choose equality in these things, and they give this principle 'lexical priority' over the second principle; that is, they agree that the equal liberties of all are not to be sacrificed for any gain in respect of income, wealth or power (the matters dealt with in the second principle). They choose that the society to which they belong should have a basic structure of institutions which puts liberty first.

Why should they? Because, says Rawls, it would be irrational for any of them to take chances with his liberty. He does not know what position he will hold in society, nor what things will be valued by the person he turns out to be. But he does know that there are 'social primary goods', that is, things which every rational person wants whatever else he wants. These include liberty and opportunity, income and wealth, and the bases of self respect. A person in the original position will choose the basic liberties in priority to any distribution of income, wealth and power, because he knows that, by so doing, he will have the best chance of obtaining for himself the social primary goods and of pursuing whatever other ends his particular plan turns out to encompass. He would not opt for principles which would allow a dictator to take away political liberties on condition that the dictator increased everyone's wealth, because, whereas he does not know whether he would value the increase in wealth (beyond the minimum which constitutes a primary social good), he does know that he would miss the political liberties, for they contribute to the social primary goods of liberty and self-respect.

Rawls makes one qualification on the priority of liberty. The people in the original position will choose the two principles which constitute the 'special conception' of justice, only on the assumption that their society has reached a stage at which liberties can be effectively secured. On the assumption that that stage has not been reached they will choose a more 'general conception' of justice, which requires that all social primary goods, including liberty, are to be distributed equally unless an unequal distribution would be to the advantage of the least favoured. It is not clear what Rawls has in mind for the take-off point of the priority of liberty. Presumably, if conditions of a society are chaotic so that minimum security required as a basis of liberty and self-respect cannot be obtained, the people in the original position would allow that their basic liberties might be traded for firm government; and, presumably, if economic development is at such a low level that many people may starve without draconian, liberty-restricting measures, the same trade-off would be agreed to. But once this minimum stage has been attained, the people in the original position insist on their lexically-ordered two principles. The only limitations on liberty are to be justified for the sake of the total system of basic liberties, such as rules of order in debate. From behind the veil of ignorance, people would not agree to their liberties being restricted for the sake of economic prosperity.

The first clause of the second principle allows for social and economic inequalities, but only if they are for the benefit of the least advantaged. This is Rawls's famous 'difference' principle. The people in the original position would choose this, not knowing whether they would be favoured or disfavoured by any inequality, because the worst they could be would be 'least advantaged'. They would not opt for a set-up which allowed greater inequalities, because that would be risking being worse off, should they be the least advantaged; and it would be perverse to opt for complete equality even if that meant that everyone was worse off including the least advantaged. Rawls leaves open the question whether private enterprise or public ownership of the means of production does maximise the position of the worst off members of society; but claims that whichever does must, for that reason, be the more just – assuming the priority of liberty. Furthermore, we do not know what 'the right to hold personal property', which is one of the lexically prior basic liberties, entails. If it includes the right to accumulate wealth without limit, there might not be much left to be divided at the second stage, in accordance with the difference principle.

Try testing these principles, as Rawls tells us to do, against your considered judgments about justice. Suppose we have a rich man and a poor man arguing about whether their society is just.

Poor man: How can it be just, when you can afford champagne and I only get beer.

Rich man: But I get a higher salary than you because I'm cleverer and so contribute more to society; and also, my father was cleverer than yours and saved money which he left to me. Your lack of talent is not your fault, of course, but you can't complain that it's unfair if my greater contribution is more rewarded.

Poor man: Your greater talents are not your fault either. They are just an accident of birth. If we all work our best, why shouldn't we be paid the same?

Rich man: On that argument, why shouldn't we be paid the same whether we work or not? If people have to be paid to give them an incentive to work, isn't it right that those who happen to have talents and need long training should be given extra incentives? For if they weren't, there'd be less produced to pay for old-age pensions and so on. If my wealth were shared out, industry would collapse and you'd be worse off than you are now. Would that be worth it, just for the satisfaction of knowing that I was no better off than you?

Poor man: I don't believe that industry would collapse.

Now Rawls constructs his original position on the assumption that the poor man is right in regarding being born with talents as morally irrelevant; hence he stipulates that the veil of ignorance hides from each chooser whether he has greater or less intelligence or abilities. He also constructs it on the assumption that the rich man is right in denying pure envy a legitimate place in reasoning about justice; hence each person in the original position is defined as the sort of individual who is concerned exclusively with his own maximum good, and consequently they choose what would favour them most should they be least advantaged over against a set-up which would give them less but make men more equal. If, on reflection, you do not agree that ability and/or envy are morally irrelevant, you would construct the thing differently.

The rest of the second principle of Rawls's special conception of justice makes reference to two things which qualify the call for arrangements to be so ordered as to confer maximum benefit on the least advantaged. First, he invokes a 'just savings' principle. The people in the original position would know (knowing human psychology) that they would have some concern (once the veil of ignorance lifts) for at least the next generation, so they will agree that all social assets should not be immediately squandered. Secondly, they will not debar anyone from attaining any office even if it carries special power or wealth, provided 'fair equality of opportunity' is guaranteed. Top jobs would be open to all, without reverse discrimination against the best endowed individuals. But it would be agreed that as much as possible should be done, by way of education provision and so forth, to counteract disadvantages such as those flowing from family background, so that the equality of opportunity will be 'fair'.

Objections to Rawls's contractarian procedure may be levelled at its alleged objectivity. Its merit is supposed to be that it provides a common check for people who now disagree. If I say to you: 'You only call this law just because it benefits you (or because it accords with some religious principle you have)', and you offer counter jibes in terms of my subjective interests and views, we can both be asked whether people who did not know their own particular situation would have agreed to it. Then we shall have to give reasons which at least purport to leave out special pleadings. Against this it may be argued that Rawls's original-position people are not truly neutral. They have controversial evaluations built into them, and their conclusions must therefore be controversial.

One may cavil at the conception of the primary good of 'self-respect' which Rawls attributes to his people. In arguing for the priority of liberty, he says that this primary good leads them to favour freedom of conscience so much that they will not trade it for economic gain. But is this conception of self-respect, as he claims, something that all rational people desire –

and hence a 'primary social good'? Perhaps people's self-esteem has more to do with the size of their car than their ability to engage in free moral and political speculation. Many, no doubt, hold that it is better to be a philosopher than a rational pig; but then such prior evaluations of human excellence were supposed to be eliminated from the original position. Further, self-respect may be a relative matter, depending on how far we fall short of others in achievement. If that is so, why should not 'envy' be taken into account? Conversely, self-respect may be impossible unless we feel that we are benefiting others; so why should Rawls assume that the people in the original position calculate only on the basis of self-interest? Some sort of 'service to others' may be a primary social good. Perhaps Rawls's people are too pig-like. Rawls makes it clear that his 'contractarian' approach to justice is open for adoption by someone who does not accept his particular version of the contract situation. 'Reflective equilibrium' may lead to modifications in the original position in order that principles emerging from it match our considered judgments. Can this process produce accord between those whose considered judgments differ, especially if they vary, not merely about what they regard as just, but about what is essentially 'human'?

In *Anarchy, State and Utopia*, Nozick attacks all theories of justice which advocate any patterned distribution of resources, on the ground that they are incompatible with autonomy. With whatever pattern one began, it could not survive if one allowed people freedom to spend their own money as they choose. They might all opt to buy tickets to watch an outstanding sportsman perform so that the sportsman (Wilt Chamberlain) will end up disproportionately rich.[9]

Nozick offers an alternative theory of justice, 'the theory of entitlements'. According to this theory, the justice of social arrangements has nothing to do with the way in which the total wealth and power of a society is distributed, but is exclusively concerned with the justice of people's present holdings. There are three principles. The 'principle of acquisition' requires that holdings over resources, which were previously owned by no one, were acquired in a just way. The 'principle of transfer' requires that holdings devolved to the present owners through just transactions. The 'principle of rectification' comes into play only when either of the other two has been violated.

The 'principle of acquisition' presupposes that there must be some means by which original titles to resources can be acquired, carrying an ownership right which comprises free transmissibility (so that the 'principle of transfer' can apply). Nozick invokes the state-of-nature theorising of John Locke, but his application of Lockean principles is not easy to follow. I have argued in *Property and Justice* that Locke's

9   *Anarchy, State and Utopia* pp 160-64.

celebrated defence of private property in the fifth chapter of his *Second Treatise of Government* contains two distinct arguments for natural property rights, and that Nozick deploys them both. The first argument invokes self-ownership: since everyone owns his own body and his labouring activities, he owns whatever he creates by mixing his labour with the products of nature. The second argument I have called 'creation-without-wrong': if someone turns natural products into a new item but leaves 'as much and as good' for everybody else, he is rightful owner of that new item.

The self-ownership argument can be summarised in four steps:
1. If I am not a slave, nobody else owns my body. Therefore
2. I must own myself. Therefore
3. I must own all my actions, including those which create or improve resources. Therefore
4. I own the resources, or the improvements, I produce.

Nozick runs these four steps backwards, in order to demonstrate that redistributive taxation is 'on a par' with forced labour. If the state expropriates any of the fruits of my labour, it is denying my moral ownership of them (contrary to step 4). Therefore, it is implicitly denying step 3, that I own all my labouring activities; and hence also step 2, that I own myself. Now since the only alternative to my owning myself is that someone else owns me, the redistributive state is implicitly denying even step 1, that I am not a slave. Hence, redistributive taxation turns me, at least partially, into the slave of the community.[10]

The fallacy in the self-ownership argument is (as I argue) patent, because of the spectacular *non sequitur* between steps 1 and 2. From the fact that I am not a slave it does not follow that I 'own' myself in a sense which has any bearing on ownership of external resources. Nobody 'owns' me, not even me. There may be grounds for objecting to the kind of redistributive taxation called for by Rawls's difference principle, but a libertarian critique which invokes notions of self-ownership and partial slavery is devoid of normative force.

The creation-without-wrong argument asserts that if a person
1. creates a new item of social wealth and
2. wrongs no-one in doing so, it follows that
3. he ought to be accorded ownership of that new item.

Nozick contends that Locke's enough-and-as-good proviso may be restated in such a way as to yield just original acquisitions. So long as the appropriation did not (and continues not to) make other people worse off, all things considered, than they would have been had it not occurred (or were it not still insisted on), then the appropriation is just; and in

10   Op cit pp 169-72.
11   Op cit pp 175-82.

making this comparison one may take into account all the familiar incentive and market-instrumental advantages of private property institutions.[11]

The creation-without-wrong argument is more plausible than that based on self-ownership. Nevertheless, there are serious objections. One has to do with the social character of labour. One need not go all the way with Proudhon in assuming that all men are equally responsible for any accretion in social wealth, in order to point out that it is most unusual to find a single individual creating something on his own. Even where one can, it is not obvious that step 3 follows from the combination of steps 1 and 2. Why does the non-wrongfulness of the actor's creative endeavour entail in him a power to impose obligations on all other persons not to intermeddle with that which he has created, especially if those obligations are to have the timeless quality that would be needed to enable him and his successors to transmit ownership for ever?

Even if some abstract natural-right principle of just acquisition could be established, the question would arise whether Nozick's historical entitlement theory actually applies to any society we know. Recall Maine's suggestion that individual titles, at least to land, began with dispossession (see chapter 17, above). Presumably, Nozick might invoke his 'principle of rectification', about which he says very little. If the heirs of the wrongfully dispossessed owner cannot be traced, are present holdings just even if we know that they are vested in the successors of someone whose original acquisition was unjust? Another libertarian, Murray Rothbard, argues that this must be so. Consequently, he maintains, whereas in South America land ought to be handed over to the peasantry without compensation being paid to the successors of the *Conquistadores*, land titles in North America are secure. That is so (it seems) because, in North America, the colonial expropriators committed genocide so efficiently that no heirs of the original just owners can be identified.

3 Communitarianism

The 1980s witnessed an attack upon liberal philosophical positions, whether egalitarian or libertarian, in the name of a revived 'communitarianism'. Notable contributions to this critique have been made by Alasdair MacIntyre, Michael Sandel and Charles Taylor. The principal target has been the assumption that the justice of social arrangements can be assessed from the standpoint of atomistic, right-bearing individuals. Liberal-individualists, it is said, take the egoistic and self-sufficient individual as a given. They then propose competing views about the mutual rights and duties of such beings and define the just society as one which provides conditions of co-operation under which these deontological requirements will be respected. In that way, liberals suppose that desirable communal living is derivative from that which detached human entities are entitled to demand, the 'priority of the right over the good'.

These supra-communal individuals are, so it is urged, figments of liberal invention. The only selves which have ever existed are human persons situated within, and at least partially constituted by, the communities in which they live. It is foolish to predicate conclusions about just human association from the standpoint of rootless beings, entering into contracts or dealing with one another in a mythical state of nature. Furthermore, such an approach down-plays those moral values which result from community-created roles and settled traditions. MacIntyre, for example, finds no place in the theories of either Rawls or Nozick for the moral significance of desert, arising when people foster the good of their communities. He looks back to Aristotelian and medieval conceptions of the virtuous individual, wherein there was no clash between that which was in one's own interest and the role one should play as a member of the community. He finds little in the large-scale societies of modern states which echoes these older conceptions. Sandel charges Rawls in particular with a metaphysical conception of the person, which makes no room for the moral demands which matter – those which depend on real atttachments and commitments to persons with whom we associate. Taylor sees as paper-thin any conception of autonomy which is not based on a substantive concept of the self, one which (reversing liberal priorities) derives from the good society.

These philosophers are principally engaged in demolition and in a nostalgic evocation of what we have lost. Their attacks on individualism nevertheless chime with a populist call for a greater sense of community in social arrangements. Surely, it is not enough that people refrain from wrongs or the breaking of contracts. Rather, we should engender a sense of community in which members are concerned with each other's welfare as part of their own conception of what it is to live good lives. A society which promotes a sense of belonging and shared public concerns is a worthy aspiration. Participation in public decision-making, at all levels, should not be seen in terms of mere political rights, but as an index of social excellence. Seek first the good society, and enriched individual living will follow. Are there not social goods which are not reducible to a collection of fulfilled, individuated life-plans?

In a series of essays and lectures now published in his book *Political Liberalism*, Rawls asserts that the foundation of his theory is political, not metaphysical. He denies that liberalism has any specific conception of the self, certainly not one of egocentric self-assertion. He no longer portrays his theory of justice as one of general application. Rather, it is a device for testing the soundness of the intuitions we have about a well-ordered liberal society. In such a society, each person may form a conception of the good both for himself and for the community in which he wants to live. If we are to co-exist, however, we must look for an 'overlapping consensus': a shared political structure which makes room for competing deeper views by providing surface institutions.

I find the meta-ethical communitarian critique of liberalism unconvincing. The mere fact that liberal philosophers employ thought-experiments, like 'veils of ignorance' or 'states of nature', does not establish that they believe that persons so situated are of the same ilk as flesh-and-blood individuals. As to politics and law reform, it is difficult to make a judgment between liberalism and communitarianism without further information about which variety of each someone has in mind. Liberalism may, as we have seen, be egalitarian or libertarian. Presumably, no communitarian would suggest that any settled community, with defined role-values, must be better than any society which liberalism might aspire to. For all his harking back to the Aristotelian virtues, MacIntyre does not advocate the re-introduction of slavery. I have suggested that the public culture, as distinct from the appalling governmental practices, of the modern world does embody a 'minimalist conception of justice', to which liberals and communitarians would alike assent. It contains only three elements.

First, there is 'natural equality': if treatment of a certain kind is due to one human being, X, nothing less is due to another person, Y, merely because Y is an inferior type of human being to X. If treatment of citizens varies according to age, disability or gender, the differentiation has to be justified on some ground other than that the young or the old, the disabled or the disfavoured gender, are inherently inferior kinds of human beings. That leaves open the question whether, as liberals would have it, no exercise of power is warranted if it presupposes any priority among conceptions of the good; or whether a government may treat all its citizens alike in the light of a communitarian consensus as to what is the best life for everyone to lead.

The second element is the assumption that autonomous choice, over some range of actions open to individuals, is of value to all human beings. Some liberals and some communitarians might differ as to how wide that range can be; but no modern communitarian would argue that we are all so much the products of our communities that it never makes sense to speak of individual choice or responsibility.

The third element consists of the *prima facie* banning of unprovoked invasions of bodily integrity – without some such justification as medical treatment, promotion of public health, self-defence, just punishment, the maintenance of order or legitimate struggle. Mill's harm principle takes this assumption for granted. Communities of the past would have denied that it applied to violence directed towards 'strangers' or dependent family members, but presumably modern communitarians do not espouse values which would allow for such exceptions. They might, however, question the Millian harm principle on another ground: it wrongly denies government intervention to protect what a community sees as constitutive of its distinct communal values.

Have communitarians a valid ground of complaint against at least libertarian liberals, in that the latter allow for no communal responsibility to recognise either the deserts or the basic needs of citizens? As we saw in chapter 2, above, David Hume advocated a purely conventional basis for justice. Whatever conventional property rules have emerged, we do better to enforce them than to try to alter them by reference to a supposed public interest, even if they avail the profligate or the miser:

> 'The relation of fitness or suitability ought never to enter into consideration, in distributing the properties of mankind; but we must govern ourselves by rules, which are more general in their application, and more free from doubt and uncertainty.'[12]

Following Hume, F. A. Hayek argues that it is the sole business of government to enforce spontaneously-evolved 'rules of just conduct' without reference to need or desert. The justice of individual rules can be tested only by their compatibility with other conventional rules, the ultimate touchstone being a socially-evolved 'order of actions'. By this compatibility test, the substantive and remedial justice of law may be assessed, in the manner of common law case-by-case evolution. But, for Hayek, the notion of 'social justice', by which judgment might be passed on entire bodies of law, is 'wholly devoid of meaning or content'.[13] It is also dangerous. It was initially invoked in favour of the destitute, but it has proved to be 'the thin end of the wedge by which the principle of equality under the law was destroyed'.[14] It allows for demands which can be satisfied only by a totalitarian state. Part of the explanation for the appeal of this chimerical notion lies in inherited dispositions of compassion towards the unfortunate which were appropriate in a face-to-face community, but which should have no place in the open society instituted by the post-medieval enlightenment. If we value freedom, we must steel ourselves to an overriding belief in the morality of the market:

> 'It may at first seem paradoxical that the advance of morals should lead to a reduction of specific obligations towards others: yet whoever believes that the principle of equal treatment of all men, which is probably the only chance of peace, is more important than special help to visible suffering, must wish it. It admittedly means

12 *A Treatise of Human Nature* book 3 p 283.
13 *The Mirage of Social Justice* p 96.
14 Op cit p 142.
15 Op cit p 91.

that we make our rational insight dominate over our inherited instincts. But the great moral adventure on which modern man has embarked when he launched into the open society is threatened when he is required to apply to all his fellow men rules which are appropriate only to the fellow members of a tribal group.'[15]

Thus Hayek and conservative communitarians agree that the large-scale societies of the modern day exhibit characteristics quite unlike the values which permeated older small-scale communities; but whereas for the latter this development is doleful, for Hayek it is something to be celebrated. Supporters of the view that the community owes duties to meet the basic needs of its citizens may base themselves either, contrary to Hayek's strictures, on communitarian values which affirm that the good society is one which takes inter-dependence seriously; or on egalitarian liberal claims which suppose that such provision is the subject of individual rights.

It seems to me that the libertarian fallacy of both Nozick and Hayek lies in the following trick. It assumes that, just as the third element of the minimalist conception of justice bans violence to the person, so also it prohibits invasion of a domain which includes private ownership of individuated portions of the external world. However, whereas we are all born with bodies that can be violated, nothing attaches resources to us as a matter of natural right. Property institutions are the product of social convention and law and must offer reasons to those excluded from any resource for the obligation not to intermeddle. How could such obligations be well grounded unless those subjected to them are sufficiently in community with others that, at least, their basic needs are met and their desert-claims receive respectful consideration?

4   Feminist jurisprudence

Liberal conceptions of justice and of law have been the subject of attack by a burgeoning literature which, since the early 1980s, has come to be called 'feminist jurisprudence'. In some American and Australian law schools, it has intruded into university politics in a fashion comparable to that of the critical legal studies movement (see chapter 8, above). The promotion prospects of women members of departments may turn on what attitude they take towards it.

'Feminism' comprises a range of philosophical, political, social and literary projects and attitudes united only by the commitment to take seriously the distinct experiences of women. Those feminists who attack 'liberalism' do so on the following ground. When liberals insist that just arrangements are those which foster equally the autonomy of all the individuals of which a society is composed, the 'individual' presupposed is almost always a male. At the abstract level women are ignored altogether, since the prototypical human being is masculine; and when concrete problems of women are considered, they are depicted by reference to, and in contrast with, a normative standard fashioned for the treatment of males.

Liberal law, it is said, aims to provide general rules about the rights and responsibilities of citizens; but they are standardly male citizens. When liberal reformers of the past (including liberal feminists) have succeeded in instituting changes in the law to take account of the interests of women, they left untouched whole swathes of what really matters to women. Formally equal political rights are of little value, given the economic dependence of most women. Equal rights of entry into the professions can do nothing to counteract the social forces which stereotype women as homemakers, and hence do not in practice confer equal promotion opportunities. Above all, supposedly neutral legal rules are suspect because, in the light of womens' real situations, they turn out not to be neutral at all.

For example, the law purports to prohibit homicide to all, allowing for the justification of self-defence and the partial excuses of provocation and diminished responsibility. If anyone deliberately kills another for simple revenge, that is murder (whether the killer be male or female). Recent English cases have highlighted the tragic dilemmas of women who have suffered years of violent abuse and eventually killed their partners.[16] The liberal response would be to explore whether any of the existing excuses can be tailored to take account of such circumstances. But that, according to a critical feminist perspective, is to ignore the actual experience of the accused woman. She should not be squeezed into these abstract categories at all.

Another example can be taken from the law of rape. For serious crimes in general, the legal-liberal approach balances the state's policing functions against the citizen's right to freedom from unmerited coercion through the dual doctrines of *mens rea* and burden of proof: no-one is to be held guilty unless the tribunal of fact is satisfied beyond reasonable doubt that he or she acted intentionally or at least recklessly. The House of Lords has ruled that this applies to rape, so that if it may have been the case that a man honestly believed his victim to be consenting, he is entitled to an acquittal.[17]. A liberal response might be as follows. In other areas of criminal liability, such as manslaughter, falling below an objective standard of proper care is sometimes enough. That ought to be so for rape, so that a careless belief in consent, even if honestly held, should not exonerate. A critical feminist response deplores concentration on the

16   *R v Ahluwalia* [1992] 4 All ER 889; *R v Thornton (No 2)* [1996] 2 All ER 1033.
17   *DPP v Morgan* [1976] AC 182.

rapist's state of mind. One should look at the matter from the point of view of women who, in our society, are regularly subjected to coerced sex or the fear of it.

I once had the temerity to address a sixth form at a girls' school in the following terms:

'If you were on a jury when a woman had been charged with shoplifting, and if she said that she picked up the goods absent-mindedly, you would be instructed to acquit unless you were sure she was lying. Is that right?'

Unanimous answer: 'Yes!'

'If a young woman complains that her boyfriend has raped her and he says she consented to intercourse, you would be told to find him not guilty unless you were sure he was lying. Is that right?'

'No! The girl should always be believed!'

Two strands of recent theorising are commonly distinguished as 'cultural' or 'radical' feminism. The former is associated with the work of the developmental psychologist, Carol Gilligan. She suggests that from early childhood girls and boys are taught different patterns of social appraisal which typically persist into adult life. Men value autonomy and devise systems of ethics comprised of abstract rules. Women value connectedness and nurture and pass moral judgments which are specific to particular contexts. These different 'voices' should both be respected. The male aspiration towards abstractness should not (she contends) be regarded as a superior kind of rationality.

Radical feminism finds this tame. In all societies there has been but one official voice, that of the dominant male. Suppression and silencing has been the universal experience of women. The state, the law and the social institutions which the law supports or allows to flourish are all structured in the interests of one class, men, and against the interests of another class, women. Whether a society espouses liberal or socialist principles, the experience of individual women is one of relative economic deprivation compared with men, sexual objectification for the gratification of men, and systematic subjection to personal violence by men.

The most influential of those radical feminists who have turned their attention to law is Catharine Mackinnon. She argues that we can generalise from the pervasiveness of the patriarchal structures supported by law so as to characterise the state as itself 'male'. She dismisses the jurisprudence of Austin, Hart and Dworkin as alike expressive of a male

18 *Toward a Feminist Theory of the State* pp 169-70.

point of view.[18] The only feminism worth having is one which exposes the systematic stereotyping and denigration of women. Its primary methodology should be 'consciousness raising', wherein women share their true (as distinct from socially-constructed) experiences and thus may, eventually, reveal or construct a specifically feminine point of view. As things are, discourse of all kinds is man-made and has concocted a concept of woman as a passive and subservient 'other'. It is not merely that abstract individuals have traditionally been invoked by using male pronouns. Many writers (feminist or not) today endeavour to counteract this phenomenon by adopting the following maxim of 'politically correct' terminology – always use the plural or 'she', unless you have a particular male individual in mind. For Mackinnon, the masculinity of discourse goes much deeper than that. Sexual metaphors for 'knowing' are, she maintains, no coincidence. She instances a phrase which I have often heard repeated as illustrative of male scientific discourse – 'a penetrating observation'.[19] (Why must one assume that the metaphor is taken from sex rather than from light passing through glass?)

Other radical feminists, while accepting the general line of Mackinnon's condemnation of contemporary societies, disagree with her grand-scale theorising. The state should not be simply dubbed 'male', since it contains pockets of oppression, discrimination and exclusion which are not gender-specific. Black or disabled people (women and men) may suffer at the hands of white or able-bodied people (men and women). Further, is it not an over-simplification to suggest that there is a singular 'woman's view' awaiting empowerment by the process of consciousness-raising? Some women whom Mackinnon would classify as mere liberal feminists, or some who do not choose to embrace the label 'feminist' at all, may feel insulted if they are told that the experiences they report are not authentic because they reflect a consciousness created for them by men.

There is also disagreement about what a 'feminist jurisprudence' should be taken to include. It would presumably not be enough to offer criticisms of particular branches of law. Many 'liberals' would affirm, for example, that the law contains no adequate machinery for rewarding homemaking and child-care. Who would not agree that modern societies have failed to redress – although they have uncovered – the miseries of domestic violence and abuse towards women and children? A 'feminist jurisprudence' addresses the law as a whole. It finds in law a systematic playing out of male power. Radical feminists then diverge about whether law could be used as part of the cure.

19 'Feminism, Marxism, Method and the State' (1983) 8 Signs 635 at p 636, n 4.
20 *Toward a Feminist Theory of the State* p 244.
21 *Feminism and the Power of Law* p 160.

Mackinnon displays the characteristic American attitude that, with the help of the constitutional text, anything is possible. The statutory and constitutional law of equality 'provides a peculiar jurisprudential opportunity, a crack in the wall between law and society'.[20] Given the law's lip-service to 'equality', it is open to radical lawyers to insist on concrete rights which reflect women's real experiences – against pornography, in favour of what is called 'reverse discrimination', and rights to control every aspect of their reproductive functions (including the disposal of foetuses which they choose to abort). With comparably typical British gloom, Carol Smart seeks to warn feminists 'to avoid the siren call for law'.[21] She notes that legal intervention in the areas of pornography, rape and child-abuse have done as much harm as good and she is suspicious of invoking more 'rights'. Feminists who seek law reform may be contaminated with law's inherent oppressive power. Better to marginalise law and seek other means for changing social attitudes.

The problematic of women's sexuality, as (feminists claim) it is constructed by men, recurs again and again through the literature; and the crime of rape is taken to be its darkest emblem. Mackinnon writes:

'Perhaps the wrong of rape has proved so difficult to define because the unquestionable starting-point has been that rape is defined as distinct from intercourse, while for women it is difficult to distinguish the two under conditions of male dominance.'[22]

'Rape should be defined as sex by compulsion, of which physical force is one form. Lack of consent is redundant and should not be a separate element of the crime.'[23]

Taking these two claims together, what would the law be like? It seems that the crime would be established if the victim averred that, although she had always 'consented' to intercourse with her partner, her consent was based on compulsion resulting, say, from economic dependence. Presumably, the law would not arraign a man for rape if his adult partner was eager to testify that she had been, and still wished to be, a willing participator in intercourse – or might her testimony be suspect if some *amicus curiae* could establish that her consciousness had been distorted by the setting of male dominance in which she had grown up?

The response to such questions would, I suspect, be that they are typical of the legal-liberal and 'male' aspiration towards abstract definitions as controls on the application of public force. There comes a point at which interchange of opinions between men and women over such matters runs

22 *Toward a Feminist Theory of the State* p 174.
23 Op cit p 245.

into the sand. Witness the depressing spectacle of male students required to write examination answers about feminist jurisprudence who suppose that they must rehearse the views of leading members of the school and that they are officially debarred from saying what they actually believe.

Perhaps a genuine feminist jurisprudence shared by open-minded investigators of both sexes is impossible. That would follow from Robin West's analysis of the gender-lines which (she maintains) necessarily pervade theory itself. Borrowing both on cultural and radical feminism, she sets out the duality of distinctively female self-awareness. Women both aspire to connectedness and nurture, from which stance sexual relations and motherhood may be valued; and also resent the invasion of their individuality constituted by consensual sex or planned pregnancy. Both aspects of femininity are silenced by male law. Only in a post-patriarchal society could these rifts be healed, men and women come to share a common humanity and justice at last be attained.

Bibliography

Justice and law

Devlin P. *The Judge* (1979) ch 5
Finnis J. M. *Natural Law and Natural Rights* (1980) ch 7
Hall J. 'Justice in the Twentieth Century' (1971) 59 Calif L Rev 752
Hart H. L. A. *The Concept of Law* (2nd edn, 1994) ch 8
Honoré A. M. *Making Law Bind* (1987) ch 9
Lucas J. R. *On Justice* (1980)
MacCormick D. N. *Legal Reasoning and Legal Theory* (1978) ch 4
Miller D. *Social Justice* (1976)
Pettit P. *Judging Justice* (1980)
Pound R. *An Introduction to the Philosophy of Law* (revised edn, 1954) ch 3
Ross A. *On Law and Justice* (1958) ch 12
Sartorius R. E. *Individual Conduct and Social Norms* (1975) ch 7
Solomon R. C. *A Passion for Justice* (1995)
Taylor C. 'The Nature and Scope of Distributive Justice' in Lucash (ed) *Justice and Equality Here and Now (1986)*
Walzer M. *Spheres of Justice* (1983)
Wasserstrom R. A. *The Judicial Decision* (1961) ch 5

Liberal individualism

Ackerman B. A. *Social Justice in the Liberal State* (1980) chs 2, 6 and 7
Barry B. M. *The Liberal Theory of Justice* (1973)
Cohen G. A. *Self-Ownership, Freedom, and Equality* (1995) chs 1 and 3

Daniels N. (ed) *Reading Rawls* (1975)
Dworkin R. M. 'What is Equality? pt 2 Equality of Resources' (1981) 10 PPA 283
Harris J. W. *Property and Justice* (1996) ch 11
Locke J. *Second Treatise of Government* (Gough ed, 1976) ch 5
Munzer S. R. *A Theory of Property* (1990) chs 9 and 10
Nozick R. *Anarchy, State and Utopia* (1974) pt 2
Paul J. (ed) *Reading Nozick* (1982) pt 4
Proudhon J. P. *What is Property?* (Kelley and Smith trans, 1994)
Raz J. *The Morality of Freedom* (1986) pts 2 and 3
Rawls J. *A Theory of Justice* (1971)
Rothbard M. N. 'Justice and Property Rights' in Blumenfeld (ed) *Property in a Humane Economy* (1974)
Waldron J. *The Right to Private Property* (1988) chs 6 and 7
Williams B. 'The Idea of Equality' in Laslett and Runciman (eds) *Philosophy, Politics and Society* (2nd series, 1972)
Wolff R. P. *Understanding Rawls* (1977)

Communitarianism

Avineri S. and De-Shalit A. (eds) *Communitarianism and Individualism* (1992)
Buchanan A. 'Assessing the Communitarian Critique of Liberalism' (1989) 90 Ethics 852
Gardbaum S. 'Law, Politics, and the Claims of Community' (1992) 90 Mich L Rev 685
Green L. *The Authority of the State* (1990) ch 7
Harris J. W. *Property and Justice* (1996) pt ii
Hayek F. A. *Law, Legislation and Liberty vol 2: The Mirage of Social Justice* (1976)
Hume D. *A Treatise of Human Nature* (Green and Grose eds, 1974) bk 3, pt ii
Kamenka E. and Ursoon-Tay A. 'Beyond Bourgois Individualism: the Contemporary Crisis in Law and Ideology' in Kamenka and Neale (eds) *Feudalism, Capitalism and Beyond* (1975)
MacIntyre A. *After Virtue* (1981)
Rawls J. *Political Liberalism* (1993)
Sandel M. J. *Liberalism and the Limits of Justice* (1982)
Sher G. *Desert* (1987)
Taylor C. *Sources of the Self* (1989)

Feminist jurisprudence

Bartlett K. T. 'Feminist Legal Method' (1990) 103 Harv L Rev 829

Gilligan C. *In a Different Voice* (1982)

Graycar R. and Morgan J. *The Hidden Gender of Law* (1990)

Harris A. 'Race and Essentialism in Feminist Legal Theory' (1990) 42
   Stan L Rev 581

Itzin C. (ed) *Pornography, Women, Violence and Civil Liberties* (1992)

Lacey N. 'Closure and Critique in Feminist Jurisprudence' in Norrie (ed)
   Closure or Critique (1993)

Mackinnon C. A. 'Feminism, Marxism, Method and the State' (1983) 8
   Signs 635

   − *Feminism Unmodified* (1987)

   − *Toward a Feminist Theory of the State* (1989)

Morris J. (ed) *Encounters with Strangers: Feminism and Disability* (1996)

Olsen F. (ed) *Feminist Legal Theory* (1995)

Rhode D. L. 'Feminist Critical Theories' (1990) 42 Stan L Rev 617

Scales A. C. 'The Emergence of Feminist Jurisprudence' (1986) 95 Yale
   LJ 1373

Smart C. *Feminism and the Power of Law* (1989)

Thornton M. (ed) *Public and Private: Feminist Legal Debates* (1996)

Weisberg K. (ed) *Feminist Legal Theory: Foundations* (1993)

West R. 'Jurisprudence and Gender' (1988) 55 U Chi L Rev 1

Index